Ralph del Colle was born in New York City on October 3, 1954, and was raised in Mineola, Long Island. He attended Xavier High School in Chelsea and received a BA in History and Literature of Religions from New York University, and MDiv, MPhil, and PhD degrees from Union Theological Seminary. Ralph taught for seventeen years in the Marquette University Theology Department; prior to that he taught at Barry University, Miami Shores, Florida, and at St. Anselm College, Manchester, New Hampshire.

Ralph's lively Christian faith and interest in church unity led to his participation in ecumenical dialogues. He served as a representative to the International Catholic-Pentecostal Dialogue for the Pontifical Council on Christian Unity for twelve years and also served on the Catholic-Reformed Dialogue and Catholic-Evangelical Dialogue, both for the U.S. Conference of Catholic Bishops. He was invited by the Pontifical Council to serve as a representative to the World Council of Churches Assembly in Harare, Zimbabwe, in 1998. In 2002–2003, he served as the President of the Society for Pentecostal Studies and in 2003 Ralph received the Archbishop's Vatican II Award. Ralph's scholarly work, especially his work on the Holy Spirit, made significant contributions to the field of Systematic Theology.

Ralph died in July of 2012, slightly more than four weeks after he was diagnosed with a rare form of liver cancer. He was fifty-seven.

A Man of the Church

A Man of the Church

Honoring the Theology, Life, and Witness
of Ralph Del Colle

Edited by
MICHEL RENÉ BARNES

☙PICKWICK *Publications* • Eugene, Oregon

A MAN OF THE CHURCH
Honoring the Theology, Life, and Witness of Ralph Del Colle

Copyright © 2012 Wipf and Stock Publishers. All rights reserved. Except for brief quotations in critical publications or reviews, no part of this book may be reproduced in any manner without prior written permission from the publisher. Write: Permissions, Wipf and Stock Publishers, 199 W. 8th Ave., Suite 3, Eugene, OR 97401.

Pickwick Publications
An Imprint of Wipf and Stock Publishers
199 W. 8th Ave., Suite 3
Eugene, OR 97401

www.wipfandstock.com

ISBN 13: 978-1-62032-601-5

Cataloging-in-Publication data:

A man of the church : honoring the theology, life, and witness of Ralph Del Colle / edited by Michel René Barnes.

xviii + 342 p. ; 23 cm. —Includes bibliographical references.

ISBN 13: 978-1-62032-601-5

1. Del Colle, Ralph. 2. Ecumenical movement. 3. Theology, Doctrinal. I. Barnes, Michel R. (Michel René). II. Title.

BX9 M12 2012

Manufactured in the U.S.A.

Cover art, front: Interior St Joan of Arc Chapel, Courtesy of Marquette University.
Cover art, back: Courtesy of Marquette University.

Contents

Editor's Preface | vii
Introduction by Timothy Cardinal Dolan | xi
A Letter from The Pontifical Council for Promoting Christian Unity by Monsignor Juan Usma Gómez | xiii
List of Contributors | xv

I: A Last Word

    1 Spirit Christology: Dogmatic Issues — Ralph Del Colle | 3

II: The Vocation of the Theologian—Reflections on the Work and Witness of Ralph Del Colle

    2 The Ecclesial Vocation of the Theologian
       — Bruce D. Marshall | 23

    3 Courage — John Webster | 40

    4 The Humble Greatness of Theology — C. C. Pecknold | 56

    5 The Work and Witness of Ralph Del Colle: Ecumenical Friendship
       — D. Stephen Long | 65

    6 Embodying Grace: The Super/natural Witness of Ralph Del Colle
       — James K. A. Smith | 82

    7 Speaking the Truth in Love: Ralph Del Colle and the Methodist-Roman Catholic International Dialogue
       — Geoffrey Wainwright | 88

    8 The Our Father, Prayer of the Crucified: In Tribute to Ralph Del Colle, Who Prayed the Our Father with Jesus his Savior
       — Thomas G. Weinandy, O.F.M., Cap. | 96

    9 Snowden's Secret: Gregory of Nyssa on Passion and Death
       — Michel René Barnes | 107

III: Dimensions of Christological, Pneumatological, and Trinitarian Theology

    10 *Diastasis* in the Trinity — Edward T. Oakes, S.J. | 125

11 The Divinity of Christ and Social Justice
— D. Thomas Hughson, S.J. | 148

12 "He Will Baptize You with the Holy Spirit": Recovering a Metaphor for a Contemporary Pneumatological Soteriology
— D. Lyle Dabney | 176

13 A Chaste Marriage: Matthias Scheeben's (Western) Doctrine of Deification — Richard J. Barry | 185

14 Spirit-Christology and the Shape of the Theological Enterprise
— Andrew Grosso | 206

IV: Theological Dimensions of Biblical Interpretation

15 The Facecloth of John 20:7 — David Coffey | 225

16 The Book of Job and God's Existence — Matthew Levering | 231

17 Reformation Controversy and Biblical Interpretation
— R. R. Reno | 241

18 Baptism, Unity, and Crucifying the Flesh
— Rodrigo J. Morales | 249

V: Ecumenical Dimensions of Christian Theology

19 Mary and Inculturation — Peter J. Casarella | 265

20 Ghosts of Westphalia: Fictions and Ideals of Ecclesial Unity in Enlightenment Germany — Ulrich L. Lehner | 283

21 "An Irony of Enthusiasm": The Reversal of Luther's Epithet in the Enlightenment — Paul R. Hinlicky | 302

22 Reading Kant Ecumenically: Prolegomena to an Anthropology of Hope in the Aftermath of Modernity — Philip J. Rossi, S.J. | 316

Epilogue: The Homily Preached at the Funeral of Ralph Del Colle
— Joseph G. Mueller, S.J. | 331

Opera: The Theology and Witness of Ralph Del Colle (1954–2012) | 335

Preface

IN JUNE OF 2012 Ralph was diagnosed with a rare and aggressive form of liver cancer; estimates on how long he had left ranged from weeks to months. When some of us in the Department learned of Ralph's illness we decided that we wanted to recognize his many accomplishments. We contacted some of his friends in the academic world to contribute to a Festschrift in his honor. We hoped to publish the book and present it to Ralph, so we worked with very short deadlines. The tasks of organizing, funding, and editing this volume were shared amongst Ralph's friends and colleagues in the Department of Theology at Marquette University: Michel Barnes, Lyle Dabney, Ulrich Lehner, Steve Long, Mickey Mattox, and Joseph Mueller, S.J. This Festschrift has had two purposes. The first was to give Ralph a sense of how important he was to so many people. Despite the fact that Ralph died before this collection could be published, it achieved this purpose, for Ralph knew of this Festschrift and its contributors, and saw a photo proof of the cover. He was very moved by the collection, and asked us to include an essay he was working on furthering his thoughts on Spirit-Christology. The second purpose of this Festschrift was to honor Ralph's many and diverse accomplishments. We hope that we have accomplished this.

Theologians are, relatively speaking, a dime a dozen. There are many theologians who basically work a "day job," and the product of that day job is not theology but helping along the revolution. Theology was never a day job for Ralph: it was an intellectual, spiritual, emotional, and social vocation. With his death, Ralph's thought is now free of its Departmental/Institutional/Guild normalization: his theology can take on a life of its own. It is now more difficult to pigeonhole his work, or to dismiss him by locating him on some political/ideological spectrum. Ralph is dead, but his theology is about to become very much alive. Ralph felt that he had much more to say, much more to do, and this was undoubtedly true. But in his death Ralph is about to accomplish something that did not happen in his life: Ralph's theology will become a light. Ralph's passage into death—the last four weeks of his life—gave us a firm hermeneutical guide into

Preface

the true meaning(s) of his theology. Ralph Del Colle's theology cannot be separated from his life. Perhaps that is true of every good theologian, but it is especially true of him. For Ralph, theology emerged from a profound prayer life and an earnest desire to embody the perfection to which Christ called his disciples in the Holy Spirit. He waited upon the Spirit with an attentiveness few achieve.

Since his death on Sunday, July 29th, 2012, Ralph Del Colle's theology is not only inseparable from his life, but it has also become inseparable from his death. His death at 57 was not the vocation his friends, family, or he himself anticipated, or for which anyone prayed. Even as he was dying Ralph was a powerful witness. Soon after the initial diagnosis on June 21st, Ralph knew that he was dying and thereafter he never wavered from accepting that very soon he would be dead. He spoke honestly about death, and required those around to speak this truth. Yet Ralph also refused any bravado. He showed those around him how to die as a faithful disciple of Christ.

The New Testament passage that Ralph chose for his funeral Mass was Philippians 3:17—4:1:

> Brothers, join in imitating me, and keep your eyes on those who walk according to the example you have in us. For many, of whom I have often told you and now tell you even with tears, walk as enemies of the cross of Christ. Their end is destruction, their god is their belly, and they glory in their shame, with minds set on earthly things. But our citizenship is in heaven, and from it we await a Savior, the Lord Jesus Christ, who will transform our lowly body to be like his glorious body, by the power that enables him even to subject all things to himself. Therefore, my brothers, whom I love and long for, my joy and crown, stand firm thus in the Lord, my beloved.

Those of us who heard this passage in church that morning could easily imagine Ralph reading these words aloud to us. Ralph would have read these words not to call attention to himself, but to recall the struggle that belonged to every Christian: the struggle to set our minds on spiritual good, and the struggle to preserve the faith from enemies of the cross of Christ. The cover of this volume is a photograph of St. Joan of Arc chapel on the campus of Marquette University: we chose this photo as a cover because Ralph could regularly be found at this small chapel, for Mass or for personal prayer. Ralph did not flinch over the fact that the chapel was

Preface

dedicated to Joan of Arc: he spent much of his life trying to give God his own passions for His service.

Without the generous spirit shown to us by Jim Tedrick and Christian Amondson at Wipf & Stock Publishers, this volume could not have been published, and we are grateful for their gracious participation. We are also grateful to his Eminence, Timothy Michael Cardinal Dolan, Archbishop of New York, who volunteered to write a preface for this Festschrift, and to Monsignor Juan Usma Gómez, Head of the Western Section, Pontifical Council for Promoting Christian Unity, Vatican City, for his letter describing Ralph's contributions to Ecumenical dialogue. We also need to thank Julia Pananen Barnes, who worked long hours under deadline copyediting the essays.

May the angels escort Ralph into paradise; at his coming may the martyrs welcome him, and conduct him to the holy city Jerusalem. May a choir of angels receive Ralph, and may he find rest with Lazarus, who once was poor.

Michel René Barnes

Introduction

TIMOTHY CARDINAL DOLAN

It is an honor for me to be in the company of so many others who praise the God of Life for the gift Ralph Del Colle was to all of us.

I first met him in his vocation as a seasoned, articulate theologian, but, in my seven happy years as archbishop of Milwaukee, came to consider him an inspiration and a friend.

Upon arrival in Milwaukee, Bishop Richard Sklba, my faithful and learned auxiliary bishop, asked if I wanted to continue regular meetings with a distinguished group of theologians who assembled two-or-three times a year.

I'm glad I replied, yes—for there I came to know Ralph! There I came to marvel at his insights into, for example, the Catholic-Jewish dialogue, eschatology, the Eucharist, the ecclesial vocation of the theologian, and Christology—all topics this group considered.

The serenity of his presentation, the sincerity of his voice, and his mastery of the sources verified my initial hunch that this was a man of consecrated study and a sustained interior life. To those virtuous traits I add charity, as he proved so patient in my endless questions about matters theological, and my frequent requests for help on particular projects.

But what inspired me most was to see him so faithfully there at 8 am Mass on Sunday morning at the cathedral. I must admit that the presence of this astute scholar prompted me to be more attentive than usual to the preparation of my homily!

Then came the word of his cancer . . . and he became an even more effective professor.

In my telephone conversations with him those last weeks, the tranquility I had always sensed was even more evident. It was so clear to me that the God who was the object of his scholarship was also his father, his Lord, his physician, his savior, his best friend. This man of such nuanced

Introduction

and sophisticated theological precision was "like a little child" in his trust of Jesus and Mary, in his simple plea that I would pray for his healing—"either now or in eternity," to borrow his phrasing—through the intercession of Blessed Pope John Paul II.

As these acclaimed intellects unite to honor his memory with erudition worthy of their colleague in this providential *Festschrift*, I am confident that, through the mercy of Jesus, Ralph Del Colle has received the eternal answer to Blessed John Henry Cardinal Newman's "Prayer for a Happy Death" which Ralph told me he was making his own:

> O, my Lord and Savior, support me in my last hour in the strong arms of Thy Sacraments and by the fresh fragrance of Thy consolations. Let the absolving words be said over me, and the holy oil sign and seal me; and let Thine own Body be my food, and Thy Blood my sprinkling; and let my sweet Mother, Mary, breathe on me, and my Angel whisper peace to me, and my glorious saints and my own dear patrons smile upon me, that, in them all and through them all, I may receive the gift of perseverance, and die as I desire to live, in Thy faith, in Thy Church, in Thy Service, and in Thy love. Amen.

Requiescat in pace.

Timothy Michael Cardinal Dolan
Archbishop of New York
August 8, 2012
Feast of St. Dominic

A Letter from The Pontifical Council for Promoting Christian Unity

MONSIGNOR JUAN USMA GÓMEZ[1]

THE PONTIFICAL COUNCIL FOR Promoting Christian Unity relied on the theological competence of Professor Ralph Del Colle over many years, and he always generously offered his expertise in the firm conviction that unity is God's will and the irrevocable path for all Christians.

Since 1998 he was a member of the Pentecostal-Catholic International Dialogue, and took part in the Informal Conversations with the Seventh–Day Adventists (2001–2002), as well as in the official Catholic delegation attending the General Assembly of the World Council of Churches in Harare in 1998.

Professor Del Colle was particularly appreciated for his faithfulness and his love for the Church, lived in a firm awareness of his Catholic identity.

With his deep knowledge of official Church teaching, he always strove to make it available as a gift to share among Catholics and other Christians. Theological research and a life of faith were inseparably linked for him.

His analytical skills, his intellectual honesty, and his insight were put at the service of the truth. At the same time, he always nurtured a deep spirituality, a profound human sensitivity, and a genuine openness. He drew from the wellspring of a rich sacramental and devotional life throughout his entire life.

A dedicated spirit and a joyful approach always marked his contribution to the meetings of the dialogue. Attentive not only to the general discussion but also to its varied nuances, Professor Del Colle never turned away from any issue, even when his personal life was touched. While he

---

1. Head of the Western Section, Pontifical Council for Promoting Christian Unity, Vatican City.

A Letter from The Pontifical Council for Promoting Christian Unity

retained his lively and perceptive sensitivity, he succeeded in combining it with his determination to support his positions and beliefs. He demonstrated the ability both to confront controversial questions and to engage in a challenging exchange with other Christians, as well as the willingness to overcome rifts and tensions in a proactive and constructive way. The bonds of communion, and even deep friendship, that he was able to create enabled the dialogue to deal with a range of themes, sometimes very difficult ones, without ever diluting them or diminishing their significance.

In particular, the Catholic-Pentecostal International Dialogue is indebted to Professor Del Colle in its last two stages. His expertise and understanding of the Pentecostal world made him at times a bridge and at other times a challenge that inspired deeper clarifications on respective positions. From its very beginning, he was convinced that discernment is the key in this dialogue in particular, affirming that the "Pentecostal distinctiveness . . . its defining characteristic is the 'pentecostal outpouring of the Holy Spirit,' which ought not to be considered as a claim, i.e., we have the outpouring, but as a witness, i.e., the Spirit has fallen." The dialogue, therefore, is part of the process of our discernment of the Spirit's work, including the possibility of a new outpouring. And, as he stated on different occasions, "This discernment requires our authentic receptivity to what God is offering." Always fully aware that unity is God's gift, Ralph Del Colle faithfully awaited the surprises of the Spirit.

Contributors

Michel René Barnes is Associate Professor for Patristics at Marquette University. His publications include *The Power of God: Dynamis in Gregory of Nyssa's Trinitarian Theology*, as well as articles on Gregory and Augustine, including "De Régnon Reconsidered." He co-edited the collection *Arianism After Arius*.

Richard J. Barry has a Master of Theological Studies from the University of Notre Dame, and is pursuing a PhD in systematic theology at Marquette University.

Peter J. Casarella teaches Catholic Studies and is Director of the Center for World Catholicism and Intercultural Theology at DePaul University. He edited *Cusanus: The Legacy of Learned Ignorance* and co-edited *Christian Spirituality and the Culture of Modernity*, *Cuerpo de Cristo*, and *A World for All?*

David M. Coffey, Professor Emeritus of Systematic Theology at Marquette University. His publications include *Deus Trinitas*, *Grace: The Gift of the Holy Spirit*, and *The Sacrament of Reconciliation*.

D. Lyle Dabney is an associate professor of Systematic Theology at Marquette University, specializing in Modern Protestant Theology. His publications include: *Die Kenosis des Geistes: Kontinuität zwischen Schöpfung und Erlösung in Werk des Heiligen Geistes*; and he translated and edited *Is There Life after Death?*, by Jürgen Moltmann, as well as edited (with Bradford Hinze), *Advents of the Spirit: Introduction to the Current Study of Pneumatology*.

Andrew Grosso, Rector of Trinity Episcopal Church in Atchison, KS, Missioner for Theological Formation for the Episcopal Diocese of Kansas, and Adjunct Professor of Systematic Theology at Nashotah House Theological Seminary, Nashotah, WI. He is the author of *Personal Being: Polanyi, Ontology, and Christian Theology* (Peter Lang, 2007), a revised version of a dissertation he completed under the direction of Ralph Del Colle.

Contributors

Paul R. Hinlicky, Tise Professor of Lutheran Studies at Roanoke College, Salem, VA. His publications include *Paths Not Taken, Luther and the Beloved Community* and *Divine Complexity*.

D. Thomas Hughson, Emeritus Associate Professor of Theology at Marquette University, Milwaukee. His publications include *Believer as Citizen: John Courtney Murray in a New Context* (Paulist, 1993), "Social Justice in Lactantius's 'Divine Institutes': An Exploration," in Johan Leemans editor, *Reading Patristic Texts on Social Ethics* (CUA Press, 2011) 185-205, "Missional Churches in Secular Societies: Theology Consults Sociology," *Ecclesiology* 7 (2011) 173-194 and "Beyond Ecumenical Dialogue," *One in Christ* 46 (2012) 24-37.

Ulrich L. Lehner, Associate Professor of Religious History and Historical Theology at Marquette University. His publications include several books on Early Modern Religion, among which *Enlightened Monks* won the 2012 Gilmary Shea Award of the American Catholic Historical Association. He is currently co-editing the *Oxford Handbook of Early Modern Theology* and *Transnational Catholic Enlightenment*.

Matthew Levering is Professor of Theology at the University of Dayton. His publications include *Predestination, Jesus and the Demise of Death*, and *The Feminine Genius of Catholic Theology*.

D. Stephen Long is Professor of Systematic Theology at Marquette University. His publications include *Christian Ethics: A Very Short Introduction*, *Hebrews: A Theological Commentary*, *Speaking of God: Theology, Language and Truth* and *The Divine Economy: Theology and the Market*.

Bruce D. Marshall is Lehman Professor of Christian Doctrine and Director of the Graduate Program in Religious Studies at the Perkins School of Theology, Southern Methodist University. He is the author of *Trinity and Truth* (Cambridge University Press, 2000), *Christology in Conflict: The Identity of a Saviour in Rahner and Barth* (Blackwell, 1987), and a number of papers on Christology, sacramental theology, and the theology of Thomas Aquinas.

Mickey L. Mattox is an associate professor of Historical Theology and Reformation Studies at Marquette University. As research professor at the Institute for Ecumenical Research in Strasbourg, France, from 2000-2003, he worked as a consultant for international dialogues sponsored by the

Lutheran World Federation. His publications include *The Substance of Faith: Doctrinal Theology in the Tradition of Martin Luther*, *Changing Churches? An Orthodox, Catholic, and Lutheran Theological Conversation*, and *"Defender of the Most Holy Matriarchs:" Martin Luther's Interpretation of the Women of Genesis in the Enarrationes in Genesin, 1535–1545*.

Rodrigo J. Morales is an Assistant Professor in Judaism and Christianity in Antiquity at Marquette University. He is the author of *The Spirit and the Restoration of Israel: New Exodus and New Creation Motifs in Galatians*, and has published articles in *Nova et Vetera*, the *Zeitschrift für die Neutestamentliche Wissenschaft*, and *Biblische Zeitschrift*.

Joseph G. Mueller, S.J., Associate Professor of Theology at Marquette University, Milwaukee. His publications include *L'Ancien Testament dans l'ecclésiologie des Pères: Une lecture des Constitutions apostoliques*.

Edward T. Oakes, S.J., is Professor of Systematic Theology at University of St. Mary of the Lake/Mundelein Seminary and President-elect (for the year 2014) of the Academy of Catholic Theology. His most recent book, *Infinity Dwindled to Infancy: A Catholic and Evangelical Christology* (Eerdmans) won the 2012 Book Prize from the Center for Catholic and Evangelical Dialogue. He is also the author of *Pattern of Redemption: The Theology of Hans Urs von Balthasar* (Continuum) and co-editor of *The Cambridge Companion to Hans Urs von Balthasar* (Cambridge).

C. C. Pecknold, Assistant Professor of Historical and Systematic Theology at The Catholic University of America, Washington, DC. His publications include *Transforming Postliberal Theology* (T. & T. Clark) and *Christianity and Politics: A Brief Guide to the History* (Cascade).

R. R. Reno, Editor, *First Things*. His publications include *Fighting the Noonday Devil*, *Brazos Theological Commentary on Genesis*, and *Sanctified Vision*.

Philip J. Rossi, S.J., Professor of Theology and Interim Dean of the Klingler College of Arts and Sciences at Marquette University, Milwaukee. His publications include *The Social Authority of Reason: Kant's Critique, Radical Evil and the Destiny of Humankind*, *Together Toward Hope: A Journey to Moral Theology*, "Reading Kant from a Catholic Horizon: Ethics and the Anthropology of Grace," "Finite Freedom, Fractured and Fragile: Kant's Anthropology as Resource for a Postmodern Theology of Grace,"

Contributors

and "Sojourners, Guests, and Strangers: The Church as Enactment of the Hospitality of God."

James K. A. Smith, Professor of Philosophy, Calvin College, Grand Rapids, MI. His publications include *Desiring the Kingdom*, *Thinking in Tongues*, *The Fall of Interpretation*, and *Who's Afraid of Postmodernism?*

Geoffrey Wainwright, Cushman Professor Emeritus of Christian Theology, The Divinity School, Duke University. His publications include: *Doxology: The Praise of God in Worship, Doctrine and Life* and *Embracing Purpose: Essays on God, the World and the Church*.

John Webster is Professor of Systematic Theology at the University of Aberdeen. His publications include *Holy Scripture*, *Confessing God*, and *The Domain of the Word*.

Thomas G. Weinandy, O.F.M., Cap. Executive Director, Secretariat for Doctrine, United States Conference of Catholic Bishops. PhD in Historical Theology, King's College, University of London. His publications include *Does God Change?: The Word's Becoming in the Incarnation*; *Does God Suffer?*, *The Father's Spirit of Sonship: Reconceiving the Trinity*, and *Athanasius: A Theological Introduction*.

I

A Last Word

1

Spirit Christology: Dogmatic Issues

RALPH DEL COLLE

[Editor's Note: It has famously been said that no one begins at the beginning; we all begin in the middle. In the same way, we all come to our end in the middle as well. In the midst of his final days, Ralph Del Colle was at work on this essay. Although it is by no means complete—as he himself recognized—he asked that we include it in this collection as a final witness to his own theological concerns and as a marker indicating where his voice in the contemporary theological debates was silenced. The skeleton, if not always the body, of his argument is clear. He sought to demonstrate that Pneumatology should rightly *enrich* traditional Christological and Trinitarian dogma, against those who see Spirit Christology as offering *an alternative* to those formulations. This essay manifests, therefore, two themes, indeed, perhaps *the* two themes, that run through the length and breadth of his scholarly activity: his passion for Pneumatology and his commitment to the Western, above all the Roman Catholic, theological tradition. But beyond that, this essay demonstrates something about Ralph Del Colle himself, something more than simply his doctrinal concerns or denominational identity, namely that he lived and died as what Patristic theologians once called ἄνθρωπος τῆς ἐκκλησίας, "a man of the church," one who was committed to the struggle for the truth of the church's theological witness throughout its history. May this essay help us to remember and honor him as such.]

A Man of the Church

INTRODUCTION

My interest in examining the dogmatic issues that accompany Spirit Christology has to do with how pneumatology, especially in the Western Catholic tradition, ought to inform our christological constructions. That is, I take it, the whole point of Spirit Christology. At the risk of oversimplification, I will identify the two major contemporary options for this new christological model as 1) a trinitarian Spirit-Christology, and 2) a post-trinitarian Spirit-Christology. By post-trinitarian, I do not necessarily mean unitarian or pre-trinitarian. The former implies rejection of the dogma of the trinity and the latter assumes a pre-conciliar theological milieu, which is clearly impossible, although appeal is often made to that era, whether it is to New Testament Christologies or to ante-Nicene and pre-Chalcedonian Christologies. The Spirit Christology proposed from this perspective is understood as part and parcel of a larger project to revise the classical presentation of trinitarian and christological doctrine. The focus usually has to do with the cogency of maintaining the intra-trinitarian distinctions in the so-called immanent trinity, the exclusive dominance of Logos Christology, and questions of pre- or post- existence relative to Jesus as the Christ, and/or the use of the Chalcedonian terminology of natures and person.

The ascription "post-trinitarian" is intended to underscore that the classical distinction between Son and Spirit is now subsumed under a schema in which the triadic structure of the Christian confession—soteriologically speaking, <God, Christ, Spirit>—is conceived as an account only of God's saving activity and presence in the man Jesus and in the experience of the Christian community. The distinct hypostases (or persons) of Son and Spirit are relegated to what is understood negatively to be have been a process of "hypostization" which basically comes down to something getting in the way between God and the *humanum*—I am thinking of the work of Geoffrey Lampe and Roger Haight especially. In other words, the symbolic representation of the dynamism that is the divine-human encounter in Jesus and the Spirit becomes objectified into existent mediators of that encounter, the results of which are Christolatry, on the one hand, and a neglect of pneumatology on the other. To stalwart adherents of trinitarian orthodoxy this evaluation is indeed a departure from the classical norms.

All of this is to say that the debate between the two positions can be waged on a number of levels: 1) fundamental—the nature of religious language and theological predication, 2) hermeneutical—how to interpret the norms of Nicaea and Chalcedon, 3) dogmatic—how to integrate the doctrines of God, Christ, and salvation. I propose to consider the common ground between the two positions, what Roger Haight observed as the two foci of Spirit Christology: ". . . Spirit Christology that sees Jesus during his life time as one in whom God as Spirit was at work . . . [and the] dimension of Spirit Christology [that] applies to the risen Jesus, the Jesus alive, with God, and called the Christ.[1]"

Borrowing from James D. G. Dunn, upon whom Haight also drew, we can phrase the issue in terms of the following two questions.

1. How is the divinity of the incarnate Christ a function of the Spirit?
2. How is the humanity of the risen Jesus a function of the Spirit?[2]

As I will concentrate on the dogmatic configuration attending classical trinitarian Spirit-Christology let me summarize the difference between the trinitarian and post-trinitarian positions in a series of concise bullet points:

- In trinitarian Spirit-Christology the relationship between Jesus and the Spirit in both cases must negotiate the intra-trinitarian relationship between the Son and the Spirit. In other words, Spirit-Christology will include both a filiological and a pneumatological dimension.
- In post-trinitarian Spirit-Christology the relationship between Jesus and the Spirit reconceives the intra-trinitarian distinctions (Son/Spirit language) as referring to the modality of Jesus' historical revelation of the divine and the Christian experience of the God revealed in Jesus and now present among us.

Therefore,

- Trinitarian Spirit-Christology would answer Dunn's first question by stating that the Spirit actualizes the incarnation of the divine Son and enables the intensification of Jesus' Abba relation through the course of his journey from Jordan to Gethsemane to Golgotha.
- Post-trinitarian Spirit-Christology answers this question by stating that Spirit is the presence of God in Jesus that enables authentic revelation along the contours of that same evangelical narrative.

---

1. Roger Haight, "The Case for Spirit Christology," *Theological Studies* 53 (1992) 270.

2. James D. G. Dunn, "Rediscovering the Spirit," *The Expository Times* 84 (1972) 12.

- Trinitarian Spirit-Christology would answer Dunn's second question by stating that the risen Jesus is present in the Spirit who is poured forth upon the community of faith.
- Post-trinitarian Spirit-Christology answers this question by stating that the presence of God as Spirit has a Christ-character about it that invokes the memory of Jesus.

What is really being controverted in these two positions is the hypostatic rendering of the trinitarian distinctions, or from the point of view of the Christian experience of salvation, what may be termed the inseparability but non-identity between the *Christus praesens* and the *Spiritus praesens*. Of course, I am framing the issue from the perspective of the divine economy. From the more classical position, Spirit Christology raises two questions. First, how does one distinguish the christological and pneumatological missions? Second, how does the mission of the Holy Spirit so inform the mission of the Son that we have an authentic Spirit Christology? If we do not adequately answer the first question we inevitably end up with a rather limp pneumatology, and with help from a narrow understanding of the *filioque*, one that for all intents and purposes is subordinated to Christology.

From the point of view of the Christian experience of salvation, we may query how the agency, identity, and presence of the risen Christ and the Holy Spirit, the *Christus praesens* and the *Spiritus praesens*, are to be distinguished within the economy of the triune God. If this cannot be answered—if, for example, the agency of the risen Jesus is subsumed by that of divine Spirit—do we not end up with a binity of divine transcendence and divine immanence as the basic criteria for terms of distinction in God? Or, at the level of the divine economy do we not fall into a modalism of Christ and the Spirit? If this is the case, the irony of post-trinitarian Christology (which I believe succumbs to these charges) for us in the Western Catholic tradition is that, whereas once we tended to instrumentalize the work of the Spirit relative to that of Jesus Christ—the usual charge, we now reverse that process by instrumentalizing the person of Jesus Christ relative to the presence of Spirit. Either way, in my judgment, a truly pneumatological Christology is short-circuited.

Therefore, the first major dogmatic issue to be resolved has to do with the comportment of the terms of Spirit Christology with orthodox Trinitarian dogma, namely, that the christological and pneumatological dimensions of Spirit Christology bespeak the filiological and pneumatological aspects of divine agency and presence. In other words, the distinction but inseparability between the *Christus praesens* and the *Spiritus praesens* underscore how the divine persons or hypostases of the Son and Holy Spirit are related to each other in reference to 1) the life, death and resurrection of the incarnate Son, and 2) the presence and agency of the risen and exalted Christ in the power of the Holy Spirit. This will resolve the specifically christological issues concerning the person and work of Christ. Second, we then must negotiate the relationship between Christology and speculative trinitarian theology, namely, how the temporal missions and eternal processions of Son and Spirit impact Spirit Christology. Within this horizon I will address what is for some the bane of Spirit Christology relative to the ordering or *taxis* of the trinitarian persons, namely, the *filioque*. At that point it will become clear why Spirit Christology complements but does not displace Logos Christology.

I. THE SPIRIT IN JESUS

Proceeding from the premises already elucidated Spirit Christology entails the recognition that every aspect of the mystery and work of Jesus Christ is a work of the Holy Spirit. His conception and nativity, viz., Incarnation, his life and ministry, his death and resurrection, viz., the redemption, abide under the agency and work of the Spirit. Indeed, this is the evangelical witness of the New Testament. Jesus is conceived in the womb of Mary when the Holy Spirit comes upon her (Lk 1: 35). According to tradition Mary's virginity was sustained in the birth of Jesus because, as St. Thomas Aquinas says, "all these things took place miraculously by Divine power" (*Summa Theologica* III, Q 28, A 2, ad. 3). I will return to the Mariological aspects of Spirit Christology. Jesus grows in wisdom and grace (Lk 2: 52): grace as given by the Spirit—another exposition that I will also engage in. At his baptism the Spirit descends upon Jesus to inaugurate his public mission (Lk 3:22). Thus filled with the Spirit Jesus is led by the Spirit into the desert (Lk 4:1) and returns from his temptation in the power of the Spirit (Lk 4:14). His preaching, healings, miracles and exorcisms are accomplished in the power of the Spirit, captured in words of the Matthean Jesus, "But if by the Spirit of God that I drive out demons, then the kingdom of God has come upon you" (Matt 12:28). Perhaps Jesus' Spirit-endowed life and ministry is best summarized in the Johannine statement that he possessed the Spirit without measure (Jn 3:34). This is consistent with messianic prophecy that Jesus is anointed with the Spirit (Lk 4:18–19) and that his Spirit-inspired ministry culminated in his self-offering through the eternal Spirit on the cross (Heb 9:14). And perhaps, although it is ambiguous, Paul alludes to the role of the Spirit in the resurrection of Jesus from the dead: "If the Spirit of the one who raised Jesus from the dead dwells in you, the one who raised Christ from the dead will give life to your mortal bodies also, through his Spirit that dwells in you" (Rom 8: 11).

Thus far I have briefly summarized the New Testament witness to what can be designated as the pneumatological dimensions of Jesus' life and ministry. The coherence of the proposal must be consistent with the *transitus* of Jesus in his earthly ministry, inclusive of his saving passion and death, to his session at the Father's right hand through resurrection and ascension. In kerygmatic terms, we speak of the passage of Jesus the proclaimer of the kingdom of God to the apostolic kerygma of the Christ who is proclaimed. In a pneumatological key, Jesus the Spirit-bearer becomes Jesus the Spirit-baptizer. It is this latter *transitus* that is the key for Spirit Christology. Each relates to the two issues and questions already noted: the presence and role of the Spirit in the earthly Jesus and the presence and agency of the risen Jesus in the outpouring of the Holy Spirit. I now turn to the speculative issues that attend Christology, specifically, Spirit Christology. First, let me say a word about speculative Christology.

Speculative Christology is that exercise within Christology that attempts to elucidate the mystery of the person of Christ, the eternal Son of God incarnate who is fully human and fully divine. Necessitated by the need to counter heterodox trends and associated with right doxology and true contemplation, speculative Christology is essentially a spiritual exercise that deepens the Church's knowledge of divine revelation in Jesus Christ. To adjudicate the meaning and relationship between nature and person is not a philosophical imposition upon Christian doctrine but rather a theological exegesis of the salvific self-offering of God in Jesus Christ. In order to properly identify this reality and be formed by its truth, reference must be made to its metaphysical and ontological verity, respectively its underlying structures and its grasp on our existence.

As we take up our first issue—the presence and agency of the Spirit in the earthly Jesus let us also recall James Dunn's correlative question: how is the divinity of the incarnate Christ a function of the Spirit? Consistent with the complementarity of Logos and Spirit Christologies I am not predicating divinity in Christ, his being truly divine, as Spirit. Spirit Christology understood as inspiration Christology (a la John Hick) is not sufficient to account for the mystery of the Incarnation. The Holy Spirit is not made flesh, the eternal Son is. Of the three divine persons, he is sent from the Father and conceived by and anointed with the Holy Spirit. The filiological aspect of Christology requires that the *Abba* relation of Jesus to the God of Israel constitutes the predication of divinity in Christ. To avoid all forms of adoptionism we must be clear that Jesus does not become the Son of God or that a man becomes divine. Rather, humanity is assumed by the eternal Son through the agency of the Holy Spirit such that Jesus' *Abba* relation determines his human existence as one lives out of his relationship and communion with the Father, the God of Israel, and wholly does his will. Jesus is indeed the Word who reveals the Father and is God to the extent that the filial relation that subsists in God is incarnate as a human being in Jesus of Nazareth.

IIA. JESUS IN THE SPIRIT

In order to appreciate this saving mystery, I turn now to the question of how the divinity of Jesus is a function of the Holy Spirit. Let me be clear, again. I am not proposing that the Holy Spirit should be predicated as the divinity of the man Jesus. More accurately, this is the position of post-Trinitarian Spirit Christology described above wherein God as Spirit—not a third hypostasis in the Godhead—is adverbially predicated of Jesus. As Geoffrey Lampe puts it: Jesus acts divinely. Or, in terms of inspiration Christology, Jesus is filled with the Spirit more than anyone else, a Christology of degree. There is truth here. Indeed Jesus was filled with the Spirit without measure, the Spirit-bearer who would become the Spirit-baptizer. In the language of the theology of grace, Jesus is full of grace. So was Mary. I introduce the Blessed Virgin—even for those who for whom Marian dogma and veneration is not a theological factor—because she presents an image of one whose fullness of grace is analogous to but distinct from that of Jesus. It is the difference between the predication of divinization, which both our Lady and Our Lord possess, and the predication of divinity, which said only of Christ. Both divinization and the incarnation of divinity are the work of the Spirit and may be expressed in the language of grace. It is that to which I turn with the guidance of Thomas Aquinas.

IIB. DOGMATIC EXPLICATION

In the *tertia pars* of the *Summa Theologiae* Thomas elaborates on the threefold grace of Christ. Although the efficient cause of grace for St. Thomas *ad extra* is common to the three divine persons, the appropriation of grace to the Holy Spirit is consistent with presence of the indwelling Trinity in the just according to the invisible missions of the Son and the Holy Spirit. The order of theological reasoning proceeds from Christian experience to God who is known in that experience, which then further illuminates our experience. Formally, this means we move from the economic trinity, i.e., the biblical witness to the Trinity, to the immanent trinity and then back to the economic trinity. In other words, by reasoning to the truth of the faith, viz., the speculative moment in dogmatic theology, we enter more deeply into the mystery of the Trinity. Specifically, to know the risen humanity of Christ in the power of the Spirit directs one to the incarnate divinity of Christ in the same Spirit, which then illuminates our mystical union with Christ. I will proceed by tracing these steps in reference to the theology of grace, inclusive of the grace of Christ, and then we will examine the trinitarian deep structure of Spirit Christology.

Two aspects of the Christian experience of God and the God who is revealed in that experience require adjudication. From the perspective of the latter, from God to us, we must speak of the divine missions of the Son and Holy Spirit. From within this framework, one of Christian anthropology and of Christian experience, we focus on the grace offered and received. The *Christus praesens* and the *Spiritus praesens* are appropriated means of specifying the divine presence in light of the trinitarian missions. The Son and the Holy Spirit are sent, the former visibly in the Incarnation and the latter visibly at Jesus' baptism (in the form of dove) and at Pentecost (flames of fire). Although distinct, these visible missions are inseparable. The Holy Spirit's descent on Jesus at his baptism in the likeness of a dove is directed toward the christological mission of the incarnate Word. As with the descent of the Holy Spirit upon the Virgin Mary at the Annunciation, the christological mission is enabled by the work of the Holy Spirit. It would also appear that, in these instances, the mission of the Spirit precedes that of the Son, an order or taxis that seems to invert the *filioque* as some systematic theologians have noted. I will return to this matter.

Thomas Aquinas also refers to the invisible missions of the Son and Holy Spirit, specifically as this relates to the indwelling of the Holy Trinity in the just. This entails some intricate trinitarian issues that require adjudication. For example, does one posit a distinct indwelling for each of the divine persons? Or, by virtue of a proper mission of the Holy Spirit, the third person inhabits the Christian and the other two do so through *perichoresis*? I will reserve further consideration of this question for another time. However, for Thomas the invisible missions of the Son and the Spirit further demonstrates their distinction but inseparability, so much so, that the *Catechism of the Catholic Church* can designate the missions of the Son and the Holy Spirit as the "joint mission of the Son and Spirit" (no. 689). The invisible missions, as with the trinitarian missions in general, consist of the following elements as defined by Aquinas.

> Mission signifies not only procession from the principle, but also determines the temporal term of the procession. Hence mission is only temporal. Or we may say that it includes the eternal procession, with the addition of a temporal effect. For the relation of a divine person to His principle must be eternal. Hence the procession may be called a twin procession, eternal and temporal, not that there is a double relation to the principle, but a double term, temporal and eternal. (*Summa Theologiae*, Ia, Q 43, A 2, ad. 3)

Our interest is in the temporal terms of the missions.

Thomas distinguishes the invisible missions of the Son and the Spirit by virtue of the properties of the divine persons that constitute them as subsistent relations in the intra-divine processions. In the case of the Son Thomas argues that Word and Image are proper names whereas the Holy Spirit is properly nominated as Love and Gift. Thus Thomas can eloquently describe the interrelationship of their invisible missions as follows:

> The soul is made like to God by grace. Hence for a divine person to be sent to anyone by grace, there must needs be a likening of the soul to the divine person Who is sent, by some gift of grace. Because the Holy Ghost is Love, the soul is assimilated to the Holy Ghost by the gift of charity: hence the mission of the Holy Ghost is according to the mode of charity. Whereas the Son is the Word, not any sort of word, but one Who breathes forth Love. Hence Augustine says (De Trin. ix 10): "The Word we speak of is knowledge with love." Thus the Son is sent not in accordance with every and any kind of intellectual perfection, but according to the intellectual illumination, which breaks forth into the affection of love, as is said (John 6:45): "Everyone that hath heard from the Father and hath learned, cometh to Me," and (Psalm 38:4): "In my meditation a fire shall flame forth." Thus Augustine plainly says (De Trin. iv, 20): "The Son is sent, whenever He is known and perceived by anyone." Now perception implies a certain experimental knowledge; and this is properly called wisdom [sapientia], as it were a sweet knowledge [sapida scientia], according to Sirach 6:23: "The wisdom

of doctrine is according to her name." (*Summa Theologiae*, Ia, Q 43, A 5, ad. 2)

Note the relationship between the missions and grace. The latter neither collapses the missions into each other nor denies the unity of divine activity *ad extra* on the principle that all actions of the triune God *ad extra* are one, viz., the unity of operation follows the unity of the divine nature. Although the offer of grace is common to the three divine persons, nevertheless, the distinct presence of these persons is also evident, as Thomas makes clear:

> Since mission implies the origin of the person Who is sent, and His indwelling by grace, as above explained, if we speak of mission according to origin, in this sense the Son's mission is distinguished from the mission of the Holy Ghost, as generation is distinguished from procession. If we consider mission as regards the effect of grace, in this sense the two missions are united in the root which is grace, but are distinguished in the effects of grace, which consist in the illumination of the intellect and the kindling of the affection. Thus it is manifest that one mission cannot be without the other, because neither takes place without sanctifying grace, nor is one person separated from the other . . . " (*Summa Theologiae*, Ia, Q 43, A 5, ad. 3)

This speculative construction on the relationship between trinitarian missions and grace—in my view unsurpassed in the theological tradition—illustrates how a trinitarian Spirit-Christology requires the predication of the threefold personhood in the mystery of the Triune God. Contemplating these missions in the communication of divine grace forms the gestalt of the Christian experience of God. The objective trinitarian predications of processions, missions, and grace are certainly consistent with Thomas's logic. Thomas further specifies the particulars relative to the telos of divine grace in the sanctification of the just:

> This mode of manifestation [the manifestation of the invisible missions of the divine persons in visible creatures] applies in different ways to the Son and to the Holy Ghost. For it belongs to the Holy Ghost, Who proceeds as Love, to be the gift of sanctification; to the Son as the principle of the Holy Ghost, it belongs to the author of this sanctification. Thus the Son has been sent visibly as the author of sanctification; the Holy Ghost as the sign of sanctification. (*Summa Theologiae*, Ia, Q 43, A 7)

Indeed what may appear to be a conflation of the Risen Christ and the Holy Spirit in certain readings of St. Paul—consider James Dunn's axiom: "as the Spirit is the divinity of Jesus, so Jesus is the personality of the Holy Spirit"[3]—in fact, bespeaks the distinction of persons. It is by the Spirit in the affection of divine charity that one knows the person of the Son as the risen Lord and it is through spiritual knowledge imparted by the indwelling Son that the breath of divine charity in shed abroad in our hearts (Rom 5: 5). Matthias Scheeben, the nineteenth century neo-scholastic (of sorts) distinguishes these interior missions in the following near mystical terms.

> Indeed, in a certain sense this supernatural love [the Holy Spirit as the outpouring of the paternal love of the Father and of the filial love of the Son] is enkindled and inflamed by the Holy Spirit as its object . . . for He is the living expression, the breathing forth of the divine love for us.[4]

And,

> The Son of God becomes the object of our happiness (in the future life, and with due proportion also in the present life) only because the Light of which He Himself is born, the Light of the divine nature and cognitive faculty, is irradiated in us as in Him, and produces a reflection of the Father's nature in us as, similarly, it does in Him. And conversely, this Light is irradiated in us only inasmuch as we know and perceive the Son as the mirror of the Father, and in Him the Father Himself.[5]

Scheeben in his account of invisible trinitarian missions, like Thomas, is able to distinguish the presence of the divine persons. This may be accepted not only as a faithful account of Pauline theology. "For it is the God who said, 'let light shine out of darkness,' who has shone in our hearts to give the light of the knowledge of the glory of God in the face of Jesus Christ" (2 Cor 4: 6). And, "And, all of us, with unveiled faces, seeing the glory of the Lord as though reflected in a mirror, are being transformed into the same image from one degree of glory to another; for this comes from the Lord, the Spirit" (2 Cor 3: 18). It also demonstrates the relationship between grace in us and the threefold grace of Christ to which I now turn as a necessary foundation for a trinitarian Spirit-Christology.

---

3. Ibid.
4. Matthias Scheeben, *The Mysteries of Christianity* (St. Louis: B. Herder, 1946) 174.
5. Ibid., 175.

A Man of the Church

St. Thomas is explicit that of the three types of grace in the Christ—the grace of union, habitual grace, and capital grace—Jesus' habitual grace is identical to his capital grace. The grace by which Christ is holy in his dispositions and operations is the same grace that as head of the Church he communicates to the members of his body. By this fullness of grace the instrumentality of Christ's human nature is active relative to the Godhead and not merely passive. The fullness of grace in Christ is inclusive of the grace that justifies, the sevenfold gifts of the Holy Spirit that supernaturally perfect the operations of the soul, and the gratuitous graces (charismata) that manifest divine power to others; all of which are given by the Holy Spirit in the outpouring of the grace of the Holy Spirit on the Church. These are to be distinguished from the grace of union by which the humanity of Christ is created and assumed by the eternal Son of God. The grace of union substantially sanctifies Christ but requires habitual grace to sanctify the dispositions and operations of his human nature. In this respect the fullness grace in Christ surpasses that of Mary, the holiest of the saints, since her fullness is proportioned to her maternal mission whereas the grace of Christ extends to the universality of his redemptive mission regarding the exigencies of human nature to be perfected both in the state of the *viator* and in glory.

In the experience of the invisible missions, the Christian knows the abundance of this grace poured out in its fullness and also attains knowledge of the divine persons present and indwelling. The christological grace of union is at the basis of this distinction between the effusion of grace flowing forth from the risen Christ and the divine person himself, who in his incarnate and glorified humanity is the author, principle, and source of this grace. One must be cautious so as not to reduce all grace in Christ to habitual grace becoming capital grace such that the operation of grace does not extend to the divine personhood of Jesus and for which there is no analogy for the grace present in Christians. This leads us to the distinctiveness and uniqueness of the pneumatological dimensions of grace in the person of Christ himself.

The distinction between the grace of union and habitual grace in Jesus is not just that Jesus is the source of grace as no other. He is the source of grace because he is the incarnate Son by virtue of the hypostatic union. The grace of union gives rise to habitual grace in Christ, but neither the grace of union nor habitual grace function as a medium by which the hypostatic union takes place. The grace of union is not the means of the union but the efficient cause of the union, its gratis so to speak simply being that from above the human nature is created and simultaneously united to the divine nature in the person of the Son. Thomas expresses this distinction with force and clarity.

> ... grace is taken in two ways:—first, as the will of God gratuitously bestowing something; secondly, as the free gift of God. Now human nature stands in need of the gratuitous will of God in order to be lifted up to God, since this is above its natural capability. Moreover, human nature is lifted up to God in two ways: first, by operation, as the saints know and love God; secondly, by personal being, and this mode belongs exclusively to Christ, in Whom human nature is assumed so as to be in the Person of the Son of God. But it is plain that for the perfection of operation the power needs to be perfected by a habit, whereas that a nature has being in its own suppositum does not take place by means of a habit. (*Summa Theologiae*, IIIa, Q 2, A 10)

The implications for how the Spirit is present in Jesus are noteworthy. Indeed this is consistent with the biblical witness that Jesus possesses the Spirit without measure (as we have already noted), and that he is anointed with the Holy Spirit and power (Acts 10: 38). But here we must distinguish between Jesus as the God who anoints and the Jesus as the man anointed. Without any implication of Nestorian tendencies, we must still affirm the Chalcedonian distinction between the two natures of Christ. The human nature of Christ as the instrument of the Divine Word is still finite. Therefore, the operations of his human nature proceed from a finite soul negating the notion that habitual grace in Christ is infinite. Nor for that matter in another vein, can we posit that the human soul of Christ comprehends the divine essence. The former cannot circumscribe the latter. All the more then must we affirm that the anointing of human nature with the Holy Spirit is why he possesses the fullness of grace but only with the qualification that such fullness proceeds from the grace of union. Again, Scheeben puts it eloquently.

> This is the divine ointment which, flowing down from the wellspring of the Godhead into the creature and submerging the creature in God, constitutes not merely a deified man, but the true God-man. This is the mystery of Christ par excellence. He is anointed not merely by divine deputation for the discharge of an office, nor even merely by the outpouring of the Holy Spirit in His deifying grace, but by personal union with the principle of the Holy Spirit. Hence, the divine ointment is contained

in the very make-up of Christ's being, and constitutes Him a divine-human being.[6]

We have now arrived at the trinitarian issue that has been the bane of an orthodox trinitarian Spirit Christology in the Western Catholic tradition, namely the *filioque*. Many trinitarian theologians who have developed a more pneumatologically oriented Christology have either dismissed or qualified the *filioque*. Jürgen Moltmann alters the *filioque* in the interest of accentuating the distinct agency of all three divine persons in the parabola of the eschatologically generated fulfillment of the divine economy. Therefore, in the divine economy of trinitarian glorification one moves from the sequence of Father–Spirit–Son (Incarnation through resurrection) to Father–Son–Spirit (Lordship and Outpouring) to Spirit–Son–Father (Session and Parousia).[7] Hans Urs von Balthasar is well known for his trinitarian inversion to account for the mission of the Spirit directing that of the Son in his earthly life and ministry. The inversion by which the Son under the "rule of the Spirit" obeys the Father is "the projection of the immanent Trinity onto the 'economic' plane, whereby the Son's 'correspondence' to the Father is articulated as 'obedience.'"[8] Finally, David Coffey has argued that a return or mutual love model of trinitarian relations (wherein the Father bestows the Spirit on the Son) must complement the procession model (with the *filioque* in place) in order to accentuate the Spirit's agency and his proper mission relative to that of the Son.[9]

Indeed, it may seem more trinitarian to argue that the Father bestows the Spirit on Jesus and that Jesus in the Spirit does the will of the Father. That is true as long as we do not predicate divinity in the incarnate Jesus as Spirit. Likewise, the outpouring of the Holy Spirit from the Father and the Son underscore the distinct personhood of the Son in his glorified humanity as we have seen by examining the invisible missions of the Son and Holy Spirit. This is borne out sacramentally as well wherein the *epiclesis* of the Spirit is invoked for the action and presence of the Son, most especially in the Eucharist. The Eucharistic *epiclesis* for the coming of the Holy Spirit on the bread and wine is distinct but inseparable from the

---

6. Ibid., 332–33.

7 Jürgen Moltmann, *The Trinity and the Kingdom* (San Francisco: Harper & Row, 1981) 94.

8. Hans Urs von Balthasar, *Theo-Drama Theological Dramatic Theory: III. Dramatis Personae: Persons in Christ* (San Francisco: Ignatius, 1992) 191.

9. David Coffey, *Deus Trinitas: The Doctrine of the Triune God* (New York: Oxford, 1999) 46–65.

substantial presence of Christ in the Eucharistic elements—"his Body and his Blood, with his soul and his divinity" (*CCC*, no. 1413) as the Council of Trent put it. The analogy with the Incarnation is obvious. Only the Son becomes incarnate, so too, Christ is present under the Eucharistic species, not the Holy Spirit.

The same principle applies to the procession of the Holy Spirit from the Father and the Son in the act of the Incarnation. The procession of the Holy Spirit is inseparable from the eternal generation of the Son. In the temporal missions of the Son and Spirit the distinction of persons is preserved by extension of their temporal missions from their eternal processions as we have seen. Since this is a consequence of habitual or sanctifying grace, as I have stated, this cannot be analogous to the grace of union that constitutes the hypostatic union. In Jesus of Nazareth, the work of the Holy Spirit entails both the grace of union and habitual grace. The latter is manifest in the fullness of grace unique to Jesus (as compared, for example, with Mary relative to its scope and extension) and during his earthly ministry is the fruit of the Father's anointing of him with the Holy Spirit, e.g., Jesus' baptism at the Jordan whereby Jesus is the Spirit-bearer. In the outpouring of the Holy Spirit, Jesus the Spirit-baptizer received from the Father the gift of the Holy Spirit and as mediated through his incarnate, paschal and glorified humanity fulfills the messianic promise that God's Spirit will indwell the reconstituted People of God (Ezek 37: 14). However, in the hypostatic union the Spirit's work is even more unique and distinctive.

The conception of Jesus in the womb of Mary by the Holy Spirit does indeed entail the bestowal of the Spirit upon her such that the Divine Son becomes incarnate. However, one cannot disassociate the procession of the Holy Spirit from the Son in consideration of the anointing of his humanity as in creating and uniting it with the eternal Son—no temporal sequence implied. The eternal Son assumes a human nature (through creation and union) as his own on the basis of his own hypostatic identity relative to the Father and the Spirit. The only-begotten One becomes flesh by the Spirit he breathes forth with the Father who is the principle origin of the third person. It is precisely as Image and Word of the Father that the eternal Son becomes human by power of the Holy Spirit. The Father sends the Son with the Holy Spirit proceeding from both in one spiration (not a double spiration) anointing the human nature of Jesus as the Son's own humanity. Again I turn to Scheeben:

> When the Fathers say that Christ is anointed with the Holy Spirit, they mean that the Holy Spirit has descended into the humanity of Christ in the Logos from whom He proceeds, and that He anoints and perfumes the humanity as the distillation and fragrance of the ointment which is the Logos Himself.[10]

I conclude with one final corroboration of this truth from the perspective of the earthly Jesus as the incarnate Son. Jesus' knowledge of the Father and the Holy Spirit is evident in the gospels and is expressed dramatically in Luke:

> At that same hour Jesus rejoiced in the Holy Spirit and said, "I thank you, Father, Lord of heaven and earth, because you have hidden these things from the wise and intelligent and revealed them to infants; yes, Father, for such was your gracious will." (Lk 10:21)

Jesus lived in the Spirit and in communion with the Father. This is analogous to our own experience of grace for it is by this Spirit, what Paul identifies as the Spirit of his Son, that we cry out Abba! Father! (Gal 4: 6). However, Jesus' relationship with the Father constitutes his identity as the Son of God whereas the Christian's relationship is the consequence of one's new identity in Christ by virtue of baptism as a son or daughter in the Son, his natural filial relation versus our adopted one. This leads to one further distinction.

It is by the grace of the Holy Spirit that the Christian is indwelt with the Spirit and knows the divine persons in their invisible missions including the Father who sends the Son and Spirit. In Christ it is the Holy Spirit himself who works by his grace to constitute the God-man, not just a deified man although indeed his human nature is deified by habitual grace. Therefore, Jesus' knowledge of the Father and the Holy Spirit (even of the divine Son in a reflexive manner to the extent that the Son's knowing

---

10. Scheeben, *Mysteries of Christianity*, 332. Scheeben becomes even more precise in footnote no. 7 on the same page. "Not so much the Holy Spirit in Himself, as rather the source from which He issues, but including, besides this source, all its wealth and overflow, is the unguent with which Christ is anointed. In other words, the ointment is not the *Spiritus Sanctus spiratus*, but the *Spiritus Sanctus spirans* together with His *spiramen*; it is not the latter's operation through the former, as with the saints, but the former's operation through the latter, that produces the Saint of saints. Moreover, the execution of the hypostatic union, which is the reason why the dignity of the Son of God pertains also to the Son of man, is ascribed to the Third Person, the representative of the divine love, only by appropriation." This last point might be contested regarding the distinction between a proper and appropriated mission but the substance of these remarks is quite illuminating.

cannot be circumscribed by Jesus' human intellect) proceeds from the grace of union that substantially sanctifies his human nature along with the habitual grace that divinizes his dispositions and operations. This inseparable differentiation of his sanctification and divinization, requires that Christ even as *viator* possesses the beatific vision, beholding the divine essence that is not really distinct from the divine persons. In this manner and according to the modalities of both the grace of union and habitual grace we can posit a Spirit Christology within which Jesus' possession of the Spirit without measure is the unique basis of his incarnate deity and the incompatible source of divine life for all.

II

The Vocation of the Theologian—
Reflections on the Work and Witness
of Ralph Del Colle

2

The Ecclesial Vocation of the Theologian

BRUCE D. MARSHALL

WITH RARE GRACE, CONSTANCY, and serenity Ralph Del Colle has embodied for all who know him the ecclesial vocation of the theologian. In gratitude to God for the purity of his witness to it, I offer this brief reflection on our common vocation.

I

In May of 1990, on the Feast of the Ascension of the Lord, the Vatican's Congregation for the Doctrine of the Faith published a substantial "Instruction" on the nature and mission of theology. Its official title, in the manner of Vatican documents, came from the Latin words with which it opened: *Donum veritatis*, "The Gift of Truth." The text quickly became known, however, by its subtitle, which quite precisely summarizes its contents: "The Ecclesial Vocation of the Theologian."

It is not so much upon this important Vatican document itself as upon the thought embodied in its subtitle that I want to reflect briefly here. The theologian's calling and task are from the Church, and so his responsibility is to the Church. Theology, to be sure, seeks wisdom about God, and responds to God's own call to know him and love him. But the God about whom theology seeks wisdom is the God known to the Church, the God who has entrusted the most sublime truths about himself to fishermen and tentmakers, and to their successors down to this day.

A Man of the Church

Theology's purpose is therefore to serve the Church, to help build up the people of God in their knowledge of the truth that sets us free.

The publication of "The Ecclesial Vocation of the Theologian" in 1990 was greeted with a storm of protest from Catholic theologians in the United States and Western Europe, though there were also those who welcomed its appearance, if for the most part more quietly. The protest grew more vociferous in August of the same year, when Pope Blessed John Paul II issued his Apostolic Constitution *Ex corde ecclesiae*, on the nature and mission of the Catholic university. *Ex corde ecclesiae* gave teeth to the earlier document from the CDF by underlining the existing canonical requirement that Catholics on the theology faculties of Catholic universities have explicit permission to teach from their bishop. By requiring this permission—the much-contested "mandatum"—the Holy See signaled that it intended to enforce the teaching of "The Ecclesial Vocation of the Theologian." As theology exists to serve the Church, so the theologian must answer to those divinely empowered to teach the truths of the faith authoritatively in the Church, namely her bishops in communion with the successor of Peter. The theologian must, in other words, answer to the Church's Magisterium, her living authority to teach, embodied in particular human beings.

Even this brief description intimates what lay at the heart of the strident opposition to "The Ecclesial Vocation of the Theologian" and *Ex corde ecclesiae*. To many American Catholic theologians these documents seemed to call for a hopelessly authoritarian and oppressive infringement of the necessary freedom of the theologian. Theology is an intellectual enterprise, and theologians are intellectuals. They must therefore be free to follow evidence and arguments wherever they lead, unencumbered by outside interference, especially the interference of those who—like most bishops—are not themselves intellectuals. As an intellectual, the theologian is answerable to the truth, above all the truth about God, as she or he sees it, and not to any authority external to her conscientious undertaking of intellectual discernment.

By requiring that what Catholic theology professors actually profess be consonant with the teaching of the Church as interpreted by her bishops, many thought the Vatican was doing more than attempting to stifle much-needed creativity and innovation in theology, though that was bad enough. Rome was undermining the whole enterprise of Catholic theology, by failing to recognize that theology is by nature *Wissenschaft*. It is an activity of rigorous critical reflection, a "science," in the broad sense of an activity for scholars trained in its distinctive requirements. Like any such scientific or scholarly activity—physics, economics, or art history, to name a few—theology's results can properly be assessed only by its own practitioners, and not by those inexpert in its critical methods and demands. The Church, many feared, was trying to do away with real theology, and replace it with a peculiarly flat-footed sort of authorized catechesis.

At the root of this last objection lay, it seems, the suspicion that the Vatican was trying to scuttle perhaps the most basic and hard-won achievement of Catholic theology in modern times, which was to have secured the legitimate and necessary place of reason, of free critical inquiry, in relation to the claims of faith. Since Vatican II, so the objection went, the Church has accepted the right of modern philosophical and historical science, and more recently of social and political theory, to scrutinize her teachings. The theologian's creativity and ingenuity, which the Vatican wanted to stifle, are needed in order to carry out this scrutiny, and to decide what must be done in light of its results. It is precisely the theologian's job, in other words, to show how Christian doctrines can be adapted to the manifold demands of reason as they bear in upon us in our contemporary context. *Donum veritatis* and *Ex corde ecclesiae* were nothing less, many supposed, than an attempt to rob the Catholic theologian of this precious responsibility, and to return Catholic theology to the evil pre-Conciliar days when theologians cringed before an authoritarian fideism emanating from Rome.

II

It will be plain, I hope, that the issues at the center of this Catholic debate are not of concern to Catholics alone. The struggle to harmonize scriptural faith and modern *Wissenschaft* has a long history in Protestantism as well. That struggle continues to this day, if not always in just the way I have described. An appreciation of the ecclesial mission of theology and the ecclesial vocation of the theologian is, I think, essential to grasping the coherence of faith and reason, and thereby to understanding the nature of theology as a rigorous intellectual enterprise.

In what follows I will attempt to develop an argument for the irreducibly ecclesial character of the theologian's work and vocation without any direct appeal to the divinely established authority of the Catholic Magisterium over teaching in the Church. I bracket the distinctive teaching office of the Magisterium here not because I doubt the reality and reach of its authority, but for purposes of inquiry—in fact, for two such purposes. One is to make an argument based on assumptions that Protestants as well as Catholics can accept, since the problem that comes to the surface in recent debates about the ecclesial vocation of the theologian (the right relationship between faith and critical reason) is shared by modern Catholic and Protestant theology.[1] The other is to gain more understanding of theology as an inherently ecclesial enterprise than is likely to be reached if the argument ends too quickly.

This last is a specifically Catholic concern. When the issues raised by *Donum veritatis* and *Ex corde ecclesiae* come up for discussion among Catholic theologians, those who embrace the teaching of these two documents tend to begin by insisting that all Catholics—theologians included—must accept the teaching of even the Church's ordinary Magisterium with, at the very least, religious submission of mind and will.[2] They are of course right to maintain this principle. But in this context it tends to be a conversation-stopper. When we seek reasons for believing that theology must be an ecclesial vocation, we are unlikely to find them if we start off by declaring, in effect, that Catholic theologians are obligated to see their work in this way lest they fail of religious submission. Newman observed that "when men understand each other's meaning, they see, for the most part, that controversy is either superfluous or hopeless."[3] So it is here. Upon hearing this declaration those who (rightly) accept the need

---

1. This paper began as a lecture given before an audience mainly of free Church Protestants, at the 2012 Christian Scholars Conference sponsored by the universities of the Church of Christ. I am grateful for the questions and comments I received there, especially from my respondent, Prof. Matthew Tapie. Addressing the present question with that audience helped impose on me the useful discipline of making a case for the ecclesial vocation of the theologian without relying on an appeal to the authority of the Magisterium.

2. In the language of *Donum veritatis* itself: (§23): "When the Magisterium, not intending to act 'definitively,' teaches a doctrine . . . the response called for is that of the religious submission (*obsequium*) of will and intellect." This is contrasted with those teachings that are proposed by the Magisterium "in a definitive way," which "must be firmly accepted and held," and those proposed as "found in Revelation," which call for "the assent . . . of theological faith" (ibid.). In making these distinctions *Donum veritatis* employs the language of *Lumen gentium*, 25 and the 1983 *Code of Canon Law* (canons 750 & 752). For the English text of *Donum veritatis* see http://www.vatican.va/roman_curia/congregations/cfaith/documents/rc_con_cfaith_doc_19900524_theologian-vocation_en.html; the Latin typica is in *Acta apostolicae sedis* 82 (1990), pp. 1550–1570.

3. John Henry Newman, "Faith and Reason Contrasted as Habits of Mind," in *Newman's University Sermons*, Introductions by D. M. MacKinnon and J. D. Holmes (London: SPCK, 1970 [originally published 1871]), p. 201.

for religious submission to the Church's teaching will probably see little need for further discussion of the theologian's vocation, and those who don't, or are unsure, will probably want to talk about this particular matter with someone else. Either way, we will be unlikely to find reasons that help us see some of the deeper grounds on which the ecclesial vocation of the theologian, and the ecclesial authority that requires it, rightly rest.

III

Especially to some Protestants, it might seem as though the problem of balancing authoritative Church teaching with the intellectual vocation of the theologian is solved easily enough: just get rid of the Church. The underlying problem, after all, is how to square divinely revealed truth with the legitimate requirements of reason. If we drop the idea of the Church as the authorized guardian of revealed truth, then the theologian no longer lives under an authoritarian shadow, fearful of having somebody else's theology arbitrarily imposed on him in the name of the Church. By not putting the Church between God and the believer, so the argument runs, we leave the individual Christian, including the theologian, where she ought to be: alone with the revealing God. God speaks through scripture, of course, but presumably everybody who wants to do theology at all acknowledges that in some basic way theology has to be authorized by scripture, and accepts the ultimate authority of the God who speaks through the text. The theologian can go about his scientific work, confident that the intrinsic authority of God himself and the luminosity of the text through which God speaks will keep his theology on the right track, upholding correct Christian teaching without ecclesial intervention. Perhaps the intellectual vocation of the theologian is, after all, only a problem for Catholics.

Getting the Christian community out of the intersection between divinely revealed truth and theological reason is, I think, easier said than done. To see why, it may help to recall Friedrich Schleiermacher's way of describing the difference between Protestantism and Catholicism. These two forms of Christianity differ, Schleiermacher proposes, in that Protestantism makes the individual's relationship with the Church depend on his relationship with Christ, while Catholicism makes the individual's relationship with Christ depend on his relationship with the Church.[4] At first glance this might seem to mean that for Protestantism, an individual can, indeed should, have

---

4. See *The Christian Faith*, proposition (*Leitsatz*) to §24, trans. H. R. Mackintosh and J. S. Stewart (Edinburgh: T. & T. Clark, 1928), p. 103.

a relationship with Christ without having any relationship with a Church, or at least prior to having any such relationship. The genius of Protestantism, which Schleiermacher obviously wants to defend, would then consist precisely in its refusal to interpose the Christian community between the believer and Christ, while Catholicism insists on doing just that.

Schleiermacher's explanation of his thesis, however, is characteristically subtle. A vital relationship with Christ is in fact always joined to a vital relationship with the Christian community. "In no individual," he writes, "does Christian piety originate independently and of its own accord, but only from and in the community."[5] This applies in Protestantism just as much as it does in Catholicism. The two differ not over whether the individual's faith, her apprehension of divine truth, is always mediated by the believing—and teaching—community, but over *which* community mediates this apprehension of divine truth in the right way. More precisely, for Schleiermacher, the difference between the two forms of Christianity lies in the way each regards the basic "facts" of Christian communal existence, such as the ordained ministry. Protestantism sees these as instituted by the Church itself in order to serve Christ's effective work in the world, while Catholicism sees them as a legacy authoritatively bequeathed by Christ to the Church so that the Church itself can carry on Christ's effective work in the world.[6] My present concern is not to assess the adequacy of this way of distinguishing Protestantism from Catholicism. The point, rather, is to observe that even where one might least expect to find it—in the outstanding theological genius of liberal Protestantism—the Church is always already present in the relationship between the believer, theologian included, and Christ.

For the moment I will not argue further for the claim that any individual's believing relationship with God in Christ depends upon the Church. If it's true, though, that Christian faith is always ecclesially mediated, then this fact about faith goes to the heart of what theology is. It will help to think through this suggestion with a bit of care.

IV

Theology is often thought of as faith seeking understanding. That's certainly a good definition of theology as far as it goes. Whatever else we

---

5. *Christian Faith*, §24.4, p. 106. The translation, however, is my own as are all others in this paper.

6. See *Christian Faith*, §24.4, pp. 106–07.

may think theology is, or needs to be, surely it is at least this. Faith seeks understanding, it starts to become theology, when it searches out reasons for the truth of what it believes. By seeking reasons, faith looks for light, for a clearer and more luminous apprehension of the truths about God that God has given us in faith, and of the radiant bonds that unite these truths of faith. Taking a cue from Thomas Aquinas, we could say that faith itself is already a participation in God under the aspect of the first truth and measure of all truth, albeit a partial and imperfect one under the conditions of this life. As such faith is also a participation in the uncreated light by which alone this first truth can be seen, even in the dim mirror of this present life.[7] When faith is conceived in this way, theology becomes faith's deliberate effort to intensify its present participation in the first truth by the light reasons provide—to make of what it has been taught by God nothing less than "a certain imprint of God's own knowledge" in our own minds.[8]

Giving reasons is, of course, an activity of critical reason; it's the activity for which reason exists. The demand for reasons is what makes theology a science, and distinguishes theology from the divine gift of faith, which rightly accepts the truths God teaches about himself in the Church, but does not as such give reasons for what it believes. Animated by the Holy Spirit, faith recognizes the voice of God in the teaching of the Church, and believes what God says because God, who is the truth itself, says it. Faith knows that no authority in heaven or on earth can make false what God says is true, and embraces with joy the mysteries of God's own life that he has opened up to us in the human words of the Church—the truths "that eye has not seen and ear has not heard . . . but God has revealed to us by his Spirit" (I. Cor. 2:9–10). Yet faith also knows that no appeal to authority, even divine authority, yields understanding. Divine authority teaches us what is true about God, and about the world in relation to God, but not why it is true.

When it's a question of what is true about God, for example whether God is incarnate of the Virgin Mary, or whether God is three persons distinct from one another but not distinct from the one God himself, then the

---

7. On the first see *De potentia* 6, 9, c: "That the divine word dwells in us happens by faith, which is a kind of participation by us in divine truth (*quaedam participatio in nobis divinae veritatis*)." On the second see *In Ioannem* 1, 4 (no. 120): "There is a twofold participation in the divine light. One is perfect, which happens in glory, according to Ps. 35:10: 'In your light we will see light.' The other is imperfect, namely that which we have by faith."

8. *Summa theologiae* I, 1, 3, ad 2.

authority of God, speaking through the Church's interpretation of scripture, is both necessary and sufficient to settle the question. But when it's a question not of knowing whether these sublime states of affairs obtain, but of understanding why they obtain, we need reasons that connect one thought to another. We understand the divine mysteries of Christianity discursively, by coming up with arguments that establish a connection between one truth and another.

Here Thomas Aquinas is again helpful. He observes that the teacher of theology has not done his job when he has established, however correctly, what we are to believe on divine authority, ecclesially mediated. His job is to give reasons, and thereby help the learner begin to see the light the teacher already sees, the light shining from the Christian mysteries themselves and exposing their wondrous harmony.[9] "In the classroom, the theological master carries on disputations . . . in order to instruct his hearers so that they may be led to an understanding of the truth of which he speaks. For this it is necessary to rely on reasons which get at the root of this truth, so that the hearers may know how it is that what is said, is true. Otherwise, if the teacher settles the question by authorities alone, the hearer will indeed be certain as to what is true, but he will acquire no knowledge or understanding, and will go away empty."[10]

Theology so understood is evidently a science, a *wissenschaftlich* intellectual discipline, and theologians are scientists, intellectuals who, with their discipline, ought to be at home in the university. Indeed it was theology's rigorous intellectual demands that gave rise, around the turn of the thirteenth century, to the university as it still exists, more or less, today. At the same time, theology and the people who practice it differ from other sciences and other scientists in one particularly important way. Theologians answer to the Church, and not simply, or primarily, to the university or to their own intellectual guild.

Every intellectual enterprise, it's important to recall, is responsible to a community, and not only to the ingenuity or insight of its individual practitioners. In fact academics insist on this with considerable vehemence, as anyone who has undergone a tenure evaluation well knows. Peer review is the gold standard when it comes to determining the quality of scientific work and the value of its results, and any evaluation that comes from

---

9. To borrow a phrase from Matthias Joseph Scheeben, who gives a particularly penetrating modern account of theology as the science of the Christian mysteries. See *Die Mysterien des Christentums*, §4; in English as *The Mysteries of Christianity*, trans. Cyril Vollert, S.J., (St. Louis: B. Herder Book Co., 1946), p. 19.

10. *Quodlibet* IV, 9, 3 c.

outside the guild is at best second-rate. Academics reflexively assume that the community to which intellectual enterprises answer, first and last, is made up of those who practice the enterprise, for the most part found in universities. Whether physics, economics, or art history is practiced well or poorly, whether its results are true, false, or uncertain, is, we normally suppose, a matter for physicists, economists, and art historians to decide.

There are many reasons for this characteristic insistence that sciences ought to be monitored by those who practice them, and not by outsiders. Not all of these reasons are noble. Power is one of them, perhaps especially in fields where large amounts of funding are at stake from governments and other agencies. Those who have achieved high status in their science are not immune from using what power they have to shape the direction of research and funding in their discipline according to their own beliefs and interests. But there are also good reasons for intellectual disciplines to be judged by those who are fully engaged in them, in particular the fact that like Christian faith, any science is mediated to the individual by the community that already practices it. This requires the individual scholar to trust the judgment of the community of scholars or intellectuals to which he belongs.

This is especially clear if we think about how a science is learned. As Aristotle observed, and as very much remains the case in acquiring an intellectual discipline today, "the learner should be one who believes."[11] The learner must trust that what the teacher says is true, even if she cannot understand it or see why it is true. Only in this way will understanding eventually come, and the learner begin to be a scientist. In trusting her teacher, though, the student does not simply accept what the teacher says as warranted because it embodies the teacher's individual judgment. Rather the learner assumes that what she accepts is warranted in the judgment of the whole scientific community to which the teacher also belongs. If she had a different teacher she would, in the end, learn the same thing. And if the student becomes a scientist herself and a teacher of others, she will continue to trust the judgment of the scientific community to which she belongs, both as to what she teaches and as to what she continues to learn. In that sense the individual's science, both her store of knowledge and her practices of inquiry, never cease to be mediated by the scientific community to which she belongs.

---

11. *De Sophisticis Elenchis* 2 (165b3). Cf. Aquinas's observations on this text, *Summa theologiae* II–II, 2, 3, c.

Any intellectual discipline, then, is mediated to its practitioners by a community. Authority over the practice of that discipline is inseparably bound up with this communal activity of mediation, of forming individuals in an intellectual practice. Receiving her practice from a particular community, the individual scientist is answerable to the standards of that community when it comes to judging the quality of her practice and the correctness of her results. Bearing this point in mind may help us appreciate how theology too answers to communal standards, but in a distinctive way.

Theology is a scientific discipline, but the community to which theology answers, we have said, is the Church. The Church is made up mostly of those who are not intellectuals, and who do not practice theology. In this the Church differs from, say, the Catholic Theological Society of America. Yet we would not want to say that in the end theology answers to the CTSA, rather than to the community of Christians to which theologians too belong. Ultimately, if for the most part indirectly, the intellectual discipline of theology answers to a community overwhelmingly comprised of non-intellectuals. How can this be?

Theology is, at minimum, faith seeking understanding. The faith theology seeks to understand is mediated to theologians by the Church, which receives that faith, forms individuals in it, and hands it on to them. The theologian thus depends on the Church for the faith he seeks to understand, even if the theologian is not himself a believer.[12] As the community which mediates to individuals the complex network of beliefs and practices which constitute the Christian faith, the Church has the responsibility to judge what is and is not in accord with its faith. By carrying out this responsibility, the Church makes judgments about whether its faith has been rightly understood. When it discerns whether proposals for belief and practice are in accord with its faith, the Church is deciding whether the theologian's results are true or false, and thereby whether theology has been done well or poorly.

The Church's responsibility to judge whether the truth claims with which it is presented, including those of theologians, are in accord with its faith is not, therefore, a mere juridical stipulation. This responsibility can, of course, be canonically codified, and in the Catholic Church it is. But the Church's responsibility to assess the truth claims of theologians stems from the very nature of the Christian faith as a communally mediated

---

12. Whether and in what sense theology can be done by those outside the community of Christian faith is a question I will not pursue here. The present point is simply that the argument of this paragraph doesn't depend on the assumption that the theologian is a believer.

system of belief and practice. The Christian faith itself is an interconnected network of judgments, of beliefs held true. Only as such can it be possessed and handed on. When the Church finds itself compelled to assess whether a theologian's claims are or are not in accord with its faith, the Church necessarily makes judgments about the truth or falsity of what the theologian teaches.

This may seem like an obvious non-sequitur. Pulmonologists seek to understand the act of breathing and correct deficient cases of it, but no one would say that the community of breathers is competent to make a rigorous intellectual assessment of the act of breathing, or to assess whether pulmonology was well or poorly done. Why should the community of Christian believers be thought competent to make a rigorous intellectual assessment of the act of believing, and to judge whether theology has been well or poorly done?

The chief reason lies in the disparity between the two cases. Neither the act or breathing nor what one breathes is communally mediated at all, but the act of believing and what one believes are. The science of pulmonology is communally mediated to individuals, but it is handed on by the community of pulmonologists, not the community of breathers. The parity here is not between the community of breathers and the community of believers, but between the community of pulmonologists and the community of believers. Each mediates a highly ramified system of beliefs and practices to individuals, and assesses their mastery of what the community aims to hand on.

Precisely as an intellectual, then, the theologian answers to, and is rightly loyal to, what a decidedly mixed community of mostly non-intellectuals believes to be true. The observation that being good at theology and being good at believing don't necessarily go together reinforces this point. As we all know, being an accomplished, even a highly accomplished, theologian doesn't make one a model believer, or even a particularly competent one. Conversely, the most accomplished Christians, the saints whom scripture bids us to emulate, are for the most part not theologians, or people of learning at all. Yet they have a kind of instinctive grasp of the whole Christian faith, what Aquinas calls a connatural knowledge of divine things, which enables them to size up cases of speech and action by Christians far more readily, and far more reliably, than any theologian who lacks this sort of grasp. Think of Blessed Mother Theresa of Calcutta, or St. Thérèse of Lisieux. Both had only a rudimentary education, and read little besides the bible and the works of a few saints and spiritual writers.

A Man of the Church

Yet anyone who was unsure what to say or do as a Christian, whether peasant or scholar, could trust their judgment more than that of the most accomplished theologian. The Church, in other words, includes people who are not intellectuals, but who are markedly holier than you or I. For just that reason they get to tell you and me what we should believe and what we should do.

V

To the understanding here outlined of the roots of the theologian's ecclesial vocation it will no doubt be objected that the legitimate and necessary prophetic office of the theologian has been suppressed, if not eliminated entirely. Part of the theologian's responsibility, perhaps a large part, is to criticize the Church. The theologian may need to be critical, not only in the sense of "rigorous," as here assumed, but in the sense of "negative." Part of the theologian's job is to use the insight gained by his reflective activity to change the Church for the better, to propose new ways of believing and acting which will reform the Church and bring the Church closer to being the community God intends it to be. By making the theologian's work subject, by its very nature, to the judgment of the Church, I have guaranteed, so the objection might go, that the theologian's work will simply reflect the status quo in the Church, and precluded the possibility of theological reform of the Church.

Not at all. I assume that the theologian, like every human being, must speak and act in accordance with his conscience. This may bring the theologian into conflict with the Church. Indeed if the theologian advocates views contrary to those presently held by the Christian community to which he belongs (leaving aside the complex question of how such a community should decide what is genuinely "held" by it), he should expect conflict. No one, after all, has an a priori right not to be disagreed with. If, after open-minded critical reflection on the disputed matter—including self-critical reflection—the theologian still believes he is right and the Church is wrong, he not only may, but must, continue to hold the view which in good conscience he believes to be true. Whether the theologian appreciates the necessarily ecclesial nature of his enterprise will, however, have a lot to do with where he goes from there. It will deeply affect the character of the dissent to which he regards himself in conscience bound.

Faced with this situation, the theologian might respond by rejecting, privately or publicly, the very idea that the results of his critical reflection can be subject to the judgment of those who are not themselves intellectuals, or are intellectuals of a lower caliber than himself. This underlying refusal of faith seeking understanding to be corrected by mere faith can take various forms, not least appeals to academic or intellectual freedom or to the legitimate plurality of theological views in the Church.

These are, to be sure, important values for both the Church and theology, but they are not absolute values. To suppose that reasoned faith ought in principle to trump simple faith, the faith of intellectuals to supersede the faith of the unwashed, is a failure to appreciate the necessarily ecclesial character of the theologian's task. If explicit, it manifests a studied ingratitude, a refusal to recognize or accept that the theologian wholly owes to the Christian community the faith his reason seeks to understand. This has to be thought of as false dissent. John Henry Newman captures it with his characteristic stringency. "It goes against them to believe [the Church's] doctrine, not so much for want of evidence that she is from God, as because, if so, they shall have to submit their minds to living men, who have not their own cultivation or depth of intellect, and because they must receive a number of doctrines, whether they will or no, which are strange to their imagination and difficult to their reason."[13]

What, though, of critical reason's right to scrutinize Church teaching, in order to arrive at a genuine understanding of the faith? The post-Conciliar Church has itself insisted—not least in the teaching of John Paul II and Benedict XVI— that true faith must be rational, and that faith cannot be played off against the legitimate demands of reason. The theologian, therefore, evidently has the responsibility of criticizing Church teaching when it is, at the moment, out of step with the requirements of reason. As Thomas Aquinas rightly said, grace does not destroy nature—perhaps the one Thomistic axiom that post-Conciliar theology has embraced without reservation.

Faith and reason are not opposites, to be sure, but there is a definite and ordered relationship between them, just as there is between grace and nature. Faith perfects reason, by bringing reason to the goal it naturally

---

13. John Henry Newman, "Faith and Private Judgment," in *Discourses Addressed to Mixed Congregations* (London: Longmans, Green & Co., 1916 [originally published 1849]), p. 204. Newman is here speaking of the resistance of the English educated class in his day to Roman Catholic teaching, the acceptance of which would require Englishmen to subject themselves to the religious judgment of uncouth Irish priests and bishops. But his point has broader application.

seeks: to know, as fully as possible, the truth about God. It's not reason that perfects faith, any more than it's nature that perfects grace. So if there's a conflict between the contents of faith and the deliverances of reason, it's reason, not faith, that's out of step. In that case reason needs to be brought into harmony with faith, and not the other way around. Faith is a gift of grace mediated by the teaching Church, so if reason finds itself at odds with Church teaching (allowing for different levels of assent appropriate to different sorts of teaching), reason has to take that as a sure sign that it has gone astray, that it has allowed itself to be lured away from its natural goal. Reason in conflict with the teachings of the faith is not natural reason, exactly, but reason no longer oriented toward its goal, and thus damaged reason, reason failing to live up to its own nature. That grace perfects nature means, in this case, not only that faith brings reason to a goal it cannot attain under its own power, but that faith, by correcting wayward reason, heals the damage reason has inflicted on itself.

For just this reason Aquinas, after famously stating that *gratia non tollit naturam*, goes on to say that just because grace perfects nature, "it is necessary that natural reason be subservient to faith."[14] Natural reason is the "handmaid," not the teacher and guide, of faith, precisely the faith that the individual receives from the teaching Church.[15] Consequently all of reason's products, philosophical, historical, social scientific, or otherwise, are meant to serve the teaching of the faith, as aids to faith's own understanding. Only thereby can reason itself come to rest at its final goal, and so reach its own perfection. Faith uses natural reason, puts reason to work in its service, in order to attain a deeper apprehension of what the Church teaches and faith has received. Genuine understanding of the faith comes when reason gratefully accepts this handmaid's role, and genuine understanding is forsaken when reason tries to instruct faith about what it ought to believe. Since the critical capacities of natural reason minister to faith, and not the other way around, theology, precisely at its most intellectually rigorous and critical, is the servant, not the master, of the faith of the unwashed.[16]

---

14. This quotation, and the immediately preceding allusions to St. Thomas, are from *Summa theologiae* I, 1, 8, ad 2: "Cum enim gratia non tollat naturam, sed perficiat, oportet quod naturalis ratio subserviat fidei; sicut et naturalis inclinatio voluntatis obsequitur caritati."

15. See *Summa theologiae* I, 1, 5, sc.

16. The theological epistemology here briefly sketched can be developed in many ways. For one such account of reason's service to faith, see the concluding part of Scheeben's *Mysterien des Christentums* (§§104–110), on "The Science of the Christian

Thus the theologian, faced with a conflict between the teaching of the Church and his own conscience, might respond by embracing the truth that grace does not destroy, but does perfect, nature. The theologian might accept the right of the Church, inherent in her role as communal mediator of the Christian faith, to judge his teaching, even though his judges may not be his natural intellectual equals. To accept the right of the Church to reject one's dissenting views does not mean, of course, that one gives them up. That can happen properly only if one comes to a change of mind accepted in good conscience. But it does mean that one will not, publicly or privately, contest the right of the Church to reject one's views, even though the theologian counts this rejection as mistaken.

This is loyal dissent, rooted in the theologian's appreciation of the ecclesial nature of his enterprise and not in the privileged status of his own judgment, or that of his guild. Its clear mark is acceptance of the discipline the Church may impose upon one's dissent. This means, as the Vatican document with which we began rightly observes, that the theologian may find himself called to suffer on behalf of the truth. "For a loyal spirit, animated by love for the Church, such a situation [ecclesial reproach of the theologian's teaching] can certainly prove a difficult trial. It can be a call to suffer for the truth, in silence and prayer, but with the certainty, that if the truth really is at stake, it will ultimately prevail."[17]

In following this advice of the Congregation for the Doctrine of the Faith, the loyally dissenting theologian is much like the scientist whose views are rejected by his intellectual community, but who remains convinced he is right. In that situation he will justifiably continue with his scientific work, hoping to prove to the guild that his conclusions are correct and his arguments sound. In the meantime, however, he will not view the skepticism about his work among his peers as an unwarranted intrusion

Mysteries, or Theology" (pp. 733-796 in Vollert's English translation). For another, see Bruce D. Marshall, *Trinity and Truth* (Cambridge: Cambridge University Press, 2000).

17. *Donum veritatis*, §31. The history of the Church over the last century or so offers some signal examples of theologians willing to accept this "difficult trial." One was Yves Cardinal Congar, who became one of the most active and influential theologians at Vatican II. As his posthumously published diaries vividly reveal, he was deeply anguished over what he and others saw as the wholly unjust suppression of his theological views by Church authorities in the decade from the late 1940s to the late 1950s. But throughout this trial he remained true to his vows of obedience as a Dominican and as a priest, and made no public criticism of, or even comment upon, the Church's disciplinary actions (which included suspension from teaching and other public activities, such as participation in ecumenical discussions). See Yves Congar, *Journal d'un théologien (1946-1956)*, ed. Étienne Fouilloux (Paris: Cerf, 2000).

upon his intellectual freedom. In fact he will see it, frustrating though it might be, as the necessary safeguard of his conclusions in the long run. If, as he believes, the truth is here at stake, then the truth will come to be recognized for what it is.

It belongs to the wonder of the truth that it can always make itself known to minds that seek it. The scientist disbelieved by his peers will therefore not try to combat their skepticism by seeking to gather an alternative community of scientists who agree with him, who will vote to further his views at the annual meeting of the guild, and so forth. He will keep doing his experiments. Even less should the theologian, who seeks a deeper knowledge of the truth that God himself is, a truth not inert but supremely living and active, think he needs to take the cause of the truth into his own hands, against the community which has taught him the truth about God in the first place. He should keep doing theology until he changes his mind or his views prevail.

The theologian's willingness to accept the judgment and discipline of the Church even when he believes the Church to be mistaken—to suffer for the truth at the hands of the Church—surely demands a high view of the Church. In this the theologian goes beyond even the conscientious scientist in his estimate of the community of teaching to which he belongs, and to whose judgment he submits his own. What sort of community—more pointedly, what actually existing community—is worthy, if we may put the matter this way, of that suffering for the truth to which the theologian may in conscience believe himself called?

It will have to be that community of which the words Newman puts on the lips of the dying Gerontius are true:

> And I hold in veneration,
> For the love of Him alone,
> Holy Church, as his creation,
> And her teachings, as his own.[18]

A community that can forget the truths it has been taught by Christ, so as to need the prophetic office of the theologian to bring it back into line, is evidently not the Church which may legitimately call upon its members to suffer for the truth. A community that can forget the truth upon which its own existence depends is not that community for which one can responsibly make this sacrifice, since it's a community that, *a fortiori*, cannot be

---

18. John Henry Newman, *Prayers, Verses, and Devotions* (San Francisco: Ignatius Press, 1989), p. 694.

relied on to recognized the truth, theological or otherwise. Only that community which can't forget the truth (cf. Jn. 16:13–15), however great the failures and errors of her individual members—including those in authority—can be relied upon to recognize the truth. In this sort of community, but only here, one can responsibly suffer for the truth. It can be right to suffer for the truth at the hands of the Church only if the relationship between Christ, the Church, and the believer is as Newman's verse describes. And if the Church really is what Newman succinctly describes, then she can rightly ask this of us, and we should be willing to accept it. Readiness to suffer for the truth, it has to be said, isn't a virtue widely prized among theologians today. But it should be.

Feast of St. Lawrence of Brindisi, 2012

3

Courage

JOHN WEBSTER

I

CHRISTIAN MORAL THEOLOGY SEEKS clear knowledge of the nature and conditions of human action in order to guide its performance. Because moral theology is moral *theology*, and because the matter of theology is God and all things in relation to God, it inquires into God and creatures, their differing natures, and the history of their fellowship which is created, preserved and brought to completion by divine love. Moral theology is thus an element in faith's intelligent apprehension of the triune God, his inner perfection and his outer works. In this, faith is instructed by the gospel, the loving address of God of which the prophets and apostles are appointed and authoritative ambassadors. Attending to this instruction—contemplating as it presents itself, and avoiding coveted partial or untruthful representations—moral theology seeks to say: This is the God who is the origin, preserver, governor, judge and end of all human action; these are the creatures summoned to life-movement by this God; these are the properties of their conjunction in its temporal course; these are modes of action which are necessary and fitting enactments of creaturely nature and which are to be the objects of creaturely exertion; these are modes of action which inhibit, damage, or deny creaturely life-movement in conjunction with God.

If this is so, Christian moral theology has both ontological and deontological interests; it treats both the metaphysical and the perceptive. There is, however, an order to these inquiries: deontology follows ontology, because action follows being. The order of discovery may, of course, run in a different direction: consideration of the principles of moral being may be prompted by puzzlement over a precept. But precepts are the imperative force of being, of what is the case in the world because of its conjunction with God. This is why Christian moral theology is not an unreservedly practical science. It concerns itself with the principles of human practice. Access to these principles is often occasioned by practical life-movement; yet what kind of movement is this if not the movement of reconciled *creatures*, those who move themselves truthfully only when they do so in accordance with their given nature and state, and whose nature can only be grasped in its transparency to the divine charity which is its origin and its preserving power?

As metaphysics of morals, Christian moral theology is a contemplative science, which helps to kindle, direct and evaluate moral activity by pausing over moral nature. We are to enact our life-movement in such a way that we conform to our good. This enactment requires the exercise of moral reason, that element of our intelligent nature by which the good—that which the loving creator purposes for the creatures he has made to be *thus*—becomes an object of knowledge, desire and will. In our corrupt state, our capacity for contemplative knowledge of our moral nature is damaged: by hatred of God and others, by inordinate self-love, and by ruinous desire through which we are drawn to or flee from the wrong things, to the wrong degree or in the wrong way. Ignorant, deficient in charity, and with our desires disordered, we need instruction and illumination, the renovation of our loves, and the moderation and ordering of our passions. We need, that is, the work of God which renews the spirit of the mind as part of the creation of the new nature.

Renewed moral reason is intrinsic to the exercise of the Christian graces, including the grace of courage. Acting courageously, and avoid the opposing vices of recklessness and irresolution, requires truthful assessment of our nature, and capacities, of what provision we may expect from the hands of God, and of the setting in which courage is required. Courageous persons will be persons of well-formed moral intelligence who act out of a lively apprehension of their nature and situation as it is configured, upheld, and moved by the works of divine justice and benevolence. Such intelligence, steady and attentive to the Spirit's teaching, will understand that the call to exercise courage reaches creatures at a particular point in the temporal unfolding of their fellowship with God: not that of primal integrity, nor of entire corruption, nor of perfect restoration, but that time in which accomplished reconciliation, effected by the Son at the Father's behest, is being realized as the Spirit's renovating work proceeds. For creatures whose lives take place in this penultimate dispensation (in classical theological terms, the third of the four "states of humanity"[1]), courage is possible, fitting and necessary. Courage is possible because the new nature created after the likeness of God (Eph 4:24) has been given to us, and with it the renewal of our powers, including that *firmitas animi* which is the essence of courage. Courage is fitting, because our future good, which is the motive force of our capacity to resist evil and face fear, is secure: courage is the natural action of those whose lives are tethered by divine promises. Courage is necessary, because our future good is not yet possessed.

Having knowledge of these things—knowledge acquired by contemplation of God and God's works, and reinforced by the exercise and application of courage in face of difficulties and disappointments—courageous persons will be able to evaluate threats to their well-being, to make discriminations about when and how to act in face of evil, to moderate the emotions generated by objects of dread, and to act in obedience to the divine summons. Such discriminating and acting are the stuff of moral exhortation; but moral exhortation is the application and reinforcement of moral science, that by which moral science is brought to term, and that whose imperative force derives from its indicative principles.

So much by way of orientation. What, on this basis, is to be said of the nature and acts of courageous persons, of the extensions and deformations of courage, and of the divine gifts by which it is moved? For guidance I have looked to its treatment by Ambrose,[2] Augustine,[3] and Gregory,[4] but most of all to the lengthy treatise *de fortitudine* which takes up eighteen questions and sixty-six articles of the *secunda secundae* of Aquinas's *Summa theologiae*. The authority of the latter presentation derives from its sure grasp of the conjunction of reason, virtue and emotion in courage, as well as from the ease with which it shuttles between moral theory and human detail. It is also bound up with the way in which Aquinas grounds the act

---

1. See here Augustine *Enchiridion* 118; the classic Reformed account remains the early eighteenth-century account by Thomas Boston, *Human Nature in Its Four-Fold State* (Edinburgh: Banner of Truth Trust, 1964).

2. *De officiis* I.35–39.

3 *De morib. eccl. cath.* I.15, 22.

4. *Moralia in Iob* XX.2.

of courage in a theology of God, creation and redemption, even though such considerations rarely break the surface of the text. The structure and content of what follows derives in large part from Aquinas's treatment.[5]

II

Grasping the nature and function of courage requires an understanding of the task of human virtue, especially of its task in face of the lingering corruption of our nature to which the Spirit's continuing work of sanctification directs itself. "[I]t is the function of human virtue to make both man and his activities at one with reason" (123.1 resp.). This, in turn rests upon a conception of the function of reason as that through which human creatures are able to apprehend the ends of action, most of all that our "ultimate end is happiness, in other words God" (123.7 resp.). Virtue, of which courage is an instance, is an element of "following right reason."

Two matters immediately call for comment here. First, the exercise of courage follows the intelligence of moral truth: "the function of virtue is to preserve a man in the good proposed by reason"; and the object of "reason's good" is, quite simply, "truth" (124.1 resp.). Aquinas assumes the accessibility, singularity and non-relativity of truth. Moral reason is not correlative to the schematisations of moral cultures or ways of life, but is that through which creatures come to acquire a sufficient (though not, of course, comprehensive or intuitive) knowledge of the nature of things and their course under the direction of God. In moral reason, what matters is not our seeing but that which we see. If we are to act virtuously, we "must first know what the good is":[6] not merely hold something *as* good, but see the good.[7]

---

5. I have generally quoted from the Blackfriars edition (*Summa theologiae* vol. 42) though its translation is patchy; in-text references are to this volume. I have profited from J. R. Bowlin, "Rorty and Aquinas on Courage and Contingency," *Journal of Religion* 77 (1997) 402–20; S. Hauerwas and C. Pinches, *Christians Among the Virtues. Theological Conversations with Ancient and Modern Ethics* (Notre Dame: University of Notre Dame Press, 1997) 149–65; H. McCabe, *On Aquinas* (London: Continuum, 2008) 165–68; J. Pieper, *The Four Cardinal Virtues: Prudence, Justice, Fortitude, Temperance* (Notre Dame: University of Notre Dame Press, 1966) 117–41; J. Porter, *The Recovery of Virtue. The Relevance of Aquinas for Christian Ethics* (Louisville: Westminster John Knox, 1990); L. H. Yearley, *Mencius and Aquinas: Theories of Virtue and Conceptions of Courage* (Albany: SUNY Press, 1990).

6. Pieper, *Four Cardinal Virtues*, 122.

7. Yearley's otherwise perceptive presentation of Aquinas's conception of courage, in which human flourishing is relative to ways of life and social location, falls into

Second, the quality of acts of courage is determined by the goods which they pursue and our relation to which they preserve, and not simply by the forcefulness of the exercise of human power. Courage is not mere vitality indifferently directed, but power directed to that which reason perceives. It is an aspect of the *sequela rationis* (123.3 resp.) which characterises good human action; by courage we are preserved *in bono rationis* (124.1 resp.).

Following reason is difficult, sometimes acutely so. This is because the disorder of sin extends to the emotions, those primary movements of attraction and flight which are intrinsic to our created nature, but cast into disarray once our original integrity has been forfeited. Such is the disarray that we are easily defeated in following the good proposed by reason. Some pleasure attracts us inordinately and draws us from hearing reason's superintendence; or, in a contrary movement, we experience "revulsion of will from the end suggested by reason because of some oppressing difficulty" (123.1 resp.). The first disorder—"the pull exercised by some pleasure towards something which right reason rejects" (123.1 resp.)—is countered by temperance, the second by courage. To exercise temperance and courage is not to suppress emotion (to do so would frustrate the operation of our nature) but to regulate and moderate attraction and withdrawal so that they serve rather than inhibit active adherence to reason's good. The obstacle to such adherence is not affectivity *tout court* but unformed and unruly affectivity. Correction of this deformation cannot be achieved simply by commands. What is needed is our preservation in the pursuit of the good by those virtues which rectify, moderate and steer the affections so that they serve the establishment of the order of reason in human affairs.

III

Courage is firmness of mind, *firmitas animi*; it is a consistent and persistent set of the mind on some known good by which action is directed. Ambrose speaks of "the courage of the mind": "rightly is that called fortitude, when a man conquers himself, restrains his anger, yields and gives way to no allurements, is not put out by misfortunes, nor gets elated by good success, and does not get carried away by every varying change as by some chance wind . . . [W]hat is more noble and splendid than to train the mind, keep down the flesh, and redirect it to subjection, so that it may

---

difficulties over this point; Hauerwas and Pinches are unguarded in their reliance on Yearley's social idealism.

obey commands, listen to reason, and in undergoing labours readily carry out the intention and wishes of the mind?"[8] Aquinas picks up the point: most generally described, courage is the steadfastness with which good is pursued, and in this sense it is "a condition for each and every virtue" (123.2 resp.; see also 123.11 resp.; IaIIae 61.2 resp.). In a more specific sense, however, courage may be taken to mean "firmness of mind in enduring or repulsing whatever makes steadfastness outstandingly difficult, that is, particularly serious dangers" (123.2 resp.). It is this particular determination of courage—that steadfastness "by which a man refuses to yield to hostile forces deterring him from good" (124.2 ad 1)—with which Aquinas is especially concerned in his treatise.

It is important to recognise the external orientation of *firmitas animi*. The worth of courage does not simply consist in purposive exercise of our powers, and in the sense of integrity and command of self which such exercise engenders. Courage is not simply a matter of "laying claim to one's own character, giving it a shape and thereby making it one's own."[9] What matters in courage is not so much the expansion of the self as its extension beyond itself towards the good—a matter whose importance can readily be seen in distinguishing courage from mere daredevilry.

Courage is firmness of mind exercised in relation to difficulties which engender fear. In his earlier discussion of fear in the *prima secundae*, Aquinas identifies the object of fear as "future evil which exceeds the power of the fearful person so that he is incapable of resisting it" (IaIIae.41.4 resp.). Faced with such evil, fear takes flight. In one sense, fear is natural disinclination from that which is "repulsive to one's natural desire for one's own existence" (IaIIae.41.3 resp.). But because the impulse to have and maintain oneself is subordinate to our orientation to God as our ultimate good, it cannot be permitted to run its course isolated and unchecked, because it may inhibit pursuit of that ultimate good as presented to us by reason. The task of courage in this matter is to restrain fear and so "remove the hindrance which holds back the will from following reason" (123.3 resp.). More specifically, "retreat from a difficult situation is characteristic of fear, for fear connotes withdrawal before a formidable evil . . . Accordingly, courage is chiefly concerned with fears of difficulties likely to cause the will to retreat from following the lead of reason" (123.3 resp.).

Chief among the fears which courage restrains is fear of death. Aquinas is characteristically concerned with any virtue *simpliciter*, in its

---

8. Ambrose *De officiis* I.36
9. Bowlin, "Rorty and Aquinas on Courage and Contingency," p. 406.

maximal modulation, since a virtue "always presses to its own utmost objective" (123.4 resp.), and in that its distinctive properties are most fully manifest. And so "courage is properly employed in sustaining all misfortunes. But a man is not unreservedly considered brave just because he endures any sort of trouble, but only because he endures the very greatest evils well" (123.4 ad 1) *Circa majora major fortitudo consistit* (123.5 obj. 2). Death is "the most dreaded of all bodily ills" because it "removes all bodily goods"; and so *virtus fortitudinis est circa timores periculorum mortis* (123.4 resp.).

We may prescind from the question of whether courage is chiefly concerned with death in warfare, with martyrdom or with other mortal dangers, and focus on why it should be that "dangers of death" (123.5 resp.) are the primary object of courage. Aquinas picks up a passage from Augustine:

> Among all things that are possessed in this life, the body is, by God's most righteous laws, for the sin of old, man's heaviest bond, which is well-known as a fact, but most incomprehensible in its mystery. Lest this bond be shaken and disturbed, the soul is shaken with the fear of toil and pain; lest it should be lost and destroyed, the soul is shaken with fear of death. For the soul loves it from the force of habit, not knowing that by using it well and wisely its resurrection and reformation will, by the divine help and decree, be without any trouble made subject to its authority.[10]

Why do we fear death? Because we are both embodied and vulnerable. Our present mode of existence, in which we have life in conjunction with having a body, means that we are not inviolable, that we are susceptible to damage and loss. Moreover, because we are fallen, awareness of our mortality fills us with dread that loss of the body will mean the end of life. This fear is intense, not only because of disordered attachment to our present state of embodiment, but because love of life is super-eminent and natural. "Fear springs from love" and "it is natural to love one's own life" (123.4 ad 2; see also IaIIae 94.2 resp.). Courage does not despise this natural love of life. Its task is not to eliminate fear by eradicating the love of life which produces fear of its injury or loss, but rather to moderate that fear and overcome the withdrawal from reason's good caused by the bondage to the body which in turn causes us to ignore our ultimate end.

---

10. Augustine *De mor. eccl. cath.* I.22.

Such, then, is the object of courage: fear of evil which inhibits movement towards good. Courage is chiefly displayed in acts of endurance, though subordinately in attack, that is, in vigorous action against an opposing force. The division of courage into endurance and attack will be important in Aquinas's detailed anatomy of the parts of courage (QQ 128–138), but the priority of endurance is established in the first question of the treatise. "The chief act of courage is not so much attacking as enduring, or standing one's ground amidst dangers" (123.6 resp.). The precedence of endurance is instructive for Aquinas's understanding of courage as a whole. Endurance is a richer, more spacious mode of action, and one less exposed to corruption than the action of aggression. Partly this is because we endure assault from a stronger force, but attack things which are weaker; partly because one who endures faces immediate danger rather than the future dangers which attack may expect; partly, again, because endurance is extended over time, whereas attack is sudden and of short duration. Underlying these distinctions is Aquinas's sense that—appearances notwithstanding—endurance denotes greater interior power since it involves "the act of the soul clinging most bravely to some good" (123.6 ad 2). Maintaining one's position unchanged rather than the élan of spirit in striking out of evil: this is more characteristic of true courage. Seeing this makes Aquinas cautious about audacity and the use of anger (123.10), and quick to qualify the kind of delight which follows from the exercise of courage (123.8 resp.), and it pushes him to modify the notion of attack into magnanimity and magnificence. And it is one of the factors which leads him to consider martyrdom an act of the highest perfection, since it is linked to endurance (the primary act of courage) rather than to aggression (courage's secondary act).

The endurance of martyrs is an act of the highest courage most of all because its primary impulse is love. In the course of his treatise, Aquinas says relatively little about this (Augustinian) theme beyond such occasional remarks as "well-ordered love is found in any virtue whatsoever" (125.2 resp.; see also 139.2 ad 2, and IIaIIae.23.8). But it grounds the entire treatise, for only love of God can impel us to follow reason's direction, to endure temporal evil and loss of temporal goods, to face death.

IV

One of the ways in which moral intelligence enables specification, and therefore more effective performance, of a virtue, is by discriminating it from its opposing vices. Contrast illuminates and clarifies, and thereby directs the energies of the soul: not that, but *this*, in *this* way. In Aquinas's anatomy, there are three opposing vices: fear, fearlessness, and audacity, each instructive about the nature of courage.

Not fear, but disordered fear, is sinful. Fear is proper to our constitution as affective creatures who love and preserve their given life, and flee from all that would precipitate its loss. Fear, however, can be disordered. For Aquinas, the ordering of appetites, whether of attraction or repulsion, in accordance with reason, is basic to their operation: "the good of a human action lies in due order," and "due order demands that appetite be subject to the rule of reason" (125.1 resp.)—subject, that is, to the truth of our nature in relation to God. But again, our affective life is not immune to corruption; it is a domain of sin. Sin muddles the order of the appetites; we pursue what should be shunned, we shun what should be pursued. Fear is an instance of the latter disorder. "When appetite avoids particular things which reason commands us to endure, so that we may not abandon other objectives which we should pursue, such fear is disordered and becomes sinful" (125.1 resp.). And so "fear is a sin in that it is disordered, that is, insofar as it avoids what reason demands should not be avoided" (125.3 resp.). Fear avoids the good because of the pain involved in its pursuit of the good; courage, by contrast, bears pain for the sake of the good.

But this discrimination of courage from fear is insufficient; further specifications are needed, because courage is opposed not only by fear as its defect but by fearlessness and audacity as its excesses (the idiom of defect and excess, and the identification of true virtue as a mean, has remarkable explanatory power). Why is fearlessness (*intimiditas*) sinful? The root of the vice is not simply a swollen head which believes itself sufficient to deal with all comers, or dim-wittedness which fails to grasp the dangers which it faces. Most of all, fearlessness is "insufficient love" (126.1 resp.), a failure to love life as we ought. "[I]f a man falls behind the due measure of love of temporal goods, this is against the basic tendency of his nature, and is consequently a sin . . . It is possible for someone to fear death and other temporal evils less than he should, because he loves life and its goods less than he should" (126.1 resp.).

The fearless person has only a semblance of courage, because courage values life but is prepared to endure its deprivation for the sake of the good of reason. Because this is so, courage involves "a calculated and reasonable fear" (126.2 resp.), whereas fearlessness is a deficiency of this fear, a failure to "fear what we ought to fear" (126.2 resp.). Courage does not ignore or underestimate threats to well-being: it *endures*. Fearlessness, by contrast, is indiscriminate attack, not directed to the good of reason, but simply a rush of self-confident vitality.

Fearlessness is close cousin to audacity. When governed by reason, audacity can be a kind of godly daring which does not shy from opposing that which opposes life (this positive sense of *audacia* is set out earlier in IaIIae.45). But the *passio* of daring "sometimes lacks the balance of reason, either through excess or through deficiency, and in this way becomes wicked" (127.1 resp.). Immoderate daring is not courage but recklessness; not clear-sighted facing of fear, but "an imperfectly-formed spiritedness"[11] which lacks calm, truthful apprehension of the good and its opponents. Courage, by contrast, involves the "measure of reason" (126.2 resp.), that is, moderation by which we avoid the deficiencies and excesses which inhibit orderly enactment of our affective nature. Moderation is not bland, cautious "balance"; it is truthful exercise of virtue in relation to good, and the distinction of true virtue from its inflated or shrunken versions.

V

Courage is a movement of life whose practise involves discriminating and sober assessment of the possibilities and limits of our situation and its threats, and of the capacities which we bring to that situation. Acting courageously requires knowledge and love of God our highest good, and of the subordinate goods of created life. And it also demands moderation of the emotions, so that, fittingly directed they assist in and do not detract from pursuit of these goods.

Courage is not an isolated element in the moral life. It makes its contribution to human flourishing as it both informs and is informed by other human powers.

As one of the cardinal virtues, courage "never stands alone,"[12] being inseparable from prudence, justice, and temperance. Courage is only a human excellence when exerted prudently, justly and temperately; the other virtues require steadfastness of mind for their perfect operation. Gregory, for example, comments (negatively) that "each separate virtue is of less worth in proportion as the others are wanting . . . one virtue without another is either none at all or but imperfect," and (positively) that the "first four virtues . . . are severally so far perfect in proportion as they are

11. Yearley, *Mencius and Aquinas*, 122.
12. Ambrose *De officiis* I.35.

mutually joined to one another."[13] Detached from justice, courage is mere crushing force; detached from prudence, it is mere daring.

Courage is also allied to a range of corollary and subordinate virtues, and its full description must be completed by a presentation of these. Aquinas is especially drawn to this feature of courage; much of the bulk of the treatise is taken up with close analysis of the "parts" of courage (QQ 128–38). His aim is to fill out his anatomy of courage by displaying its association with other constituents of well-developed moral character.[14]

Aquinas opens his treatment by recalling the division of courage into attack and endurance already introduced when discussing the principle act of courage (123.6), and proceeds to offer further subdivisions, Aristotle and Cicero providing much of the content, though it is substantially reshaped as Aquinas annexes it for his own purposes. Courage as attack—the assertion of our nature and movement of life against that by which it is threatened—is distributed as magnanimity (expansion of the soul in readiness for strenuous action) and magnificence (accomplishment of great deeds). Courage as endurance—sustaining our life movement when faced with formidable opposing evils—is divided into patience (by which we resist dejection) and perseverance (by which we overcome the weariness which causes us to lose heart). Each of these four parts of courage is analysed along with the several vices to which they are opposed. The essentials can be displayed by considering magnanimity and patience.

Courageous action arises from a certain greatness of soul characterised by aspiration, that *extensio animi ad magna* which furnishes the energy and resolution required by fortitude. "A man is called magnanimous chiefly because he has the spirit for some great act" (129.1 resp.). It is this which the courageous person takes to situations in which the virtue is to be exercised; by it, "the mind is strengthened for a strenuous task" (129.5 resp.). Of itself, magnanimity does not suffice; only as it is joined to courage does it become strength of mind for a task which is not only strenuous but requires steadfastness in face of mortal peril. Yet without this subordinate virtue we would be immobilised by danger and incapable of courageous sustaining of the movement of life.

---

13. Gregory *Moralia* XX.2; see here Pieper, *Four Cardinal Virtues*, 123–25; the point is considered by Aquinas at 123.11, 12.

14. Yearley, *Mencius and Aquinas*, 33f. finds the account vitiated by false harmonisation of divergent moral cultures, by excessive symmetry and by occlusion of certain virtues as they are subsumed under courage. On the contrary: far from prosecuting "a rational coherence that falsifies the actual state of affairs" (34), Aquinas is trying to preserve the irreducibly compound nature of the moral life.

Not all extensions of the spirit are praiseworthy. As courage is to be distinguished from fearlessness and audacity, so magnanimity is to be differentiated from its excesses: presumption, ambition and vainglory. Presumption takes upon itself what is beyond its powers. At first blush, the soul's movement in presumption is scarcely distinguishable from that in magnanimity, in that there is an *extensio animi*; but it is a disorderly extension, against the order of divine reason in which acts are to be proportionate to the given powers of the agent. And so "it is . . . perverse and sinful, being as it were against the natural order, for anyone to take upon himself to tackle what is above his powers" (130.1 resp.). "The presumptuous man . . . goes too far . . . in respect of his own capacities, which the magnanimous man does not exceed. In this sense presumption is opposed to magnanimity by excess" (130.2 resp.). More deeply, there is in presumption a disturbance of the creature's relation to God: sometimes a failure to realize that we are to rely upon divine help (130.1 ad 3); or perhaps excessive confidence in God's mercy (130.2 ad 1), and lack of fear of God.

Ambition is an "inordinate appetite for recognition" (131.1 resp.). In this extension of the soul, an incidental product of magnanimity—the "respect accorded to someone in witness of his excellence" (131.1 resp.)—becomes the end to which the agent aspires. All manner of distortions follow: failure to grasp that "man is not the source of his own excellence," or that excellence is "a divine gift" (131.1 resp.); failure to use excellence justly, for the benefit of others (131.1 resp.); transgression of the rule of reason in the appetite for what is good (131.1 ad 1). Vainglory introduces similar distortions of magnanimity. As ambition has a disturbed relation to the good of honour, vainglory has a disturbed relation to glory—that is, to that human radiance which is "the manifestation by someone of a thing which in our eyes seems beautiful, whether it is a physical or spiritual good" (132.1 resp.). The disturbance lies in the vanity of the desired glory: "a desire for empty or vain glory does denote a fault, for it is sinful to seek any vain thing" (132.1 resp.). Glory is empty when that for which one seeks glory is unworthy, or when the person from whom one seeks it is unworthy, or when the desire for glory is not applied to honouring God or helping our neighbour.

Presumption, ambition and vainglory are distortions of the life-movement of magnanimity; courageous persons, knowing that they lie close to hand even in the exercise of steadfastness of mind, will shun them. Yet the distortions should not dissuade us from recognising that there is, indeed, an orderly, virtuous and necessary extension of the soul.

Disorderly extension cannot be overcome by the soul's *retraction*, for such retraction is itself a repudiation of our nature.

This refusal to extend the soul to great things—pusillanimity—causes a person "to fall short of his capability" and so to fail "to achieve an aim commensurate with his powers" (133.1 resp.). The underlying principle here—that human creatures do indeed have capacities—is of great consequence in apprehending courage and acting courageously, as well as in distinguishing courage from associated vices. Courage is possible and necessary because to be a creature is to be empowered to act. "It can be said that the pusillanimous man is worthy of great things because of the disposition to virtue which is in him, whether because of good natural qualities, or knowledge, or material endowment. He becomes pusillanimous when he refuses to employ these to attain virtue" (133.1 ad 2). The refusal is sinful because it opposes "natural inclination to undertake action commensurate with its capability," thereby contradicting the "law of nature" (133.1 resp.). Law is both indicative and imperative; it indicates both the structure and end of the being with which we have been endowed and the necessity of enacting that being, for it is partly constituted by a set of abilities. Without the exercise of these abilities, we exist in self-contradiction and "hold back from the greatness of which [we are] worthy" (133.2 resp.).

Courage is empowered by the magnanimous extension of the soul in correspondence with the law of our nature. The deep foundation of this is a theology of createdness—a point of significance if we are to distinguish an account such as that of Aquinas from later conceptions of courage as self-assertion *tout court* (Spinoza is exemplary).[15] Like all creaturely virtue, courage is a moved human movement: no less a movement for being moved, no less moved for being a movement.

The life-movement of courage involves steadfastness of spirit in face of countervailing forces, and so has patience as one of its corollaries, for patience serves endurance. Courageous persons encounter the need to retain the good of reason against the *impetus passionum*, the pressure exerted by strong emotion. In particular, they need to resist the sorrow (*tristitia*) generated by sustained exposure to difficulty in pursuing the good of our nature. It is for this reason that "patience . . . is associated with courage as an ally to a main virtue" (136.4 resp.), for "the task of patience is to ensure that we do not abandon virtue's good through dejection . . . however great" (136.4 ad 2). Courage requires both refusal of flight from fearful evils and refusal of dejection. Patience is a capacity to suffer, but it

---

15. Spinoza, *Ethics* III proposition 59; IV proposition 4.

entails no abandonment of our proper movement of life and its orientation; indeed, its very task is to prevent the closing down of the soul which sorrow effects.

Yet patience takes us beyond our natural capacity to put up with what is burdensome. Its spring is "supernatural love" (136.3 ad 3). There are certainly approximations to patience in our dealings with temporal, bodily matters (acquisition of health may involve endurance of temporary pain); but properly understood, patience is *a caritate causatur*. This, because patience is not mere toleration of difficulty but toleration of difficulty "for the sake of future good" (136.3 ad 1)—that future good being the perfection of our nature in union with God. Disorderly affection inhibits us in this by concupiscence which tugs against the "inclination of reason" (136.3 ad 1). Only by charity—by the reordering of our love so that it is fixed upon God above all things—can that tug be resisted; and "we cannot have charity unless by grace" (136.3 resp.).

With this, we reach the penultimate question of the treatise, *de dono fortitudinis* (Q 139). Its brevity and late placement may suggest that it is an afterthought. Not so. The question is best read as making explicit what has been assumed all through Aquinas's scrutiny of the phenomena of courage, namely that creatures realize themselves only as they are realized by divine goodness. In both its integral and its corrupted state, our nature needs divine help to will and to do any good whatsoever (IaIIae.109.2 resp.)—this, because we are not self-moved. After the fall, however, even though creatures are not "shorn of every natural good" (IaIIae.109.2 resp.), we require healing in order to reach the full scope of virtue. We must be moved in order to move. Certainly, we can exercise a certain steadfastness of mind "according to our proper and connatural mode" (139.1 resp.). But this is not enough: a further divine work is needed for courage to reach its fullest extension. This is the Spirit's work. "The Holy Spirit moves the human mind further, in order that one may reach the end of any work begun and avoid threatening dangers of any kind. This transcends human nature, for sometimes it does not lie within human power to attain the end of one's work or to escape evils and dangers, since sometimes these press in upon us to the point of death" (139.1 resp.). Most of all, attaining the end of the human creature beyond the temporal and out of reach of any possible danger requires a grace we do not possess until given by the Spirit. "[H]e leads us to eternal life, which is the end of all good works and the escape from all dangers. And he pours into our minds a certain confidence that this will be, refusing to admit the opposing fear. In this sense courage is defined as a gift of the Holy Spirit" (139.1 resp.).

What, then, of precepts? What of the deontology which ensues from the ontology? Here, again, Aquinas's brevity is striking, a single question with two articles. Why so? Partly because—unlike, say, Ambrose—he is not directly about the work of exhortation; but partly because the moral training which the *Summa theologiae* undoubtedly offers is undertaken in the indicative mode. "Precepts in law are directed towards what the lawmaker intends" (140.1 resp.). The imperative force of law derives from its reference to the law-giver's intention, and behind that the law-giver's identity and character. All the more reason, then, to pause over the contemplative work of moral theology without which an account of courage may quickly be reduced to the merely statutory.

VI

There is a way of loving life which leads to its loss. This is a love of life which identifies life with its temporal, bodily form. Such love of life is a stranger to courage, because when it encounters the gravest of threats to that life—death itself—it is filled with fear and retreats, refusing the extension of the soul which steadfastly maintains that nothing—no tribulation or distress or persecution or famine or nakedness or peril or sword—can separate us from the love of God in Christ Jesus our Lord. The courageous person can therefore hate "his life in this world" (John 12.25)—that is, can endure its temporal dissolution with properly moderated fear, because of the super-eminent worth of the good which lies on the far side of death, and which is worthy of all love.

"He who loves his life loses it, and he who hates his life in this world will keep it for eternal life": this is the metaphysical principle of courage. "When it is said 'he that loveth,' there is to be understood *in this world*; he it is who shall lose it," says Augustine.

> "But he that hateth," that is, in this world, is he that shall keep it until eternal life. Surely a profound and strange declaration as to the measure of a man's love for his own life that leads to its destruction, and of the hatred to it that secures its preservation! If in a sinful way thou lovest it, then thou dost really hate it; if in a way accordant with what is good thou has hated it, then

hast thou really loved it. Happy they who have so hated their life while keeping it, that their love shall not cause them to lose it.[16]

> The Lord is my light and my salvation: whom shall I fear? The Lord is the stronghold of my life: of whom shall I be afraid? . . . Wait for the Lord; be strong, and let your heart take courage; yea, wait for the Lord! (Psalm 27.1,14)

---

16. Augustine, *Tractates on the Gospel According to Saint John* LI.10.

4

The Humble Greatness of Theology

C. C. PECKNOLD

THEOLOGY IS A CRAFT like any other. It is not unlike building a house or tilling a field. Tools must be acquired, and we must learn the skills of using them through apprenticeship and practice. The theologian learns to interpret, to describe, to critique, to connect, to argue—each in the field he has chosen, each according to her talent. We hope that our peers will judge our work well, and maybe that *festschriften* will eventually be written expressing that regard for our achievements.

On the other hand, theology is a craft like no other. It proceeds on revealed principles and is ordered to an end that far exceeds the grasp of reason. Indeed, when Thomas tells Reginald that "all that I have written seems like straw to me," the Angelic Doctor rightly values his work in relation to the most excellent end, namely the *visio Dei*. Theology ordered to this end is eventually like a ladder one no longer needs—not in the way of Wittgenstein, whose ladder is metaphysical, but in the way of St. Thomas, for whom the ladder is like so many modes of signifying when one comes face to face with the *res signifcandi*.

There is a paradox here for the theologian. The theologian is called to know, love, and speak well of God. What science could be greater than one which is not only ordered to the *summum bonum*, but whose first principles are revealed by God? It is a science ordered to the glory of God. What could be greater? And yet the final words of Thomas to Reginald remind us that *humility* is the virtue that we most associate with truly great exemplars of theology. Augustine's phrase "humble greatness" comes to mind whenever I think of Ralph Del Colle, and so in honor of the example he set, the virtue humility is the topic of this essay—primarily with reference to Augustine and Aquinas, who are exemplars as well to anyone who seeks to renew Catholic theology from the deepest wells. The essay concludes with some methodological reflections on the future of theology that befit the humble greatness that was Ralph Del Colle's.

I. SIC ET NON

Humility, of course, is nearly synonymous with Christian knowledge. And yet the praise of the Psalmist—"in thy light we shall see light"—indicates that theology is the queen of the sciences precisely because it is divinely illumined knowledge (Ps 35:10). The theologian participates in a knowledge that is greater than can be grasped by reason, yet must be understood by reason. Immediately the Psalmist sees fit to pray for assistance: "let not the foot of pride come to me, let not the hand of the sinner move me" (Ps 35:12).

The theologian thus seems set on a course both humble and great. Saint Paul understands the mind of Christ to consist precisely in this sort of humble greatness in his letter to the Philippians (Phil 2:5–11). Saint Augustine says that humility is the first rung on the ladder of perfection and, in his argument with pagan moral philosophy, argues that humility brings greater glory than pride ever can. Saint Benedict has twelve degrees of humility, and Saint Anselm has seven. Humility is at the heart of the whole idea of apprenticeship to masters, communal formation, *manuductio*, obedience, and especially Christian friendship. It is not the form of all the virtues—that is reserved for *caritas*—but *humilitas* may rightly be said to be necessary to receive all the theological virtues, making it central for the task of *sacra doctrina*. It is the virtue required for Christian formation—as Chesterton once wrote, humility makes firm the feet which may grip the ground like trees.

Some have not thought humility a virtue at all. "Greatness," *not* humility, was the thing for Aristotle; and David Hume famously derided humility as one of the "monkish virtues." He loathed celibacy, fasting, penance, mortification, self-denial, silence, solitude, and the chief virtue required for all: humility. All were meaningless pursuits, and the virtue required of them could not be considered a virtue because it did not lead a person to fortune, or to social prestige, or to proper employment. Humility is bad for the profit motive (as every theologian can attest!). He never once considers that mastery of the world might not be the chief end of dependent rational animals. Hume never pauses to reflect upon the humility required to learn from others, as he undoubtedly did. To be fair, Hume did think modesty—allied with the virtue of temperance—might be a way of evoking sympathy in others, and thus serve some social function. But isn't this the kind of sentimental humility we rightly distrust as disordered, and that usually irks us as disingenuous?

For Nietzsche, humility is at the heart of "slave morality." The gentle meekness of Christianity makes people into slaves of the powerful. He thinks this slave morality is unnatural. Such "monkish virtues" undermine the raw, natural power of our will to dominate. It is precisely the *libido dominandi* that he thinks we should embrace. Humility is a pathetic tactic of the weak, whose resentment of the strong has led them to a "revaluation of all values." Christian humility has led us astray from what is truly alive and good: our noble powers of mastery. Nietzsche advocates the overthrow of humility precisely to restore things to their natural order, wherein masters are considered good and noble, and slaves weak and sickly. In the line that runs from Hume to Nietzsche, we can see that humility is not always considered a virtue—indeed, it has been considered a vice.

Based on these atheistic treatments of humility, one can be forgiven for thinking that humility must be a virtue that can only be considered rightly from a theistic point of view, and that atheism must, by necessity exclude humility as a virtue. There are two things to say about that: one word from Augustine and the other from Aquinas. Both words point us back to Christ, who is the way of humility, the bridge across the thorny hedgerows of pride that constantly put obstacles in the way of the theologian (who is a creature, and thus needs help).

II. AUGUSTINE AND AQUINAS

Augustine distinguishes between godly humility and the humility experienced by plebes in a fraternity or at the naval academy. It is the former, rather than the latter, that Augustine considers a virtue. It seems all other forms of humility are prone to perversion; they are seedbeds of vice rather than virtue. If Hauerwas or Milbank ever sound dismissive of humility, you can bet it is the latter—which is especially corrosive in its sentimental forms (thanks to Hume for that). Augustine despises this kind of humility as well. My students can never understand why his rhetoric, especially in the *City of God*, seems so aggressive, critical, and bold with his Roman readers when he makes humility the seedbed for the reception of grace. Boldness and humility are not contradictory for Augustine. Godly humility is wholly different from the corrosive forms of humility about which we rightly worry. Godly humility is the cure for pride, the disordered love of self that infects us all (and not only the various secretly self-loathing or megalomaniac bloggers out there). This humility is caused by reverence for God. And true reverence for God only comes to us because of God's love, which descends into the economy of the flesh—the incarnation, death, and resurrection are at the heart of Augustine's understanding of godly humility. He often likes to conjoin, in proto-Chalcedonian fashion, a two-natured understanding of the single virtue that God communicates to us out of his goodness and love: "Humble Greatness." Like the *parabola* of Philippians 2:5–11, Augustine sees this godly humility as not only a beginning, but also the ascetic path to *ascent to glory*. Imitating his humility opens us to receive "grace upon grace." It is the virtue we most need if we are to be elevated to the only kind of greatness that will ever make us happy: *becoming partakers of the divine nature*.

Aquinas, seeking to reconcile Augustine and Aristotle, says (*ST* II–II, q. 161) that humility is a virtue that is caused by reverence for God but nevertheless has an analogical relation to the humility that is part of the natural virtue of temperance. Like Augustine, Aquinas sees humility as a cure for pride—and not just a one-time cure, but a virtue whose habituation in daily life can remove the obstacles that the sin of pride constantly places before our understanding—and this is why humility is also necessary for our ascent to wisdom. It is only in humility that we can pray with St. Thomas, "Take from me the double darkness on which I was born—sin and ignorance. Give me a sharp sense of understanding, a retentive memory, and the ability to grasp things correctly and fundamentally." For Aquinas, there is an analogical relationship between humility as an *infused* virtue and the kind of humility that one can *acquire* prudentially—the relationship matters to Aquinas because he believes that elevation to godly is not foreign to our human nature; rather, it perfects and expands our capacities for true virtue, true holiness. Only godly humility will do. Augustine, of course, will say that a natural virtue without reference to God will lead to evil, but this does not preclude a reflection on humility as part of a natural virtue that is capable of elevation. Of course, there are tensions here beyond the scope of this essay, but some reflection on the virtue of temperance is not without value for the theologian thinking about godly humility.

While Augustine recognizes a kind of humility in prudential judgments, Aquinas prefers to align humility with the acquired virtue of temperance. Why? There is at least one good reason for the theologian to consider temperance a virtue worthy of emulation in making theological judgments: it seems that a great many theological mistakes come from intemperance. Heresies are often marked by intellectual intemperance (or by a misrecognition of what the *golden mean* really is), and the Ecumenical Councils of the Church often speak of the orthodox and catholic position as the most temperate one, the one that "hits the mark" and so can *boldly* be proclaimed as truth by the holy Church.

Temperance for Aquinas is, like all the cardinal virtues, a mean between extremes, and humility is a kind of mean in our appetite for greatness. When infused with God's grace and ordered to the virtue of charity, humility can most perfectly make us aware of our deficiencies; godly humility bring us constantly to an awareness of what we lack and of our need for God's help. When, at the end of his life, Aquinas famously said that all of his work was "like straw," he demonstrated that the virtue of humility was for him, as for Augustine, the virtue that attended him in his craft of theology from beginning to end—which is also to say that he was a theologian who became a saint.

Humility is a virtue that the academy tries to habituate in scholars as well. Often this effort is unsuccessful, because the humility that scholarship seeks to inculcate often is not much different than the humility of the fraternity or the military academy—it is so easily perverted into pride, envy, backbiting, strife. Theologians can benefit from the long and invariably painful process of coursework, comprehensive exams, job search after frustrating job search, tenure anxiety, promotion anxiety, rejections and refusals, painful criticisms and corrections, the pressure to publish "the big book," and the need to make one's mark, to be heroic. But quite often this is a vicious process is vicious. How could it be otherwise? This kind of humility is a seedbed for vice. And one of the vices that it produces is this inordinate desire for the wrong kind of greatness.

III. HUMBLE GREATNESS AND THE RENEWAL OF DOGMATIC THEOLOGY

Recently, in the journal *First Things,* Reinhard Hütter called for a new *ressourcement* Thomism that would heal us of the "ruins of discontinuity," Michael Root cautioned us about the problem of virtuosity in protestant dogmatic theology, and Bruce Marshall commended the renewal of Catholic dogmatic theology after what he takes to be its long, fifty-year slumber. Each of these theologians, in different ways, point to what seems like a crisis in theological formation today.

Reinhard Hütter, a long-time advocate of the ecclesial vocation of the theologian, notes the difficulty in finding good theological formation these days. He asks where "young" Catholic theologians can "find the kind of intellectual and spiritual guidance and formation that allows them to pursue a vision other than that of simply being functionaries of their academic guild" ("Ruins of Discontinuity," *First Things*, January 2011, 38). He asks, "Where will they be instructed with the greatest fidelity to the Church?"

Everywhere he looks, Hütter finds evidence of fragmentation rather than the unity and coherence of theology. He admits to being haunted by the famous image that Alasdair MacIntyre gave us in *After Virtue*—scientific discourse in ruins after a great catastrophe. The catastrophe here arises, he thinks, from what Pope Benedict XVII has called the "hermeneutic of discontinuity," an approach to theology that sees the Second Vatican Council as drawing a bright line in the history of Catholic theology, unhinged from its dogmatic past. He largely identifies this hermeneutic with a post-Kantian preference for the theme of discontinuity and revision rather than with the council itself. And he sees the *Communio* approach of patristic *ressourcement*, as well as what he calls "Ressourcement Thomism," as promising new avenues of renewal in dogmatic theology. They provide hope for renewal precisely because they patiently receive the truths they have been given, and thus participate in the handing on and the development of the Catholic faith.

Where Hütter is critical of the post-Kantian tendency towards discontinuity and revision in theology, Michael Root is critical of the Romantic tendency towards virtuosity in a cautionary essay on Wolfhart Pannenberg. Root writes,

> A curse of recent theology has been the cult of the virtuoso theologian, the creative mind who recasts the field, the Schleiermachers and Barths of the disciplines, Promethean figures who blaze the path for others to follow. Much academic work in modern theology seems less the study of God or of the Christian message about God, and more the study of the creativity of great theologians. ("Wolfhart Pannenberg," *First Things,* March 2012, 42)

A Man of the Church

While Hütter might be read as lamenting the loss of great ecclesial theologians, Root places an appropriate question that perhaps clarifies Hütter's intent: "Are great theologians always good things? Should we bemoan that there are no giants of the field around today? Certainly, mediocrity is not to be celebrated. Theology must be more than simply cataloging the answers provided by our forebears. But the enterprise of systematic theology is inherently dubious. It necessarily elevates the theologian to systematizer, to master of a subject matter that should not be mastered" (42). Root effectively cautions us against longing for the "heroic" theologian. And in this sense, he implicitly reminds us that theological renewal will only come through humility as well. Explicitly, Root concludes on the most sobering note of all: *we get the theologians we deserve.* "A critique of the sort of theology that fits the cult of the great theologian must inevitably be a critique of the ecclesial life that produces the cult" (42). In this sense, Catholics should not want heroic theologians, even though they are right to expect good ones who habitually exhibit fidelity to the Church even in their most speculative endeavors.

Finally, it is significant that in a third methodologically incisive essay in the same journal, Bruce Marshall commends Matthias Scheeben—a nearly forgotten "great" Catholic theologian of the nineteenth century. Why Scheeben? He is hardly heroic, but he is good. He perfectly reflected a mind in conversation with the Church, and he applied his staggeringly powerful intellect in service of the unity and coherence of Catholic theology, taking care to integrate different schools of theology within the Church. And as Marshall says, "he can teach a theological generation that has sold its inestimable birthright how to restore and renew dogmatic theology" ("Renewing Dogmatic Theology," *First Things*, May 2012, 40).

Scheeben saw theology as a speculative science which required specific intellectual virtues that serve the aim of seeing (rather than being seen). Marshall admires Scheeben's speculative courage, the boldness, even the audacity of his theology: "He makes precise and often elaborate conceptual distinctions, identifies relevant objections to his ideas, and offers detailed replies" (40). Marshall notes that Scheeben habitually talked about God, drank deeply and sympathetically from the wells of different theological traditions in the Church, and above all, he notes that Scheeben everywhere performed theology in *humility*—and he did so "with reverence, joy, and submission before the divine mysteries he seeks faithfully to serve" (40). In this way, Marshall sees Scheeben as a kind of an antidote to the heroic theologian, or at least an exemplar for those of us who want to be formed in those virtues required for the renewal of dogmatic theology. "Today we need to recover these three virtues: supernatural focus, sympathetic learning, and humility—if we are to restore dogmatic theology" (40).

The counsel of humility, and the counsel against what Reinhard Hütter calls "the ruins of discontinuity," and the counsel against what Root calls the heroic theologian, is not a retreat from greatness, but a call for a different kind of greatness: humble greatness. Bruce Marshall gives us an exemplar. And this is perhaps most needful of all. We have not been totally bereft of such exemplars in this present life. Ralph Del Colle was just such an exemplar. He has habitually focused his gaze upon the mystery of the most holy Trinity. He has made precise conceptual distinctions, and has always taken seriously the objections of other theologians—especially those from other Christian traditions, such as Pentecostals. I have known few theologians who do their work with such reverence, joy, and submission before the divine mysteries as did Professor Del Colle. He managed to avoid the heroic in favor of holiness. He prayed with the Church, and thought with the Church. He was the model for the kind of theologian I want to train and he was the theologian we should all want to become.

Clarity, boldness, and attractive force are marks of the most honored theologians in the history of the Church. But the virtue which makes intellectual clarity, speculative boldness, and beauty possible is, I submit, the distinctively Christological understanding of humility as "humble greatness." It is this virtue I saw in Professor Del Colle, and it is, truth be told, the reason why I admired him. It is not that I do not admire his theology—I have read and learned much from what he has written. I admire what was his craft. But the whole reason I admire him belongs to that magical virtue I saw in him, and want for myself: that speculative courage and that humble greatness which habitually speaks of God and seeks to see the truths of faith clearly and deeply. This is what the great theologians "hand on"—this is the "great" *traditio*.

What I most lament now is the lateness of the day. It is a cloistered hour. It is a time of fasting, penance, mortification, self-denial, silence, solitude, and the chief virtue required for the *askesis* which leads to glory: humility. A cloistered hour is also a time of being in communion, being with family and friends who seek our good and who can help us to attain the right ends, and being surrounded especially by those saints who pray for us. St. Augustine occupied himself with the penitential psalms at the end of his life, not because he was depressed or feared his own death—but because he had been habituated to the humility of God in Christ who arose to glory through his obedience to the will of the Father, through being made humble even to the point of death, even the humility of death on a cross. St. Thomas ceased to write theology and spent his hours in Eucharistic adoration. Perhaps every hour should become a cloistered hour for the theologian. It is late in the day for all of us. But even so, the Holy Spirit makes everything new in Jesus Christ, and his return in glory is ever closer.

5

The Work and Witness of Ralph Del Colle: Ecumenical friendship

D. STEPHEN LONG

I FIRST MET RALPH Del Colle through his published work. When I was teaching at Garrett-Evangelical Theological Seminary, I needed a good theological essay on the Trinity. Sadly, many of our students lacked basic knowledge of the Trinity. Their overriding concern was a feminist critique of the patriarchal language. Thus in class and chapel the Arian tendency to refer to the Triune persons as "Creator, Redeemer, and Sustainer" was rampant. If the Triune Persons name the relations among them, then of course referring to the Father as "Creator" implied a created relation between the Father and Son, underwriting an Arian view of the Trinity. Ralph Del Colle's essay in the *Cambridge Companion to Christian Theology*, "The Triune God," set forth the doctrine of the Trinity in all its beauty. I used it to great effect throughout my time at Garrett. Students who were not inclined to agree with his profound analysis found in it a way to understand and affirm the doctrine of the Trinity.

Although we had in common a member of our dissertation committees, Geoffrey Wainwright, I knew of Ralph's work before I met him personally. Professor Wainwright moved from Union, where Ralph received his doctorate, to Duke, where I received mine, just as Ralph was finishing and I was beginning. We never met until two decades later, when we were asked to debate pacifism and just war in the first Gulf War. Ralph marched with the Berrigans while he was at Union and regularly got arrested. He tells the story of one protest at which his colleagues were arrested, but he was not. Upon discovering this, he walked back to the police station and turned himself into the authorities so he could be arrested along with the others.

He was never taken with pacifism, however, and is not to this day. Thus we found our first encounter to be as opponents in a debate. What struck me throughout that debate was Ralph's careful quest for truth in light of charity and faith. It was not the usual academic debate in which the point is to win, but a thoughtful probing of the issues. I would go so far as to say it was "prayerful." Anyone who knows Ralph will recognize him in this description. Prayer marks his theology and his life. Praying the liturgy of the hours and attending daily Mass provide the foundation for his work and witness.

Five years after debating Ralph I found myself fortunate to be offered a position at Marquette University. I knew scholars of Ralph's caliber make a strong department. I also knew it was a place that was committed to "classical" theology within an ecumenical context. For both these reasons I was delighted to join Marquette's faculty. As colleagues, Ralph and I quickly became friends. He understood well my evangelical past and neither disregarded it nor treated it with contempt. We also shared similar woes attendant upon spending considerable time in liberal Protestant institutions, and a mutual concern about a naive belief among Catholics that they somehow were exempt from liberal Protestantism's corrosive effects. Ralph invited my wife and me to attend SEEDS, an Ignatian spirituality group that met twice monthly for prayer. Through it we became friends with him and his wife Lee. In June 2012 Ralph had just come from Mayo clinic, where he received the diagnosis of liver cancer, when he attended a SEEDS gathering. We prayed, laughed, and wept that evening as we sought to support Ralph and Lee through this difficult time.

Ralph's work and witness always had an ecumenical focus. Some persons might find this surprising. He is a traditionalist Catholic deeply committed to the magisterium and its teachings. He is a constant witness to Catholic teaching in the theology department and broader university. He believes in obedience and received the *mandatum* from the local bishop. Perhaps some might find it odd, then, that he devotes so much time to Catholic-Methodist, Catholic-Pentecostal, and Catholic-evangelical dialogues. A list of his publications quickly reveals his ecumenical interest. His most recent book is *The Dialogue with Evangelicals: A Catholic Perspective*. He co-edited with David S. Cunningham and Lucas Lamadrid

Ecumenical Theology in Worship, Doctrine, and Life: Essays Presented to Geoffrey Wainwright on his Sixtieth Birthday. From his dissertation on, his work focuses on the role of the Holy Spirit in Christian theology, revealing his Pentecostal commitments. He could affirm a "Spirit Christology" and neoscholasticism. This makes Ralph's work and witness not easily categorized. It does not fall neatly into culture-war divisions of conservative or liberal. He is a traditionalist Catholic with strong interests in the history and practice of socialism, Pentecostalism, evangelicalism, and even the house-church movement, in which he participated for a brief time. He accomplished this while being unapologetically Catholic. I once walked back with him from Mass at St. Joan of Arc chapel and stated a theological concern that the church should not try to absorb Jesus into itself, but admit Jesus always stands over and against it. He responded, "That is not how Catholics think and speak about it." Yet when the InterVarsity organization at Marquette was facing difficulties and possible disciplinary action, it was Ralph who attended the meetings, provided counsel, and supported their work. I could always count on him to support my own ecumenical work. He demonstrated in word and deed how ecumenism flowed from his deep Catholic commitments. In thinking how best to honor such work and witness, I decided it would be fitting to publish the story of another ecumenical friendship, that of Karl Barth and Hans Urs von Balthasar. That friendship bore, and promises still to bear, ecumenical fruit.

Von Balthasar arrived in Basel in December 1939. Barth had moved there five years earlier, having been removed from his teaching post at the University of Bonn for his anti-Nazi stance. Von Balthasar wrote him in April 1940 and asked for a "conversation," telling Barth he already had held many such conversations with him in his mind.[1] One year later, Barth invited von Balthasar to attend his seminar on the Council of Trent. He did, and the result was an extraordinary friendship that influenced both Protestant and Catholic theology. It is no overstatement to say that their friendship directly contributed to Vatican II. Barth was fascinated by it, and used its documents as the basis for his final graduate seminar. Von Balthasar arranged for Joseph Ratzinger to come and speak to that seminar. Barth's last public lecture was held in tandem with von Balthasar on the implications of Vatican II. Barth lectured on "the renewal of the church," while von Balthasar spoke on its "unification." I had the opportunity to spend a month doing research in Basel during my sabbatical leave

---

1. Manfred Lochbrunner, *Hans Urs von Balthasar und seine Theologen-Kollegen: Sechs Beziehungsgeschichten*, (Würzburg: Echter, 2009) 269.

in spring 2011. Because Ralph expressed interest in my work, I find it fitting to present here some of the most important results of my research, especially the arguments Barth and von Balthasar held in the 1941 seminar that brought them together and initiated their friendship.

COUNCIL OF TRENT

Von Balthasar's preoccupation with Barth emerged from his concern over ecclesial divisions and the harm they do to the church's witness. The first line of his 1951 book, *Karl Barth: Darstellung und Deutung seiner Theologie*, presents it as a "confessional conversation [*Gespräch*] among theologians." Barth initiated the conversation.[2] Von Balthasar begins with a quote from Barth about the "enigmatic crack" [*rätselhafte Riss*] that has gone through the church for over four hundred years. The title of the first chapter, "*Zerrissene Kirche*" (the torn or divided Church), plays off this Barth quote. The "*Riss*" is the basis for the "*Zerrissene*," but what exactly is torn? Gaining some clarity on that is the first step in understanding what can only be an enigma—a divided church.

The Barth quote comes from a section in the first volume of his *Church Dogmatics*, in which he compared the Reformed emphasis on proclamation with the Catholic emphasis on Eucharist. Barth encourages his assumed Protestant readers not to recoil at Catholic terms for the Eucharist such as "*fieri*" (to become) and "*nova forma*" (new form) when applied to the "earthly elements" of bread and wine that become "the body and blood of the Lord." Although he sides with the Reformation rejection of transubstantiation, Barth also acknowledges that what occurs in Reformation preaching is as realistic as what Catholics claim takes place in the Eucharist.[3] He critiques Catholic teaching only for setting aside the earthly elements, which, he argues, does not occur in Reformed preaching.[4] Christ and the human preacher are united when preaching achieves its goal. It is "irrelevant," he argues, to ask about the "co-existence" or "cooperation" of the "two factors" (Christ and the preacher), because they are harmonious and thus one and not two. We don't need an account of secondary causality because the human and divine are united through the hypostatic

---

2. "Diese Buch ist ein Beitrag zum konfessionellen Gespräch unter Theologen." *Karl Barth: Darstellung und Deutung Seiner Theologie* (Köln: Jakob Hegner, 1951) 9.

3. *Church Dogmatics* I.1, trans. by Geoffrey Bromiley (Edinburgh: T. & T. Clark, 1975) 94.

4. *Kirchliche Dogmatik*, I.1 (Zürich: Verlag, 1980) 6.

union. As will be shown below, the discussion of secondary causality was an important theme in Barth's 1941 Trent seminar and one about which Barth and von Balthasar argued.

Barth then posed a question to Catholicism with which von Balthasar began his "confessional conversation."

> Is Christ's action, real proclamation, the Word of God preached, tied to the ecclesiastical office and consequently to a human act, or conversely, as one might conclude from this *oret* are the office and act tied to the action of Christ, to the actualising of proclamation by God, to the Word of God preached? From the standpoint of our theses this question is the puzzling cleft [*rätselhafte Riss*] which has cut right across the church during the last 400 years.[5]

Von Balthasar's "confessional conversation," as well as his presentation of Barth's work, begins here. He neither reacts to nor dismisses Barth's question, but calls for self-examination among Catholics to determine if a "cause of offense" still remains on their part. And he acknowledges, with Barth, "this whole project must begin with the admission that unity can only be the grace of the Church's Founder; this is no human product."[6] They disagreed over the extent to which Catholic teaching was supplementary and illuminating of unity in Christ or distracting and dispensable, potentially usurping his place.

Karl Barth's Seminar on the Council of Trent began on April 24, 1941, almost one year to the day after he and von Balthasar first met face to face. Barth began by claiming,

> In each time the necessary task to engage the phenomenon of Roman Catholicism is placed before the Protestant Church and for the Protestant theologian. As long as a Protestant Church and theology is and will be, it stands over and against the Catholic Church, which for it forms its greatest question.[7]

Barth's seminar focused on the Council of Trent's seventh session held in 1547. It began with the "*proemium*" (preface) to "Canons on the

---

5. *Church Dogmatics* I.1, 99.

6. Balthasar, *Theology of Karl Barth*, trans. by Edward T. Oakes (San Francisco: Communio, Ignatius, 1992) 7.

7. Protokolle are the students' written description of each seminar session. I am indebted to Hans Anton Drewes and the Barth archives for a copy of this Protokolle. It is not numbered, so I will refer to the pages based on the PDF made available to me. Council of Trent *Protokolle,* 1a, 1st Session, April 24, 1941.

Sacraments in General," and examined in detail its thirteen canons. (These canons follow the ones of justification for theological reasons. Because the sacraments "begin, augment or restore justification," the council Fathers found it necessary to follow the canons on justification with those of the sacraments.[8]) Barth emphasized two things about these canons on the Catholic side. First, all seven sacraments are necessary. Second, and Barth adds this to the first protocol at the beginning of the second session, although the sacraments are the "*conditio sine qua non*" of justification, they are not the only way Trent claimed grace was communicated.[9] The preface stipulated sacraments "begin" or "augment" justification. Barth saw different means of communicating grace in those two terms. If they begin grace, the sacraments work without the promise of faith or the need for proclamation. If they augment it, they assume something other than sacraments alone, such as proclamation.

The *proemium* and thirteen canons constitute less than two full pages of text, yet Barth devoted the entire summer semester to those two pages. The seminar met once per week. A student leader led the discussion and another took notes and recorded it. Throughout the seminar students were asked to address three questions:

> First, how do we agree with the canon; that is [how do] we [also] say no to the rejected conception [the anathema]. Second, in what decisive different sense can we not join in the rejection, which underlies, or primarily underlies the canon? Third, what is our positive proposition, which we have to place over and against the canon?[10]

Barth never positioned Reformed teaching and Trent as an either-or. The Reformed found common cause at places with what Trent rejected. Take, for example, this report on canon five, which stated, "If anyone shall say that these sacraments have been instituted for the nourishing of faith alone: let him be anathema." The seminar first agreed with the canon. Sacraments do not only nourish faith. They communicate grace, which

---

8. "Proemium" to Session VII, Council of Trent, "Canones de sacramentis." "Ad consummationem salutaris de justification doctrinae, quae in praecedenti proxima sessione uno omnium partum consensus promulgate fuit, consentaneum visum est, de santissimis Ecclesiae sacramentis agere, per quae omnis vera iustitia vel incipiet, vel coepta augetur, vel amissa reparature" (Henrici Denzinger, *Enchiridion Symbolorum: Definitionum et Declarationum De Rebus Fidei Et Morum* [Friburg: Herder, 1942] 843a).

9. Council of Trent *Protokolle*, 4b, 2nd Session, May 8, 1941.

10. Council of Trent *Protokolle*, 36b, 10th Session, June 26, 1941.

"means for men the forgiveness of sins, salvation, and for God the establishment (*Aufrichtung*) of his honor and glory. The glory of God and salvation of men is what the sacrament is about ... and that is more than a mere nourishment of faith. So we speak with canon five a *no* against fideism." Von Balthasar agreed that the canon set forth "a point against fideism," but it was also to be understood in a second sense, which the seminar participants rejected: "According to the Roman teaching, the Sacrament bestows a *charakter christianitatis*." According to the seminar participants, Protestants reject this character.[11] Then they rephrased the canon, putting together their own proposition:

> The sacraments are actions (*Handlungen*) in which God himself places Jesus Christ before us and through that creates faith in us. We have thus avoided the appearance as if the sacraments worked by their own laws (*eigengesetzlich*). God remains subject of the sacramental event, even if the Church is the acting subject.[12]

Perhaps this is evidence of Barth's dialectical method at its best. Students were not to dismiss the canons out of hand. They discovered where they agreed, where they disagreed, and how they would formulate their concerns as clearly as the fathers of Trent did theirs. Far and away, however, the seminar focused on areas of disagreement. The decisive areas of disagreement during the twelve sessions focused on these three points:

1. The seven sacraments and their relation to Christ and the Magisterium.
2. The difference between "*significare*" and the Catholic language of *continere, conferre,* and *ex opere operato.*
3. The nature of the *character indelebilis* sacraments produced and whether grace is an "inherent quality" in the soul.

Each will be examined in turn.

The Seven Sacraments and Their Relation to Christ and the Magisterium

The first three sessions of the seminar were devoted to setting forth the canons, exploring the rejected proposition, and responding from a Reformed

---

11. Council of Trent *Protokolle*, 37a, 10th Session, June 26, 1941.
12. Council of Trent *Protokolle*, 41b, 10th Session, June 26, 1941.

A Man of the Church

perspective. The first reference to von Balthasar occurs toward the close of the third session, after all thirteen canons had been set forth.[13] A student reported that the Catholic Church found itself in difficulty claiming Christ instituted all seven sacraments. This cannot be, because the first reference to unction is found in the letter of James. The student reported:

> It is quite clearly indicated here, that New Testament exegesis does not have the final word on this question, and also that tradition does not have it either. Rather the ecclesial magisterium and its infallibility, gives to the thesis its final steadfastness and is regarded as the real source of revelation.[14]

This suggests three sources of revelation: Scripture, tradition, and the magisterium. The protocol does not tell us who make this claim, whether it was Barth, the seminar leader, or the participants in general, but it awoke von Balthasar and caused him to enter into the fray for the first time. The student reported,

> Dr. von Balthasar indeed corrected the question of infallibility and the interpretation of revelation. There is here in fact not three but only two rails that cross and meet, not revelation, tradition and interpretation through the assistance of the Holy Spirit. What was proclaimed "ex cathedra," was always already present in the Roman Church, even if it was only latent and not expressed.[15]

In other words, von Balthasar objects to the Protestant claim that the magisterium is a source of revelation. It gives expression to revelation, which is always already latent in the tradition. This caused a response from Barth as well. "Professor Barth, however, is of the view that this does actually concern revelation."[16] Whether or not the Magisterium is a source of revelation identifies a, if not the, key disagreement between them throughout their long friendship. Does the Catholic magisterium claim for itself the power of revelation, and thus stand over Christ? Or does it only identify that revelation and thus express obedience to him? The seminar session then came to an end without further discussion of

---

13. The numbering of the seminar sessions in the *Protokolle* is odd. This third session is numbered as "4 Sitzung, May 15, 1941," which means it comes one week after the second session on May 8th when one would expect it to be the third session.

14. Council of Trent *Protokolle*, 20a, 7th Session, June 5, 1941.

15. Council of Trent *Protokolle*, 11b, 4th Session, May 15, 1941.

16. Council of Trent *Protokolle* 11b, 4th Session, May 15, 1941.

this important point. After this session von Balthasar became much more vocal.

The seventh session dealt with canon four, which states explicitly that all seven sacraments are necessary. All seven are not necessary for each individual's justification, but through them, or the desire for them, the "grace of justification" is obtainable. In order to explain how the "desire" for the sacraments justifies even when the material reality is absent, von Balthasar appealed to the biblical story of the two thieves on the cross. The one thief desired Christ and therefore the sacraments even though he did not have them. The seminar lodged a "Protestant objection" against von Balthasar's interpretation. The "desire" found in canon four failed to mention Christ. Instead, it only mentioned a desire for the sacrament. Protestants would affirm the soteriological significance of such a desire, but only as it is for Christ. Catholics, they observed, made the desire "directly" for the sacrament and therefore only "indirectly" for Christ. Von Balthasar, in turn, objected that they were making a distinction nonexistent in Catholic theology: a distinction between desire for Christ and desire for the sacrament.[17] This disagreement was never resolved, and played itself out in a discussion of infant baptism, which was a thread throughout the seminar.

Barth and the seminar participants did not contest that sacraments are necessary, but they did question in what sense they are necessary.[18] They emphasized that faith makes sacraments effective, rather than the Catholic approach, which suggests they work as long as those who receive them present no obstacle. Barth acknowledged that this Catholic teaching went back to Augustine and was the basis for infant baptism. Because a child cannot have faith, baptism works as long as no obstacle is present. For Barth, this bases the sacrament not on the presence of faith, but on the absence of any hindrance. How then, questions Barth, can the Catholic position also affirm canon seven, in which the sacraments must be "rightly received" (*rite ea suscipiant*)? If the sacraments work *ex opere operato*, and do so based solely on no objective hindrance, receiving them in faith has no place. This leads to an important second disagreement. Because Protestantism makes faith necessary for the sacraments, it is better to say, claims Barth, that they "signify" (*significare*) grace rather than "confer" (*conferre*) it. Von Balthasar denied this distinction. The eighth seminar session on canons five through eight highlighted the difference.

---

17. Council of Trent *Protokolle*, 24b, 7th Session, June 5, 1941.
18. Council of Trent *Protokolle*, 24a, 7th Session, June 5, 1941.

The Difference between "significare" and the Catholic Language of continere, conferre, and ex opere operato

Canons five through eight were the basis for the seminar's eighth session, one of the liveliest recorded. More than in any other session, Barth and von Balthasar directly engaged each other over the language used in these canons. The heart of the seminar's discussion and disagreement centered on the extent to which the Protestant insistence on faith for the validity of the sacrament was consistent with the Catholic language that grace is "conferred" *ex opere operato* as long as the recipient offered no hindrance. The test case for this was infant baptism.

The student leader started the eighth session asserting that these canons teach that "the sacraments mediate grace apart from the faith of the believer."[19] Von Balthasar objected. "It is false to say that faith would not be necessary for the reception of the sacrament. A *dispositio* is still at least required." He then went on to explain that for Catholics, "sanctifying grace would not be possible without faith in God."[20] Canon seven insists that the sacrament be "rightly" received. Barth once again expressed surprise and stated he was unconvinced by Balthasar's explanation. He pressed the language of "*rite* (rightly)." What was to be understood by a "'worthy' reception" of the sacrament? He raised this question because Catholic teaching claims a "*conferre* apart from dignity." Von Balthasar answered, "Then it no longer confers grace." He explained canon seven more fully, which stated: "If anyone shall say that grace, as far as concerns God's part (*quantum est ex parte Dei*), is not given through the sacraments always and to all men, even though they receive them rightly, but only sometimes and to some persons: let him be anathema." In order to explain why the Catholic teaching was not contradictory, von Balthasar pointed to the "quantum ex parte dei" of canon seven. "God is always ready," he stated, to give grace to all. Those who do not yet have a proper disposition, and nonetheless prevent no obstacle to reception, will receive the grace of the sacrament. They receive a "character" that is "identical with that of the church."[21] In other words, the faith of the individual who presents no obstacle is carried by the church. This of course requires the doctrine of implicit faith that Calvin and the Reformed tradition rejected, but the central instance of this is infant baptism, which Catholics and the Reformed accepted. For

---

19. Council of Trent *Protokolle*, 25a, 8th Session, June 12, 1941.
20. Council of Trent *Protokolle*, 25a,b, 8th Session, June 12, 1941.
21. Council of Trent *Protokolle*, 26a, 8th Session, June 12, 1941.

von Balthasar infant baptism is not the norm, but an exception that is permitted because of this "character." His argument showed how inconsistent Reformed practice and theology were in allowing infant baptism but denying implicit faith. This was not lost on Barth. It prompted an ongoing conversation between the two men. We have a letter from von Balthasar to Barth shortly after the seminar that discusses infant baptism along with the important expression "significando causant." The discussion of infant baptism reoccurred in Barth's 1960/61 course on the sacraments in the Lutheran tradition and in his unfinished *Church Dogmatics* IV.4, where he cites von Balthasar's *Sponsa Verbi* as a source for his now infamous criticism of infant baptism.[22]

Canon six uses the term "signify" to explain how sacraments work. However, it correlates the term "signify" with "contain" and "confer." The grace that they signify is contained in, and conferred by, the sacraments. Reformed theology, according to the seminar participants, has no problem with "signify," but found "contain" and "confer" troubling. "Protestant theology," they explained, "sees the sacraments as a sign where the grace is only in them as it exceeds the sign." The term "contain" neglected this excess. If the sacraments "signify" grace, why must they also "contain" and "confer" it? Isn't "signify" sufficient?[23] Von Balthasar acknowledged the point but emphasized the fuller Catholic teaching that interprets the sacraments as "significando causant" (that expression is not in the canons.) They signify grace, but they signify it by causing it. Barth "regretted" this way of putting it because the "signify" and the "cause" were distinguished from each other. He stated, "If the signifying were the cause, then we could extend the palm of peace." Von Balthasar emphasized the "counter" that made Trent possible and necessary. The formulation in canon six, he stated, "was chosen against an opponent" who had divided the sign and the grace conferred. Barth denied that any Protestant actually put forth this distinction. They then agreed the distinction between sign and cause should not occur. Trent presented Protestants as dividing them; Protestants presented Catholics as the culprit. Barth and von Balthasar agreed this was a misunderstanding. Barth concluded,

> What a fearful misunderstanding occurred in the sixteenth century when the Reformers proclaimed a sacramental doctrine supposedly in opposition to the "*continere*" and "*conferre*" and

---

22 *Church Dogmatics* IV.4, trans. by Geoffrey Bromiley (T. & T. Clark: Edinburgh, 1969) 168.

23. Council of Trent *Protokolle*, 29a, 8th Session, June 12, 1941.

> Trent supposedly in opposition to the "*significare*"! The Protestants did not understand that the Catholics spoke of a "*significando* causare," whereas the Catholics had not paid attention that the Protestants said, "significando *causare*."[24]

Because of this statement von Balthasar thought Barth should concede the sacraments as a "cause" of grace worked through human means.

Von Balthasar returned to this discussion and pressed Barth further in a letter sent in the summer of 1941. He asks why Barth accepts the "*significando causant*" but not the "*causa secunda*." For von Balthasar, the two are inextricably linked. If Barth accepts that the sacraments cause by signifying, he should then accept that God uses them as secondary causes. To press his point, he asked "Is it irksome for Rembrandt to use a brush?" Moreover, he finds that the "*causa dispotiva*" of the Middle Ages, along with the "doctrine of character (understood ecclesiologically), were best illuminating" for what occurs in the sacraments. He also suggests to Barth that his theology of proclamation is similar to Trent's doctrine of the sacraments, which "does not want to say that the sacrament somehow becomes the function of faith." In other words, if preaching does what Barth claimed it did, then he already had a teaching similar to the Catholic *ex opere operato*. He related this to their ongoing debate between the *analogia entis* and *fidei*. Both give priority to God, but Barth wrongly conceived of the *analogia entis* as a "diacritical point, as a naked eye-to-eye between the Person of God and the human person." He would understand it better if he saw that it "acknowledges the absolute priority of God's Person (and his worldly media)." Von Balthasar then relates this to infant baptism. It is a "limit case" and not "normative." Yet it is proper, and how it is so must be explained. Barth "should learn from this limit: *agere sequitur esse*" (action follows being).[25]

The Nature of the *Character Indelebilis* Sacraments Produce

Von Balthasar acknowledged infant baptism was irregular but, unlike, Barth he nonetheless found it permissible because of the "character" it formed in any recipient who did not present an obstacle. In his obituary for Barth, von Balthasar referred to Barth's doctrine of baptism in the fragment of IV.4 as "very radical to catholic ears."[26] For von Balthasar, infant

---

24 Council of Trent *Protokolle*, 30b–31a, 8th Session, June 12, 1941.

25. Lochbrunner, *Hans Urs von Balthasar und seine Theologen-kollegen*, 280–81.

26. Ibid., 369.

baptism was a permissible exception because of its ecclesial character. Canon nine stated explicitly that baptism, confirmation, and orders "imprinted on the soul a sign, that is, a certain spiritual and indelible mark, on account of which they cannot be repeated." This led to some of the more interesting agreements between the Protestant participants and the Catholic canon.

The agreement is found in the "ontological character" of this indelible sign. The seminar leader for session twelve, drawing on Hebrews 1, reported agreement that this character is Christ. However, he continues, based on Ephesians 3:17, this character is also for us. Christ as the head gives it to the church. Because Christ is this sign, and he shares it with his church,

> the church cannot be destroyed. It is indelible, unrepeatable, or as Augustine formulated it, *quae ecclesia perpetua mansura*. The church cannot pass away because it shares in this character. Because it cannot be destroyed, no one can build the church again. If anyone sets up a church he is foolish for the foundation of the church is unrepeatable.

The seminar participants then offered some interesting observations relating the Reformation and ecclesiology. "The Reformers did not found a church. It cannot be newly established, but only reformed. The Reformers asserted: 'We are the old Church. There is no second church next to the Catholic Church. We are the true Church.'"[27] They agreed with Trent that on these grounds, baptism is unrepeatable.

Although they agreed Christ is the indelible character by which creation itself comes into existence, they disagreed, based on Hebrews 1 and Colossians 1, over whether humans bear this character. For the Reformed participants, Christ alone is the "image of God," and that means the "image" is not in us but in him. It has no basis in humanity qua humanity.[28] This leads to two criticisms of Catholic teaching. One concerns natural theology. Barth and the participants do not reject it. They do not posit it as a genuine possibility. One cannot reject something that doesn't exist. Because the world is already disposed to Christ, natural theology is impossible.[29] Christ's character inextricably marks the world. There can be no nature left unmarked. There is no pure nature upon which a theology could be built. The second criticism concerns the "inhering" of this

---

27. Council of Trent *Protokolle*, 50a-b, 12th Session, July 10, 1941.
28. Council of Trent *Protokolle*, 50b–52b, 12th Session, July 10, 1941.
29. Council of Trent *Protokolle*, 51b, 12th Session, July 10, 1941.

character in the individual soul.[30] Because Christ is the "character of the hypostasis" (Heb. 1:3) it does not inhere in us, but we in it. This distances Protestant from Catholic teaching because the latter makes salvation dependent upon something present in the human person qua person independent of Jesus, for Barth such dependence is the quintessence of liberal Protestantism. The seminar leader drew attention to the absence of any mention of Christ in canon nine. Because the sacraments work *ex opere operato* and produce this character, he questions whether faith in Christ matters at all. Simply participating in the church's structural mediation of grace redeems.

Von Balthasar was unconvinced this properly interpreted Catholic theology. He sought to correct it by explaining how the character is mediated by the sacraments via the "communicatio idiomatum." The sacraments should not be thought of in merely external forms. When it comes to the sacraments, he states, the "inner is not only inner and outer is not only outer." Like Christ's two natures, the external and internal mutually communicate. Von Balthasar then explains that Catholicism does not teach that someone is "guaranteed" grace simply on the basis of belonging to the church. It is the overlapping of the inner and outer from which "the reality of the character arises." The character is Christ; it is the *res* that is grace. But this *res* is genuinely mediated through creaturely means so that it can inhere in creatures. He then tries to explain the nature of this indelible character provided by the sacrament. It cannot be adequately explained in physical or moral terms. He states, "To say it gives rise to something ontological is perhaps an unfortunate expression. There is no great value in distinguishing between the physical and moral. The character lies beyond these realms."[31] The external sign and the internal grace come together to form the character. One cannot be had without the other. The *sacramentum* always refers objectivity to the *res*, but it does not guarantee it. Only when the sacrament is rightly received does that occur, but rightly received it does produce a character. "The character," he stated, "functions there at this decisive point between the *res* and *sacramentum*."[32]

With that, the seminar ended. The seminar leader thanked all the participants and concluded: "with a word of thanks to everyone who participated, especially to Herr Dr. von Balthasar who offered so much that was instructive and interesting, and with a word of regret, that both

---

30. Council of Trent *Protokolle*, 52a, 12th Session, July 10, 1941.
31. Council of Trent Protokolle, 12th session, 53 a.
32. Council of Trent Protokolle, 12th session, 53 a.

our Guest and the seminar leader [Barth] do not stand in a more prominent position and by that means our conversation would be yet more fruitful."[33] The student seminar leader expressed the wish that Barth and von Balthasar held positions in their churches that would allow their conversation to bear fruit.

VATICAN II

Perhaps the student leader could be considered prophetic. Neither von Balthasar nor Barth sought ecclesial positions, and few observers in the 1940s or 1950s would have found them influential in healing the "enigmatic crack" in, or between, their respective churches. Barth was involved in the church struggles while this seminar was going on and was alienated from nearly every corner of church and society. Two years earlier he had caused a "scandal" by referring to the "natural paganism" of the German Christians. In that same year his works were banned in Germany. He wanted to issue a public letter to all German Christians calling upon them to refuse military participation or to sabotage Germany's military efforts, but even his closest allies in the church struggles thought this was "too unusual, too novel, too bold." He chided Swiss neutrality and its ecclesial supporters and advocated for armed resistance.[34] Although he had immense influence theologically, he did not have the ear of Catholic and Protestant church leaders in Switzerland or Germany.

Von Balthasar's preoccupation with Barth had not endeared him to many Catholic leaders. They feared he conceded too much to his Protestant friend. His difficulties with incardination in the 1950s after he left the Jesuits worked against his influence over ecclesial matters. Did Vatican II change all that? In one sense, it could be viewed as a vindication of von Balthasar's preoccupation with Barth. After Vatican II he was to be made cardinal, which did not occur only because he died a few days before the ceremony. The ex-Jesuit who struggled to find a diocese in which he could be incardinated was to be given the red hat. How is that not vindication? If it were vindication for von Balthasar, would it not be also indirect vindication for Barth? Von Balthasar had personally presented his copy of the Barth book to Pope Pius XII in May 1952, who supposedly called him "the greatest theologian since Thomas Aquinas and the most influential

---

33. Council of Trent *Protokolle*, 54b, 12th session, July 10, 1941.

34. Busch, *Karl Barth*, trans. by John Bowden (Philadelphia: Fortress, 1976) 289, 305, 298.

in the twentieth century."³⁵ At Vatican II, the Catholic Church followed the way von Balthasar and others pioneered by engaging Protestantism as something other than heresy, drawing on biblical and patristic theology. Unlike Trent, it offered no anathemas. But von Balthasar never found vindication in Vatican II. Instead, he lamented some of it, as did Barth, finding in it a dilution of Catholic theological substance. Like Barth, he feared that Vatican II represented more of a capitulation to Schleiermacher than the Christological renaissance he envisioned. Schleiermacher rather than Barth entered the Vatican windows opened to the world. After spending nearly three decades denying Barth's claim that liberal Protestantism and Catholicism were two sides of the same coin, von Balthasar for the first time feared Barth might be right. His published celebration of Barth's eightieth birthday in 1966 and his obituary for him in 1968 make explicit his concerns.³⁶

CONCLUSION

Vatican II produced a brief glimmer of hope for a Catholic-Protestant rapprochement; that hope has all but disappeared in the twenty-first century. Any substantive Protestant and Catholic convergence in the near or distant future appears unlikely. Of course a facile unity on the "liberal margins" of both traditions is easily accomplished, but this does not constitute a substantive convergence. The Anabaptist theologian John Howard Yoder suggested that too many ecumenical and interfaith conversations take place at the "liberal edges" of the various traditions where the participants "were relatively least bound to the classical core of their respective traditions."³⁷ Von Balthasar certainly agreed, and feared this was the ecumenical result of the *aggiornamento* of Vatican II. For Yoder, such discussions have limited usefulness because participants normally already agree. This cannot be said of Barth and von Balthasar. They spoke unapologetically from the heart of their traditions, and nonetheless produced the beginnings of an ecumenical convergence that still awaits consummation. The more Barth emphasized the Christological substance of Reformed theology and von

---

35. Although widely reported, tracking down a direct citation from Pius XII where he said this is so far not forthcoming. One reference can be found in James B. Torrance, "Karl Barth" in *The Encyclopedia of Religion*, vol. 2 (Mircea Eliade, Editor in Chief; New York, NY: MacMillan Publishing Company, 1987), 68.

36. Lochbrunner, *Hans Urs von Balthasar und seine Theologen-kollegen*, 352.

37. John Howard Yoder, *The Jewish-Christian Schism Revisited*, ed. By Michael G. Cartwright and Peter Ochs (Grand Rapids: Eerdmanns, 2003) 34.

Balthasar that of Catholicism, the closer they came to each other. Ralph Del Colle's work and witness carry on that tradition.

6

Embodying Grace: The Super/natural Witness of Ralph Del Colle

JAMES K. A. SMITH

CAN A PRAISE BE at once a lament? Is praise a moment within lament? Does lament preface praise as a mere prelude, left behind once we get to the finale of praise? Or are lament and praise more intertwined than that—inextricably bound up like the messy beauty of a good-but-broken creation? Might they be bound together in that sometimes marvelous, sometimes awkward dance that is the relation between nature and grace? Can we praise and lament simultaneously? Indeed, can we do otherwise?

Could there be a more lamentable occasion for praising a friend and colleague? I am grateful for the opportunity to honor the work and life of Ralph Del Colle, even while I lament the occasion. I will give thanks to our gift-giving God for blessing us with such a teacher, even while I protest to the same God that this is not the way it's supposed to be—ever mindful that the God to whom I'm grateful, and before whom I protest, is also the risen Son who suffered the violence and brokenness of the world on the cross, rising in triumph from the grave, thereby demonstrating that love is stronger than death. Our laments could never surprise a crucified King of creation.

In praising God for the gift of Ralph Del Colle, I'm thinking of Paul's marvelously compact rendition of the Gospel in Ephesians 4:10–16, which seems especially fitting in this context:

He who descended is the same one who ascended far above all the heavens, so that he might fill all things.) The gifts he gave were that some would be apostles, some prophets, some evangelists, some pastors and teachers, to equip the saints for the work of ministry, for building up the body of Christ, until all of us come to the unity of the faith and of the knowledge of the Son of God, to maturity, to the measure of the full stature of Christ. We must no longer be children, tossed to and fro and blown about by every wind of doctrine, by people's trickery, by their craftiness in deceitful scheming. But speaking the truth in love, we must grow up in every way into him who is the head, into Christ, from whom the whole body, joined and knitted together by every ligament with which it is equipped, as each part is working properly, promotes the body's growth in building itself up in love. (NRSV)

Ralph Del Colle was one of those gifts of the ascended Christ precisely because he was a wise teacher. As a teacher, he was concerned with honoring the prophets—and fostering a spirituality that makes room for God's surprise. At the same time, he was passionate about the unity of the faith, as evidenced by all of the energy he devoted to ecumenical dialogue. And at every turn, Ralph was an exemplar of what it means to speak the truth in love.

Some theologians we know only through their *oeuvre*, without knowing a thing about them as a person. Their books are stand-ins for their person, and we can sometimes fall into the illusion that we know *them* because we've read their books. Or we can be quite disappointed to finally meet them as persons and experience a disheartening disjunction between theoretical beauty of the oeuvre and moral ugliness of the person. My relationship with Ralph Del Colle was almost completely the inverse: I knew Ralph the theologian primarily as a person, with only a growing familiarity with his published *oeuvre*. But given the unique graces of Ralph as a person, and his distinctive emphases as a theologian, this order of knowing (him) seems just right. Ralph's theology was something he carried in his person—it was a distinctive Christian comportment that embodied grace, the central theological concept at the heart of his corpus. I have long treasured Ralph not just because he was smart, but because he was *wise*, and that wisdom was felt in his person more intensely than it might have been communicated merely through his writing. Indeed, I fear that those only acquainted with Ralph's corpus might not have fully absorbed his theological wisdom that can only be encountered in embodied conversation. In this respect, we can be envious of his students, who I suspect know what I'm talking about.

I don't want to pretend to be an intimate of some sort of inner circle. I knew Ralph through our common involvement with the Society for Pentecostal Studies, though Ralph's involvement there was both more steady and more intense than my own sometime participation. Much of my encounter with Ralph's theology was not in the lecture halls of ivory towers, or the cool distance of the printed page, but in hotel rooms across the country as the SPS gathered annually in the vicinity of colleges and universities willing to show hospitality to Pentecostal and charismatic scholars (that's a smaller pool than you might think). Inevitably, a crew of us would end up in late night conversations that were a significant part of my own theological education, especially as a neophyte in Pentecostal and charismatic traditions. I have fond memories of (very sober![1]) animated conversations that regularly featured Amos Yong and I listening and laughing as Ralph, Dale Irvin, and Frank Macchia regaled us with stories of Union Seminary—Donald Dayton sort of harrumphing in the corner, interjecting historical context. Absent from these conversations was the usual showboating and politicking that characterizes a lot of academic gatherings; instead, I associate these conversations with wisdom, joy, and delight—and Ralph contributed on all three fronts.

In these contexts, Ralph was both a theological bridge-builder and an ecumenical accountability partner. He stood as a bridge-builder because he affirmed the unique gifts of different streams of the body of Christ. In his tireless efforts on Roman Catholic-Pentecostal dialogue, Ralph was a key conversation partner because his theological sensibilities—and pilgrimage—enabled him to affirm and identify with Pentecostal spirituality while at the same time valuing his ecclesiastical location in mother church.[2] But Ralph's bridge-building shouldn't be confused with some bland, middle-of-the-road-ism, a proverbial "third way" (that usually leads to nowhere). To the contrary, Ralph's work was bridge-building because he was also unafraid to call people to the mat—to let ecumenical encounter be a mutual prophetic call to grow into the fullness of Christ. So his stance of deep sympathy for Pentecostal spirituality, for example,

---

1. These were holiness folk, after all!

2. In his SPS Presidential Address, Ralph describes himself as "one who had migrated from charismatic prayer back to the liturgical prayer of my upbringing." See Ralph Del Colle, "Aesthetics and Pathos in the Vision of God: A Catholic-Pentecostal Encounter," *Pneuma: Journal of the Society of Pentecostal Studies* 26 (2004) 99–117 (99).

did not preclude him from challenging Pentecostals to account for their catholicity. Conversely, his location within the Roman Catholic communion did not prevent him from seeing Pentecostal renewal as a challenge to the presumption of Roman Catholic ecclesiology. I suggest that this is precisely why Ralph was also persistently interested in those thorny theological challenges at the nexus of nature and grace, the natural and the supernatural, anxious to not see Christian traditions abandon one because of their (over)valuing of the other.

This sensibility and mission is wonderfully displayed in Ralph's recent essay, "Whither Pentecostal Theology? Why a Catholic is Interested"[3]—an essay that is Exhibit A for the animating impetus of Ralph's work and a model of what I'm trying to describe here. While he unapologetically identifies as a Roman Catholic, it is precisely his interest *as a Catholic* that leads him to ask the question, "Whither Pentecostal theology?":

> So, whither Pentecostal theology is not intended as some sort of external tribunal directing where it ought to go. My interest, that is, my Catholic interest, is an attempt to think with Pentecostal theologians about the significance of Pentecostalism for the church catholic as well as the [Roman[4]] Catholic Church. You might say that because I consider the Pentecostal movement to be a move of God, it is important that its theological articulation be heard by fellow Christians as we attempt to [be] faithful to the Lord and his mission, even as we seek the unity of the church in response to his high priestly prayer that we all may be one (Jn 17:21).[5]

A succinct summary of Ralph's life's work, this paragraph—and the essay that it opens—exemplifies his two-fold concern to advance constructive theology and common Christian witness. Perhaps better, he was interested in constructive theology *in order to* advance common Christian witness. Here we have systematic *for the sake of* mission, theology *for* catholicity.

It is also perfectly fitting that the focus of this essay is the exegesis of a prayer, specifically a prayer that was the theme of the Ninth Assembly of the World Council of Churches that met in Porto Alegre, Brazil: "God, in your grace transform the world." It is a prayer that is indigenous to

---

3. Ralph Del Colle, "Whither Pentecostal Theology? Why a Catholic is Interested," *Pneuma: Journal of the Society for Pentecostal Studies* 31 (2009) 35–46.

4. Consider this editorial interjection my one little protest from my location within the traditions of the magisterial Reformation. We are not quite content to let Rome own "the Catholic Church." We see ourselves within "the Catholic Church," too.

5. Ibid., 36.

both Catholic and Pentecostal spirituality because both are characterized by what Ralph brilliantly describes as an "epicletic posture"—a stance of being-before-God with a deep sense of need and vulnerability and dependence, asking for gifts because we've been commanded to do so, and because we know that all is gift.[6] "Come, Holy Spirit" is the first prayer we exhale when we're given breath by the Creator. So what Catholics and Pentecostals share in common—a gift that they can share with the church catholic—is an appreciation for the centrality of the Spirit in transformative grace. Indeed, Ralph contends that "one cannot understand either Catholics or Pentecostals without appreciating how significant the notion and reality of transformative grace is operative in their understanding and praxis."[7] This is why "[t]he language of grace is also the language of pneumatology."[8]

Ralph's gifts to theological dialogue often come in the form of incisive, faith-full questions, and this essay is no exception. For this prayer—"God, in your grace transform the world"—raises a host of questions at the intersection of nature and grace, creation and redemption, church and world. "How does one preserve the gratuity and supernatural dimension of grace when the scope of God's gracious and salvific self-communication is the entire creation?"[9] Or: "How is the Spirit working in the church and in the world?"[10] Or: "how does one identify the transformative effects of the Spirit's work in the world, that is in culture and society, which all will admit some resemblance to the kingdom consummated and is in a real sense present in the life of the church?"[11] "What type of transformation is expected in society compared to that in the church?"[12] "[I]s the world the object of God's transformative processes?"[13] You will only feel the force of these questions if you remember that they are posed to Pentecostals. These are the questions of a friend who is genuinely interested and concerned to see where Pentecostal theology will go as it grapples with such questions.[14]

---

6. "What do you have that you have not received?," St. Paul asked (1 Cor 4:7)—a favorite citation of St. Augustine.

7. Del Colle, "Whither Pentecostal Theology?," 37. A lot is at stake in that "... *and reality* ..."

8. Ibid., 38.

9. Ibid.

10. Ibid.

11. Ibid., 42.

12. Ibid., 43–44.

13. Ibid., 45.

14. I think one could see Amos Yong's magisterial work, *In the Days of Caesar:*

Ralph's own forays into these questions always sought to hold together the gratuity of grace with a robust theology of creation (and corresponding theological anthropology) that avoids a "desiccated view of nature"[15]: "Since nature is the object of perfection it is important to have a thorough account of nature so that nothing is lost to the healing and elevation that grace effects."[16] While Ralph could sometimes be gracious to the point of being coy, I don't think it's any secret that he worried that Pentecostalism might not yet have such a "thorough account of nature." On the other hand, he would emphasize that "[o]ne needs to be cautious about the reduction of grace to some sort of religious naturalism."[17] This, he notes, is not a danger for Pentecostals[18]—it might be more of a danger for his co-religionists in Rome, which is precisely why he thought of Pentecostal spirituality as a gift to the wider church catholic.

The questions are posed *as* theology; the conversation *is* its own fruit. There is in Ralph's very methodology a deep sense that the Spirit is leading us into all truth, which is why dialogue is next to godliness, and why questions are prayers.

Pentecostalism and Political Theology (Grand Rapids, MI: Eerdmans, 2010) as an oblique—if not direct—reply to Ralph's questions in this regard, especially since Ralph specifically highlights political questions at several points in "Whither Pentecostal Theology?" (esp. 43–44).

15. Ralph is clearly ploughing the same fields as Henri de Lubac and *le nouvelle théologie* in this respect. Future reception of Ralph's work will need to do so against this horizon. For an important framing of the issues in this conversation that would help Pentecostals "triangulate" with evangelical discussions, see Hans Boersma, *Nouvelle Théologie and Sacramental Ontology: A Return to Mystery* (Oxford: Oxford University Press, 2009). I hint at something similar in James K.A. Smith, *Thinking in Tongues: Pentecostal Contributions to Christian Philosophy* (Grand Rapids: Eerdmans, 2010) 99–101.

16. Del Colle, "Whither Pentecostal Theology?," 39.

17. Ibid., 40.

18. Though one could wonder whether recent Pentecostal attempts to root the Spirit in something like "spirit" is a trajectory about which Ralph might be concerned.

7

"Speaking the Truth in Love": Ralph Del Colle and the Methodist-Roman Catholic International Dialogue

GEOFFREY WAINWRIGHT

Methodism was among the first of the Christian world communions to respond to the invitations to bilateral dialogue issuing from the Roman Catholic Church after the Second Vatican Council. The Joint Commission for Dialogue between the Roman Catholic Church and the World Methodist Council—its composition being from time to time renewed—has met in a series of five-year periods since 1967. The quinquennial reports have become stenographically known (even on the Catholic side) by the place and date of their presentation to regular meetings of the World Methodist Council and (in notional simultaneity) to the Holy See. Thus, we have Denver 1971, Dublin 1976, Honolulu 1981, Nairobi 1986, Singapore 1991, Rio de Janeiro 1996, Brighton 2001, Seoul 2006, and Durban 2011. The reports typically bear some such statement as the following concerning their status:

> The Report published here is the work of the International Methodist-Roman Catholic Dialogue Commission. Commission members were appointed by the World Methodist Council and the Holy See's Pontifical Council for Promoting Christian Unity (PCPCU). The authorities who appointed the Commission have now allowed the statement to be published so that it may be widely discussed. It is a joint statement of the Commission, not an authoritative declaration by the Roman Catholic

Church or by the World Methodist Council, which will study the document in due course.

On the Catholic side, the process of "reception" (as ecumenists like to say) has typically been encouraged by the accompanying publication of an official commentary on the part of a respected theologian with the purpose (roughly speaking) of signaling the strengths and weaknesses of the Report from a Catholic point of view. Such a theologian is appointed by the PCPCU upon agreement of the Congregation for the Doctrine of the Faith, which body has indeed to approve all theologians appointed by the PCPCU to membership on ecumenical dialogue commissions. Ralph Del Colle was the respected Catholic theologian appointed to furnish the official commentary on Brighton 2001 (the proper title of the 122-paragraph Joint Commission Report being *Speaking the Truth in Love: Teaching Authority among Catholics and Methodists*).

Ralph began by noting that Brighton 2001 was

> the fourth report of the international Catholic/Methodist dialogue that has explored fundamental theology and foundational ecclesiological issues. Three previous phases produced the following Reports: *Towards a Statement on the Church* (1982–1986), *The Apostolic Tradition* (1986–1991), and *The Word of Life* (1992–1996) in the fourth, fifth and sixth five-year series respectively. The just concluded seventh phase on teaching authority in the church follows in logical sequence, thus taking up one of the thornier issues of ecumenical dialogue. The expectation of "full communion in faith, mission and sacramental life"(15) remains the goal of these rather substantial theological exchanges.[1]

Ralph correctly noted that these "more systematic" theological treatments began in 1982, following Honolulu 1981 and its move "[t]oward an Agreed Statement on the Holy Spirit" which, he says, "set the tone for the future phases and has lent a strong pneumatological cast to the entire dialogue." No one familiar with Ralph's own theological life and thought

---

1. For this document, I quote from Ralph Del Colle, "Commentary and Reflections on *Speaking the Truth in Love: Teaching Authority among Catholics and Methodists*, the Report of the Joint Commission between the Roman Catholic Church and the World Methodist Council 1997–2001 Seventh Series" on the Vatican website, http://www.vatican.va/roman_curia/pontifical_councils/chrstuni/documents/rc_pc_chrstuni_doc_071101_speaking_the_truth_com_en.html, accessed August 8, 2012. There are no paragraph or page numbers in this edition. The numbers in parentheses in what I quote from this text refer to paragraph numbers of *Speaking the Truth in Love*.

will be surprised by the approbatory tone of that initial remark; indeed, it could be added that the subsequent Reports from this dialogue have blossomed into a fully trinitarian mode of discussion.

Brighton 2001 bears in fact a rather unusual structure, and Ralph detected a methodological promise contained in it:

> *Speaking the Truth in Love* is divided into two parts. Part One explores the theological convergences (and differences) between the two traditions in a rather systematic manner. The Second Part is more descriptive, intending to map how understanding and practice internal to each tradition may be understood by the other. A summary conclusion of "recognizable commonalities" and "outstanding differences" then leaves the two communions with a prospectus for further work to carry the dialogue forward. It is an interesting method and works to overcome any complacency if both communions are to be faithful to their ecumenical calling. It also grounds the theological issues that have arisen in the actual ecclesial life of both communions. This is by far the most prudent method by which to engage each tradition with the other in the search for Christian unity.

Ralph reverts to two matters in particular where Methodists should pursue their own self-understanding and life in dialogue with Catholicism. The first matter relates to Methodism's origins in the eighteenth-century Church of England and the Wesleyan revival and—especially in relation to the Catholic Church—Methodism's place in the deeper ecclesiological history and the broader ecclesiological picture. The second matter concerns Methodism's teaching and practice in the domain of sacramentality. These two matters have indeed occupied the Joint Commission in its subsequent Reports: Seoul 2006 (*The Grace Given You in Christ: Catholics and Methodists Reflect Further on the Church*) and Durban 2011 (*Encountering Christ the Saviour: Church and Sacraments*).

The deepest and broadest matters of ecclesiology to be discussed together by Methodists and Catholics were seen by Ralph to be framed in terms of teaching, both as substance and as act. Certainly,

> both accept "the Scriptures, the Creeds and the doctrinal decrees of the early Ecumenical Councils"(22). Both order their doctrine according to their[2] relationship to the core of the faith: Catholic "hierarchy of truths," Wesleyan "analogy of faith" or "grand scheme of doctrine" (23). Both acknowledge

---

2. This edition of Ralph's text should read "its" here instead of "their."

development of doctrine (24) and the ministry of theologians (25). The rule of prayer as in *lex orandi, lex credendi* (26), the orientation to mission (27), and the imperative toward "entire external union" (28) all factor into the proper exercise of teaching authority.

However,

doctrinal standards are mentioned but the equivalence between the two traditions is not balanced in the same way. The accumulation of decrees and pronouncements by episcopal synods, the Pope and the Roman Curia weigh more heavily in the Catholic Church than do the doctrinal reading of Scripture by Methodist Conferences according to the standard texts of "the Sermons of John Wesley, his Notes on the New Testament, and the Articles of Religion" (22). What remains unclear from the Report is the normativity of these standard texts for Methodism.

Ralph posed the question for Methodism in this way:

On the Methodist side the relationship between John Wesley and Anglican doctrinal formularies is noted (86, 89, 90) along with the early emergence of the Conference (90, 91, 94–96) and Wesley's provision of American Methodism with liturgy, ordained ministry and general superintendency (92). The latter could actually be expanded to provide further insight as to whether Methodists consider this an emergency situation for the church in the new Republic analogous to the Lutheran situation in the sixteenth century, or whether it is normative for subsequent Methodist practice.

Similar questions could be put to British Methodism, even though the "distinction," in fact the separation, of Methodism from the Church of England took rather longer and contained certain characteristic features of its own. Ralph's reference to the sixteenth century, and implicitly "the Reformation," prompts this writer to suggest that the Catholic Church may also now be ready to reread certain features in its own history in a new light. Regarding Methodism and Catholicism, Ralph declares that "the two traditions are indeed different precisely because their histories entailed distinct receptions of the apostolic tradition."

Ralph finished his commentary on the first part of *Speaking the Truth in Love* by noting that

there still remains lack of agreement on the degree of certainty that preaching and teaching are "truly that of Christ and his

> Church" (82). The phrase is a Catholic one and when Methodists respond that they can be sure about essentials, both sides acknowledge agreement here as well. They disagree, however, about what those essentials are (82). Their agreement that oversight is a matter of love and a means of grace to support "holiness in living, . . . faithfulness in teaching, and . . . participation in God's mission to the world" (84) demonstrates the strong convergence that the Report aims for and should not be underplayed. However, *Speaking the Truth in Love* should also be commended for registering the difficulties that remain.

Certainly the Methodist/Catholic dialogue's Seoul Report of 2006 (*The Grace Given You in Christ: Catholics and Methodists Reflect Further on the Church*) showed the partners to have at least begun a process of "mutual reassessment" in the "new context" of ecumenism.[3] The Seoul Report made much of Pope John Paul II's 1995 encyclical *Ut unum sint* and of the recognition that ecumenical dialogue entails both an "exchange of ideas" and an "exchange of gifts."[4] Such exchanges between what are now dialogue partners rather than controversial opponents could lead to a conquest of respective historical weaknesses and even a correction of respective historical errors. Positively put, perhaps the most pregnant and challenging sentences in Seoul 2006 would be these, from the start of chapter 3:

> The very considerable agreement reached over the years of our recent dialogue, amply summarized in Chapter Two, indicates that Catholics and Methodists do, in fact, hold in common many beliefs and priorities regarding the Church. It is time now to return to the concrete reality of one another, to look one another in the eye, and with love and esteem to acknowledge what we see to be truly of Christ and of the Gospel, and thereby *of the Church*, in one another. Doing so will highlight the gifts we truly have to offer one another in the service of Christ in the world, and will open the way for an exchange of gifts which is what ecumenical dialogue, in some way, always is [citing *Ut Unum*

---

3. The text can be found on the website of the Centro pro Unione; Interconfessional Dialogues; "Methodist-Roman Catholic International Dialogue," http://www.prounione.urbe.it/dia-int/m-rc/doc/e_m-rc_seoul.html, accessed August 8, 2012. The title of the first chapter of this document is "Mutual Reassessment: A New Context for Mutual Reassessment." This edition of the text has no page numbers, but it has retained the paragraph numbers, which I will use in my references to the text.

4. For the exchange of ideas, see no. 63. For the exchange of gifts, see nos. 13, 63, 97, 107-35, 141, 151-52, 156-57, 161-62, 167.

Sint, 28]. . . . In our striving for full communion, "we dare not lose any of the gifts with which the Holy Spirit has endowed our communities in their separation."[5] The Holy Spirit is the true giver of the gifts we are seeking to exchange. The present chapter identifies the principal ways in which Methodists and Roman Catholics are able to recognize each other's ecclesial character, before describing those elements and endowments that they could suitably receive from, and give to, the other. Practical proposals for that exchange follow in Chapter Four. (no. 97)

As already mentioned, Ralph Del Colle highlights a second major matter in which Methodists should pursue their own self-understanding and life in dialogue with Catholicism: Methodism's teaching and practice in the domain of sacramentality. There is, of course, always overlap between questions of ecclesiology and questions of sacrament, sacraments, and sacramentality. In his commentary on *Speaking the Truth in Love*, Ralph appropriately concentrates on "the sacramentality of office," where indeed lies "the major area of difference between the two communions relative to teaching authority in the Church": "Whether, by virtue of ordination, ministry is not only a sign but a 'guarantee of the active presence of Christ by the power of the Holy Spirit, especially in particular acts of authoritative discernment and proclamation' (68) is what divides Catholics and Methodists."

It should be recorded that starting at least from Nairobi 1986, the Joint Commission for Dialogue between Catholics and Methodists began to affirm the sacramental dimension of ecclesiology: "The Mystery of the Word made flesh and the sacramental mystery of the eucharist point towards a view of the Church based upon the sacramental idea, i.e. the Church takes its shape from the Incarnation from which it originated and the eucharistic action by which its life is constantly being renewed."[6] This paragraph from Nairobi 1986 is crucially cited in paragraph 77 of Seoul 2006, where it declares, quoting *Speaking the Truth in Love*, no. 49, that the "agreement between Catholics and Methodists on the need for 'graced, free and active participation in God's saving work' lies at the very heart

---

5. Here the Seoul Report cites United Methodist-Roman Catholic Dialogue, USA, *Through Divine Love: The Church in Each Place and All Places* (2005), no. 178.

6. *Towards a Statement on the Church*, no. 10. The text can be found on the website of the Centro pro Unione; Interconfessional Dialogues; "Methodist-Roman Catholic International Dialogue," http://www.prounione.urbe.it/dia-int/m-rc/doc/e_m-rc_nairobi2.html, accessed August 8, 2012. This edition of the text has no page numbers, but it has retained the paragraph numbers.

of the possibility of our moving towards a common understanding of the nature and mission of the Church which makes use of concepts associated with 'sacramentality.'" Given agreement on a generally sacramental view of the Church, Ralph had been willing to admit that Catholicism might then learn from Methodism lessons that "would enhance the participation of the laity in receiving and maintaining the truth."

Seoul 2006 recorded a "very considerable" (no. 97) or "extensive" (no. 141) measure of agreement between Methodists and Catholics in ecclesiology. It was chiefly in the area of what might be called the instrumentality of grace that "divergences" between Methodists and Catholics "require further exploration and discussion":

> There remain aspects of teaching and ecclesial elements which Catholics regard as essential to what we must hold in common in order to have full communion and to be fully the Church of Christ. These include a precise understanding of the sacramental nature of ordination, the magisterial role of the episcopate in apostolic succession, the assurance asserted of certain authoritative acts of teaching, and the place and role of the Petrine ministry (no. 92).

Here we encounter again a number of questions that were raised by Ralph Del Colle in his commentary on Brighton 2001. At least some of these topics were then treated in the ninth round of the bilateral dialogue, leading to Durban 2011. Under the title *Encountering Christ the Saviour: Church and Sacraments*, and with the Paschal Mystery as the key concept, this text registered the achievement of an outstanding level of agreement concerning baptism, the eucharist, and even sacramentally ordained ministry (including "ministerial priesthood and the common priesthood of the faithful"[7]). If, as appears to be the case, Methodists can agree that God unfailingly bestows specified grace through rightly administered sacraments, then perhaps the next question they should consider, in dialogue with Catholicism, is whether, in appropriate circumstances, the Church may also be infallibly taught—a question that was at least broached in Nairobi 1986 and may have underlain discussions in the intervening rounds.

Already from my first reading of Ralph Del Colle's commentary on *Speaking the Truth in Love* at the time of its appearance, I found help for

---

7. The title of the fourth section of chapter 4. For the text, see World Methodist Council website; 2011 World Methodist Council Meeting; Roman Catholic Dialogue Report, http://worldmethodistcouncil.org/wp-content/uploads/2012/02/Roman-Catholic-Dialogue-Report.pdf, accessed August 8, 2012.

the continuing conduct of the Methodist/Roman Catholic dialogue, the Joint Commission of which I joined in 1982 and chaired on the Methodist side from 1986 to 2011. That same phrase, "speaking the truth in love," characterized the intention and practice of Ralph's theological work from my first acquaintance with him as a student at the Union Theological Seminary in New York in the early 1980s. I am grateful to have known him as a friend and fellow laborer.

8

The Our Father, Prayer of the Crucified: In Tribute to Ralph Del Colle, Who Prayed the Our Father with Jesus His Savior

THOMAS G. WEINANDY, O.F.M, CAP.

DURING HIS CRUCIFIXION, WHAT was Jesus' mental disposition? What was the form and content of his prayer? Despite the unimaginable physical pain and emotional distress, we know that during the course of his crucifixion Jesus' heart and mind were consumed with love—love for his Father and love for each human person. We know, too, that Jesus was not undergoing his crucifixion in a passive manner, as if he merely were submissively enduring what was happening to him. Rather, he was using what was being done to him as a divinely ordained event by which he would ardently give his life as an act of sacrificial love to the Father. This Spirit-filled offering of his life to his Father was done lovingly in our stead and on our behalf. Jesus on the cross must have prayed to his Father out of love for his Father, and he must have prayed for us out of love for us. We know that, in his cry of abandonment, Jesus prayed the whole of Psalm 22, according to which, in the midst of horrendous suffering, the afflicted man trusts in the Lord and is confident that he will be delivered from the present evil only to manifest God's glory among all the nations.

With this in mind, I want to suggest that one of the prayers that Jesus prayed while on the cross was the prayer that he taught his disciples to pray, the Our Father. This thought first came to me when I was recently celebrating Mass. When it came time for the Our Father, I looked up from the Missal (since it is now one of the few prayers of the new Roman Missal that I know by heart) and looked at the crucifix before me. I thought to myself: "Jesus prayed the Our Father when he was on the cross." Immediately the Our Father, in its totality, took on a fuller and richer meaning. Some may immediately object that there is no biblical evidence that Jesus prayed the Our Father during his crucifixion. That is true. Nowhere do the Gospels state that Jesus did so. However, as I hope to demonstrate, only if Jesus did pray the Our Father while he was nailed to the cross does it assume its most profound significance and acquire the fullness of its truth. Only because Jesus prayed the Our Father on the cross was the fullness of its salvific potential and historical consequence actualized. Moreover, everyone else who prays the Our Father does so only in union with, and in imitation of, the crucified Jesus, as that prayer has been imbued with the meaning and authority that the cross has indelibly conferred upon it. Thus, I will assume, for the sake of this essay, that the crucified Jesus actually did pray the Our Father. I will, then, examine the Our Father in the light of Jesus having prayed it while upon the cross.

OUR FATHER

Most scholars are confident that when Jesus taught his disciples to pray "our Father," the Aramaic word he spoke for "father" was *abba* so as to designate their filial loving intimacy with the Father and the Father's paternal loving intimacy with them. Two interrelated truths can be perceived in the crucified Jesus saying "our Father." First, Jesus, as man, addressed God as Father, and he did so precisely because he alone is the eternal Son of the Father, begotten and not made, consubstantial with the Father. Jesus, therefore, enjoys the privilege and the right to address God as Father, as *Abba*, in a singular and definitive manner.

Second, Jesus did not say "my Father" or simply "Father." He addressed his Father as "our Father." He did so because it is specifically on the cross that Jesus was obtaining the salvation of all who would become, throughout the whole of human history, members of his body, members of his Church, and so adopted children of the Father. Thus, Jesus was praying the Our Father not simply for himself but as the head of his body and thus for all men and women. It is indeed only because Jesus reconciled us to the Father through his sacrificial death that we now obtain, through faith and the indwelling of the Holy Spirit, the privilege and the right to address, in union with Jesus, God as our Father, as *Abba*.

A Man of the Church

WHO ART IN HEAVEN, HALLOWED BE THY NAME

With the words "who art in heaven, hallowed be thy name," Jesus confessed who the Father is and thus in what manner he and all of us are to appear before him. Jesus confessed that his and our Father is in heaven, that is, he lives and exists in a divine manner, in a way that differs in kind and not simply in degree from all else. The acknowledgment that his Father is in heaven, within the context of the cross, was also an act of faith in that he trusted that his Father, as the heavenly Father, providentially governs all earthly events, even this event, and so continues to have his loving and protective hand upon him. Moreover, Jesus, having said "our," included all of humankind under the care of his heavenly Father. When we pray the Our Father, in union with Jesus, we are confessing with him that we too trust, in all circumstances even in the midst of our own suffering and death, that we are in the safety of our heavenly Father's hand.

Precisely because the Father is the heavenly Father, his name is to be hallowed, that is, acclaimed to be holy and separated from all that is profane. The Father's name is hallowed by the very fact that he is the Father of all, including his Son. However, everyone has a sacred duty to hallow the name of the Father, that is, to acknowledge and bear witness to the Father's holiness. Even the divine Son, from all eternity, hallowed the name of his Father, because the divine holiness that was bestowed upon him comes from the Father. What is significant, under the present circumstances of the cross, is that Jesus, as the incarnate Son, was perfectly hallowing the name of his Father. Jesus' suffering and death on the cross was in itself the supreme acknowledgement and the ultimate testimony to his Father's holiness, for in this very act of laying down his life on the cross, Jesus is ardently worshipping and fervently glorifying his Father. The offering of his holy and innocent life was the perfect sacrifice of praise. Moreover, on the cross Jesus was doing away with all that is not holy—sin and death, as well as the devil, the father of all that is sinful and profane. We too hallow our Father's name not only when we pray the Our Father, but also, and especially, when we do so in association with acts of sacrificial love for others, for we are imitating the sacrificial love of our crucified savior.

When Jesus prays that the name of his Father be hallowed, hidden within that proclamation is an entreaty that his own name be hallowed as well. During the Last Supper Jesus affirms, "Now is the Son of man glorified, and in him God is glorified; if God is glorified in him, God will also glorify him in himself, and glorify him at once" (John 13:31–32). As his perfect Word and eternal Image, the Father forever hallows and glorifies the name of his Son for the Son expresses his own name in its entirety. Moreover, the Son eternally hallows and glorifies his Father, from whom he was begotten as the Father's perfect Word and Image. The event of the cross is the earthly historical act by which and in which the Father and Son mutually hallowed and glorified one another. "Father, the hour has come; glorify your Son that the Son may glorify you. . . . I glorified you on earth, having accomplished the work which you gave me to do; and now, Father, glorify you me in your own presence with the glory which I had with you before the world was made" (John 16:1, 16:4).

Of course, this is true of all of us who are in communion with the Son and, like him, glorify the Father in our sacrificial acts of love. In these very same acts, the Father glorifies us, for he allows us to manifest the working of the Spirit in our lives. This mutual glorification finds its supreme expression in the act of martyrdom, in which the crucifixion is most fully replicated and so the mutual hallowing and glorifying is most fully witnessed. Through the cross, both Jesus and all of us hallow the name of the Father.

THY KINGDOM COME, THY WILL BE DONE, ON EARTH AS IT IS IN HEAVEN

These three expressions found their full significance when Jesus prayed them in the midst of his passion. His passion and death were the culminating acts by which Jesus, in his very person, was establishing his Father's kingdom. Through his sacrificial death, the reign of sin was destroyed and the power of death was vanquished. In conquering this twofold evil on the cross, Jesus opened the gates to God's kingdom, the kingdom of the resurrected life of holiness and immortality. While Jesus, in his very resurrection, was the first to experience the fruit of his cross, his prayer for the coming of his Father's kingdom was prayed on behalf of all. Now all who believe in him can, in union with him, enter the Kingdom of God, the Kingdom of the Spirit of life and truth.

The coming of God's kingdom is predicated upon the doing of his will. Jesus, unlike Adam and Eve, did the will of his Father, for all eternity in heaven and now here on earth. "I can do nothing on my own authority; as I hear, I judge; and my judgment is just, because I seek not my own will but the will of him who sent me" (John 5:30). This seeking to do his Father's will found its ultimate expression in the Garden of Gethsemane. Echoing the Our Father itself, Jesus prayed: "*Abba*, Father, all things are possible to you; remove this cup from me, yet not what I will, but what you will" (Mark 14:36). In filial love and obedience, Jesus confidently entrusted himself to his *Abba*, Father. The cross was Jesus' supreme act of obedience. "And being found in human form he humbled himself and became obedient unto death, even death on a cross" (Phil 2:8). This loving obedience was what destroyed the reign of sin and death. The Letter to the Hebrews tells us that Jesus received a body so that as man he could willingly offer his life for our sanctification. "By that will we have been sanctified through the offering of the body of Jesus Christ once for all" (Heb 10:10). Because of this filial and loyal obedience, his Father "highly exalted him and bestowed on him the name which is above every name, that at the name of Jesus every knee should bow, in heaven and on earth and under the earth, and every tongue confess that Jesus Christ is Lord, to the glory of God the Father" (Phil 2:10-11). This filial submission to the will of the Father also ushered in the new creation. "Then as one man's trespass led to condemnation for all men, so one man's act of righteousness leads to acquittal and life for all men. For as by one man's disobedience many were made sinners, so by one man's obedience many will be made righteous" (Rom 5:18-19). Here we discover the depth and significance of Jesus praying the Our Father as he suffered on the cross. Not only did Jesus pray the words of the Our Father on the cross, but the cross itself is the enacting of the Our Father. By faithfully doing the will of his Father on earth, even unto death, the Incarnate Son established the kingdom of God on earth, the kingdom for which he prayed. The three expressions in this part of the Our Father are now fulfilled in Jesus and will come to complete fulfillment at the end of time when all who have done the will of the Father on earth, and so continued to make real the kingdom of God on earth, will forever, in loving joy and gratitude, do the will of the Father forever in heaven.

As implied above, Jesus used these three expressions not only on his own behalf but also on behalf of his body, the Church. As the head of his body, Jesus declared in the name of the whole church, "Thy kingdom come, thy will be done, on earth as it is in heaven." Moreover, whenever we echo the words of Jesus we do so in union with our heavenly Lord. With one voice, in the one breath of one Spirit, the head and members pledge to further the kingdom of God by doing the Father's will both here on earth and in heaven. It is in the midst of the suffering body of Christ here on earth that this threefold expression finds its most vivid manifestation. For as Jesus established the kingdom through his loving obedience to the Father even unto death, so by sharing in and completing his suffering, the

Church most clearly bears living testimony to the Father's kingdom and contributes to that kingdom's continuing reality.

GIVE US THIS DAY OUR DAILY BREAD

The Last Supper is Jesus' commentary on his immanent passion and death. In the course of the meal, he took bread, blessed and broke it, and gave it to his disciples, saying, "Take, eat; this is my body." He then took the cup filled with wine and said, "Drink of it, all of you; for this is my blood of the new covenant, which is poured out for many for the forgiveness of sins" (Mt 26:26–28). Jesus, through his words and actions, was prophetically revealing that his passion and death on the cross would be the new paschal sacrifice that would establish a new and eternal covenant with God, his Father. It would be a covenant of new life. Jesus, in the Last Supper, was dramatically portraying and anticipating his own sacrificial death on the cross, and already he was allowing his disciples to share in it through the reception of his body and blood under the forms of bread and wine, the bread of life and the cup of salvation.

After Adam had sinned, God said to him, "In the sweat of your face you shall eat bread" (Gn 3:19). Through his sweat and blood on the cross, Jesus, the new Adam, gained the new bread of eternal life both for himself and for his Church. The cross freed Adam and his descendants (including Jesus himself) from the curse, and so the new Adam would provide the new bread of life that his Father would send down from heaven.

Thus, when Jesus prayed on the cross, "Give us this day our daily bread," he had in mind a meaning with two interrelated requests. He was petitioning his Father to give him the bread of everlasting risen life. In addition, as head of the Church that is born from his pierced side, he was asking the Father to give the bread of new life to the members of his body. In raising him from death by the power of the Holy Spirit, the Father answered Jesus' twofold petition. "He who eats my flesh and drinks my blood abides in me, and I in him. As the living Father sent me, and I live because of the Father, so he who eats me will live because of me" (John 6:56–57). There is a three-fold communion here. Jesus as God and now as the risen Savior lives because of the Father, and when we partake of Jesus' risen body and blood, we abide in him and he in us; thus we, in union with Jesus, abide with the source of all life, the Father. In this way, since Jesus vanquished sin and death through the sweat of his brow, the Father truly makes him the bread of life. In the light of the cross and the resurrection,

Jesus could truly declare, "I am the living bread which came down from heaven" (John 6:51). Being the living bread, he now provides his body, the Church, with living bread; that is, he nourishes his body on, and with, his very own risen self and in so doing makes us one in him. "Because there is one bread, we who are many become one body, for we all partake of the one bread" (1 Cor 10:17).

When we, as members of the body of Christ, petition our Father for our daily bread, we do so in union with him. We pray not simply for natural bread, though that be important, but we pray especially to receive the living bread that is Jesus' resurrected body. The Father answers this petition in providing for us the Eucharist, in which we both share in the one sacrifice of Christ and partake of his risen body and blood; we obtain communion with the risen Christ and so, in his Spirit, commune with the Father.

By praying the Our Father within the liturgy of the Mass, we are uniting ourselves to that same event in which Jesus himself prayed it most fittingly—his passion and death. Thus, it is most apt that we pray the Our Father immediately after the Eucharistic prayer, for we have conjoined ourselves to the one sacrifice of Christ, having placed ourselves on the cross with and in him. At this point, cleansed of sin and so now properly disposed and appropriately prepared, we can most fittingly cry out, "*Abba*, Father," to the Father who will provide for us our daily bread, Jesus himself.

This petition also contains an eschatological entreaty. While we wish to share here on earth the living bread that is Christ, we also yearn, along with him, for the day when we will be fully transformed into his likeness by living fully in and with him who is our eternal and heavenly bread. As the crucified Christ entreated the Father to make him into the living bread through the resurrection, so within the sacrifice of the Mass, we entreat the Father to bring us also to the fullness of life since we partake, already here on earth, of the bread of immortality, the risen Lord Jesus Christ. As we have already participated in the heavenly supper here on earth, so we long to share in its full reality in heaven. We do so in the hope of Jesus' promise: "He who eats my flesh and drinks my blood has eternal life and I will raise him up at the last day" (Jn 6:54).

AND FORGIVE US OUR TRESPASSES AS WE FORGIVE THOSE WHO TRESPASS AGAINST US

In the cross we find the forgiveness of our sins. When Jesus prayed, "Forgive us our trespasses," he did so as our Savior, as the head of his body, the Church. Only when Jesus spoke the words on the cross did these words achieve their true end, for it is on the cross that Jesus is truly offering his holy and innocent life to the Father as a sacrificial petition for the forgiveness of our sins. Moreover, it is because Jesus prayerfully enacted these words from the cross that the Father heard and answered his prayer once and for all. The resurrection confirmed that Jesus' appeal for forgiveness has been realized.

It is only because the Father looked favorably upon his Son's plea from the cross, precisely insofar as it was from the cross that it was made, that we are able confidently to say to the Father, "Forgive us our sins." We say these words in union with our crucified and risen Savior and this very union is the sole assurance that the Father will look kindly upon our entreaty. Without the cross and Jesus' petition from the cross, there would be no forgiveness of sins, and for us to petition the Father in this way would be pointless and futile.

However, the plea for the forgiveness of our trespasses is predicated upon the next clause, "as we forgive those who trespass against us." As we forgive others, so we are asking the Father to forgive us. Again, Jesus fulfilled this requirement perfectly on the cross. "Father, forgive them; for they know not what they do" (Luke 23:34). While the primary referents were those who had condemned him and had now crucified him, Jesus was also forgiving all of those who would persecute the members of his body, or would harm the just and injure the innocent.

As Jesus prayed, so he has directed all of us to pray. In and with him we too ask the Father to forgive us as we forgive others, even in the midst of our suffering for righteousness' sake. "For if you forgive men their trespasses, your heavenly Father also will forgive you; but if you do not forgive men their trespasses, neither will your Father forgive you your trespasses" (Matt 6:14–15). Moreover, to forgive reflects the merciful love of the Father. "In this is love, not that we have loved God but that he loved us and sent his Son to be the expiation for our sins" (1 John 4:10). The Father's perfection resides in his mercy (see Matt 5:48; Luke 6:36). The Father is the source of all mercy, and only Jesus is as perfect as the Father, for only he is as merciful as the Father. Nonetheless, in communion with the Father and the Son, sharing in the merciful love of the Holy Spirit, we too are able to forgive.

LEAD US NOT INTO TEMPTATION, BUT DELIVER US FROM ALL EVIL

As mentioned at the outset, we know for sure that, while on the cross, Jesus prayed at least one prayer, Psalm 22. The first verse is a cry of dereliction: "My God, my God, why have you forsaken me?" While Jesus had committed himself to drink the cup during his agony in the Garden, now on the cross he suffered the emotional experience of being abandoned by his Father. In trust and faith, Jesus humanly knew that his Father had not truly done so; nonetheless, his greatest human temptation was to think he had lost his loving *Abba*, Father. "Why are you so far from helping me, from the words of my groaning?" (Ps 22:2) In praying the Our Father, the crucified Jesus, in the midst of feeling abandoned, also prayed that his Father would "lead him not into temptation," that his Father would free him from the grip of this lying fear and deceitful anguish. He was praying that the Father would send upon him the comforting love and enduring strength of the Spirit.

As we have seen throughout this exposition, Jesus was also praying on behalf of his body, and when we pray "lead us not into temptation," we are doing so as members of his body. He was interceding on our behalf that the Father would always send us the wisdom to see the lie within every temptation and to provide us the strength of the Holy Spirit to overcome every temptation. Moreover, in the midst of her suffering, cares, and concerns, the Church must pray that the Father will free her from the greatest of all temptations to fear: the fear of being abandoned by God. We too at times feel that we no longer reside in the loving presence of the Father, and yet, in union with Jesus, we too know in confident faith and unwavering trust that, despite its seeming reality, this temptation is simply that, a temptation. If the Father never abandoned his crucified Son, we know he will never abandon the Church or any of us who now live in communion with his risen Son.

The final solution to being led into temptation is to be delivered from evil, the evil from which temptation arises. Thus, Jesus concluded with the request that the Father "deliver us from evil." The evil from which Jesus wished to be delivered is not simply that of being subject to the hands of wicked men and so his suffering of the cross. Rather, Jesus requested that the Father deliver him and all of us from sin, the source all evil, and thus also from the curse of sin, death. Ultimately, Jesus wanted to be freed from the kingdom of Satan, the father of lies from whom all evil comes.

The cross portrays a marvelous irony. When the crucified Jesus prayed that the Father "deliver us from evil," his prayer was simultaneously being answered. The cross is the petition, and the cross is the answer. In his sacrificial passion and death, the definitive petition, Jesus, as one of us, reconciled us to the Father and so obtained the Father's loving forgiveness. On the cross Jesus put death to death. The cross itself was the instrument of Satan's downfall. Thus, the cross itself is the agency by which Jesus and all of us in him are delivered from evil. The cross itself was the Father's answer to Jesus' and our plea for deliverance.

The resurrection was the Father's complete answer to Jesus' plea for deliverance, for in the resurrection the Father inaugurated his kingdom, a kingdom free from sin and death, a kingdom of righteousness and immortality. In answer to Jesus' petition for deliverance from evil, the Father made Jesus himself the answer. Jesus crucified prayed to the Father that we be delivered from evil, and the Father's answer to this petition is Jesus risen. The person of Jesus, our crucified Savior and risen Lord, is himself our deliverance from all evil. Through faith and baptism we unite ourselves to the risen Jesus as our Savior and Lord, and so share in his victory over evil and obtain the new life of his Holy Spirit.

What we see here is that the first petition of the Our Father, "thy kingdom come," and the last petition, "deliver us from evil," go together. The coming of God's kingdom delivers us from all evil. Moreover, the acts that bring about God's kingdom are the same as those that deliver us from evil—the death and resurrection of Jesus. In Christ we live within the Father's kingdom and so are delivered from evil.

While the resurrection is the assurance that our plea for deliverance from evil has been answered, Jesus, ever before the throne of his Father, continually intercedes for us who are members of his body. Moreover, when we pray the Our Father, we are joining our voices with Jesus' voice, confident that the Father is ever watching over us and protecting us even in the evil world in which we still reside. Thus, the petition "deliver us from evil," is inherently eschatological. Only at the coming of Jesus in glory at the end of time will our deliverance from evil be fulfilled and the fullness of the life in Christ be ours.

> Therefore are they [the saints] before the throne of God, and serve him day and night within his temple; and he who sits

> upon the throne will shelter them with his presence. They shall hunger no more, neither thirst anymore; the sun shall not strike them, nor any scorching heat. For the Lamb in the midst of the throne will be their shepherd, and he will guide them to springs of living water, and God will wipe away every tear from their eyes. (Rev 7:15–17)

CONCLUSION

I hope that I have demonstrated that Jesus did actually pray the Our Father during his suffering on the cross, and even if one is not convinced, I hope that I have shown that, at the very least, he prayed the content of the Our Father. Only if Jesus prayed the Our Father was the content of the Our Father fulfilled. The cross is the doing of the Our Father. On the cross Jesus addresses his heavenly Father in sacrificial love, and here he perfectly hallows his name. Because of this, all of the petitions of the Our Father are fulfilled. The cross makes possible the Father's kingdom because on the cross Jesus accomplished perfectly on earth the will of his heavenly Father. In raising Jesus from the dead, the Father provides for us the daily bread of eternal life—Jesus himself. In his sacrificial death, Jesus obtained the forgiveness of our sins and reconciled us to the Father. In the Father's forgiveness we are empowered in the Spirit to forgive others. Lastly, the cross enables us to overcome all temptation and delivers us from all evil, even death itself. By raising him from the dead, the Father testifies that Jesus fulfilled the Our Father. In the risen Jesus we find the Father's unqualified answer to all the Our Father's petitions. In perfectly enacting the Our Father on the cross, Jesus himself becomes the Father's perfect response.

Having been conformed to the likeness of Christ through the indwelling of the Holy Spirit, we can now pray the Our Father in spirit and in truth. Moreover, we too, as members of Christ's body, enact and so make real the Our Father through our deeds of sacrifice. In so doing we hallow the Father's name by doing his will and thus further his kingdom on earth. We also long for Jesus' coming in glory, when we will worship the Father in the fullness of the Spirit and love one another as perfect sons and daughters of the Father.

9

Snowden's Secret: Gregory of Nyssa on Passion and Death

MICHEL RENÉ BARNES

During the spring break of my freshman year of college, I did what most undergraduates newly freed from the yoke of their parents do: I gathered up a bunch of important novels to read, one of which was *Catch-22* by Joseph Heller. The climax of the novel occurs when the main character, Yossarian, a bombardier aboard a World War II B-25 Mitchell bomber, goes to the aid of Snowden, a waist gunner who had been wounded by flak. Snowden is lying on the cold metal skin of the aircraft, in shock, but showing little evidence of injury. Desperate to help, Yossarian figures that there must be some small wound under the gunner's flak vest, so he removes it. Here is what Yossarian finds:

> Snowden *was* wounded inside his flak suit. Yossarian ripped open the snaps of Snowden's flak suit and heard himself scream wildly as Snowden's insides slithered down to the floor in a soggy pile and just kept dripping out . . . . He forced himself to look again. Here was God's plenty, all right, he thought bitterly as he stared—liver, lungs, kidneys, ribs, stomach and bits of the stewed tomatoes Snowden had eaten that day for lunch. Yossarian hated stewed tomatoes and turned away dizzily and began to vomit, clutching his burning throat.[1]

---

1. Joseph Heller, *Catch 22*, 9th printing (New York: Dell, 1963) 449.

Yossarian called what he saw "Snowden's secret," and it became the rule by which he measured claims to truth.

Gregory of Nyssa has a rule of truth, too, a secret he is trying to make plain, and his secret is also a sad fact about the weakness that holds our bodies together and the strength that breaks them apart. This essay is about Gregory's understanding of the morally toxic state in which humans reproduce themselves. I will bring together passages from three of Gregory's writings for the sake of the illumination they can shed on each other and on Gregory's theological anthropology generally. The three passages are related to one another by a common subject, Gregory's understanding of the relationship between sin, death, and sexual reproduction.

The three principal texts of Gregory that I will be discussing are *On Virginity, On the Life of Macrina,* and *Homily on the Fifth Beatitude.* I intend to trace a thread common to these three texts. Mainly for the sake of thematic comparison, I will refer with some regularity to two other works by Gregory, *On the Soul and Resurrection* and the *Catechetical Oration* or, as I call it, the *Great Catechism.* All but the last of these writings could be termed "ascetical," as they are labeled in one translation of some of Gregory's writings.[2] However, in the fourth century during which Gregory lived, these works, including a large part of the *Catechism,* would have been recognized as falling within the realm of moral psychologies. What intrigues me about these texts is how Gregory displays in them his understanding of the links among passion, sexual reproduction, and death. This is an essay about what could justifiably be called Gregory's doctrine of "original sin" (though not without upsetting some of his modern readers).

Dating Gregory's writings is a scholar's nightmare. The dating of a given text can vary by ten or fifteen years among respected authorities on Gregory. Strong scholarly arguments date all the works to which I have so far referred to the early part of Gregory's career. *On Virginity* is usually thought to be Gregory's earliest writing, dated 371–75. *The Life of Macrina,* Gregory's hagiographic account of his eldest sister's last days, could not have been written before 379 (when Macrina died), and probably was composed soon thereafter. Gregory's homilies on the Sermon on the Mount are thought to date from 375 to 380, more likely closer to the former date than to the latter. *On the Soul and Resurrection* purports to be an account of the conversation Gregory had with Macrina the night before she died. Thus, *On the Soul and Resurrection* is linked to the *Life*

---

2. *Saint Gregory of Nyssa: Ascetical Works,* trans. Virginia Woods Callahan, Fathers of the Church 58 (Washington, DC: Catholic University of America Press, 1967).

of *Macrina* and is usually thought to have been written within a year of his sister's death. Of all the texts I will be discussing the date for the *Great Catechism* (or *Catechetical Oration*) is the most debated by scholars. Raymond Winling summarizes this debate in his introduction to the Sources Chretiennes edition of the *Great Catechism* and persuasively argues that the work predates Gregory's engagement with Eunomius, which means prior to 380.[3] In short, all the important works that I will be discussing are dated prior to Gregory's completion of Book One of his *Against Eunomius*.[4] In what follows, I will refer, briefly, to two works that date from late in Gregory's career, his writing against Apollinarius (called *The Antirhetorus*, not earlier than 383, probably 385) and his *Commentary on the Song of Songs* (around 390). This rushed overview of the relevant texts makes clear that I am dealing, for the most part, with writings early in Gregory's career from a short period of time, something like 375–380.

The first passage I want to examine comes from *On Virginity*.

> I affirm that this very thing, this sweetness that surrounds their lives, is the spark which kindles pain. They are human all the time, things weak and perishing; they have to look upon the tombs of their progenitors; and so pain is inseparably bound up with their existence, if they have the least power of reflection. This continued expectancy of death, realized by no sure tokens, but hanging over them the terrible uncertainty of the future, disturbs their present joy, clouding it over with the fear of what is coming.[5]

For my purposes here, the interesting line in this quotation is "they have to look upon the tombs of their progenitors; and so pain is inseparably bound up with their existence." "They" refers to married people, parents in particular, who are sad from looking upon the tombs of their own parents. Marriage and parenthood—the two are inseparable for Gregory—form a portal into crushing pain.[6] How fortunate we are, then, that the Church

---

3. See *Discours Catechetique*, Sources Chretiennes Vo. 453 (Paris: Cerf, 2000) 125–30.

4. Later I will refer very briefly to Gregory's *On the Making of Man*, which I date to just prior to Gregory's first book *Against Eunomius*.

5. *On Virginity* 3, *Nicene and Post-Nicene Fathers, Second Series*, trans. Philip Schaff and Henry Wace, vol. 5 (1890; repr., Peabody, MA: Hendrickson, 1994) 346. This volume is the most easily available English translation of many of Gregory's works, and is hereafter cited as NPNF 5, followed by page number(s).

6. See my "'The Burden of Marriage' and Other Notes on Gregory of Nyssa's *On Virginity*," *Studia Patristica* 37 (2001) 12–19.

offers us the sanctuary of "virginity," that is, celibacy in the monastic life. As Gregory says elsewhere in *On Virginity*, every chronicle of human horrors begins with marriage, and certainly the great Greek tragedies such as the *Oresteia* trilogy, *Oedipus the King*, and *Medea* bear him out.

The problem of parental anguish is a theme that remains with Gregory throughout his literary career. It is present in Gregory's account, in *Life of Macrina*, of his mother's crushed response to the death of her son, Naucratius. More importantly, in *On the Death of Infants*, likely the very last work Gregory wrote, he accounts for God allowing the death of newborns and infants by claiming that because God foresees that these children will grow up to be evil and cause their parents much agony and grief, He takes the infants while they are still innocent.[7]

Gregory's remark in *On Virginity* about looking upon the tombs of progenitors merits attention, for my purposes, because it resembles a passage written in the midst, as it were, of a death in the family. Sometime during 379–380 Gregory writes a short biography of Macrina, his sister. As a whole, the *Life of Macrina* focuses primarily on her youth, on the last few days of her life, and on her death. Gregory writes about his experience just before the burial of Macrina in the family crypt. Such crypts were—as they still are in parts of Mediterranean Europe (my family has one in Martique)—high cement or stone boxes into which one deposited the body of the dead family member. The top of the box is lifted off, the body is lowered down to rest atop the remains from previous generations, and the stone top is returned to cover the box. As Gregory faces the prospect of opening his family's tomb, he is immobilized by panic. Gregory knows that he will see the decomposed bodies of his parents when the lid is slid aside. What strikes Gregory is not, it seems, simply the pain or horror of such a sight: what strikes Gregory is what seeing *that* sight is *equivalent to seeing*.

> When the proper ceremony was finished [and it was time to open the family crypt], the fear of the divine command not to uncover the shamefulness of father and mother came upon me. "How," I said, "shall I ward off such a judgment if I look upon the common shame of human nature in the bodies of our parents, since they have surely fallen apart and disintegrated and been changed into a disgusting and disagreeable formlessness?"[8]

---

7. This is not the most credible or appealing argument that Gregory ever offered, but it does illustrate just how fundamental Gregory took the dynamic of parental pain to be, even for God's Providence.

8. *Life of Macrina*, in Callahan, *Saint Gregory of Nyssa: Ascetical Works*, 188. See also

In short, the sight of his parents' decomposed bodies is, in Gregory's mind, the sight of their sexuality; their full nakedness is uncovered. Their exposed decomposition is their sexual nakedness; their decomposed bodies put their sexuality, their "shamefulness," on display.

Once Gregory has understood that decomposition is sexuality on display, he is reminded of the story in Genesis 9:20–27. A drunken Noah has allowed his night covers to fall, revealing his nakedness. Noah's adult sons understand the sight of his nakedness as the sexuality that must not be uncovered and looked upon (according to the prohibitions at Lev 18:7). Noah's sons solve the problem of an uncovered parent by holding a bedcover between them and walking backwards until the bedcover falls over their father's body and covers him. Gregory solves the problem of looking upon his parents' sexual nakedness by having a sheet slid under the top of the tomb as soon as it is opened, so that when the lid is taken away entirely what one sees is only the sheet. Macrina's body is laid upon that sheet, the tension in the sheet is relaxed and the body slips into the box, with the sheet left in the box, still covering her parents.

The boldness of Gregory's judgment on the meaning of his parents' corrupted bodies is made clearer if we consider this passage from the *Life of Macrina* in the context of other writings by Gregory normally considered to be closely contemporaneous. The work *On the Soul and Resurrection* is a dialogue which features Macrina on her deathbed in a conversation with Gregory that is briefly described in the *Life*. However, there is no mention at all of sexual reproduction in *On the Soul and Resurrection*, much less a specific association between it and death. The principal specific passions (*pathē*) addressed are grief and anger. Anger and grief were the great concerns of Greco-Roman moral psychology, as we see in Cicero's *Consolation*, Seneca's *On Anger*, as well as Galen's *On the Diagnosis and Cure of the Passions of the Soul*, which is devoted to both passions, anger and grief, and which Gregory certainly read. When, in *On the Soul and Resurrection*, Gregory recalls that the conversation has previously enumerated our psychological kinships with the beasts, the list includes "anger . . . fear, desire of pleasure."[9] Sexual desire is presumably included implicitly in Macrina's distinctions of types of pleasure, but anger is stated explicitly. There is nothing in *On the Soul and Resurrection* that gives theological sense to the interpretation Gregory gives to seeing his parents' corpses in their

---

The Life of St. Macrina, trans. Kevin Corrigan (Eugene, OR: Wipf & Stock, 2005) 51.

9. NPNF 5, 449.

tomb.[10] In *Life of Macrina* Gregory's reaction to the possibility of viewing his parents' corpses has no hint of the process leading to resurrection; his mind looks backwards from his parents' death, and not forward. In this work Gregory did not portray his decomposing parents as poised for reconstitution, but as signs of the sinful origins of death. That this would be so despite the chronological, dramatic, and doctrinal proximity of *On the Soul and Resurrection* is intriguing.

Some historical and literary contexts are useful for a better understanding of Gregory's thoughts on marriage, virginity, and death. Here I draw from the work of Ton H. C. van Eijk. He traces the history of ascetical judgments on marriage, virginity, and death from Plato to Gregory of Nyssa. For my purposes in this essay, the following facts are worth noting. In the *Acts of Paul and Thecla*, "resurrection is reserved to those who have practiced continence."[11] In the *Gospel of the Egyptians*, the Christian (that is, encratite) community has already experienced resurrection and thus must refrain from sexual intercourse (following Luke 20:34–36), since procreation (characterized particularly as "the female" act) feeds death.[12] Methodius links virginity to "affinity with divinity."[13] Basil of Ancyra (in the *On Virginity* traditionally attributed to Basil of Caesarea) emphasizes that sexual reproduction comes after the fall and that the virgin "already lives in Paradise and already is incorruptible" and angelic.[14]

Van Eijk remarks that "Gregory takes up the view of that marriage gives nourishment to death."[15] Gregory likewise repeats Basil's view on the origin of marriage and the status of virgins. Van Eijk does not remind the reader of the obvious fact that since Macrina's spiritual name is Thecla, Gregory is engaged with aspects of the asceticism expressed in the *Acts of Paul and Thecla*. In *On the Soul and Resurrection*, Gregory has clearly rejected the judgment that only those who have practiced continence will experience their own resurrection, but in the *Life of Macrina* it seems that death is, in some special way, associated with those who have sexually

---

10. In *On the Soul and Resurrection* NPNF 5, 462, Macrina describes resurrection as a remedy against the decay of old age and of those mutilated by disease and catastrophes.

11. Ton H. C. van Eijk, "Marriage and Virginity, Death and Immortality," in *Epectasis: Mélanges patristiques offerts au Cardinal Jean Daniélou*, Jacques Fontaine and Charles Kannengiesser, eds. (Paris: Beauchesne, 1972) 209–35, at 212.

12. Van Eijk, "Marriage and Virginity, Death and Immortality," 214–16.

13. Ibid., 222.

14. Ibid., 226.

15. Ibid., 234.

reproduced; the decay of his parents' bodies does not bring Gregory to reflect upon their future resurrection.

In *On the Soul and Resurrection*, Macrina tells Gregory that "resurrection is the reconstitution of our nature in its original form."[16] However, nothing is said in *On Virginity*, *Life of Macrina*, and *On the Soul and Resurrection* about what roles death and decomposition have in that reconstitution. But in the *Great Catechism*, death and decomposition are included as dynamics in the process of reconstitution. In this work death is our necessary reduction to the tiniest parts that allows the process of reconstruction to our original form to begin at our resurrection. Gregory's descriptions of sin inhabiting or mixed in with our nature—and there are several such descriptions in the *Catechism*—are consistently *entrées* into metaphors for the ways that such sin is removed from us by death. The most famous of these metaphors presents the clay pot that is broken into dust so that it can be remolded into its perfect form.[17] Such an evaluation of the part death and decomposition plays in our restoration cannot be found in the three early "ascetical" works. What, then, has Gregory done in his account of Macrina's funeral? Gregory has made the sight of his parents' decomposed bodies the sight of their sexuality. There is no precedent for this in Gregory's moral psychology and anthropology other than the passage from *On Virginity* that I quoted above.

On Virginity allows us to recognize one other feature of Gregory's analysis in the *Life of Macrina*: sexuality is principally a feature of a married couple.[18] While *we* might assume that sexuality is a feature of *all* humans, Gregory does not think this way. The fact that, in *Life of Macrina*, the dead bodies in the grave are those of *his parents* means that the bodies are those of people who have obviously engaged in sexual reproduction. It is important that Gregory specify that by opening the tomb he will see the bodies of both his parents; that is to say, the bodies of two people who were sexually active and who indeed reproduced themselves in Gregory. On the basis of this detail, Gregory offers a *pesher* of Genesis 9:20–27 that may be characterized as anything from insightful to idiosyncratic or bizarre. To

---

16. *On the Soul and Resurrection* NPNF 5, 464.

17. An appeal to an analogy of clay pots occurs at *On the Soul and Resurrection* 77B–D, NPNF 5, 446, in support of the claim that God can reconstitute dispersed bodies as a potter remolds clay.

18. In *On Virginity* III the vicissitudes of life are contained within the frame of marriage; at *On Virginity* VIII controlling sexual desire is the task of the good husband. In general Gregory talks as though single people do not experience the pull of sexual desire.

see the decomposed bodies of his parents is to see their sexuality. Their uncovered decomposition is their sexual nakedness. If we understand that sexuality is principally a feature of a married couple, then we can know why, in his *Life of Macrina*, Gregory describes his sister's birth in angelic terms. It is generally known that Gregory's protology does not allow for the possibility that children be born in Paradise, but he does nonetheless use the literary motifs of prelapsarian life to describe Macrina's birth. For example, Macrina's mother delivers her painlessly, indeed, she sleeps through Macrina's birth, echoing, I suggest, Adam sleeping while Eve is "born." Her mother suffers none of the birth pangs given as punishment for the fall. An angel is there to receive the newborn Macrina. All of this happens at Macrina's birth because she is never going to marry, that is, never going to engage in sexual reproduction. She is not going to be the kind of holy person her mother or grandmother were; she is going to remain a virgin. In short, in order to talk about concupiscence, Gregory needs the forensic example of a married and reproducing couple. This is a different notion from Augustine's account of sexuality, which locates the passion squarely in the individual alone. In *Confessions* Augustine can explore the reality and consequences of his own concupiscence without implicating his parents or his son.[19]

That Gregory is interested primarily in the nature and consequences of human sexual reproduction, and not simply of human sexual desire, is made evident again in the third passage I want to bring to bear. This is a quotation from Gregory's *Homily on the Fifth Beatitude*.

> At the outset it is from passion we get our origin, with passion our growth proceeds, and into passion our life declines; evil is mixed up with our nature through those who first allowed passion in, those who by disobedience gave house-room to the disease. Just as with each kind of animal the species continues along with the succession of the new generation, so that what is born is, following a natural design, the same as those from which it is born, so man from man is generated, from passionate passionate, from the sinful its like. Thus in a sense sin arises together with those who come into existence, brought to birth with them, growing with them, and at life's end ceasing with them.[20]

19. Perhaps this has to do with the difference in Stoic influences between Gregory and Augustine. Perhaps it has to do with Gregory's proximity to Syriac Christian traditions of the *icydyos*, the solitary ones.

20. *Homily on the Fifth Beatitude*, Stuart Hall, trans., in *Gregory of Nyssa: Homilies*

Gregory states that whatever is born has the same nature as that from which it is born. We are the products of a passionate nature, and our nature, therefore, is itself passionate, that is, containing passions and subject to them. Indeed, that passionate nature of which we are the product comes to the fore for our production. We are not simply born of a passionate nature; we come to be because of and through a passionate act. The passion in the act and the passion of the nature transmitted by the act are one and the same: "X from X through X," where "X" is always "passion."

In the *Life of Macrina*, Gregory implies that the decomposition of his parents' bodies is their sexual nakedness. Here in his *Homily on the Fifth Beatitude*, Gregory implies that sexual nakedness is death, that is, decline and then decomposition.[21] What is born dies, not because something has to be alive in order to become dead, but because a life begun by birth is a life given over to death since the birth and the life arise from passion, which constantly accompanies them. Death is not a black-robed figure standing at the end of our lives; it is the green- or blue-gowned figure catching us as we leave our mother's birth canal. Unlike Macrina, most of us do not have an angel waiting on our delivery.

It does no good to think that passion has simply to do with an individual will, whether one emphasizes "individual" or "will." The existence of the will—that a will exists, as well as what kind of will it is—is determined by its nature. Human nature—in the sense of that image of *anthropos* that extends from the first to the final, completing, specific human—has not changed because of the fall. But human nature as that which moves towards completeness through each additional generation until the last one—that human nature has been changed. This change, Gregory says in the *Great Catechism*, is inexorably mixed with human nature in history. The addition to our nature is not a positive addition; it is functionally destructive, like sand in the Vaseline or a wrench in the works. This

---

on the Beatitudes; An English Version with Commentary and Supporting Studies, Hubertus R. Drobner and Alberto Viciano, eds., Supplements to Vigiliae Christianae 52 (Leiden: Brill, 2000) 71. Another translation, more widely available, is in Hilda C. Graef, trans., *The Lord's Prayer; The Beatitudes*, Ancient Christian Writers 18 (New York: Newman, 1954) 150–51.

21. At Letter 31.7a-b Gregory distinguishes two degrees of sin in the act of grave-robbing. If a thief merely rifles the grave, e.g., taking stones from the grave to use in building, that act is not a sinful offense. But if the thief disturbs the "ash of the body returned to dust" then this is "condemned with the same sentence as *fornication*. . . ." Anna M. Silvas, *Gregory of Nyssa: The Letters; Introduction, Translation and Commentary*, Supplements to Vigiliae Christianae 83 (Leiden: Brill, 2007) 224, emphasis added.

changed nature is reified as sexual reproduction and the product of sexual reproduction.

Many of the statements in the quotation from the *Homily on the Fifth Beatitude* have parallels in Gregory's *Great Catechism*. While the homily says evil is mixed up with our nature, the *Catechism* observes that "[e]vil has been mixed up with our nature like some noxious ingredient spoils the taste of honey"[22] and that "there has been inbred in the soul a strong natural tendency to evil."[23] Again, whereas the homily affirms that a human is born from a human, the subject of passion from that which is subject to passion, the *Catechism* notes, "All things born are subject to the impulse of those that beget them."[24] But in the *Catechism* statements such as these are brought together to form a narrative about an almost benign order in our spiritual and physical self-destruction; Gregory calls it the "movement of nature."[25] In the *Catechism* 16 Gregory speaks of the sensual pleasure that goes with reproduction and the death that is made necessary by birth, but birth and death are endpoints in a natural process that includes growth and the maintenance of our bodies. Gregory even goes so far as to speak here of birth as the renewing of the species against the encroachments of death, a kind of immortality. The sensual pleasure that goes with conception is still regarded as the cause of vice in our nature, and for that reason Gregory points out that Christ was conceived without an act of passion, which left His humanity free from passion. Gregory initially says that because he is born, Christ must necessarily die, which would indeed be an application of his general theory of birth. But then he says that in the case of Christ "death was not a consequence of birth"; rather, birth was accepted by Christ so that He could die. Death remains, however, a consequence of birth for everyone else.

What serves in the *Catechism* as the basis for Gregory's benign account of death is a strongly articulated doctrine of the resurrection. The fact and the effect of Christ's resurrection and the eventual resurrection of all humans write a happy ending to the story of humanity, a story that would otherwise be left a relentless tragedy. In the *Catechism* death is not so much the product of sin as it is the means to redress the presence of sin. Death is our reduction to the tiniest parts so that the process of

---

22. NPNF 5, 482.
23. NPNF 5, 484.
24. NPNF 5, 506.
25. NPNF 5, 488.

reconstruction can begin at our resurrection. It becomes necessary to destroy the village to save it.[26]

In the *Great Catechism* 8, when Gregory wants to suggest the temporary, extrinsic character of our mortality, he uses the metaphor of the dead skins of animals with which Adam and Eve were clothed after the fall. The dead skins stand for mortality, he says, which is properly an attribute of animals. The skins are worn and removed as a coat is worn and removed. "This liability to death, then, taken from the brute creatures, was provisionally made to envelope the nature that had been created for immortality."[27] In *On the Soul and Resurrection*, the "dead skins" are understood as the "form of our irrational nature which we have put on through our association with passion." When, in the *Catechism*, Gregory wants to suggest the intrinsic cause of our mortality, he uses the metaphor of a clay pot filled with molten lead that has hardened and made the pot useless. Gregory means the metaphor to express the following process. The human will of Adam misjudged what was good and opted for sensual pleasure; consequently, an inclination to material goods contrary to our original inclination to intelligible, immaterial goods operates in our wills.[28]

Gregory affirms that this addition to our nature exists in our faculty of sense perception (*aisthētikon*), a faculty which stands halfway between our mind (*nous*) and the sense world of our body and may be involved in making judgments about sense perceptions. It is mainly the *aisthētikon* that "contracted a fellowship with evil" and got evil mixed up in our nature.[29] In our *aisthētikon* the "opposite" now becomes reified with a kind of inclination to the material, sense-perception is unable to perform its proper function because of this objectified condition of passion, and thus the *aisthētikon*, with the body it works through, must be dissolved and rebuilt.

The *aisthētikon* is discussed by Macrina in *On the Soul and Resurrection*: "through it our soul becomes associated with the traits which are joined with perception. These are the traits which, when they occur in us, are called 'passions.'"[30] After the fall the *aisthētikon* in the individual hu-

26. Major Chester L. Brown USAF, February 2, 1968, Bến Tre village, S. Vietnam.

27. NPNF 5, 483.

28. NPNF 5, 483. The Greek text may be found at Grégoire de Nysse, *Discours catéchétique*, ed. E[kkehard]. Mühlenberg, trans. Raymond Winling, Sources chrétiennes 453 (Paris: Cerf, 2000) 188.

29. NPNF 5, 484.

30. Catharine P. Roth, trans., *On the Soul and the Resurrection* (Crestwood, NY: St. Vladimir's Seminary Press, 1993) 56. The NPNF 5 translation of this is on 442, and

man is no longer simply the mental part of us that processes sense data; it now has the capacity to incline the mind to sensibles, a capacity it should not have. Through the *aisthētikon* the body's desires mix in with our rational desires, Gregory notes, as a noxious ingredient dissolves throughout a batch of honey. This addition to our person is not lifted off as a coat is thrown off. The pot containing the lead has to be shattered and reduced to particles that are mixed with water, kneaded, and rethrown into a new, uncontaminated, functional pot. The mental faculty for sense perception is dissolved along with the body, so that it can be reconstructed without the imbedded tendency towards material goods, that is, without passions. This is the *good* reason why we have to die. What was once called the sign and presence of irrational nature is later called the sign and presence of mortality. What, in *On the Soul and Resurrection*, was the burden of our transformed nature is now, in *Catechism*, the temporary but useful passage through death.

Gregory's thought on sexual reproduction includes one distinctive feature we always need to remember. While sexual reproduction is now the only way in which human nature is passed on to other humans, nothing intrinsic to human nature as such requires this manner of transmission. That human nature now requires sexual reproduction is evidence of the disfiguration that nature suffers in its present material form. For Gregory, the purpose of sexual reproduction is *not* the "preservation of the species" because God saw that it was not good that his image should pass from the land of the living. The purpose of sexual reproduction is rather to fill out the number of human individuals who in their fullness or *plerōma* make up human nature. It is this ideal human nature that is made in the Image of God. Our fall from angelic reproduction had to be replaced by another form of reproduction so that the *plerōma* of our nature would, despite our fall, be fulfilled. All of this is articulated by Gregory in *On the Soul and Resurrection* and *On the Making of Man*.

Given what seems to be Gregory's strong emphasis on the sexual transmission of death, it may be surprising to see that Johannes Zachhuber has argued that in many of his writings, Gregory did not regard Adam as the source of human nature, perfect or disfigured.[31] In works like *Contra Eunomium* 1 and 2, Gregory's principal interest in Adam is to show that he was certainly as human as were his offspring, even though Adam

completely obscures the technical language Gregory employs in this passage.

31. Johannes Zachhuber, *Human Nature in Gregory of Nyssa: Philosophical Background and Theological Significance*, Supplements to Vigiliae Christianae 46 (Leiden: E. J. Brill, 2000) 158.

was not born from a human. The equal humanity of Adam and Abel has trinitarian applications for an argument for continuity of nature between the Father and the Son. Zachhuber states that in these writings Gregory does not speak of Adam as the father of us all, or as the original source of our human nature.[32] The doctrine that humans are humans because they descend from Adam, and humans are what they are because of what they receive from Adam, Zachhuber claims, is more typical of Apollinarius' anthropology.[33] Zachhuber is then somewhat surprised to see, in a *Homily on the Lord's Prayer*, Gregory explicitly stating that human nature is not free from defilement since Adam lives in each one of us, we share in Adam's nature, and we participate in his exile, for we all die in Adam, according to Paul (1 Cor 15:22).[34] I can add one other example of Gregory adopting what Zachhuber calls "the Apollinarian pattern."

In the *Antirrheticus*, which one might call his "Against Apollinarius," Gregory argues against the Apollinarian doctrine that Christ "had flesh before the ages" and did not receive his humanity from Mary. Gregory's argument is that the human race sprang from Adam, and if Christ does not spring from the human race, he is not human but something else. Saint Luke, after all, is at pains to show that Christ descended from Adam. The argument that the human race springs from Adam and our sinfulness follows from that origin is an argument that we would expect Gregory to make, given its traditional status at the time, but I think Zachhuber is right to say that much of the time Gregory does not make anything like this argument. Nonetheless, the argument "from Adam" does appear in the *Homily on the Lord's Prayer*, the *Antirrheticus*, the *Homily on the Fifth Beatitude*, and, in part, in the *Great Catechism*.

The link between passion, sexual reproduction, and death also figures in Gregory's account of the Incarnation. I have already noted above that in the *Great Catechism* Gregory points out that Christ was conceived without an act of passion, which left His humanity free from passion. Gregory initially says that because he is born, Christ must necessarily die. But then, denying that Christ's death flowed as a consequence from his birth, Gregory affirms that Christ accepted birth so that he could die. However, in the *Commentary on the Song of Songs*, Gregory takes this logic a step further and makes a startling point: Christ's flesh was taken from the

---

32. Zachhuber, *Human Nature in Gregory of Nyssa*, 154–62.
33. Zachhuber, *Human Nature in Gregory of Nyssa*, 132–42.
34. Zachhuber, *Human Nature in Gregory of Nyssa*, 182.

fullness of mankind, that is, from the eidos-like nature of humanity which is, according to Gregory, the human site of the image of God.³⁵

> All flesh implies birth, with marriage as the means for bringing it about. The person, however, who is not subject to a birth of flesh . . . does not submit to the actions effected by human nature nor to the passions arising from the mind. . . .Christ [does not] partake of [the] birth common to mankind. Rather, *our God assumed our human nature from the multitude of men which he had begotten.* . . . Nature did not cooperate in this birth, but served it. . . .His conception is virginal; his birth undefiled and without pangs. . . .He was free from birth resulting from marriage, for his existence does not come from marriage. No terminology pertaining to human birth can rightly pertain to Christ's incorruptible, painless birth. . . .Therefore, Christ was chosen, and unfamiliar with any of birth's consequences. His mortal existence did not begin in pleasure, nor did it come forth through pain.³⁶

There is no statement here that Christ took his human nature *from Mary*. However virtuous and virginal Mary was, her flesh was not perfect and original, just as Macrina's was not perfect and original. I do not doubt that Gregory believed that Christ received "flesh" from his mother Mary, but for Gregory this reception does not completely explain the character of Jesus' humanity: a perfect humanity. Gregory must involve another "humanity" from another source, namely, the ideal human nature in the "image of God" (still) of Genesis 1:26.

The conclusion that I draw from all these passages is that Gregory's moral psychology is sometimes misrepresented by his modern readers. In this presentation, Gregory is concerned about the moral content of intentions, with interior acts of the will in themselves. In the important case of sexual desire, the picture that is presented is one of Gregory worrying over the moral content of interior acts of the will. I do not think that Gregory has this worry. I think that Gregory is concerned with moral and immoral *action*, physical action. Interior states are significant only insofar as they are part of the action of our bodies. I am saying that Gregory is concerned

---

35. "Our whole nature, then, extending from the first to the last, is, so to speak, one image of Him Who Is." Gregory of Nyssa, *On the Making of Man* 16, NPNF 5, 406.

36. *Commentary on the Song of Songs*, trans. Casimir McCambley, The Archbishop Iakovos Library of Ecclesiastical and Historical Sources 12 (Brookline, MA: Hellenic College Press, 1987) 236–37. Sometimes scholars seem to treat the *Commentary* as if it were Gregory's consolation prize for breeders. It is not. It is for those who have not only traded *in* their sexuality, but also traded *up*.

not with any interior "lusts," but with the physical act of sexual intercourse that precedes and causes reproduction. I cannot find any passage in which Gregory analyzes sexual desire simply as an interior state or as an act of the will. When Gregory speaks about out-of-control lust, he always talks about adultery, which is not only an action, but also an act of a *couple* having sex.

I have an unpleasant explanation for the prior, usually sympathetic, modern misreading of Gregory: we are all Augustinians now. We assume that immoral acts are constituted principally by an interior state, and that physical action is not intrinsically part of the moral definition of "passion." The center of sin is sinful consciousness; our moral analysis tends not simply to regard intention as the beginning of sin, but as the essence of sin. I would call this "street Augustinianism." There are so many ways in which people hasten to contrast Gregory and Augustine in their accounts of broken lights and mended lives that I hesitate to add one more, though this is actually a contrast between Gregory and us his readers. The center of Gregory's moral analysis is the passionate *act*, and not the passion alone. The best way that I can illustrate the distinction I am making is by a thought experiment. One can imagine in the *Life of Anthony* that there would be an episode in which the devil tempts Anthony by appearing as a woman. However, we can also imagine that if Augustine had written the *Life of Anthony*, the devil would have tempted Anthony by putting the *idea* of a woman in his mind. I think that Gregory's understanding definitely is more like Athanasius' than Augustine's, although I cannot suppress the suspicion that Gregory would have had the devil appearing before Anthony as a woman who said, "I want to bear your children."

An urban legend claims that a piece of graffiti from the 1980s said, "Life—sexually transmitted and 100% fatal." Given a magic marker or a can of spray paint, Gregory could have written that on the hard sandstone walls of Cappadocia. He did indeed say as much even if not quite so succinctly. (Graffiti encourages brevity; the Second Sophistic did not.) Yossarian learned from looking at Snowden the secret that we are fragile collections of messy bits of flesh, and that the laws of death are written in physics. The decomposed corpses of Gregory's parents taught him that the source of our bodies is the end of our bodies, and that the laws of death are written in biology. Before Gregory's time, Christian discussion of the experience of death was largely preempted by the apologetic need to argue for the resurrection, since such an event seemed absurd to the pagan mind. This apologetic gave way to rococo speculation about what our bodies will be like upon resurrection. If our bodies are then perfect, Origen speculates, will they then be spherical, since a sphere is the perfect shape? Gregory's strong medical background sweeps such delicacy aside. He reminds us of what a foul biochemical event death actually is. And how much it intrudes at the origination of our destiny.

As Ralph Del Colle, whom we honor in this festschrift, faced his own death, he always spoke honestly and without sentimentality about the fact that he was dying. He did not gloss over realities. When Ralph had the strength, he talked theology with those who visited him. Gregory of Nyssa watched his sister die with her strength of faith sustaining her and nourishing those who witnessed her passing, though this nourishment did not keep back the enormous loss he felt at her passing. Ralph's family and friends have witnessed the same courage born of faith. We, like Gregory, have been nourished, and we, like Gregory, cannot contain our grief. No matter how much courage with which death is faced, the fact remains that it is not proper to the nature God gave us, and we wait—sometimes patiently, sometimes not—for the end of death and the beginning of true life.

III

Dimensions of Christological, Pneumatological, and Trinitarian Theology

10

Diastasis in the Trinity

EDWARD T. OAKES, S.J.

THE CHRISTIAN DOCTRINE OF the Trinity is puzzling enough, but it gets an added fillip of complexity with the notion of *diastasis* (distance): that is, that there can be posited a certain "gap" or "standing over against" between the trinitarian persons. But if that gap is granted, how can such a position not lead to tritheism, if it does not constitute tritheism already? If God is one, must not whatever distinctions are granted within the Godhead be seamless, lest the divine unity be undermined? In other words, distinction (*diakrisis*) yes, distance (*diastasis*) no.[1]

Because they assume such a distance, models of the Trinity that favor social analogies are continually running into the objection that they will inevitably lead to tritheism. But that objection has troubles of its own. For

---

1. Although both terms imply separation of some kind, *diakrisis* (usually translated as "distinction") implies a milder contrast (for example, it means "resolved form" in Aristotle's *Metaphysics* at 403b and 341b15), whereas *diastasis* is usually translated with stronger terms, such as "parting," or "difference" (at Aristotle's *de Caelo* 312a13), and in certain contexts can even mean "breach" (Aristotle *Politics* 1303b15). Without claiming that the Greek fathers kept terminological rigor here, I shall be using *diakrisis* ("distinction") as the uncontroversial term that refers to relational *contrasts* between the persons of the Trinity, whereas *diastasis* ("separation") will refer to issues in trinitarian theology that are more controversial, because more problematic, for the axiom has always been: "The belief of this faith in the unity of the Trinity is as follows: 'the Father [says the Athanasian Creed] is God, the Son is God, the Holy Spirit is God.' Therefore, Father, Son, and Holy Spirit are one God, not three gods. The cause of this union is absence of difference." Boethius, *De Trinitate* I, 1, in: Boethius, *Theological Tractates*, trans. S. J. Tester, Loeb Classical Library (Cambridge: Harvard University Press, 1973) 7.

one thing, tritheism is a paper heresy, one never advocated as an explicit position by any orthodox (or heretical!) theologian in the history of the Church, certainly not by those often most accused of it, such as the Cappadocians, Richard of St. Victor or Jürgen Moltmann—even Joachim of Fiore was no explicit tritheist. Monophysites agree that they are monophysite, but disagree that their monophysitism is a heresy. Arians appeal to Arius and thus willingly call themselves Arians. But no one *admits* to being a tritheist.[2]

True, certain proposals for coming to terms with the trinitarian mystery can sound like they might (or, according to their critics, will inevitably) *lead* to tritheism. But that very objection shows that no one (not even those later declared heretics in other matters) wants any trinitarian proposal to terminate in that impossible conclusion, so that it becomes the burden of those facing that objection to show that their proposals still preserve the core monotheism of the Christian confession of God, which everyone confesses.[3]

So just what is at stake here? Given strict monotheism, the problem comes, first of all, from certain key passages in Scripture that at least imply

---

2. In his justly famous book *God in Patristic Thought* (London: William Heinemann, 1936) G. L. Prestige accuses Leontius of Byzantium (*c.* 485–543) and John Philoponus (early sixth century) of tritheism, but the charge in the former case arises from Leontius' terminological sloppiness in attributing not just two natures (*physeis*) to Christ but also two essences (*ousiai*), and in the latter case from Philoponus' monophysitism, which, in order to make it less heretical-sounding, forced him, as with Leontius, to some unhappy christological formulations. At all events, even Prestige admits that Leontius' primary interest was in Christology ("It is fair to remark that Leontius was almost wholly occupied with Christology, and that his views were developed with that subject mainly in view," 272) and that Philoponus was a self-described Monophysite ("Philoponus was a Monophysite of a moderate type, who propounded a doctrine based on the teaching of Cyril ... The extracts preserved do not give any full account of his Trinitarian views," 282–83). Neither man called himself a tritheist, and so Prestige proves my point.

3. According to Thomas Aquinas there are only three basic trinitarian heresies, despite later elaborations: Photinianism, Sabellianism (modalism), and Arianism (subordinationism) (*ScG* IV 4–6). But Photinus' heresy was really a form of adoptionism, and thus is really a christological heresy. Thus there are, deep down, only two trinitarian heresies: one that suppresses any notion of threeness in the Godhead (modalism), and the other that makes the Second (and sometimes) Third Person in the Trinity *ontologically* subordinate. As Athanasius never tired of pointing out, such ontological subordinationism leads either to ditheism (or tritheism), since one must posit a "really real" God (the Father) and then two "lesser gods" (Son and Spirit); or that position makes the subordinate person(s) effectively creatures. In other words, the very *universal* unacceptability of tritheism was Athanasius' greatest weapon against the Arians.

diastasis and that obviously won't go away with airy objections to a nonexistent tritheism; I am referring primarily (but by no means exclusively) to those passages in which God (or the Father) is said to *act upon* the Son, especially here: "He who did not *spare* his own Son but gave him up for us all, will he not also give us all things with him?" (Rom 8:32); and here: "God so loved the world that he *gave* his only begotten Son" (John 3:16a). Other verses even imply an adversarial relationship: "Christ redeemed us from the curse of the law by becoming a curse for us" (Gal 3:13a), or here: "For our sake he [God] made him [Christ] to be sin who knew no sin, so that in him we might become the righteousness of God" (1 Cor 5:21). Other verses seem to assert an open subordinationism: "The Father is greater than I" (John 14:28c) and "He is the image of the invisible God, the firstborn of all *creation*" (Col 1:15).

Semantically cognate to these verses implying distance and distinction between Father and Son are all those passages that speak of the Son being *sent* by the Father. The verb "to send" makes no sense, after all, unless the one being sent indeed goes forth to some distant land as ambassador to foreign parts.[4] This implication is particularly strong in the Greek verb *apostellein* (to send *forth*).[5] The New Testament uses the noun "apostle" only once when describing Jesus, at Heb 3:1 ("fix your thoughts on Jesus, the apostle and high priest whom we confess"); but the Gospel of John is awash in the verbal (especially participial) forms of either *apostellein* or *pempō* (both of which mean "to send")[6], verbal forms that are especially

---

4. Notice how the English idiom "to go the distance" implies the fullest willingness to be of assistance to someone. Similarly, we speak of someone "going the extra mile," a cliché drawn, often unawares, from the Sermon on the Mount. See also: "He loved them to the end" (John 13:1). See too: "In the fullness of time God sent *forth* his Son, born of woman, born under the law" (Gal 4:4).

5. This is an insight common to exegesis: "As a compound of *stellein* [to send], it [*apostellein*: to send *forth*] has an additional emphasis as compared with it. This emerges especially when it is used figuratively or almost technically. Thus it is more sharply accentuated in relation to the consciousness of a goal or to effort towards its attainment.... *apostellein* expresses the fact that the sending takes place from a specific and unique standpoint which does not merely link the sender and recipient but also, in virtue of the situation, unites with the sender either the person or the object sent. To this extent it is only logical that *apostellein* should also carry with it the significance that the sending implies a commission bound up with the person of the one sent." Entry for *apostellō* in *Theological Dictionary of the New Testament*, ed. Gerhard Kittel, trans. Geoffrey W. Bromiley (Grand Rapids: Eerdmans, 1964) 398; cited hereafter as TDNT.

6. The nuances between the two verbs is much controverted in Johannine exegesis; but since both verbs mean "to send," and since sending always implies that the one sent must *depart* in some fashion from the sender, the subtleties between these two verbs

frequent on the lips of Jesus, who regularly speaks of "the one who sent me" or "the Father who sent me," as here:

> I have testimony weightier than that of John. For the very work that the Father has given me to finish, and which I am doing, testifies that the Father has sent (*apestalken*) me. And the Father who sent (*pempsas*) me has himself testified concerning me. (John 5:36–37)
>
> Jesus answered: "The work of God is this: to believe in the one he has sent (*apesteilen*)." (John 6:29)
>
> No one can come to me unless the Father who sent (*pempsas*) me draws him, and I will raise him up at the last day. (John 6:44)
>
> Just as the living Father sent (*apesteilen*) me and I live because of the Father, so the one who feeds on me will live because of me. (John 6:57)
>
> *I have not come of my own accord*; he who sent (*pempsas*) me is true, and him you do not know. I know him for I am from him and he sent (*apesteilen*) me. (John 7:28b–29)
>
> *I have not come on my own*; but he sent (*apesteilen*) me. (John 8:42)
>
> I am the one who testifies for myself; my other witness is the Father who sent (*pempsas*) me. (John 8:18)

The implication of these verses for trinitarian doctrine becomes clear when they are paired with other "I" statements in the nominative case in the same Gospel. So far, the participial form of *pempō* (*pempsas*) and the aorist form of *apostellō* (*apesteilen*) all have as their direct object the accusative form of the first person pronoun, *me*, that is, where Jesus is the direct object of the sending Father. But in the nominative form (*egō*) of the same pronoun the focus shifts, and stress is laid on Jesus' full equality with God:

> Before Abraham was, I am. (John 9:58)
>
> I and the Father are one. (John 10:30)
>
> He [the Spirit] will take what is mine and declare it to you. *All* that the Father has is *mine* [nominative case]; therefore, I

---

need not detain us here. In any case, for those who think there is exegetical mileage to be gained from the distinction, the verses adduced below will give the Greek forms for each use of the translation of the English verb "to send" or its variants.

said that he will take what is mine and declare it to you. (John 16:14b–15)

When these two sets of verses are combined, they lead to the question how the *Son himself*—in his full equality with God—has been sent *forth*.[7] The notion of ambassadorship has certainly been preserved but also radicalized.[8] In other words, in whatever way one understands the Father and Son being "one," their relationship must be such that, *out of that union*, the Son can actually "depart" for the earth by becoming incarnate and fulfilling his *mission* (the Latin nominal form for a "sending").[9]

Such a mission, for the New Testament, entails another feature of inner-trinitarian relations that renders such a mission possible: *kenosis* or self-emptying. Few verses in the New Testament are more controverted than Phil 2:7a: "he emptied himself, taking the form of a slave." Debate on this verse has tended to focus more on christological issues, especially after the collapse of the Lutheran/Anglican Kenotic Christology movement in the late nineteenth and early twentieth centuries, which so stressed the emptying of divine attributes in the incarnation that it made incarnation virtually synonymous with Ovidian metamorphosis (for example, Niobe turning into a fountain and thereby losing entirely her human nature).[10]

---

7. Recall that Paul says, "God did not spare his *Son*" (Rom 8:32a), and in Philippians speaks both of Jesus' equality with God and his *obedience* (implying subordination) to God (Phil 2:6, 8). The notion of distance implied in the sending is made explicit here: "In saying 'He ascended,' what does it mean but that he had also descended into the lower parts of the earth. He who descended is he who also ascended far above all the heavens, that he might fill all things" (Eph 4:9–10).

8. "Hence it must be stated that, in so far as the idea of the ambassador plays any role in John, it does not influence the Christology but is rather colored by it. In this respect the whole complex . . . derives its distinctive character from the fact that this ambassador is not a man, not even a pre-existent or primal man, but the Son in whom the Father attests His presence and Himself offers salvation or judgment." *TDNT*, 445.

9. Although I am concentrating here, for sake of brevity, on the Father sending the Son, all of this applies *a fortiori* to the Spirit: *a fortiori*, because Scripture speaks at times of the Son sending the Spirit and at times of the Spirit acting upon the Son. As Bruce Marshall rightly notes, "the scripturally narrated economy of salvation gives us *too much* evidence about how to distinguish and relate the Father, the Son, and the Spirit. . . . [T]he New Testament depicts not only actions by the incarnate Son Jesus of which the Spirit is the term (the Son breathes the Spirit upon the apostles, sends the Spirit to them, and so forth), but also actions of the Spirit of which the Son is the term (the Spirit drives Jesus into the wilderness, incites him to preach good news to the poor, is the power who raises him, and so forth)." Bruce Marshall, "Trinity," in *The Blackwell Companion to Modern Theology*, ed. Gareth Jones (Oxford: Blackwell, 2004) 183–203; here 197.

10. For details of the rise and fall of this movement, see Thomas R. Thompson,

A Man of the Church

To sum up a long and complicated story briefly, this movement collapsed because it assumed that Christ had to "leave behind" in heaven certain divine attributes (omniscience and omnipotence chiefly) in order to become fully human, an assumption grounded in a prior assumption that the *vere Deus* ("truly divine") must stand in opposition to the *vere homo* ("truly human") of Chalcedon. There must be, in other words, a *reduction* of the divine to "make room" for the human: the Son must, so to speak, empty himself so fully (or fully enough) that, in effect, he ceases to be divine (Ovid again).

This dilemma is obviously a false one, but its falsity becomes especially apparent inside a trinitarian framework. In other words, the act of the Son "giving himself *away*" (the orthodox interpretation of kenosis, as opposed to "giving *up* a portion of his divinity," as the kenoticists maintained) must be seen as the revealed reflection and expression of the Father's eternal act of giving himself away in his eternal generation of the Son. Thomas Aquinas takes up just this connection between Christ's *status exinantionis* in the incarnation and the Father's eternal begetting of the Son in his reflection on two verses from the Gospel of John: "The Father loves the Son and *shows* him all he does" (John 5:20) and "By myself I can do nothing; I judge only as I *hear*, and my judgment is just, for I seek not to please myself but him who sent me (John 5:30). Here is Thomas' interpretation:

> The Father's *showing* and the Son's *hearing* are to be taken in the sense that the Father *communicates knowledge* to the Son, as He communicates His essence. The command of the Father can be explained in the same sense, as giving Him [the Son] from eternity knowledge and will to act, by begetting him. . . . So the Son has the same omnipotence as the Father, but with another relation; the Father possessing power as *giving*, signified when we say that he is able to beget; while the Son possesses the power of *receiving*, signified by saying that he can be begotten. (*ST* I q.42 1.6 ad 2 and 3)[11]

"Nineteenth-Century Kenotic Christology: The Waxing, Waning, and Weighing of Quest for Coherent Orthodoxy" in *Exploring Kenotic Christology: The Self-Emptying of God*, ed. C. Stephen Evans (Oxford: Oxford University Press, 2006) 74–111.

11. Italics are the translators' to denote quotes from Scripture, underlines are made by me for emphasis; translation here from the five-volume editions of the Dominicans of the English Province (Westminster, MD: Christian Classics, 1981) I: 219. The same method of showing emphases will be used in the rest of the citations in this paper for the *ST*. It should also be mentioned that Thomas here cites Hilary's *De Trinitate* ix, who makes this crucial distinction: "The unity of the divine nature implies that the Son

Under the rubric that Christology is a truth about God just as Trinity is a truth about Jesus, the conclusion follows that the self-emptying that took place at the incarnation is grounded in trinitarian relations. Thus the question is forced upon us: Just what kind of "self" does the Son have that is available for him to "empty" in order to take on God's curse? How can he "obey" (or even "hear") if he is not capable on his own of freely obeying? Further: in what way does it make sense to speak of God *simpliciter* or of the persons of the Trinity has "having" or "being" a self?[12]

St. Augustine famously said that Christians speak of three "persons" in the Trinity not because the term is adequate but because otherwise all confession of the Trinity would become impossible.[13] The same surely must be said of "self" or "himself" (*seauton*). It's hard enough to define what constitutes a human self, so how can that word be applied to God *simpliciter* or to the three persons of the Trinity?[14] If a self possesses individual, reflexive *self*-consciousness and will, how can that apply to the "three" of God without undermining monotheism? If self, *pace* Hume, is some kind of centered awareness denoting interiority and perspectival consciousness, how does that apply to God?

---

so acts of himself [*per se*] that he does not act by himself [*a se*]."

12. This issue of "self" is complicated because, in contrast to Greek, Latin, the Romance languages, and German, only English requires the suffix *self* in the reflexive pronoun (myself, yourself, herself, himself, itself, themselves), whereas other languages content themselves with *se* or *sich* and the like (German can say *sich selbst* for emphasis instead of the usual *sich*). But because all forms of the reflexive pronoun refer back to the subject of the sentence, the point is hardly crucial: *He* emptied himself. What does that mean and how is that possible? The problem, in other words, is inherent in any language and is not rooted in the quirks of English grammar.

13. "So the answer 'three persons' is given, not that something should be [adequately] said, but so as not to remain wholly silent" (Augustine, *De Trinitate*, V.10). There is obviously a significant semantic overlay between *self* and *person*, an issue to be taken up shortly.

14. Quoting David Hume here almost becomes obligatory: "When I enter most intimately into what I call *myself*, I always stumble on some particular perception or other, of heat or cold, light or shade, love or hatred, pain or pleasure. I never catch *myself* at any time without a perception, and never can observe anything but the perceptions . . . If anyone upon serious and unprejudic'd reflexion, thinks he has a different notion of *himself* I must confess I can reason no longer with him. All I can allow him is, that he may be in the right as well as I, and that we are essentially different in this particular. He may, perhaps, perceive something simple and continu'd, which he calls *himself*, tho' I am certain there is no such principle in me." David Hume, *Treatise of Human Nature* (Oxford: Oxford University Press, 1928) 252. If the philosophical definition of "self" is problematic, then the same applies *a fortiori* to the Trinity.

A Man of the Church

It would obviously be impossible to resolve the philosophical enigma of the human self here (assuming it is even resolvable); but I do wish to point out one aspect of selfhood that has been more stressed in modern times than in the past: self in some way implies being *sent*—or at least (for those who deny providence entirely, like Martin Heidegger), being *thrown*. Heidegger was famous for coining the term *Geworfenheit* (thrownness) to name what all recognize as the fundamental characteristic of one's being-there (*Dasein*) in the world: none of us chose to be born. Still less did we choose our sex, our parents, our siblings, our native language, our race and nationality, the period of history into which we were born (or "thrown"), and so forth.

Absent a belief in God and his providence, such a realization leads, at best, to bafflement, at worst to a sense that life is fundamentally a nightmare.[15] But what if someone, for whatever reason, believes in God and so subscribes to a confident trust in God's providence? From this perspective, *thrownness becomes mission*, as in Gerard Manley Hopkins's poem "As kingfishers catch fire." The grammar of the poem is typically dense, but its echoes with the Gospel of John are patent:

> Each mortal thing does one thing and the same:
> Deals out that being indoors each one dwells;
> Selves—goes itself; *myself* it speaks and spells,
> Crying *What I do is me: for that I came*.[16]

The semantic ranges of self and person obviously overlap, but not entirely. Whereas self implies enigma, person implies relation. Indeed, it

---

15. As in Christopher Durang's witty playlet *The Actor's Nightmare*, in which the audience is told by the stage manager, after a certain delay of the proceedings, that the actor hired for the one-man show has absconded with the evening's box-office take. Since a refund is impossible, the manager asks for a volunteer to entertain the audience for the next hour. When no one in the real audience volunteers (obviously), the manager looks down at the first row and hauls a man up on stage against his will to perform *ad lib*. The hapless "actor" then proceeds to race through lines and fragments he has picked up from his (apparently extensive) theatergoing, and in so doing gives a hilarious riff on *Hamlet*, *A Man for All Seasons*, *I Love Lucy*, advertising slogans, and the like. Of course, that romp through Western theater and contemporary culture is all part of Durang's script, and the hapless "actor" is indeed the hired actor for the evening. I don't want to overburden Durang's *jeu d'esprit* with too much Heideggerian murkiness, but the parallels with that German's *Geworfenheit* should be clear: we too are thrust upon the stage of the world and have to make the best of it, speaking lines that have been circulating (often as shopworn clichés that have lost their power) long before we were born.

16. Gerard Manley Hopkins, "As kingfishers catch fire," in *Gerard Manley Hopkins: Poems and Prose*, ed. W. H. Gardner (New York: Penguins, 1953) 51; Hopkins's italics.

is the claim of not a few theologians, not least in the writings of Joseph Ratzinger, that it was precisely due to the Christian doctrine of the Trinity that the concept of person nowadays carries such a relational connotation:

> Let us listen once again to St. Augustine: "In God there are no accidents, only substance and relation." Therein lies concealed a revolution in man's view of the world: the sole dominion of thinking in terms of substance is ended; relation is discovered as an equally valid primordial mode of reality.... The "I" is simultaneously what I have completely and what least of all belongs to me. Thus here again the concept of mere substance (= what stands in itself!) is shattered, and it is made apparent how being that truly understands itself grasps at the same time that *in* being itself it does not belong to itself; that it only comes to itself by moving away from itself and finding its way back as relatedness to its true primordial state.[17]

All well and true; but such a formulation hides another aspect of the term "person" in its normal, ordinary, "philosophical" sense: *incommunicability*. In fact, I think it can be argued that, to the ordinary ear, this latter meaning trumps the relational meaning, as when an envelope says "personal," it means, in effect, "private." This latter meaning, in fact, goes all the way back to St. Thomas, despite his obvious debt to previous relational interpretations of the word:

> Now, a rational creature exists under divine providence as a being governed and provided for in himself [*secundum se*], and not simply for the sake of his species, as is the case with other corruptible creatures. For that individual that is governed only for the sake of the species [all the other animals] is not governed for its own sake [*propter seipsum*]. But the relational creature is governed for her own sake [*propter seipsam*]. (*ScG* III, ch. 113)[18]

17. Joseph Ratzinger, *Introduction to Christianity*, trans. J. R. Foster (San Francisco: Communio Books, Ignatius, 2004) 184, 190. See too: "Although some rudimentary concepts of the individual existed in antiquity that Gregory [of Nyssa] likely used, a more developed notion of person did not exist prior to the Cappadocian fathers." Lucian Turcescu, *Gregory of Nyssa and the Concept of Divine Persons* (Oxford: Oxford University Press, 2005) 115.

18. John Crosby makes this large claim of this section of the *ScG*: "Chapters 111–114 of Book III seem to me to constitute the most 'personalist' passage in the entire corpus of St. Thomas. The modern reader sees to his amazement that St. Thomas here has already made his own the Kantian idea that each person in a sense exists for his own sake (is an end in himself), as well as the Kierkegaardian idea that each individual person exists in a sense 'above' the human species. On the other hand, one has to admit that these personalist insights do not yet occupy the place of prominence in the

If one combines these two meanings of "person," relationality and incommunicability, the question becomes all the more exigent: what does it mean to relate to some other "person" or "self" without a concomitant, *sui generis*, and unique *awareness* of that relation? In other words, does person or self not just imply, but more strictly entail, consciousness? And if so, does that mean there are three separate "consciousnesses" in God, three separate wills, three separate "points of view"? What is it "like" for the Father to beget the Son eternally? What is it "like" for the Son to gaze back at the Father who begot him? Is that "experience" just "like" the Father's "experience"? Does it even make sense to speak of God *having* an experience, which implies both passage through time and a gaining of wisdom, something obviously impossible with God? And is not consciousness inherently discursive, which is also ruled out in the case of God?

Yet if we rule out self-consciousness, awareness, incommunicability and "experience" in God (or the three divine persons individually), and leave only relationality, how can we speak of God's personal nature, let alone of the three persons of the Trinity? Does not Paul himself admonish the Ephesians in these terms: "And do not *grieve* the Holy Spirit of God, in whom you were sealed for the day of redemption" (Eph 4:30)? And does this not imply a unique (and passible!) experience unique to the Holy Spirit? Admittedly, the modern use of the term consciousness does not sit easily with the medieval notion of intellection (the primary term for describing God's eternal act of self-knowledge and knowledge of his creation); but there can scarcely be intellection without an awareness of that intellection. But who is the subject of that intellection, God *simpliciter* or the three persons individually? Here at least is G. L. Prestige's reply, given on the last page of his influential *God in Patristic Thought*:

> [I]n God there are three divine *organs* of God-consciousness, but one centre of divine *self*-consciousness. As seen and thought, He is three; as seeing and thinking, He is one. He is one eternal principle of life and light and love. . . . To claim more is perilous to Christian monotheism. To claim less is treacherous to Christian history.[19]

---

philosophical anthropology of St. Thomas which they deserve. It is as if he glimpses in these chapters a new world whose time has not yet come." John F. Crosby, III, "The Incommunicability of Persons," *The Thomist* 57/3 (July 1993) 403–42; here 404 n. 2. Of course, to grant that point is simultaneously to concede that Thomas has thrown down a severe challenge to trinitarian theology.

19. Prestige, *God in Patristic Thought*, 301; emphasis added. This passage concludes the book.

Whether the content of Prestige's formulation of the issue is as felicitous as is its rhetoric might be doubted; but *that* there is an issue cannot be doubted, as can be seen in the way Aquinas can simultaneously claim that *person* can be said of God *simpliciter* as well as of the three hypostases of the one Godhead. For example, in the twenty-ninth question of the *Prima Pars*, he devotes the third article to the question "Whether the Word 'Person' Should be Said of God" and the thirtieth to "Whether the Word 'Person' Signifies Relation," and the answer to both questions is Yes:

> It would seem that the name *person* should not be said of God . . . *I answer* that *Person* signifies what is most perfect in all nature—that is, a subsistent individual of a rational nature. Hence, since everything that is perfect must be attributed *to God*, forasmuch as His *essence* contains every perfection, this name *person* is fittingly applied to God; not, however, as it applied to creatures, but in a more excellent way; as *other names also*, which, while giving them to creatures, we attribute *to God*. (*ST* I q.29 a.3)

The italicized words point to the initial logic established in this article: the word *person* denotes a *perfection*, and since God's *nature* is entirely perfect (because *simple*!), God may be denoted (analogically, to be sure) by the word "person." But that would mean that "person" applies to God's *essence*, not to inner-trinitarian relations.[20] But orthodox dogma teaches that God is one in nature but three in (relational) persons. How can that dogma be reconciled with what was said above? This issue is taken up by the next article:

> It would seem that this word *person*, as applied to God, does not signify relation but substance. . . . *I answer* that a difficulty arises concerning the meaning of this word *person* in God, from the fact that it is predicated plurally of the Three in contrast to the nature of the names belonging to the essence; nor does it [essence] in itself refer to another, as do the words which express relation.
>
> Hence, some have thought that this word *person* of itself expresses absolutely the divine essence; [just as does the] name *God* and word *Wise*. But to meet heretical attack, it was ordained by conciliar decree that it was to be taken in a relative sense, and especially in the plural. . . . Used, however, in the singular, it may be *either* absolute or relative. But this does not seem to be a very

---

20. Note how Paul often speaks of God *simpliciter* acting upon his Son. We have already cited Rom 8:32; but there is also: "The grace of our Lord Jesus Christ, and the love of God, and the fellowship of the Holy Spirit be with you all" (2 Cor 13:14).

satisfactory explanation. For, if this word *person*, by force of its own signification, expresses the divine essence only, it follows that inasmuch as we speak of *three persons*, then—far from the heretics being silenced—they would have still more reason to argue. Seeing this, others have maintained that this word *person* signifies in God *both* the essence *and* the relation. Some of these said that it signifies directly the essence, and relations indirectly, since *person* means, so to speak, *by itself alone* [*per se una*]; and unity belongs to the essence. . . . Others, however, said on the contrary that it signifies relation directly, and essence indirectly, inasmuch as in this definition of "person" the term nature is mentioned indirectly; and these come nearer to the truth. (*ST* I q.29 a.4; translation modified)

It is at this point that the interpreter wants to throw up his hands at all these trinitarian conundrums, quote St. Augustine, and be done with it: "For nowhere else is a mistake more dangerous, or the search more laborious, or discovery more advantageous than when are seeking the unity of the three, of Father, Son, and Holy Spirit."[21] But such despair ignores another point the bishop of Hippo made: since the Trinity is a part of revelation, and therefore a part (an essential part!) of the Church's proclamation, human speech about the Trinity is our lot: *necessitas loquendi*.

Another strategy—also a *pis aller* in its own way—is to examine the different connotations conjured by the favored Greek and Latin terms to describing the threeness of the Trinity: *hypostasis* on the Greek side, *persona* on the Latin. Now since *hypostasis* literally means "substance," and *persona* "mask," the claim is made that the fate of language virtually forces Greek theologians to favor a "social" (or to their opponents a "tritheist") model; while the Latins are stuck with the "modalist" tag, with Gregory of Nyssa and Augustine representing the two types, respectively.

Recent scholarship has demolished this typology,[22] even if it still remains deeply embedded in the secondary literature. I need not rehearse

21. Augustine, *De Trinitate* I, 5. He continues: "So whoever reads this and says, 'This is not well said, because I do not understand it,' is criticizing my statement, not the faith; and perhaps it could have been said more clearly—though no one has ever expressed himself well enough to be understood by everybody on everything."

22. The touchstone and gold standard here is Lewis Ayres's influential work of revisionist scholarship, *Nicaea and its Legacy: An Approach to Fourth-Century Trinitarian Theology* (Oxford: Oxford University Press, 2004). The money quote is here: "Pro-Nicenes assume the impossibility of there being degrees of divine existence, and they assume God to be the only truly simple reality. The generation of the Son and the breathing of the Spirit thus occur *within* the bounds of the divine simplicity. Because God is indivisible, the persons cannot be understood to work as three divided

that debate here, except to note how it has inhibited debate on the issue of most concern to me here. As to how that debate has been impaired by this too-neat typology, I shall rely on the nuanced and typically elegant way David Hart handles this issue:

> It is precisely here that the artificial distinction between "Greek" and "Latin" theology has worked the most injurious mischief, by prompting many to rush to one end or the other of a scale that must be kept in balance. We must say, at once, that the divine simplicity is the "result" of the self-giving transparency and openness of infinite Persons, but also that the distinction of the Persons within the one God is the "result" of the infinite simplicity of the divine essence. Otherwise, we will find ourselves trading in mythology: speaking of God as an infinite psychological subjectivity possessed of plural affects, or as a confederacy of three individual centres of consciousnesses; in either case reducing God, the transcendent source of all being, to a composite being, an ontic God, in whose "subjectivity" there would remain, even within the immanent divine life, some sort of unexpressed interiority (or interiorities), some surfeit of the indeterminate over the determinate, some reserve of self in which identity is constituted as the withheld.[23]

Hart makes the further point that the recognition of the inadequacy of human language to describe trinitarian relations (above all, the use of "person" to specify the threeness in God) must be counterbalanced by another consideration: the fact that the human person really *is* created in the image and likeness of God. True, *our* "being is synthetic and bounded.... In God, though, given the simplicity of his essence, there is an absolute

---

human persons work. Linking divine simplicity and inseparability of operation draws us inexorably towards the persistent pro-Nicene assertion that the nature of God is unknowable.... [We] never find descriptions of the divine unity that take as their point of departure the psychological inter-communion of three distinct people.... I mean that we do not find pro-Nicene authors offering as an analogical base for discussing the unity of God the sort of unity observed between three people engaged in a mutual project or sharing of a common goal....Where we do see the analogy of three rational beings used it is noticeable both that the terminology used of the individual persons is not defined by reference to a distinct psychological content and that the persons are always described as having an essential and metaphysical unity through the indivisibility of *physis*: in such texts it is most frequently the logic of difference and unity between individuals as distinct members of a general class that is at issue" (281, 292).

23. David Bentley Hart, "The Mirror of the Infinite: Gregory of Nyssa on the *vestigia Trinitatis*," in *Re-Thinking Gregory of Nyssa*, ed. Sarah Coakley (Oxford: Blackwell, 2003) 111–31; here 116.

coincidence of relation and unity."²⁴ But despite that infinite gulf between God and the human person, something more must be said:

> We should perhaps do well to remember that it is one thing to move about in the realm of analogy, within which one merely seeks out locutions and similitudes by which creaturely language and thought can pass, however imperfectly, from created towards divine being; but it is another thing altogether to move in the far more mysterious realm of the *imago Dei*, where one must seek first not what we may say of God, but what God says of himself in fashioning us as the creatures we are, called from nothingness to participate in the being that flows from him, and to manifest his beauty in the depths of our nature. . . . It is precisely here, though—in contemplating where the image of God is impressed upon his creatures, and how—that Trinitarian reflection can achieve its fullest and supplest expression.²⁵

If we add one more consideration to these reflections, we will finally gain the proper perspective from which to understand the meaning of diastasis in the Trinity—this influential passage from Vatican II: "Christ, the final Adam, by the revelation of the mystery of the Father and His love, fully reveals man to man himself and makes his supreme calling clear" (*Gaudium et spes* §22). It is one thing, in other words, to see how God is "speaking" of his nature by creating the human person in his image and likeness; but it is far more significant to see the nature of man *fully* revealed in Christ, the final Adam. Of course the latter perspective does not trump the former; still less are they at war with each other, as Thomas teaches: "Just as the procession of the Persons explains the production of creatures from the first principle, so the same procession explains their return thereto as to their destiny [in Christ]."²⁶ But the point is that we can stumble toward an understanding of the Trinity using our weak language only because we are *already* grounded in Christ, who is himself the revelation of the triune God, a confluence of factors fused together by St. Paul:

---

24. Ibid.

25. Ibid., 112.

26. Thomas Aquinas, *I Sent.* d 14 q 2 a 3. I owe this citation to William Hill who glosses it this way: "God's revelation of himself as a Trinity precludes any subsequent understanding of him as a self-enclosed Absolute; henceforth he is manifest—primordially, in his own being—as a self-communicating deity. If in his own reality he is a communicating plenitude, then the mystery not only of salvation but of creation also is thereby illumined." William J. Hill, OP, *The Three-Personal God: The Trinity as a Mystery of Salvation* (Washington, DC: Catholic University of American Press, 1982) 273.

> He [Christ] is the image of the invisible God, the firstborn over all creation. For by him all things were created: things in heaven and on earth, visible and invisible, whether thrones or powers or rulers or authorities; all things were created by him and for him. He is before all things, and in him all things hold together. And he is Head of his body, the Church; he is the beginning and the firstborn from among the dead, so that in everything he might have the supremacy. For God was pleased to have all his fullness dwell in him, and through him to reconcile to himself all things, whether things on earth or things in heaven, by making peace through his blood, shed on the cross. (Col 1:15–20)

When all of these considerations are taken together, the meaning for trinitarian diastasis emerges into view: for the reconciling work accomplished by Christ proclaimed in Colossians happened because of Christ's descent to the depths of a now unreconciled creation: "What does 'he ascended' mean except that he also descended to the lower, earthly regions? He who descended is the very one who ascended higher than all the heavens, in order to fill all things" (Eph 4:9–10).

Let us grant, then, that some sort of diastasis in trinitarian relations must be posited if these two Pauline passages cited above are to make any grammatical sense. What must also be granted is that such a diastasis must not be taken "too far," meaning here in the way Jürgen Moltmann does:

> Expressed in rather inadequate figurative language, God is transcendent as Father, immanent as Son, and as Spirit open to the future.... We must be careful not to picture the Trinity as a closed circle of perfect existence in heaven ... [or] to think of the Spirit as return.[27]

In this weird position Moltmann manages to "bowl a spare," so to speak, meaning he has knocked down with one ball two pins at each end of the spectrum. That is, in the very act of speaking in the language of the modalists (who spoke of God "coming across" as Father in the Old Testament, as Son in the New, and as Spirit in the era of the Church), he begins to sound tritheistic. Or as William Hill dryly notes: "Paradoxically, it is not unusual for trinitarian thought with modalistic strains to veer over into tritheism as a corrective maneuver."[28] Yet, if Moltmann's formulation is

---

27. Jürgen Moltmann, "The Crucified God: A Trinitarian Theology of the Cross," *Interpretation* 26 (1972) 278–99; here 298–99.

28. Hill, *Three-Personal God*, 173. This remark does not obviate my observation that tritheism is a paper heresy, since Moltmann would never admit to being a tritheist. In other words, if he were to admit the justice of Hill's mordant observation (which

unacceptable, how can diastasis be posited (as I maintain it must be), but in such a way that it will not lead to Moltmann's excessive differentiations between the trinitarian persons?

Augustine, I believe, offers us a way out of this dilemma in one of his sermons. First of all, he frankly admits that revelation speaks of the persons of the Trinity acting out their own roles in the economy of salvation; but monotheism requires the axiom *opera omnia Trinitatis ad extra indivisa sunt*, lest it seem like three divinities are acting upon each other in the manner of Homer's deities. The apparent clash of these two realities becomes especially noticeable in the gospel scene of Jesus' baptism: after his emergence from the River Jordan he hears the Father saying, "This is my beloved Son in whom I am well pleased," with a dove hovering above (Matt. 3:16–17). Three actors acting out their parts in three different roles! For Augustine the dilemma is real:

> So what are we to do? Here you have the Son coming separately in the person of a man, the Holy Spirit separately coming down from the sky in the form of a dove, the voice of the Father separately being heard from the sky, *This is my Son*. Where now is the inseparable trinity?[29]

Superb rhetorician that he is, Augustine at this point draws on Quintilian's lawyerly advice, *concessum non datum*; meaning he opens his case by making it seem it will be even more impossible to win over the jury than it in fact is:

> Someone may say to me, "*You* have said that the Father does nothing without the Son, nor the Son without the Father; and you have produced evidence from the scriptures that the Father does nothing without the Son, because all things were made through him. . . . Now you tell me, apparently speaking against yourself, that the Son, not the Father, was born of the virgin; the Son, not the Father, suffered; the Son rose again not the Father. So either admit that the Son does something without the Father, or else admit that the Father too was born, suffered, died, rose again. Say one thing or the other; choose one of the two."[30]

presumably he wouldn't), he would seek a more careful formulation.

29. Augustine, *Sermon 52* 3; in *The Works of Saint Augustine*, Part III: *Sermons*, Volume III, *Sermons 51–94*, trans. Edmund Hill, OP (Brooklyn: New City, 1991) 51. All citations from this sermon will be taken from the Hill translation.

30. *Sermon 52* 7; Hill, 53.

The dilemma is certainly real, but for Augustine the solution is ready to hand with an important terminological distinction: "The Son indeed, and not the Father, was born of the Virgin Mary; but this birth of the Son, not the Father, from the Virgin Mary was the work of both Father and Son. It was not the Father, but the Son who suffered; yet the suffering of the Son was the work of both Father and Son. It wasn't the Father who rose again, but the Son; yet the resurrection of the Son was the work of both Father and Son."[31]

In other words, whatever "distance" obtains between the divine persons *is itself the work of all three persons*. As Augustine recognizes, distance is "economic," that is, it makes possible the "over-against relations" between Father, Son, and Spirit that we see displayed in the scene of Jesus' baptism—in which the Father *addresses* the Son and the Spirit *hovers* over the scene.[32] Granted, then, that whatever distance necessary for the incarnation to take place is grounded in the common and totally unified action of the three persons for the sake of the economy, does that diastasis obtain immanently? Initially, at least in this sermon, Augustine seems to deny inner-trinitarian diastasis: "I don't say memory is the Father, understanding is the Son, will is the Spirit. I don't say it (however it may be understood), I don't dare to."[33] But in *de Trinitate* he (famously) moves to just that position.[34]

But even that short step is too little, too late for what are called social trinitarians, who detect a latent modalism in the psychological analogies, just as their opponents object to social trinitarianism for (they charge) its latent tritheism.[35] Round and round we go, it seems. But recent research

---

31. *Sermon 52* 8; Hill, 53–54.

32. Technically, only in Luke does the Father directly address the Son: "You are my beloved Son in whom I am well pleased" (Luke 3:22c), whereas Matthew has the voice from heaven speaking of Jesus in the third person: "This is my beloved Son, in whom I am well pleased" (Matt. 3:17). But both versions require the Son to be the "Other," whether as one addressed or as spoken about.

33. *Sermon 52*, 23; Hill, 62.

34. It is for that reason that Hill dates *Sermon 52* to around 410–412, that is, several years before Augustine completed Books IX–XI of *de Trinitate* (415 at the earliest), which very definitely ascribe the role of memory to the Father, understanding to the Son, and will to the Spirit: see Hill, 62–63, endnote 1.

35. For example: "A person who extrapolated theologically from Hebrews, Paul, and John would naturally develop a social theory of the Trinity. . . . Let me propose generally, then, that the Holy Trinity is a divine, transcendent *society* or *community* of three fully personal and fully divine *entities*: the Father, the Son, and the Holy Spirit or Paraclete. . . . The Trinity is thus a zestful, wondrous community of divine light, love, joy, mutuality, and verve" (Cornelius Plantinga, Jr., "Social Trinity and Tritheism," in

into the trinitarian theology of Thomas has shown that he actually got theology off this snag: what had seemed an irresolvable antinomy between mutually exclusive analogies drawn from psychology vs. personal relations finds resolution in him, even if the point only emerged because of that same recent scholarship.

To understand that scholarship I must first bring into the discussion two gaps that everyone agrees obtain in *our* relationship with God: the infinite gulf that separates God from creation, which is inherent and ontological in the God-world relationship, and the further (and infinite!) gap that separates God from sinful man, which is adventitious and the result of man's use of his natural freedom (and which also, in mysterious ways, affects the God-world relationship; see Rom 8:20–22). It is on the first gulf that I shall be concentrating here, with a few remarks at the end on how God relates to the second through a trinitarian involvement in the atonement.

At least if the writings of Reginald Garrigou-Lagrange may be taken as typical, a certain strain of school Thomism held that the God-world relationship is best understood under the rubric *de Deo uno*, while God's redemption of sinful man falls under the *topos* of *de Deo trino*, as we see in this telling passage:

> ... the natural order or the order of creation depends efficiently and finally on the one God, the author of nature; the supernatural order, or the order of grace, depends efficiently and finally on the triune God, the author of grace.[36]

This position can no longer be maintained, as Giles Emery has shown in his numerous publications. Even as early as his *Commentary on the Sentences* Thomas was insisting on this point: that the act of creation is grounded in the procession of the divine persons: "The exitus of the persons in the unity of essence is the cause of the exitus of creatures in a diversity of essence."[37] If the procession of the divine persons is the direct *cause* of the

---

Trinity, Incarnation, and Atonement: Philosophical and Theological Essays, eds. Ronald J. Feenstra and Cornelius Plantinga, Jr. (Notre Dame: Indiana: University of Notre Dame Press, 1989) 21–47, here 27–28; emphases added. This passage nicely exemplifies both the appeal of social trinitarianism for its advocates and the dangers lurking in its formulation for its critics, especially in the words I have italicized.

36. Reginald Garrigou-Lagrange, *The Trinity and God the Creator*, trans. F. C. Eckhoff (St Louis: Herder, 1952) 253.

37. *I Sent.*, d. 2. *Exitus enim personarum in unitate essentiae est causa exitus creaturarum in essentiae diversitate*. Cited in Giles Emery, O.P., *Trinity in Aquinas* (Naples, Florida: Sapientia, 2003) 58.

creation of all creatures *tout court*, this same principle holds, *a fortiori*, of the creation of human persons:

> Since it is not only the divine essence, but *also the procession of the persons that is the reason for the production of creatures*, this entails a relation with the creature; and so something personal can also be signified with a relation to the creature.[38]

Does that then mean that to create belongs to one person (the Father) and not the other? No, as Thomas explains in his article addressing this very question: "to create belongs to God according to His being, that is, His essence, which is common to the three Persons. Hence to create is not proper to any one Person, but is common to the whole Trinity" (*ST* I q.45 a.6). But, *pace* Garrigou-Lagrange, this does not mean that the procession of the persons is irrelevant to that act of creation: "The processions of the persons are also in some way the cause and type of creation" (*ST* I q.45 a.7 ad 3). As David Walker rightly says of Thomas:

> Thus, any facile identification of the one God with the Creator and the triune God with the Redeemer leads ultimately to an inadequate interpretation of St. Thomas's theology. Moreover, it is for this reason that in his *Summa Theologiae* St. Thomas does not include the treatise on creation immediately after the treatise on the one God . . . , but only after he has first dealt with both the unity of the divine nature and the trinity of divine persons. . . . [This] knowledge of the triune God illumines and deepens St. Thomas's knowledge of the Creator and thus of truths pertaining primarily to the one God.[39]

If the procession of the divine persons is the creative ground for the infinite gulf between the infinite God and finite creation, what is the ground for the Triune God's decision to overcome the infinitely disastrous gulf that separates sinful man from the all-holy God? One way to approach this difficult question can be found in a remark from St. Anselm that startled his monks whenever he said it: he told them that he would prefer to be free from sin and to go to hell innocently than to be permitted entrance into the kingdom of heaven while still polluted with the stain of

---

38. *I Sent.*, d. 27, q.2, a.3, ad 6: *Sed quia non tantum essentia habet ordinem ad creaturam, sed etiam processio personalis, quae est ratio processionis creaturarum; ideo potest etiam aliquid personale cum respect ad creaturam significari.* Emery, 65; emphasis added.

39. David A. Walker, "Trinity and Creation in the Theology of St. Thomas Aquinas," *The Thomist* 57/3 (July 1993) 443–55; here 446.

sin.[40] But the assertion makes perfect sense when one realizes that heaven means union with the all-holy God, who "by definition" cannot tolerate sin.

I do not wish here either to outline and still less to defend Anselm's legal-satisfaction theory of atonement. What intrigues me here is not so much his psychology or his theology of atonement but this thought-experiment prompted by his remark: what if God "must" think the same? That is, assume with Anselm that God cannot admit sin in any form into his presence, so that a mere wiping the slate clean and "letting bygones be bygones" is impossible. What, then, if *God* says it would be better *for God* to enter into hell innocently than to let *man* enter heaven stained with sin?

Merely to ask these questions throws new light on those passages in the New Testament that go beyond merely positing a *vis-à-vis* "over against" relationship between the divine persons in the economy of salvation, as depicted, for example, in the baptism of Jesus. We have seen these passages before but bear quoting again:

> He who did not *spare* his own Son but gave him up for us all, will he not also give us all things with him? (Rom 8:32)

> For our sake he [God] made him *to be sin* who knew no sin, so that in him we might become the righteousness of God. (1 Cor 5:21)

> Christ redeemed us from the curse of the law by *becoming a curse* for us. (Gal 3:13a)

And finally:

> My God, my God, why have you forsaken me? (Mark 15:34b)

The first passage from Romans speaks of God's own sacrifice in yielding up his Son; the second denotes the full consequences of becoming flesh ("For the mind that is set upon flesh is hostile to God; it does not submit to God's law, indeed it cannot; and those who are in the flesh cannot please God," [Rom 8:7–8]); the third directly posits an adversarial (to be sure, an *economically* adversarial) relationship between God and his Son, taking upon himself the penalty for sin that had belonged to us; and the fourth shows in terms of great pathos the cost the Son paid in taking on that curse: despair at the distance from God that his free act to save entailed. Here is Mother Teresa of Calcutta's own interpretation of this theologoumenon:

---

40. Eadmer, *Vita Anselmi* II, 22 (*PL* 158, 90A).

> At the Incarnation Jesus became like us in all things except sin; but at the time of the Passion, He became sin.—He took on our sins and that was why He was rejected by the Father. I think that this was the greatest of all the sufferings that He had to endure and the thing He dreaded most in the agony of the Garden. Those words of His on the Cross were the expression of the depth of His loneliness and Passion—that even His own Father didn't claim Him as His Son. That, despite all His suffering and anguish, His Father did not claim him as His beloved Son, as He did at the Baptism by St. John the Baptist and at the Transfiguration. You ask "Why?" because God cannot accept sin and Jesus had taken on sin—He had become sin. Do you connect your vows with the Passion of Jesus? Do you realize that when you accept the vows you accept the same fate as Jesus?[41]

How far did this distance extend? I cite once more Paul: "What does 'he ascended' mean except that he also descended to the lower, earthly regions? He who descended is the very one who ascended higher than all the heavens, in order to fill all things" (Eph 4:9–10). If that descent was meant to fill all things, and if that was to be accomplished under God's curse, we then come to understand Thomas' explanation why Christ descended into hell, the first reason being "to shoulder the entire punishment due to guilt and thereby to atone for all its guilt."[42]

This theme can be traced throughout the tradition subsequent to the penning of these lines. Rather than trace this history here,[43] I will cite the most recent version of this theologoumenon, from the pen of Pope Benedict XVI in his recent Jesus book:

> Jesus' Baptism, then, is understood as a repetition of the whole of history, which both recapitulates the past and anticipates the future. His entering into the sin of others is a descent into the "inferno." But he does not descend merely in the role of a spectator, as in Dante's Inferno. *Rather, he goes down in the role of one whose suffering-with-others is a transforming suffering* that turns the underworld around, knocking down and flinging open the gates of the abyss. His Baptism is a descent into the

---

41. Mother Teresa's Instruction to the Sisters on April 1, 1981, cited in Brian Kolodiejchuk, MC, *Mother Teresa: Come Be My Light* (New York: Doubleday, 2007) 250–51.

42. Thomas Aquinas, *Expositio symbolum apostolorum: prima, ut sustineret totam poenam peccati, ut sic expiaret totam culpam.*

43. For which see Edward T. Oakes, SJ, "Catholic Eschatology and the Development of Doctrine," *Nova et Vetera*, 6/2 (2008) 419–46.

house of the evil one, combat with the "strong man" (cf. Luke 11:22) who holds men captive (and the truth is that we are all very much captive to powers that anonymously manipulate us!). Throughout all its history, the world is powerless to defeat the "strong man"; he is overcome and bound by one yet stronger, who, because of his equality with God, can take upon himself all the sin of the world and then *suffer it through to the end—omitting nothing on the downward path into identity with the fallen*. This struggle is the "conversion" of being that brings it into a new condition that prepares a new heaven and a new earth. Looked at from this angle, the sacrament of Baptism appears as the gift of participation in Jesus' world-transforming struggle in the conversion of life that took place in his descent and ascent.[44]

The more this *theologoumenon* is stressed, the more the question arises (needless to say) how such a stress fits in with the absolute unity of the Godhead, my answer to which comes from perhaps a surprising source (to the extent her actual views are actually known), Adrienne von Speyr, who directly addresses this issue:

> What [the Father] bequeathed to the Son—his mission with its path through the world—has now become fully the Son's possession, something the Son has accomplished so utterly that the Father's will has been fully realized and made apparent in the Son, while the Father himself withdraws into absence, so as to enable all the light to fall upon the Son, indeed, so as to take undistracted cognizance of what the Son is. *The divine unity of essence is not for one moment shattered*; the Son's equal standing with the Father is fully evidenced *and not for one moment called into question*; while the distinctness of the Persons has never been more clearly revealed than in the relationship between the Son who is abandoned and the Father who abandons him.[45]

How all of these factors in trinitarian theology can come together in a cohesive vision of God's action to save the world will be the task of subsequent theology to elucidate. But in doing so, theology will have to continue to reflect on G. K. Chesterton's insight in his book that tellingly bears the title *Orthodoxy*:

---

44. Pope Benedict XVI, *Jesus of Nazareth: From the Baptism in the Jordon to the Transfiguration*, trans. Adrian Walker (New York: Doubleday, 2007) 20; emphases added.

45. Adrienne von Speyr, *The Countenance of the Father* (Ignatius, 1997) 82; emphases added.

[I]n that terrific tale of the Passion there is a distinct emotional suggestion that the author of all things (in some unthinkable way) went not only through agony, but through doubt. It is written, "Thou shalt not tempt the Lord thy God." No; but the Lord thy God may tempt Himself; and it seems as if this was what happened in Gethsemane. In a garden Satan tempted man: and in a garden God tempted God. He passed in some superhuman manner through our human horror of pessimism. When the world shook and the sun was wiped out of heaven, it was not at the crucifixion, but at the cry from the cross: the cry which confesses that God was forsaken of God. And now let the revolutionists choose a creed from all the creeds and a god from all the gods of the world, carefully weighing all the gods of inevitable recurrence and of unalterable power. They will not find another god who has himself been in revolt. Nay (the matter grows too difficult for human speech), but let the atheists themselves choose a god. They will find only one divinity who ever uttered their isolation; only one religion in which God seemed for an instant to be an atheist.[46]

---

46. G. K. Chesterton, *Orthodoxy* (San Francisco: Ignatius, 1905), 145.

11

The Divinity of Christ and Social Justice[1]

D. THOMAS HUGHSON, S.J.

I OFFER THE FOLLOWING essay in admiring, respectful, and grateful tribute to my faculty colleague Dr. Ralph Del Colle. Though they do not represent the totality of his family and ecclesial life, his theological reflection and scholarship have been a beacon for many. Illness and death cut short his articulate collegiality and an international theological witness to Catholic tradition. His holy life has inspired us and gives confidence about risen joy. Like most Catholic theologians, Dr. Del Colle expounded Catholic doctrine with respect for Catholic social teaching. This essay intersects with Dr. Del Colle's love for the faith of the Church but does not try to represent his published or unpublished theological principles, reflections, and positions.

INTRODUCTION: RESPONSE TO A FUTURE OP-ED

A succinct op-ed by Ross Douthat, "Can Liberal Christianity Be Saved?" was an unknown futurable when this essay was in formation.[2] Douthat

---

1. The argument in this revised essay first appeared in a paper, "Classical Christology and Social Justice: Why the Divinity of Christ Matters" presented at the Second Annual Colloquium of the Marquette Lonergan Project, "Doing Catholic Systematic Theology in a Multi-Religious World," November 4–5, 2010, Milwaukee, Wisconsin. My thanks to respondents Bryan N. Massingale, Juliana Vazquez, and Darren Dias for valuable comments.

2. Ross Douthat, "Can Liberal Christianity Be Saved?" *New York Times*, July 15,

points to that larger question raised by the Episcopal Church's House of Bishops' July 2012 approval of a rite for the blessing of same-sex unions. Douthat's balanced answer nonetheless evinces a standard American assumption about all of Christianity being summed up in the varieties of American Protestantism. Douthat states that for liberal Christianity, "[F]aith should spur social reform as well as personal conversion." Of course, that description of liberal Christianity applies equally to Popes John Paul II, Benedict XVI, and Catholic Christianity. Catholic social doctrine, from Leo XIII's *Rerum novarum* to the Pontifical Council of Justice and Peace's *Compendium of the Social Doctrine of the Church* and Benedict XVI's *Caritas in veritate*, teaches why and how faith spurs social reform, and it indicates the main directions of reform. Moreover, many Black Protestants and Black Catholics similarly believe that faith spurs social reform, although they do not necessarily agree with a whole "liberal" agenda. Then too, and Douthat ignores this, the emergence of the Religious Right in the 1980s also depended on the principle that faith should spur social reform, usually reform in the direction of minimizing federal governance except for an expansive foreign policy backed by use of military force. Seldom or never has the Religious Right, old or new, sought means in public policy to help eradicate persistent racial injustice embedded in mores and institutions long since shaped by white culture.[3]

Nevertheless, Douthat's main question escapes the limits of its assumptions. Moreover, his positive, qualified answer has merit. In his view, Christianity committed to social reform can survive and flourish if one condition is fulfilled: that liberal Christianity recover "a religious reason for its own existence." Many congregants of liberal churches have ceased to be convinced about a religious raison d'être for membership since the churches' social agenda seems almost indistinguishable from a secular agenda. Liberal Christianity's best hope, advises Douthat, lies in renewing and articulating its anchorage in the content of faith. Even apart from that challenge, there is every reason to seek that articulation beyond the spelling-out of social-ethical implications in biblical texts and in the region of faith known as tradition.

Now, all Catholics and Protestants I know who are committed to social justice have an anchorage in Scripture and tradition that at least implicitly envelops their social analyses of contemporary conditions.

2012.

3. See Bryan N. Massingale, *Racial Justice and the Catholic Church* (Maryknoll, NY: Orbis, 2010) on US cultural racism.

Nevertheless, Douthat has it right that there is a problem with a social agenda in US Christianity. The problem is minimal articulation of what links social justice with traditional Christian doctrines on God, Christ, grace, sacraments, kingdom of God, apostolic succession, eschatology, and so forth. A result is confusion about the Church's social mission, with some thinking churches have adopted a secular agenda and others wondering how some church-going Christians can be indifferent to structural causes of avoidable human suffering. A solution for the problem is not out of reach. Systematic theology can assist social ethics and biblical theology in articulating the missing link. Linkage, in this essay with traditional teaching on Christ's divinity, clarifies grounds for a Christian search for social justice and keeps that search accountable to faith, Bible, Church, and tradition. I propose in this essay that commitment to social justice finds its ultimate principle in the divinity of Christ, especially as conceived in the formulation taught by the Council of Chalcedon (451 CE). First, though, what in more detail is the problem?

A PROBLEMATIC OF ECUMENICAL BREADTH

The problem is a specific variation on the typically modern division between faith and everyday life. A chronic disjunction in many Christians keeps apart their sincere faith and their lived sense of the societal implications of their faith especially in regard to social justice. Preparation and dissemination of official social teachings by churches from the Catholic, Lutheran (ELCA), Presbyterian Church USA, Eastern Orthodox, and American Baptist to Evangelicals and some Pentecostals, have not overcome the disjunction. Despite official teachings, some degree of alienation from Christian commitment to social justice troubles almost all churches. Douthat and those for whom he speaks may see the more pressing problem to be alienation of putatively justice-oriented, so-called liberal churches from the revealed content of faith. Which alienation is it? From social consciousness or from the content of faith? In either case there is a weak connection between the core of belief and an orientation to social justice. Many who share Douthat's analysis of "liberal Christianity" have decried alienation from the content of faith. Fewer in the US have concentrated on Christian alienation from social justice. So I would like to provide an illustrative case in point of how a core doctrine of faith underwrites Catholic commitment to social justice expounded by, for example, the *Compendium of the Social Doctrine of the Church*. The core doctrine at issue is the familiar, catechetical, credal yet always mysterious affirmation that Jesus Christ is one divine person in two complete, distinct natures.

Linkage between creed and social justice passes through the Church's social mission. The Church is missionary by Trinitarian nature not solely by the dominical mandate of Matthew 28. According to Benedict XVI, mission has had a social dimension from shortly after Pentecost when the apostles (Acts 6:1–6) initiated a diaconal service in Jerusalem to distribute bread to the Hebrew-speaking and Greek-speaking widows, all of whom presumably were Jewish Christians. Care for the temporal well-being of fellow followers of Christ accompanied evangelizing. That impulse and expression in ever-varying modes has continued ever since and is now called social mission. In *Deus caritas est* Benedict establishes social charity as the primary mode of social mission. Social charities under the sponsorship of the hierarchy, such as Caritas, belong to the constitution and tradition of the Church. This means that Christ and the Holy Spirit instituted the Church with an essential, constitutive social concern for people's temporal well-being alongside the mission of evangelizing unto conversion, faith, and baptism. The parable of the Good Samaritan removed territorial, ethnic, and other barriers between believers and neighbors in need. The heritage of Catholic social doctrine, Vatican II's *Gaudium et spes*, and postconciliar papal teaching all approve and call for commitment to social justice as service on behalf of love for neighbors now a global population. Benedict's *Caritas in veritate* too endorses that commitment to social justice through civic participation in the political order, especially as an element in the vocation and apostolic work of the laity.

The Church's social mission, then, has two complementary components, social charity and social justice.[4] Social charity directly reflects the love for God and neighbor built into the Church. Social justice reflects that love indirectly but really. American Catholics, sociological research shows, have more appreciation for social charity than for social justice. Hence, in discussions of social mission, it is social justice that stands in greater need of further attention, particularly in reference to the core doctrines of Christianity. People readily grasp and revere the social charity of Blessed Mother Teresa and the Missionaries of Charity in their care for the destitute, regardless of religion. However, social mission seeking social justice has a more complex, controversial character. Its doctrinal

---

4. For clear exposition of the two components, see Charles E. Curran, *The Social Mission of the U.S. Catholic Church: A Theological Perspective* (Washington, DC: Georgetown Univ. Press, 2011).

grounding is not anywhere near self-evident. But the grounding is real and valid, as I will show.

First, though, what is social justice? "Social justice concerns. . .the social, political, and economic aspects and, above all, the structural dimensions of problems and their respective solutions."[5] It analyzes how the major public institutions of the social, legal, economic, or political orders actually function in practice not simply as chartered in ideals. Social justice looks to "the structural requirements for a just society focused on the human rights and needs of each person." [6] It seeks to promote a societal condition in which all people, equal in dignity, enjoy proportionally equal access to participation in the social, economic, cultural, civil, and political life of society. Insofar as changes are needed to bring this access about, commitment to social justice ordinarily leads to advocacy for specific public policies, always a controversial matter.

The *Compendium of the Social Doctrine of the Church* summarizes the importance of social justice for Catholic faith by stating, "A large part of the Church's social teaching is solicited and determined by important social questions, to which social justice is the proper answer."[7] Racial justice logically falls under social justice but has to be broken out because otherwise the distinctive menace of White supremacy in the United States cannot be seen in regard not only to Americans of African, Asian, and Latin descent but also in regard to Native Americans. Embedded within Catholic social teaching, racial and social justice has proved difficult to hear and to accept as belonging to faith. [8]

Why is that? A study of parishioners commissioned by the US Bishops in 1998 reported that "many Catholics do not understand that the social teaching of the Church is an essential part of Catholic faith."[9] One

---

5. Pontifical Council for Justice and Peace, *Compendium of the Social Doctrine of the Church*, trans. Libreria Editrice Vaticana (Rome: Libreria Editrice Vaticana, 2004; Washington, DC: United States Conference of Catholic Bishops, 2005) no. 201, 89–90.

6. Brian Hehir, "Social Justice," in Richard McBrien et al., eds., *HarperCollins Encyclopedia of Catholicism* (New York: HarperCollins, 1995) 1203–4.

7. Pontifical Council for Justice and Peace, *Compendium*, no. 81, p. 36. Reference to *Justice in the World*, the 1971 international Synod of Bishops' statement on social justice belonging to the preaching of the gospel did not find its way into the *Compendium*.

8. See Bryan N. Massingale, "James Cone and Recent Catholic Episcopal Teaching on Racism," *Theological Studies* 61 (2000) 700–37. In the *Compendium* only 4 of 583 paragraphs treat racism.

9. United States Catholic Conference, *Sharing Catholic Social Teaching: Challenges and Directions; Reflections of the U.S. Catholic Bishops* (Washington, DC: United States Catholic Conference, 1998), 3.

reason adduced was a perception that social doctrine was peripheral to the core of faith expressed in Eucharistic liturgy and in the Creed. An indicator of a direction for remedies was "the need to see more clearly Catholic social teaching as authentic doctrine and integral to the mission of Catholic education."[10] The *Compendium* addressed that need with a papally authorized synthesis that integrated social doctrine into the official doctrine of Catholic faith. That integration is hopeful in principle.

But in practice, Jerome Baggett's 2009 analysis of 300 interviews with members of six Catholic parishes in the San Francisco Bay area opens space for some doubt that a volume from the Pontifical Council for Peace and Justice will turn the tide in favor of wider reception of Catholic social doctrine. For one thing, Baggett found that "Catholics gain access to these idioms—concepts such as the 'priority of labor over capital,' human dignity, subsidiarity, the common good, a 'preferential option for the poor,' distributive and social justice, stewardship of the earth's resources, and 'just war' criteria—when they hear them used repeatedly."[11] Indeed, he discovered that "[s]ome use social justice language to describe how institutions perpetuate racial inequality and therefore envision institution-level remedies."[12] But such people are relatively few in number. More generally, "public discourse is occurring in parishes. But it is often undermined by a tendency toward civic silencing, whereby the idioms of the church's social justice tradition are expressed less interactively, less incisively, and less regularly."[13] Parishioners, that is, have not assimilated Catholic social doctrine, at least partly because its language, its idiom, is not coin of the American realm. Parishioners' faith expressed in liturgy, prayer, and profession of the Creed does not seem to involve a societal dimension and so can be classified sociologically as privatized.

A condition not totally dissimilar can be found among many Americans in churches and movements stemming from the Reformation, despite Stanley Hauerwas's alarm at social justice saturating Protestant consciences.[14] Instead of churches' social teaching being a "best-kept

---

10. United States Catholic Conference, *Sharing Catholic Social Teaching*, 3.

11. Jerome P. Baggett, *Sense of the Faithful: How American Catholics Live Their Faith* (Oxford: Oxford Univ. Press, 2009), 186–87.

12. Baggett, *Sense of the Faithful*, 189.

13. Baggett, *Sense of the Faithful*, 187.

14. For a helpful overview of Stanley Hauerwas's contribution, see R. R. Reno, "Stanley Hauerwas," in Peter Scott and William T. Cavanaugh, eds., *The Blackwell Companion to Political Theology*, Blackwell Companions to Religion (Malden, MA: Blackwell, 2004) 302–16.

secret" as in Catholicism, according to Hauerwas social teachings have inundated Protestant clergy and laity, all but supplanting gospel and faith. Hauerwas laments, "If there is anything Christians agree about today it is that our faith is one that does justice.... We are told that justice demands that we must reshape and restructure society so that the structural injustices are eradicated forever."[15] In Hauerwas's perspective, Christian commitment to the cause of social justice has induced rather than overcome Christians' cultural captivity by the market and the state. So he urges that churches should return from a social agenda to concentrate on renewing an ecclesial identity prior to, and complete without, a social mission.[16] The churches' social mission is to witness by example to how Christ, gospel, and faith transform social existence. That witness will contribute more to the common good than churches seeking to intervene in, or to influence, public matters.

And yet he need not worry too much about Protestant conformity to an allegedly misguided message of social justice. The message has not been heard, or having been heard, has been ignored or resisted. Whichever the case, or a mix of the three, sociologist Brian Steensland found that from the 1960s on mainline Protestants in the pews have distrusted official social teachings from the clerical leadership of churches and from the National Council of Churches. His explanation for the negative reaction is that Protestant faithful heard leaders and ecumenists advocating for, and teaching, racial and social justice for minorities and the poor in the language of policy analysis rather than by invocation of explicit theological and moral justifications.[17] The result was a backlash from 1964 to 2000 against an ecumenical social agenda associated with the headquarters and

---

15. Stanley Hauerwas, *After Christendom?: How the Church Is to Behave If Freedom, Justice, and a Christian Nation Are Bad Ideas* (1991; repr., Nashville: Abingdon, 1999) 45.

16. For an objection to interest in social justice by all religions, not only Christianity, see Shivesh Chandra Thakur, *Religion and Social Justice*, Library of Philosophy and Religion (New York: St. Martin's, 1996). Thakur argues against religious concern for social justice because "religion's ultimate goal, namely the transcendental state of spiritual salvation or liberation . . . must regard earthly matters as 'ultimately inconsequential,'" 44. "Religion has to do with life in its wholeness," according to a Presbyterian Church USA statement in 1954 in, *Social Witness Policy Compilation*, 257–58 accessed on July 25, 2012 at http://index.pcusa.org/NXT/gateway.dll/socialpolicy/1?fn=default.htm$f=templates$vid=pcdocs:10.1048/Enu.

17. Brian Steensland, "The Hydra and the Swords: Social Welfare and Mainline Advocacy, 1964–2000," in Robert Wuthnow and John H. Evans, eds., *The Quiet Hand of God: Faith-Based Activism and the Public Role of Mainline Protestantism* (Berkeley: University of California Press, 2002) 213–36.

member churches of the National Council of Churches USA.[18] There is no published empirical data on Eastern and Oriental Orthodox churches in America, but it would be surprising if the situation were not the same there.

A sociological study by James D. Davidson and Ralph E. Pyle confirms ecumenical breadth in a disconnect between faith and social justice. They discovered that in Catholic and Protestant congregations between 1965 and 1995, a period when the gap between rich and poor had been increasing, congregations allocated funds, staff time, and selected themes for preaching and hymns in congruence more with a "good fortune theology" celebrating God's material blessings on the righteous than with a "social justice theology" calling for more equitable distribution of resources.[19] That finding contravenes Hauerwas's contention that a wave of social justice rolled across Protestant America. Or if it did, then unbeknownst to him, a simultaneous and ubiquitous movement rolled it back. Where is the liberal Christianity Douthat pointed to? Is it something only in Church leadership?

To give their due to Hauerwas and those mainline American Protestants rejecting a social agenda, perhaps some advocates of Christian commitment to racial and social justice had conveyed an implicit secularization that portrayed a temporal order of socio-politically institutionalized justice as the central objective in the mission of Christ. Some interpretations of the Jesus of history as a prophet of social change have gone in that direction, and been criticized for it by other exegetes.[20] Perhaps Hauerwas has articulated a broad-based recoil in American Protestantism against a surmised assumption that social justice is the *novum* of the mission of Christ, the be-all and end-all of Christianity. No official social teaching

---

18. For an example of pre-1960s social teaching, see Presbyterian Church USA, *Compilation of Social Policy*, Chapter 1, "Theological Basis for Social Action . . . 1954 statement" (see n. 15 above).

19. James D. Davidson and Ralph E. Pyle, "Public Religion and Economic Inequality," in William H. Swatos Jr., and James K. Wellman Jr., eds., *The Power of Religious Publics: Staking Claims in American Society* (Westport, CT: Praeger, 1999) 101–14. Their investigation used a spectrum between good fortune theology and social justice theology. Few congregations were at either the extreme, but more were toward the good fortune end.

20. See Ben Witherington III, *The Jesus Quest: The Third Search for the Jew of Nazareth*, 2nd ed. (Downers Grove, IL: InterVarsity, 1997) 64–92 (criticism of John Dominic Crossan) and 137–60 (criticism of Gerd Theissen, Richard Horsley, and R. David Kaylor). See also N. T. Wright, *The Contemporary Quest for Jesus*, Facets (Minneapolis: Fortress, 2002; an excerpt from *Jesus and the Victory of God*, 1996).

document from any church makes a claim that can be understood to state that. But reception cannot be controlled by texts alone.

At the same time, many but not all Black churches have a tradition of rich social teaching and preaching that links faith with a deprivatized commitment to practice of racial and social justice.[21] Still, my limited collaboration with gifted Black Protestant laity and pastors suggests another kind of problem stemming from congregational independence in the free-church and Pentecostal traditions. While side-by-side practice of worship and of commitment to racial and social justice flourish in the congregations, within and among independent congregations there is not widespread consent to any specific articulation of a strong theological bond joining the two practices of discipleship. Consequently, for some congregants theological doubt hovers around commitments to practical activities for racial and social justice. On the other hand, though far less numerous than their Protestant counterparts, Black Catholics in principle and practice have sustained a strong public record in support of the social tradition and documentary heritage of Catholic social teaching on racial and social justice.[22] The deprivatized faith of Black Catholic clergy and laity exemplifies fidelity to what Andrew Greeley identified as the Catholic imagination underlying Catholic social teaching.[23]

REAFFIRMING THE COUNCIL OF CHALCEDON

Restating the traditional doctrine of Christ's divinity may not seem well suited to helping solve the problem of Christian alienation from social justice. For one thing, attention to a Christological theme cannot be disengaged from doctrine on the Trinity, and especially the Holy Spirit. But

---

21. See Peter J. Paris, *The Social Teaching of the Black Churches* (Philadelphia: Fortress, 1985); Andrew Billingsley, *Mighty Like a River: The Black Church and Social Reform* (New York: Oxford University Press, 1999).

22. See the articles in the issue dedicated to "Catholic Reception of Black Theology," *Theological Studies* 61 (December 2000); Catholic Charities of Chicago, *Poverty and Racism: Overlapping Threats to the Common Good: A Catholic Charities USA Poverty in America Issue Brief* (Chicago: Catholic Charities: 2008), which was written by Bryan N. Massingale; Massingale, *Racial Justice and the Catholic Church* (Maryknoll, NY: Orbis, 2010).

23. Andrew M. Greeley, *The Catholic Imagination* (Berkeley: University of California Press, 2000). Greeley long has doubted the efficacy of documentary communication of Catholic social teaching and argues instead for the primacy of a Catholic imagination, transmitted by example, story, and liturgy, that generated Catholic social teaching in the first place.

human discourse proceeds part by part, and attention to the mission of the Spirit internal to, as well as distinct from, that of the Son is not the main preoccupation here. For another, there is the issue of ideological captivity. A study at greater length would have to address the extent to which Chalcedonian Christology has been, and here and there may still be, held captive to the interests of empire, nation, class, gender, or White supremacy. Some think Chalcedon's origin within a Constantinian model of Christian Empire constitutes a permanent tie with authoritarian rule under the reign of Christ.

In defense of a presupposition that Chalcedon can be extricated from ideology and allied with emancipation, I would point, for example, to James Cone's Black liberation theology in its affirmation of spirituals and gospel music as a legitimate *locus theologicus* and to the spirit of veneration for Christ human and divine they breathe, a spirit I would argue is congruent with Chalcedon.[24] Similarly, Virgilio Elizondo's explanation of *mestizo* religion and theology allows a glimpse into *mestizo* piety that likewise resonates positively with Chalcedon.[25] It might be worth noting that according to Chalcedon's teaching the Logos cannot be defined as possessing in a divine nature qualities such as gender that belong to a human nature. It goes without saying that the divine nature of the Logos is not gendered, not male, a point made in studies of Wisdom Christology. Jesus' human nature is male. In Chalcedon's meaning of "person," though not in a modern meaning, it would be accurate to say that Jesus is not a male person because Jesus is one divine person (not gendered) in two natures, divine and human (male-gendered). Jesus is a nongendered divine person with a gendered human nature. Thus, affirmation of Chalcedon's doctrine precisely of the person of Christ does not necessarily project the

---

24. James H. Cone, *Risks of Faith: The Emergence of a Black Theology of Liberation, 1968–1998* (Boston: Beacon, 1999). See James H. Cone, "Black Liberation Theology and Black Catholics: A Critical Conversation," *Theological Studies* 61 (December 2000) 731–47, for his reiteration of a long-standing challenge to White Protestant and Catholic theologians in the United States to tackle White supremacy as a theological problem. For a response see Laurie M. Cassidy and Alex Mikulich, eds., *Interrupting White Privilege: Catholic Theologians Break the Silence* (Maryknoll, NY: Orbis, 2007). On the difference between well-meant teaching against individual attitudes and analytic exposure of systemic distortion embedded in social structures and institutions, see Bryan N. Massingale, "James Cone and Recent Catholic Episcopal Teaching on Racism," *Theological Studies* 61 (December 2000) 700–30.

25. Virgilio Elizondo, *Galilean Journey: The Mexican-American Promise* (Maryknoll, NY: Orbis, 1983); Elizondo, "Jesus the Galilean Jew in Mestizo Theology," *Theological Studies* 70 (2009) 262–80.

interests of a dominant group, though such groups have used, and still use, the doctrine in this way.

I do not presuppose that Christ's humanity is primarily *instrumentum justitiae temporalis* rather than *instrumentum salutis*. Rather the theme will be that social justice is inherent in the normative social vision of salvation, *salutis*. What is at stake is who Christ is, as well as what he taught by word and deed, as Scripture and tradition relay the Christ event to succeeding generations in the Church. Value judgments about social justice flow from truths of faith, from the theological-anthropological truth that human beings are created in the image of God, from the ecclesiological truth that the Church has an orientation beyond herself to the rest of humanity, and from the Christological truth confessed at Chalcedon, that Jesus the Christ is the eternal Word of God in two distinct natures, human and divine. Explicit definition by an ecumenical council that the Word is a distinct divine person came only with Constantinople II (553 CE).

RECEPTION OF CHALCEDON: REPETITION, REVISION, OR APPROPRIATION?

Presuming that God's grace is ever-offered and prior to, as well as independent of, human thought or agency, there is room for theology as the thinking of faith to assist grace-led reception of social teachings and social justice. Theology's contribution to conversion to approval for racial and social justice involves more than invaluable, ongoing New Testament exegeses and indispensable studies in social ethics. Unexpectedly perhaps, systematic theology in the area of Christology also has something to offer in the form of recourse to the question posed by Jesus during his public ministry, "Who do you say that I am?" and to the answer taught by the Council of Chalcedon as received and developed by the Second and Third Councils of Constantinople.

Delving into ideas of Christ at issue in discipleship's relation to society at large places the inquiry within public theology, an area that fulfills part of a large theological task outlined by Bernard Lonergan in chapter 14 of *Method in Theology*.[26] Called communications, Lonergan's version of practical theology fulfills systematics and completes the mutual mediation between religion and a cultural matrix. Communications looks to more than how to pass on already attained systematic understandings to catechists, preachers, clergy, and missionaries. Communications also puts

26. Bernard Lonergan, *Method in Theology* (New York: Seabury, 1979).

systematic theology in dialogue with other disciplines, with ecumenism, and with renewal of common meaning in Church and society. Questions about Church and society also may incite a reverse movement of inquiry back to systematics before coming home again to communications. Such, at least, is the structure of this inquiry: from a question in the life of the Church to systematic Christology, and then back to engaging theology in the life of the Church and through the Church in the life of society.

This return to systematics will retrieve and develop, not revise or reformulate, Chalcedon's classical affirmation of Christ's two natures, human and divine, in the one and the same Son of God. Constantinople II explicitly taught that the incarnate Logos is a divine person. Ecumenical consensus on the divinity of Christ grounds the accessibility of this argument for most Protestant traditions. Affirmation of Christ's divinity figures in the criterion for membership in the World Council of Churches. Baptist rejection of creeds and confessions on a *sola Scriptura* principle nonetheless does not depart from convictions congruent with the early councils including Chalcedon and Constantinople II and III. Oriental Orthodox non-affirmation of Chalcedon has to do with historical, linguistic, religious, theological and cultural contexts but arguably does not oppose the Christological belief confessed at Chalcedon.[27]

However, many theologians think that Christology has been one-sidedly "from above" ever since Chalcedon, though Eastern theologians have been more likely to notice that Western faith, piety, and theology have orbited around the humanity of Jesus.[28] It may well be the case that an undercurrent in Western Christian piety apart from doctrine and theology has been an unofficial, imaginative construal of Jesus that begins and ends with a doctrinal proposition that "Jesus is God." Roger Haight thinks that this approach to Christ is "an imaginative framework that controls the reading of the gospel accounts of Jesus . . . a doctrinal imagination."[29] And yet after more than two centuries of searches for the historical Jesus, there is something to be said for the Eastern perception of a one-sided

---

27. See Kenneth Yossa, *Common Heritage, Divided Communion: The Declines and Advances of Inter-Orthodox Relations from Chalcedon to Chambésy*, Gorgias Eastern Christian Studies 11 (Piscataway, NJ: Gorgias, 2009).

28. See the remark that "the fact remains that later Christology has often tended to absolutize Chalcedon, as though it constituted the absolute point of reference," with a consequent accent on the ontological constitution of the person of Jesus as a divine person. Jacques Dupuis, *Who Do You Say That I Am?: Introduction to Christology* (Maryknoll, NY: Orbis, 1994) 105.

29. Roger Haight, SJ, *The Future of Christology* (New York: Continuum, 2005) 20.

affirmation of the humanity of Jesus in Western thought and spirituality that are more eager to be clear that "Jesus is a man" than that he is also divine. In fact, Richard Norris Jr. describes "a new type of Monophysitism— a tendency, in the face of its own strong sense of the incompatibility of divine and human agencies, to reduce Christ not to a God fitted out with the vestiges of humanity but to a human being adorned with the vestiges of divinity."[30] Belgian theologian Jacques Dupuis (1923-2003) noticed the same tendency and called it an "'inverted monophysitism'—that supposes a certain absorption of the divine nature by the human, by which the divine nature is reduced to the measure of the human."[31] In modern Western Christology inverted monophysitism seems to have had more influence than Haight's doctrinal imagination.

In that case, recovering and developing theological reflection on Christ's divinity seeks to regain the mystery of the whole Christ event in an era more given to preoccupation with hypotheses from the Third Quest for the Historical Jesus than to an excessively high Christology. Counteracting inverted monophysitism does not consist in adopting Cyril of Alexandria's pre-Chalcedonian focus on the divinity of Christ as if to ignore explicit affirmation of two natures. Instead, going beyond this new monophysitism begins with the principle that all Christology arises and remains within the structure of the whole, historical Christ event including the incarnation, resurrection, ascension, and Pentecost, to which the New Testament bears written witness. In Christology today it is arguably the divinity of Christ not the humanity that has fallen farther out of theological reflection on the whole Christ event.

Recovery and development of reflection on Christ's divinity does not lack footing in one area of contemporary New Testament research. Larry Hurtado, for example, has shown that among Jesus's earliest disciples, a Jewish, monotheistic reverence for him as somehow divine had emerged. In the Synoptics, that emergence was an incipient movement "from below" to "above." And a pre-Johannine Paul who had to have known about the self-evidently human Jesus of Nazareth crucified under Pontius Pilate already had gone "from below" in and after his conversion and was

---

30. Richard Norris Jr., "Chalcedon Revisited: Historical and Theological Reflection," in Bradley Nassif, ed., *New Perspectives on Historical Theology: Essays in Memory of John Meyendorff* (Grand Rapids: Eerdmans, 1996), 140-59, at 155.

31. Jacques Dupuis, "Universality of the Word and Particularity of Jesus Christ," in Daniel Kendall, SJ, and Stephen T. Davis, eds., *The Convergence of Theology: A Festschrift Honoring Gerald O'Collins, S.J.*, (New York: Paulist, 2001) 320-42, at 333.

moving back "from above" in Philippians, for example.³² A presupposition of permanent principle not discussed here is that in the New Testament and in Christianity generally, faith in Christ and Christology have, on both the ecclesial and individual level, the structure of a circle continually revolving "from below" in Christ's preresurrection humanity to "above" in his incarnation and risen humanity united to his divinity, and back to his preresurrection humanity in public ministry, all the while rolling forward under the impulse of new questions and insights in successive historical and cultural contexts of mission.

At the same time Roger Haight has casts doubt on the validity of any recourse to Chalcedon that retrieves rather than revises its teaching.³³ I agree with Haight when he prescribes the importance of Christology addressing "the humanly caused and systematically ingrained human suffering that so characterizes our world situation today."³⁴ He insists too that the postmodern situation changes the whole problematic in a theology of Christ by moving it to a new starting point in the "historical appearance of the historical person, Jesus of Nazareth within the new horizon of historical consciousness. The supposition and point of departure are defined by the human being, Jesus, and the question concerns what it can mean to say that Jesus is divine."³⁵ Here my agreement is qualified by recognition that New Testament research has shown that this question about what it can mean to say that Jesus is divine was raised and answered within the New Testament and in the early ecumenical councils. Thus, the question is not

---

32. Larry Hurtado, *Lord Jesus Christ: Devotion to Jesus in Earliest Christianity* (Grand Rapids: Eerdmans, 2003). See important discussions by Richard Bauckham, *Jesus and the God of Israel: God Crucified and Other Studies on the New Testament's Christology of Divine Identity* (Grand Rapids: Eerdmans, 2008); James D. G. Dunn, *Did the First Christians Worship Jesus?: The New Testament Evidence* (Louisville: Westminster John Knox, 2010).

33. Roger Haight, *Jesus: Symbol of God* (Maryknoll, NY: Orbis, second edition, 2000). There is some affinity between Haight's project and that of Friedrich Schleiermacher in *The Christian Faith* since both propose affirming the divinity of Christ without locating that divinity in the subsistent Logos. See, however, Richard Muller, "The Christological Problem as Addressed by Friedrich Schleiermacher: A Dogmatic Inquiry," in Marguerite Schuster and Richard Muller, eds., *Perspectives in Christology: Essays in Honor of Paul K. Jewett* (Grand Rapids: Zondervan, 1991) 141–62. In Muller's view (142), Schleiermacher's "absolutely powerful God-consciousness" in Jesus did not intend to deny Chalcedon on the Logos in Jesus. Haight's revision, however, does deny the subsistent Logos.

34. Haight, *Jesus*, 25.

35. Ibid., 291.

a uniquely postmodern query, though historical consciousness is modern and postmodern.

With admirable hermeneutical attention to context, Haight acknowledges that Chalcedon made sense within the classical framework of late antiquity. But he goes on to argue that "the shift to a historical imagination and point of departure undercuts the plausibility of the Johannine framework which in turn dictated the metaphysics of the divine subject, persona, and hypostasis."[36] With that position I strongly disagree because it draws upon a reading of the prologue to John's Gospel that mistakenly denies that this passage affirms the pre-existent Logos, in favor of a metaphoric interpretation of the Logos as a personified divine attribute. Haight's position here is unacceptable, too, because it ignores the heuristic not metaphysical quality of Chalcedonian concepts. To label Chalcedon's categories of person and nature "metaphysical" is to attribute to them a precision and systematic denotation they did not possess in their historical context. Metaphysical elucidation of Chalcedon was the work of Scholasticism, not part of the council in 451 CE.[37]

Chalcedon, according to Haight, confuses when what is needed first of all is a reinstatement of an original meaning that had nothing to do with a divine person in order to reformulate Chalcedon's teaching away from the pre-existent Logos as a distinct divine person. In Haight's view, Christology oriented toward social justice and minimizing avoidable human suffering simply has no path forward except to revise and to reformulate Chalcedon.

---

36. Ibid., 292.

37. See Richard Cross, *The Metaphysics of the Incarnation: Thomas Aquinas to Duns Scotus* (Oxford: Oxford University Press, 2002). On the undefined, heuristic quality of the concepts, see Bernard J. F. Lonergan, "The Origins of Christian Realism," the Seventeenth Annual Robert Cardinal Bellarmine Lecture, St. Louis School of Divinity, September 27, 1972, in Bernard J. Tyrell, SJ, and William F. J. Ryan, SJ, eds., *A Second Collection* (Philadelphia: Westminster, 1974). Similarly, Sarah Coakley praises Richard A. Norris, amid several criticisms, for insisting that "nature" and "person" in Chalcedon's definition of faith were relatively undefined so that the document is somewhat open-ended; see her "What Does Chalcedon Solve and What Does It Not? Some Reflections on the Status and Meaning of the Chalcedonian 'Definition,'" in Stephen T. Davis, Daniel Kendall, SJ, and Gerald O'Collins, SJ, eds., *The Incarnation: An Interdisciplinary Symposium on the Incarnation of the Son of God* (2002; repr., Oxford: Oxford University Press, 2004) 143–63, at 148. Coakley proposes that the Chalcedonian definition has an apophatic character, or what also might be called a mystogogical tendency, that in Eastern Orthodoxy led to its incorporation into the divine liturgy. This is true but does not remove a potential for kataphatic development of the sort that transpired before and after Constantinople III.

Without denying the validity of the project of reformulating Chalcedon's meaning, and without now discussing the merits of Haight's reconstruction of Chalcedon's original meaning and reformulation of it, I accept an alternative priority that flows in another current of Christology.[38] The scholars in this current recognize the contextual, linguistic, and conceptual differences between Chalcedon and us as grounds for keeping Chalcedon open to reformulation, but they accord precedence to expounding that council's teaching. Why would they do that? O'Collins says carefully and rightly, "I have clearly credited the teaching of Chalcedon with at least a certain intelligibility and ongoing validity."[39] I agree with Noll, who declares that Chalcedon's definition of faith "retains its momentous significance" because "the statement faithfully represents the reality about which it speaks."[40]

CRITICAL AND POSTCRITICAL AFFIRMATION

Chalcedon is first of all a place. A visit to contemporary Istanbul, tourists are advised, is best in September or October in order to avoid the broiling summer sun of July and August. Things were not so different on Thursday, October 25, 451 CE, when 370 bishops assembled at Chalcedon a bit north of present-day Istanbul on the eastern shore of the Bosporus to sign and acclaim a definition of the faith they had produced three days earlier in session five.[41] The nucleus of that definition confessed that

---

38. This current is represented by, for example, Gerald O'Collins, SJ, *Christology: A Biblical, Historical, and Systematic Study of Jesus*, 2nd ed. (Oxford: Oxford Univ. Press, 2009; 1st ed. 1999); Jacques Dupuis, SJ, *Toward a Christian Theology of Religious Pluralism* (Maryknoll, NY: Orbis, 1997); Mark Noll, *Turning Points: Decisive Moments in Christian History* (Grand Rapids: Baker, 1997); Davis, Kendall, O'Collins, *The Incarnation: An Interdisciplinary Symposium*; Kathryn Tanner, *Jesus, Humanity and the Trinity: A Brief Systematic Theology* (2001; repr., Minneapolis, MN: Fortress, 2003); Veli-Matti Kärkäinen, *Christology: A Global Introduction; An Ecumenical, International, and Contextual Perspective* (2003; repr. Grand Rapids: Baker Academic, 2005); the commentary and notes in Richard Price and Michael Gaddis, eds. and trans., *Acts of the Council of Chalcedon*, 3 vols., Translated Texts for Historians 45 (Liverpool: Liverpool University Press, 2007); Thomas Torrance, *The Incarnation: The Person and Life of Christ*, ed. Robert T. Walker, rev. ed. (Downers Grove, IL: IVP Academic, 2008); Oliver D. Crisp, *Divinity and Humanity: The Incarnation Reconsidered*, Current Issues in Theology (Cambridge: Cambridge University Press, 2007); Crisp, *God Incarnate: Explorations in Christology* (London: T. & T. Clark, 2009).

39. O'Collins, *Christology*, 245.

40. Noll, *Turning Points*, 81.

41. Price and Gaddis, *Acts of the Council of Chalcedon*, 1:44 (Table 3: Chronology

> one and the same Christ, Son, Lord, Only-begotten, acknowledged in two natures without confusion [*asugkutos*], change [*atreptos*], division [*adiairetos*], or separation [*achoristos*] (the difference of the natures being in no way destroyed by the union, but rather the distinctive character of each nature being preserved, and coming together into one person and one hypostasis [*hypostasis*]) not parted or divided into two persons but one and the same Son, Only-begotten, God, Word, Lord, Jesus Christ. . . .[42]

Richard Price supports a modern interpretation of this definition as a teaching shaped by Cyril of Alexandria, with a moderating Antiochene affirmation of two natures after the Incarnation.[43] He rejects the interpretation that Chalcedon synthesized Antiochene and Alexandrian tendencies, or forged a compromise between them. I see no reason to disagree with Price. In *Jesus the Symbol of God*, nonetheless, Haight at one point speaks of Chalcedon as a compromise and a synthesis of the two schools of thought. Yet eventually he concludes that "the Alexandrian framework controls the whole vision."[44] He sees the Alexandrian framework as problematic, however, because it conceived the Logos as a subsistent person rather than as an attribute of Christ.

For Haight the Cyrillian problem stemmed from a patristic tradition of interpretations of the prologue to John's Gospel that misread poetic, metaphoric language about divine attributes as propositions about a distinct entity, the Logos. To counteract Chalcedon's Cyrillian concept of the Logos as a divine person, Haight undertakes retrieval of an Antiochene affirmation of Christ's two natures. Dupuis and this inquiry emphasize the

---

of the Sessions of the Council of Chalcedon); vol. 2:183–205 (fifth session); vol. 3:193–203 (Appendix 2: Attendance and Ecumenicity). Emperor Marcian's Fourth Edict had 520 bishops attending. Most likely 320 bishops attended, along with some priests serving as proxies for others, so the number of episcopal votes cast differed from the number of bishops in attendance.

42. Price and Gaddis, *Acts of the Council of Chalcedon*, 2:204. For the Greek text, see Eduard Schwartz, ed., *Acta Conciliorum Oecumenicorum*, vol. 1, *Concilium universale chalcedonense*, part 2, *Actio secunda. Epistularum collectio B. Actiones 3–7* (Berlin: Walter de Gruyter, 1933), 129. The English word "definition" and Latin word *definitio* translate the Greek term *horos*. In light of ancient usage, Sarah Coakley selects for *horos* here the meaning of pattern or grid so that the definition is a "transitional 'horizon' to which we constantly return, but with equally constant forays backwards and forwards." "What Does Chalcedon Solve and What Does It Not?" 161–62.

43. See the fifth part of the General Introduction, written by Price, in Price and Gaddis, *The Acts of the Council of Chalcedon*, 1: 56–75.

44. Haight, *Jesus*, 288.

two natures but in support of, not in opposition to, Cyrillian and Chalcedonian affirmation of the person of the Logos. True enough, attention to the two natures of Christ usually serves to keep the historical humanity of Jesus to the fore lest it be thought of as dissolved into, or rendered negligible by, his divinity. However, Chalcedon's distinction of natures equally well directs attention to the divine nature of Christ. That is the path taken by Jacques Dupuis. I will follow in his footsteps, then strike out in another direction.[45]

Dupuis highlights Christ's divine nature in a marvelous theology of religious pluralism.[46] In a series of writings from 1991 to 2001, Dupuis distinguished two aspects of the divine nature of Jesus, the Logos/Son of God incarnate.[47] The most familiar aspect is the *Logos ensarkos*, Jesus the Logos as enfleshed or incarnate, historically causative of, and immanent in, the visible economy of redemption and Christianity as its sacrament. The less familiar aspect of the divine nature of Jesus is the Logos as *asarkos* (unfleshed or non-incarnate). The eternal Logos pre-existent to the Incarnation was *asarkos*.[48] After the Incarnation, *asarkos* simply refers to the fact that the hypostatically united human nature of Jesus cannot possibly contain, participate in, receive, or mediate the totality of Christ's

---

45. See "A Bibliography of the Writings of Jacques Dupuis, S.J." and Gerald O'Collins, "Jacques Dupuis: His Person and Work," in Daniel Kendall and Gerald O'Collins, eds., *In Many and Diverse Ways: In Honor of Jacques Dupuis* (Maryknoll, NY: Orbis, 2003) 231–69 and 18–29, respectively.

46. Among others works, Jacques Dupuis, SJ, *Jesus Christ at the Encounter of World Religions*, trans. Robert R. Barr, Faith Meets Faith (Maryknoll, NY: Orbis, 1991; originally *Jésus-Christ à la rencontre des religions*, Jésus et Jésus-Christ 39 (Paris: Desclée, 1989); *Who Do You Say I Am?: Introduction to Christology; Christianity and the Religions: From Confrontation to Dialogue*, trans. Phillip Berryman (Maryknoll, NY: Orbis, 2002); originally *Il cristianesimo e le religioni: Dallo scontro all' incontro*, Giornale di teologia 283 (Brescia: Queriniania, 2001); *Toward a Christian Theology of Religious Pluralism*, (Maryknoll, NY: Orbis, 1997), 2002 ed. includes documentation related to Vatican inquiry into the original edition; "Trinitarian Christology as a Model for a Theology of Religious Pluralism," in Terrence Merrigan and Jacques Haers, eds., *The Myriad Christ: Plurality and the Quest for Unity in Contemporary Christology*, Bibliotheca Ephemeridum theologicarum Lovaniensium 152 (Louvain: Louvain University Press, 2000) 83–97; "Le Verbe de Dieu, Jésus Christ et les religions du monde," *Nouvelle revue théologique* 123 (2001) 529–46; "Universality of the Word and Particularity of Jesus Christ," in Kendall and Davis, *Convergence of Theology*, 320–42.

47. See especially Dupuis, *Toward a Christian Theology of Religious Pluralism*, chs. 1 and 11; Dupuis, "Universality of the Word and Particularity of Jesus Christ."

48. On difficulties in thinking in terms of a pre-existence before the Incarnation, see Brian Leftow, "A Timeless God Incarnate," in Stephen T. Davis, Daniel Kendall, SJ, and Gerald O'Collins, SJ, eds., *The Incarnation: An Interdisciplinary Symposium*, 273–99.

divine nature. Dupuis states that "[t]he divine action of the Word is not 'circumscribed' by, 'exhausted' by, or 'reduced' to its expression through human nature."[49] This is to say that the divine nature does not turn into a non-divine nature.

He expands on the transcendence of Christ's divine nature with respect to his human nature in noting that "[t]he action of the Word reaches beyond the limits imposed on the operative presence of the humanity of Jesus, even in its glorified state, just as the person of the Word exceeds the human nature of Christ, the hypostatic union notwithstanding."[50] This recognition of difference and divine excess is not only allowable but compelled by the definition of Chalcedon.[51] It has been orthodox theology of the Incarnation since Athanasius in the fourth century.

Though Dupuis nowhere discusses the Reformation, it is the case that Luther and early Lutheran theologians took exception to Jean Calvin's assertion of the transcendence of Christ's divine nature in the *Institutes of Christian Religion*. Lutheran celebration of, and communion in, the Eucharist in multiple places and times seemed to require that Christ's glorified bodiliness be omnipresent if Christ is really and simultaneously present in far-flung celebrations of the Eucharist. Lutheran teaching on the *communicatio idiomatum* accordingly attributed, or in the term of Oliver Crisp, "transferred" divine omnipresence to Christ's risen and glorified human nature.[52] Lutheran theologians objected to Calvin's affirmation of a surplus or excess in Christ's divine nature over his human nature in the famous vocabulary of the *extra Calvinisticum*, the "Calvinist extra."[53] Calvin understood the transcendence of the divine nature with respect to the human nature of Jesus to lead to rejection of the omnipresence of the human nature of Jesus. Calvin approved the following scholastic distinction: "Although the whole [*totus*] Christ is everywhere, yet everything [*totum*, i.e., the whole that includes his human nature] which is in him is not everywhere." Paul Helm comments that "[i]f that distinction had

---

49. Dupuis, "Universality of the Word and Particularity of Jesus Christ," 334.
50. Ibid., 338.
51. Ibid., 332.
52. See Crisp, *Divinity and Humanity*, 6–26.
53. E. David Willis remarks, "There are two passages in the *Institutes* which are commonly accepted as Calvin's classical statements of the 'extra Calvinisticum.' These are II, 13, 4 and IV, 17, 30 of the 1559 edition." *Calvin's Catholic Christology: The Function of the So-Called Extra Calvinisticum in Calvin's Theology*, Studies in Medieval and Reformation Thought 2 (Leiden: Brill, 1966) 26.

been observed, then, Calvin thinks, it would have ruled out the doctrine of transubstantiation."[54]

In surveying the world's religions from a Christian viewpoint, Dupuis merely points out that the divine nature of Jesus exceeds the powers and capacities of Jesus' human nature as greatly as the divine exceeds the human. After 1994, instead of an *ensarkos/asarkos* distinction in regard to Christ's divine nature, Dupuis spoke about the universality of the Logos and the particularity of Jesus. His focus was on the universal enlightening influence of the Logos described in John 1:9: "The true Light, which enlightens everyone, was coming into the world." The divine Logos enlightened all people prior to the Incarnation.[55] Dupuis then adds that this universal enlightening is a saving influence that did not cease because of the Incarnation and that continues after the Incarnation has happened, but not only through the mediation of the historical human nature and activities of Jesus prolonged in the Church.

Dupuis did not edge away from the particularity and centrality of the fullness of light from the Logos in and through the whole Christ event. Still, Chalcedon's affirmation of two distinct natures unchanged by their union means that the hypostatic union does not remove the operations proper to each nature, more clearly taught by Constantinople III against monothelitism. But one of the powers proper to the Logos is enlightening all people. Therefore, after the Incarnation too the eternal Logos continues to be universally influential and enlightening directly by his divine nature and not only through the human nature of Jesus active in his ministry, mission, teaching, death, and resurrection and in the redemption visible and communicable in the churches and historical Christianity.

---

54. Paul Helm, *Calvin at the Centre* (Oxford: Oxford University Press, 2010) 114–28, at 116, quoting Calvin, *Institutes* 4.17.30.

55. Dupuis does not refer to Aquinas's interpretation of John 1:9. But see St. Thomas Aquinas, *Commentary on the Gospel of St. John*, trans. James A. Weisheipl and Fabian R. Larcher, vol. 1, Aquinas Scripture Series 4 (Albany, NY: Magi, 1980), ch. 1, lecture 5, 69–76, at 71–73. Aquinas explains the enlightening as divine; the Word was "light by his essence," by Whom, before the Incarnation, "all men coming into this visible world are enlightened by the light of natural knowledge through participating in this true light which is the source of all the light of natural knowledge participated in by men." On the other hand, Aquinas notes, the enlightening can be understood to happen by the light of grace, and this in three ways. Origen understood "enlightens" to mean the grace of faith admitting people to the reconciled world of the Church. Chrysostom understands "enlightens" by reference to the Word wanting all to come to knowledge of the truth about God and to be saved. Augustine explains the enlightening as the effect of the Word but only in those who receive the light of saving knowledge from Christ in a dark and perverse world.

Dupuis concluded that the universally operative Logos enlightens and inspires founders and adherents of non-Christian religions at the same time as the same Logos, as incarnate, fulfills that enlightening and becomes present in divine love as redeemer within a humanity that was created through "him" in the first place. The divine Word incarnate, Jesus the Christ, is at once the particular, historical man who taught, suffered, died and rose from the dead, and the universal Logos immanent in and active upon the cosmos, within human history, and in the lives of non-Christians.

In defending Dupuis against some theologians' misreadings, Gerald O'Collins pointed out that Dupuis's texts did not separate the universal Logos from the incarnate Logos. Instead, maintained O'Collins, "What Dupuis has consistently argued is that within the one person of Jesus Christ we must distinguish the operations of his (uncreated) divine nature and his (created) human nature. Here he lines up," O'Collins continued, "with St. Thomas Aquinas who championed the oneness of Christ's person but also had to recognize that Christ's divine nature infinitely transcends his human nature (*divina natura in infinitum humanam excedit*), *Summa Contra Gentiles*, 4, 35,8."[56] According to O'Collins, Dupuis was arguing that the Chalcedonian affirmation of Jesus' divine nature means that "the Word's divine operations are not canceled or restricted by his assumption of a human existence that has now been glorified through the resurrection."[57] I will follow Dupuis's distinction between the original, invisible, constant, and universal divine operation of the Logos and the particular, though central and eschatologically universal, operation of the Logos through the humanity of Jesus of Nazareth. However, I will turn in addition to the creating power of the Logos.

LOGOS AS CREATOR

The affirmation of Jesus' distinct divine nature can be turned from the nature/grace question of God's saving action in non-Christian religions to the origin of social justice in the Creator/creature relationship. Dupuis once mentioned "mediation in creation" by the Logos as an act that

---

56. Gerald O'Collins, "Jacques Dupuis," 24. Quotation also from an electronic version of Gerald O'Collins's "The Dupuis Case," gratefully received in an email from Daniel Kendall, October 13, 2010.

57. O'Collins, "Jacques Dupuis," 26.

transcends the human nature of Jesus.⁵⁸ Yet he never explored the theological consequences of the creating work of the Logos. I note some of these consequences in the following six steps. First, seven New Testament passages attribute divine agency in creating to the Logos (John 1:1–4) and to Christ (1 Cor 8:6; 2 Cor 5:17; Eph 2:15; Col 1:15–20; Heb 1:1–4; Rev 3:14). This became a standard, formal part of Church tradition enshrined in the creedal profession that "through him all things have come to be."

The second step is realization that the creating agency of the Logos did not, could not, cease and desist at the Incarnation. Indeed, Paul proclaimed that, "there is one Lord Jesus Christ through whom all things come and through whom we exist" (1 Cor 8:6), and Hebrews 1:3 exclaimed about Jesus "sustaining the universe by his powerful command."⁵⁹ These statements attribute creating to Jesus, it is true. How could that be, since Jesus is a visible human being? John's Gospel provided the answer: the self-evidently human Jesus not only acted with divine authority and rose in divine power but is the divine Logos who became flesh. In Chalcedonian terms, Who Jesus is upholds the universe, but through his divine, not his human, nature.

That the Incarnation did not interrupt or halt the creating agency of the Logos is the gist of a brief reflection by Athanasius in *On the Incarnation*. Speaking of Jesus as the Logos incarnate, Athanasius declares

> For He was not, as might be imagined, circumscribed in the body, nor, while present in the body, was He absent elsewhere; nor, while He moved the body, was the universe left void of His working and Providence. . . . He was, without inconsistency, quickening the universe as well, and was in every process of nature, and was outside the whole, He was none the less manifest from the working of the universe as well.⁶⁰

The divine creating agency of the Logos, Athanasius says, did not cease at the Incarnation.

---

58. Dupuis, "Universality of the Word and Particularity of Jesus Christ," 334.

59. O'Collins observes that Pauline and Deuteropauline letters attributed creation to Christ (1 Cor 8:6; 2 Cor 5:17; Eph 2:10, 2:15; Col 1:15–17; Heb 1:1–3a) before John's Gospel circulated in final form; see "Jesus as Lord and Teacher," in John C. Cavadini and Laura Holt, eds., *Who Do You Say That I Am? Confessing the Mystery of Christ* (Notre Dame, IN: University of Notre Dame Press, 2004) 51–61 at 56.

60. Athanasius, *On the Incarnation of the Word*, trans. Archibald Robertson, in Philip Schaff and Henry Wace, eds., *Nicene and Post-Nicene Fathers, Second Series*, vol. 4 (Buffalo, NY: Christian Literature Publishing, 1892) ch. 17.1–2, rev. ed. by Kevin Knight, 2009, http://www.newadvent.org/fathers/2802.htm.

A Man of the Church

The third step in my presentation of the consequences of the creating work of the Logos involves recognizing that creating is the divine operation of the Logos least conceivable as an act and attribute of Jesus' human nature. The role of the divine Logos's in mediating, with the Spirit, the act of creation that stems from the Father cannot be transferred to, mediated by, participated in, or enacted by, the human nature of Jesus. Jesus the Logos acted in and through his full, free humanity when he performed miracles of healing, changed water to wine at Cana, walked on the water or calmed the sea, he forgave and remitted sins with divine authority, initiated the Lord's Supper with an unheard-of change in the sacred meal of the Pasch, and breathed the Holy Spirit upon his disciples after the resurrection (John 20:22–23). These are referred to as Jesus' theandric acts.

One can conceive theandric acts, as did Aquinas, in terms of a divine principal cause acting with and through a free, intelligent, human, conjoined instrumental cause in a combined causality producing an effect beyond the capacity of the human instrumental cause by itself. Jesus' human subjectivity, freedom, imagination, speaking, and so forth are human realities able to be drawn into service of the divine operation of the Logos and so to bring about effects beyond the capacity of his humanity that are due to divine power. However, creating by the Logos cannot be a theandric activity in which the human nature of Jesus serves as instrumental cause for his divine nature and person acting as principal cause.[61] The humanness of Jesus' human nature includes its being created. Being created means existing in constitutive difference from the creating source; creatures are not the Creator since they have come to be, and the Creator has brought them to be. Jesus' individual humanity shares the limits of all created reality. The created cannot create itself much less anything else. Jesus' human nature was created through, and exists in dependence on, his creating act as Logos.

Of course, in Chalcedon's definition of faith, both human nature and divine nature are heuristic concepts rather than comprehensive, closed definitions. It follows that whatever is proper to human nature—even if we do not understand what that is in completeness—is inherent in Christ's human nature. Likewise, whatever is proper to God, divinity, and the

---

61. Aquinas denies that any creature can act principally or instrumentally in creating: "since creation is not from any pre-existing material to be rendered or prepared by an instrumental cause's action . . . for creative action to be attributed to any creature is impossible, either by its own proper power or instrumentally as a minister." Thomas Aquinas, *Summa theologiae*, vol. 8, *Creation, Variety and Evil (Ia. 44–49)*, ed. and trans. Thomas Gilby, OP (London: Blackfriars, 1967) 47 (*ST* Ia, q. 45, a. 5).

Logos—and we have not come to the end of grasping what that is—belongs to the divine nature of Christ. The divine nature of the Logos is the Logos acting. We do receive as true, nonetheless, that, as the prologue to the Gospel of John says, the Logos brings into existence that which has come to be. Therefore, creating cannot be separated from Christ's divine nature. The distinction between the divine person Who is the Logos and the divine nature of Jesus is a convenient, human mental distinction. The distinction between the divine and human natures in Jesus is a real distinction in Jesus.

When Chalcedon affirmed the "distinctive character of each nature being preserved," it professed that the Logos did not lose anything proper to divinity by assuming a human nature. The divine kenosis described in Philippians 2:6–11 refers to withholding manifestation of divinity, sovereignty, and power. Kenosis withheld a manifestation of divine effects, in the humanity of Jesus first of all, but was not loss of divinity. If the Logos had, in its kenosis, left behind the action of creating, then the divine nature of the Logos would have changed because of the hypostatic union, just what Chalcedon rejected in affirming that each of the two natures remains unchanged, *atreptos*.

The fourth step in drawing out the consequences of the creating work of the Logos affirms that the Logos's agency in creating is the divine act that is the ultimate principle of social justice. Indeed, Christ, the incarnate (*ensarkos*) Logos acting universally (*asarkos*) in the power of his divine nature so as to mediate the act of creation constitutes the ultimate and universal principle of social justice for Christians and non-Christians alike. All societies and all religions, not only Christianity, have seeds of social justice sown in their people by the Logos. As Creator, the Logos always and everywhere is that on Whom all creation depends, and that from Whom human nature is constituted in self-presence, that is, in the natural light of human reason, in distinction from its fulfillment through faith in Jesus. The universally and continually active Creator Logos who is Jesus the Christ must be the sole immanent divine source of order in the cosmos and history and, therefore in the social dimension of human existence.

CREATING IS ORDERING

The fifth step begins by asking why this must be so. The continuance of the creating work of Christ, the Logos-become-flesh, is an ordering principle because creation is not chaos, or rather, according to contemporary understanding, chaos has the potential for emergent order. The meaning of order in the physical universe will not be discussed here but has been a theme in dialogue between science and religion. The omnipresent, immanent activity of the Logos as Creator revealed in John's Gospel implies that the Logos is also the source of order in creation, in whatever way order can be understood. Christ as creating Logos (*asarkos*) is the ultimate source of existence and order in all creation in its every dimension, including human socio-historical existence that also flows so obviously from very concrete, historically accessible human beings. The Logos creates everything that comes to be, including human beings who in their self-transcending acts of intentional consciousness directed toward the good of order are the proximate source of social justice. Creaturely dependence on the Logos extends to the human capacity to generate meaning, and so reaches to conscience and concern for the common good, for the well-being of all members of a society. Social justice has its human inception here. Thus, in creating humanity the Logos is the source, too, of the proximate ordering principle in a society.

The concept of order probably has to be reclaimed from guilt by association with the concept of control, and Lonergan does just this in chapter 2 of *Method*, which is on the human good. He explains that in groups there is cooperation through institutions (family, mores, society, education, state, law, economy, technology, church) with defined and assigned roles and tasks carried out by individuals for the sake of the good of order. The paradigm of order is not an externally imposed unity, direction, and purpose, but a structured, intrinsic unity in multiple operations by an individual or a group. In an individual physical health is order. In a community, regular and successful cooperation for common objectives to the benefit of all and each is the good of order. Spontaneity depends on order and then sometimes reorders.

SOCIAL JUSTICE IS SOCIAL ORDERING

The good of order in a society can be achieved neither by anti-institutional anarchy, nor by a single institution or person controlling all social authority, nor by carefully designed institutions or policies that nevertheless do not result in beneficial effects. To the contrary, one can argue that achieving the good of order depends on, and instantiates, among other things, realizing a substantial degree of social justice. Social justice is crucial because the good of order involves the effective functioning of a society's be stirred to expand its scope from the visible economy of redemption centered in Jesus' humanity to affirmative cooperation with the universal action of the Logos Who Jesus is, cooperation to be sought in dialogue with adherents of other religions, or of none. Thus, Christian faith does not stop at the limits of Christ's humanity and of Christianity but casts its obedient gaze to everything coming from his divine nature, too, including creating and ordering within human history under the influence of human self-transcendence in intentional consciousness.

The Christological premise for indifference or resistance to social justice is either a tacit "Nestorian" separation between the divine and human natures of Jesus, as if not joined in the person of the Word-Logos, or a view, perhaps an extreme kenoticism, of Christ's divine nature as having changed in the Incarnation by losing or alienating the divine power to create. But to accept Chalcedon is to accept the inseparability of faith in Jesus from discipleship involving commitment to the social justice to which the Creator Logos continually labors by drawing human beings into their created capacity for self-transcending reason and love in social existence. Chalcedonian dogma clarifies the Christological ground for an impulse and mandate arising within faith for seeking dialogue and cooperation with any who promote social justice that institutionalizes human self-transcendence, a self-transcendence Christians believe is due to the Creator Logos through Whom all has come to be that has come to be.

12

"He Will Baptize You with the Holy Spirit": Recovering a Metaphor for a Contemporary Pneumatological Soteriology

D. LYLE DABNEY

THE METAPHOR OF "BAPTISM with the Holy Spirit" has never played a major role in the history of western theology. In the debates of the last century, however, attention to this trope has increased conspicuously. Developing themes in the Wesleyan tradition, the nineteenth-century Holiness Movement claimed that, in light of the Pentecost narrative in Acts 2, there was a "second work of divine grace" in a baptism with the Holy Spirit subsequent to forensic justification. And that interpretation of the metaphor then became pronounced in a new way with the rise of Pentecostalism early in the twentieth century. This claim has continued to figure prominently in the Pneumatology of the Charismatic movement. Catholic Charismatics like Kilian McDonnell and George Montague, for instance, have sought to steer the interpretation of the metaphor into the well-worn traces of their own tradition by insisting that, according to scripture and the Church Fathers, the notion belongs properly not to that which follows salvation but rather to the beginning of the event of becoming Christian itself. Thus the "general conclusion" of their book *Christian Initiation and Baptism in the Holy Spirit* states that "Christian initiation, modeled on the baptism of Jesus or on his death and resurrection, involved essentially the gift of the Holy Spirit."[1] But attention to this

---

[1] Kilian McDonnell and George T. Montague, *Christian Initiation and Baptism in*

trope in the last few decades has by no means been limited to Pentecostals and Charismatics. In the last fragment of the *Church Dogmatics* published during his lifetime, the Reformed theologian Karl Barth proposed precisely this metaphor as that which properly encompassed the basis of all our becoming Christian. Epitomizing much of his own tradition, he summed up his argument with the statement: "We thus maintain that the power of the divine change in which the event of the foundation of the Christian life of specific men takes place is the power of their baptism with the Holy Spirit."[2] In the twentieth century, therefore, the metaphor of "baptism with the Holy Spirit" has emerged in a new way, and the new interpretation of this trope by Pentecostals emphasizing subsequence to salvation has been accompanied by new statements of the Catholic and Protestant traditions stressing initiation into the same.

My argument in the following is quite simply that neither of these interpretations of the metaphor of "baptism in the Holy Spirit" are adequate either to the witness of scripture or to the challenge of giving account of salvation through Jesus Christ today. My thesis is that this metaphor is central to the witness of the New Testament to God's salvation of God's creation through Christ, and, properly understood, should be central to our witness to God's Gospel in the social world in which we now find ourselves. Baptism in the Holy Spirit, therefore, is best understood as neither that which merely leads to nor follows after a forensically conceived salvation. It speaks, rather, of the entirety of salvation itself, and as such, it bespeaks a new and different soteriological conceptuality than the traditional interpretations: resurrection and the new creation of all things. The recovery of such a language of Pneumatological redemption, I contend, is of first importance for any Christian theology that will "act its age" today. In the following, then, I will first examine the metaphor of baptism with the Holy Spirit in the context of the Pneumatology of the New Testament and then seek to demonstrate how this opens up a way of speaking of God's salvation of God's creation through Jesus Christ and in the Spirit that is faithful to both God's Word and God's world today.

---

the Holy Spirit. Evidence from the First Eight Centuries, First, Emended Edition (Collegeville, MN: Liturgical, 1991) 316.

2 Karl Barth, *CD* IV/4, 3–40, 30.

A Man of the Church

THE METAPHOR IN THE CONTEXT OF THE WITNESS OF THE NEW TESTAMENT

The fundamental question in the interpretation of this metaphor is where to begin. Pentecostals and many Charismatics—as well as the Holiness movement before them— have begun their talk about baptism in the Holy Spirit with the story about the eschatological "pouring out" of the Spirit on the day of Pentecost in Acts 2, and have interpreted this as sanctification or empowerment subsequent to justification. Without ignoring that narrative, the Catholic and Protestant traditions, on the other hand, have tended to concentrate on the gospel story of the baptism of Jesus in the Jordan river and the descent of the Holy Spirit upon him in the form of a dove, and have interpreted this in terms of the initiation of the process or event of justification. In the following I suggest that the place to properly come to understand this metaphor is neither with Jesus at the Jordan nor with his disciples in Jerusalem, but rather with John the Baptist in the wilderness. All four canonical gospels preface the testing and public ministry of Jesus Christ with the appearance of John and with the words with which the Baptist announces the coming of the one greater than he: "I have baptized you with water," John declares in Mark's formulation of the saying (1:8), "but he will baptize you with the Holy Spirit." With this metaphor Mark and all the other gospels introduce and summarize the person and work of Jesus Christ. As such, it is the conceptual framework in which both the descent of the Spirit upon Jesus at the Jordan and the outpouring of the Spirit upon the disciples at Pentecost are to be properly interpreted.

But before we look at the descent of the Spirit at the Jordan upon Jesus and again at Pentecost upon the disciples in light of John the Baptist's definition of the coming one, let's place this metaphor in the context of what we might call the "logic" of New Testament Pneumatology. As Friedrich Wilhelm Horn has demonstrated, the perspective which informs the New Testament's witness to God's Spirit is the Easter faith of earliest Christianity.[3] Against the twofold background of traditional Jewish prayers such as the "Eighteen Benedictions" (Shemoneh 'Esreh), the second of which confesses the "God who brings the dead to life," and such Old Testament texts as Ezekiel 37, in which the Spirit of God is portrayed as the

---

3 F. W. Horn, *Das Angeld des Geistes. Studien zur paulinischen Pneumatologie*, (Göttingen: Vandenhoeck & Ruprecht, 1992); idem, "Holy Spirit," *ABD*, vol. 3, 1992, 260–80, 267. Further, see Dieter Müller, *Geisterfahrung und Totenauferweckung. Untersuchungen zur Totenauferweckung bei Paulus und in den ihm vorgegebenen Überlieferungen*, Dr. Theol. Dissertation, Christian-Albrechts-Universität at Kiel, 1980.

eschatological life-giving Spirit whom God would breath anew upon the dry bones of his people and raise them from their graves to new life, the earliest Christian communities interpreted the resurrection of Jesus as an act of the Spirit of God.[4] Thus, in texts such as Romans 1:3–4, I Timothy 3:16, and I Peter 3:18 we see examples of fragments of very early hymns and/or credos, each of which, contrasting σάρξ and πνεῦμα, emphasize that it is by the power of God's Spirit that Jesus Christ has been raised from the dead. For example, if Christ "was put to death μὲν σαρκί," recites I Peter, he "was made alive δὲ πνεύματι." Paul, of course, can couch the whole of the Gospel of God in precisely these terms: God's Son "was descended from David κατὰ σάρκα and designated Son of God in power κατὰ πνεῦμα ἁγιωσύνης by his resurrection from the dead." According to the witness of the New Testament, therefore, it is by the Holy Spirit that God has raised Jesus Christ from the dead.

It is in this context of the logic of New Testament Pneumatology that the metaphor of "baptism in the Holy Spirit" can best be understood. Even those who would most vigorously contend for the historicity of the traditions concerning Jesus in the New Testament would acknowledge that the Gospels are by no means merely "video tapes" of the past, a bare, "objective" recounting of a set of past words and deeds and events. Rather, they are clearly theological redactions that lay claim to and interpret earlier Jesus traditions from the perspective afforded by later traditions, specifically, from the perspective of the witness of earliest Christianity to the resurrection of Jesus Christ. It was that perspective, the early church believed, that opened up the true identity and work of Jesus of Nazareth. This shapes the witness of the gospels to the Spirit of God in their accounts of the life, death, and resurrection of Jesus Christ. Thus Mark, the earliest of the Gospels, structures the prologue to his account of Jesus (1:2–13) in such a way that he frames the whole of his narrative in terms of the life-giving Spirit: John the Baptist testifies that the Coming One will baptize in that Spirit (vv. 2–8), the appearance of Jesus is marked by baptism, descent of that Spirit and God's voice hailing him as "Son" (vv 9–11), and that Spirit then drives the Anointed One into the wilderness to be tested (vv 12–13). The story of God's redemption of God's creation, therefore, is not simply the narrative of Jesus' death on the cross; it is the story of the whole life, death, and resurrection of Christ, told from the perspective of God's eschatological act of new creation in the power of the Spirit.

---

4 See F. W. Horn, *Das Angeld des Geistes*, 92f.

A Man of the Church

Telling their story from this perspective, all four Evangelists frame their narratives of Jesus Christ by defining the salvation he realizes in terms of Pneumatology. "I have baptized you with water," John the Baptist is depicted as declaring, "but he will baptize you with the Holy Spirit" (Mk 1:8 par).[5] With this metaphor Mark and the other Evangelists sum up all the ministry of Jesus Christ as a mediation of the Spirit. The metaphor both relates Jesus to John and differentiates him from the Baptist. Like the Baptist, his ministry will consist in a ministry of "baptism," an act of dousing with or inundating/immersing in a medium of cleansing and new life; unlike John, Jesus' metaphorical baptism will not be one of repentance and anticipation, but of fulfillment, indeed precisely the fulfillment of the promise that God would pour out his Spirit upon all his people that we find in Old Testament texts such as Isaiah 44:3, Ezekiel 39:29, and Joel 2:28f. Thus the Evangelists depict Jesus of Nazareth as the Christ, the one in whom and through whom Israel's true hopes for redemption are realized, the one who mediates the eschatological outpouring of the Spirit of God that results in the new creation of all things.

What is important to recognize here is that, according to the Evangelists, Jesus' mediation of the life-giving Spirit is not to be understood as an act simply occurring at the beginning of or subsequent to his life, death, and resurrection;[6] but is rather precisely the sum of all that is

---

[5] After being largely ignored in the scholarly literature, and then examined only in terms of historical-critical questions, this logion has in recent years begun to be the subject of theological consideration. See J. Daryl Charles, "'The Coming One'/'Stronger One' and His Baptism: Matt 3:11-12, Mark 1:8, Luke 3:16-17," *Pneuma* 11 (1989), 37-49; Simon Légasse, "L'autre 'baptême' (Mc 1,8; Mt 3,11; Lc 3:16; Jn 1,26.31-33)," in: F. van Segbroek et al. (eds.), *The Four Gospels*, (Louvain: Peeters, 1992), 257-273; Claude Coulot, "'Il vous baptisera d'Esprit Saint': le logion de Jean-Baptiste sur les deux baptêmes (Mc 1,7-8; Mt 3,11; Lc 3:16; Jn 1,26.27.33)," in: Raymond Kuntzmann (ed.), *Ce Dieu qui vient: études sur l'Ancien et le Nouveau Testament: offertes au professeur Bernard Renaud à l'occasion de son soixante-cinquième anniversaire*, (Paris: Cerf, 1995), 291-305; and above all, R. Alastair Campbell, "Jesus and His Baptism," *Tyndale Bulletin* 47 (1996) 191-214.

[6] And this is the typical mistake that is made in both the exegetical and systematic discussions of this metaphor. See, for example, Morna Hooker, *The Gospel according to Saint Mark*, 38, who represents a signal advance over most commentators in that she draws attention to the parallels Mark assumes between Jesus' baptism and that of those who follow Jesus such as is narrated in Acts 2. Nevertheless she fails to consider the fact that the salvation that Jesus is said to bring, the 'baptism in the Holy Spirit,' is precisely that which he himself undergoes. Cp the more typical exegesis of Robert Guelich, Mark 1:8-26, (WBC, 34a) (Dallas: Word, 1989) 24ff., where his interpretation (with extensive bibliography) is that this 'baptism' is to be understood simply as the forgiveness of sins rather than realizing that Mark tells the story in exactly the

communicated to us in his life and work and death and resurrection. For the "baptism with the Spirit" that Jesus Christ mediates begins with Jesus' own baptism; indeed, it is precisely as the "One Baptized in the Holy Spirit" that he is the "One who Baptizes in the Holy Spirit." In his baptism he is himself anointed by the Spirit that descends upon him as he is declared God's Son, and as a consequence of his baptism he is driven into the wilderness to be tested by Satan. And for Mark, this "testing" is not simply that period preceding his public ministry; it is that which defines the whole of his story. From the wilderness (1:12-13) to the villages of Caesarea Philippi (8:27ff., esp 33: "Get behind me, Satan!") to the garden (14:32ff., esp 36: "yet not what I will, but what you will . . . ") to his trial in the courtyard of the high priest (14:53ff.) and of Pilate (15:1ff.) to the cross (15:21ff., esp 30: ". . . save yourself, and come down from the cross!"), Jesus is tested, tried, and tempted. But unlike the first Adam or the Israel of old, this Baptized One, this second Adam and true Israel, makes manifest what it means to be God's Son: in his teaching on hillside and synagogue, in his encounters with evil spirits and the accusations of the leaders of his own people, in his acts of healing and feeding and forgiveness, in his betrayal and judgment and crucifixion that is to be understood as nothing less than Jesus giving "his life as a ransom for many" (10:45), and in his resurrection from the dead. In all of this, the life-giving Spirit of the resurrection is at work in the new creation of all things through a new baptism in the Holy Spirit. This is precisely the language Jesus employs to speak of his ministry as he rebukes his disciples' efforts to gain for themselves positions of favor in the kingdom: "Are you able to drink the cup that I drink, or to be baptized with the baptism that I am baptized with?" he asks (10:38). And in answer to his own question he declares that his disciples will indeed be baptized in the very baptism with which he is himself baptized (10:39), they will themselves be "driven into the wilderness" to be "tested" where their new humanity in the Spirit will emerge and God's new creation of all things will begin to be made known in proclamation and prayer, in suffering and glory, and in resurrection and death. Each of these individual events as well as the story as a whole are to be understood as the emergence of the end in the midst of the middle of history, as the eschatological outpouring

---

opposite way: the forgiveness of sins (2:1-12) is to be understood within the overarching category of the baptism in the Holy Spirit (1:8). A notable exception to all this is the very suggestive article by R. Alastair Campbell, "Jesus and His Baptism" who not only recognizes that this baptism in the Spirit is central to Jesus' own identity and work in the Gospels but also asks the question to which such a recognition drives one: how then are we to understand the cross in the light of Jesus' baptism?

of God's Spirit in which and through which judgment and new creation appears in the midst of the old. The story of Christ, therefore, is not simply the story of the *means* by which we are saved, it the revelation of the very *substance* of God's salvation itself in the eschatological personage of the Son of God, the re-creation of creation in the new creation of Jesus Christ's life, death and resurrection.

In the history of the Christian theological tradition, various aspects of the being and work of Christ have been pointed to as central for God's salvation of God's creature.[7] Broadly speaking, the Orthodox have emphasized the incarnation in which the Son assumes our humanity and grants us his divinity, the West has emphasized the death of Christ on the cross as the event in which God's wrath is assuaged and God's favor won, while modern Protestant theology has emphasized the example and teachings of Jesus of Nazareth. And within and across these divisions there have been various voices emphasizing being or intellect or will. Viewed from the perspective of "baptism in the Holy Spirit" as new creation in the Spirit of the resurrection, all of these are understood to be part of God's redemption of God's creation. For the life and death and resurrection of Christ *in toto* and not *in partu* is the mediation of a new gift of the Spirit, a "baptism" in the Holy Spirit, by which we are made children of God in Christ, by which we are called into discipleship to Christ and taught his ways, by which we are fed in the wilderness and rescued from the storm, by which our sins are forgiven and our bodies healed, and by which we are led into and through suffering and death to new and eternal life. This redemption is indeed an act of the pure and undeserved grace of the God who is Father, Son, and Holy Spirit; but it is an act that includes rather than excludes us from the life of God in the world. For the Spirit that the life of the Son mediates to us is precisely the Spirit who mediates our life to the Son. Just as the baptism in the Spirit brings forth the Word of God in Jesus Christ in the whole of his life, death, and resurrection, by which creation is taken up in

---

7 For that history, see Albrecht Ritschl, *The Christian doctrine of justification and reconciliation; the positive development of the doctrine*, H. R. Mackintosh & A. B. Macaulay (trans/eds), (Clifton, N.J., Reference Book Publishers, 1966); T. H. Hughes, *The Atonement. Modern Theories of the Doctrine*, (London, 1949); Hans Kessler, *Die theologische Bedeutung des Todes Jesu. Eine traditionsgeschichtliche Untersuchung*, (Düsseldorf: Patmos-Verlag, 1970); Gunther Wenz, *Geschichte der Versöhnungslehre in der evangelischken Theologie der Neuzeit*, 2 vols, (München: Chr. Kaiser, 1984–1986); Vernon White, *Atonement and Incarnation. An Essay on Universalism and Particularity*, (Cambridge: Cambridge University Press, 1991). For texts from the western tradition and an excellent bibliography, see Gerhard Sauter, ed., *Versöhnung als Thema der Theologie* (München/Gütersloh: Chr. Kaiser/Gütersloher, 1996).

a new act of re-creation, so our lives become part of God's emergent new creation in faithful words and telling deeds.

THE METAPHOR IN THE CONTEXT OF GOD'S WORLD TODAY

In our world today, I would suggest, rendering such an account of the Gospel is both faithful to God and telling for our age. The two major forms of theology, those of Scholasticism and the Reformation, that have dominated the western tradition were products of Christendom, an age that assumed a form of cultural Christianity with the Church defined as an established ecclesiastical institution having to do with the problem of divine judgment in eternity upon human sin in time. The question over which these two kinds of theology struggled was *how* God's grace in Christ was mediated now for the forgiveness of sin then. Representatives of theologies of the first sort contended that this grace is then mediated through divinely ordained channels of sacramental action, resulting in the capacities of human nature being fulfilled by grace, while representatives of theologies of the second kind have protested that such grace is mediated through the proclamation of a divinely revealed Evangel, resulting in sinful human nature being contradicted by the declaration of divine grace. Each, as I have argued elsewhere, subordinated the work of the Spirit, the one to that of the Father and other to that of the Son.[8]

But we now live in a world of "post-Christendom," an age which does not assume Christianity but rather asserts cultural and religious pluralism, an age that has forgotten the ancient language of sin but has discovered anew the specter of death. And in this context we must learn again to "act our age," to listen to and give account of the Gospel in a manner appropriate to the age in which we now find ourselves. This then is nothing less than an opportunity for Christianity to re-discover the Gospel of Jesus Christ, to discover that the issue is not just guilt but death and thus the question is not just *How?*—*How is* God's grace mediated to us?—but *What?*—*What is* the Gospel of Jesus Christ? *What* is the grace of God in Christ all about? *What* is the redemption of which we speak and in which we hope? Now this is not to dismiss the question of "how," but it is to realize that the terms in which that question was debated and the forms in which the theologies

---

8 See my lecture, "Starting with the Spirit: Why the Last Should Now Be First," in Pickard, Steven & Preece, Gordon, ed., *Starting with the Spirit*, (Hindmarsh, Australia: Australian Theological Forum. 2001) 3–27.

of grace were promulgated in Christendom are no longer adequate—any more than the terms of the theological debates of the Patristic era were adequate in themselves of the Medieval or Reformation eras. The question of how God's grace is mediated to us must now be taken up anew in the context of a better understanding of what that grace consists of: the new creation of all things in a resurrection of the dead through the baptism in the Holy Spirit by Jesus Christ.

It is that question of *What?* that enables us to act our age and give account of God's Gospel in the situation in which we now find ourselves. We live today in a social world that defines itself in terms of the second law of thermodynamics, one implication of which is that all forms of energy are constantly decaying into lower forms, from the first explosion of energy in the big bang to its final vague memory in the defuse glow and distant echo that will be the end of the space/time event of the cosmos. Our world views itself, therefore, as a part of a universe in which all things will inexorably end in death and destruction. In the midst of such an age we proclaim in word and deed the emergence of the event of the new creation of all things, witnessed in Jesus Christ and witnessed to by the community of Christians around the world. And it is in the context of such a proclamation that we can rightly speak of sin, for the forgiveness of sins is neither an act of merit nor of substitution but of new creation. When the God who said "'Let there be light'; and there was light" (Gen 1:3) says "your sins are forgiven" (Mark 2:5), the result is not simply a forensic declaration of guiltlessness but a new creation in God's righteousness. For by God's Spirit God's Word accomplishes what it commands.[9]

In conclusion: as I stated at the beginning of this essay, the metaphor of "baptism in the Holy Spirit" has never played a major role in the history of western theology. But as I hope I have demonstrated: it should. In a world at one and the same time both "postmodern" and post-Christendom," this metaphor should be recovered and figure prominently in a Pneumatological soteriology as an act of both faithfulness to God's word and faithfulness to God's world.

---

9 See Hans Küng, *Justification: The Doctrine of Karl Barth and a Catholic Reflection*, with a new introductory chapter by the author and the original response of Karl Barth, T. Collins, E. E. Tolk, and D. Granskou, trans. (Philadelphia: Westminster, [1981] c1964).

13

A Chaste Marriage: Matthias Scheeben's (Western) Doctrine of Deification

RICHARD J. BARRY

INTRODUCTION

ACCORDING TO THE MOST common theory, incongruity is at the root of all humor: it is an unexpected and welcome twist on the mundane. If this is true, then one might say that joyful laughter echoes in Ralph Del Colle's work, a mirthfulness that is profoundly appropriate to Christian theology. Who is this man who appreciates and celebrates the ideas of fiery Pentecostals and dusty neo-scholastics, sometimes on the very same page? So faithfully Catholic, so broad-minded and inquisitive, full of charismatic fervor and dogmatic precision, candid about his convictions, with warmth and charity . . . it may not seem to fit together, and yet here he is. One can only praise the Creator of such an extravagantly unexpected world, and thank him for giving Dr. Del Colle the grace to be a man of inspiring incongruity. The Church is forever blessed.

Another theologian who had a flair for the unexpected is Matthias Scheeben (1835–1888). Twenty years ago, at a time when Scheeben had been long forgotten by theologians writing in English, Dr. Del Colle was virtually alone in appreciating and developing his work.[1] Today Scheeben

---

1. Ralph Del Colle, *Christ and the Spirit: Spirit-Christology in Trinitarian Perspective* (Oxford: Oxford University Press, 1994) especially chapter 2; "Neo-Scholasticism,"

is finding new admirers, thanks in part to Dr. Del Colle's efforts. I offer this essay, therefore, with profound appreciation and gratitude to an outstanding mentor, Ralph Del Colle.

THE RHYTHMS OF RETRIEVAL

When reading accounts of twentieth-century theology, one sometimes gets the impression that the *ressourcement* movement's rediscovery of the church fathers was unprecedented. Without denying the richness of this recent "return to the sources," it must also be said that the history of Christian theology very often takes on a pattern of controversy, retrieval, and development. For example, in the mid-fourteenth century, a fissure opened in Byzantine society. At the center of the "Hesychast controversy" was a theological question: whether or not true, transformative union with God—deification—is possible in this life. Gregory Palamas, by turning to the church fathers—especially the Cappadocians—fruitfully defended the Hesychast method of prayer and redevelop the largely dormant theology of deification by grounding it in an "essence/energies distinction."[2] Or, to cite a second example of controversy, retrieval, and development, this time from the nineteenth century: hoping to free theology from the lingering dusk of rationalism which had lately enveloped Catholic thought, Matthias Joseph Scheeben also turned to the church fathers—especially Irenaeus, Athanasius, and Cyril of Alexandria—to revive a theory of "the supernatural," with special attention to deification. Or, third, more recently still, to differentiate Eastern mystical theology from Western scholasticism, and to rejuvenate an atrophied Orthodox theological tradition, Eastern theologians in the twentieth century turned again to Gregory Palamas, enthusiastically embracing the essence/energies distinction as the outstanding feature of the Orthodox tradition.

In each example, present-day disagreements inspired the return to a shared history in an effort to trace a solution. Each example also relates

---

The Blackwell Companion to Nineteenth-Century Theology (2010) 375–394; "An Ontology of the Supernatural: The Contribution of the 'Lyrical Scholasticism' of Matthias Scheeben to Charismatic/Pentecostal Theology with Reference to the Latter Rain Movement," in *Festschrift in Honor of Vinson Synan*, ed. David Moore and Chris Emerick (Cleveland, TN: CPT Press, forthcoming).

2. For a detailed history of the controversy, see Norman Russell, "Theosis and Gregory Palamas: Continuity or Doctrinal Change?," *St. Vladimir's Theological Quarterly* 50 (2006) 357.

more or less directly to the key soteriological doctrine of deification.³ But of these three examples, Matthias Scheeben's efforts in a Catholic context will be less known, and less expected, because one component of the neo-Palamite polemic is the claim that the West does not have the theological resources necessary to sustain a genuine and robust doctrine of deification. Scheeben represents a possible counter-example.⁴

This paper begins with a general overview of the neo-Palamite approach to deification, with special emphasis on its critique of Western theology. This will lead into a detailed consideration of Scheeben's own writing on grace and deification—which precedes neo-Palamism by almost a century—looking specifically at the developments in his earliest major works, *Nature and Grace* and *Mysteries of Christianity*. The goal will be to discover in Scheeben the contours of a doctrine of deification that both takes advantage of the unique and enduring insights of the Latin tradition and is also ontologically rich enough to satisfy Eastern critics.

DOUBTS ABOUT A WESTERN DOCTRINE OF DEIFICATION

In a 1925 encyclopedia article, an Augustinian monk named Martin Jugie argued that the Palamite "real distinction" between God's essence and

---

3. A definition of Θέωσις—sometimes translated theosis, deification, or divinization—would be desirable here, but one of the difficulties with this doctrine is that, from the beginning, it has been understood in various ways. In the introduction of his celebrated history on the development of the doctrine in the Greek patristic tradition, Norman Russell says that Dionysius the Areopagite supplies the first "formal definition" of the word. Denys says, "'Deification is the attaining of likeness to God and union with him so far as is possible,'" Norman Russell, The Doctrine of Deification in the Greek Patristic Tradition (Oxford University Press, USA, 2006) 1. These two components, attaining likeness and union, are fundamental whenever the word is used. The biblical text most immediately associated with the doctrine draws attention to another key component: 2 Peter 1:4 says that through God's promises we "become partakers in the divine nature." The idea of "participation," then, is also central. But, as Russell shows, the interrelated themes of likeness, union, and participation that come together in this doctrine are understood as being more or less metaphysically serious, some giving a "nominal" interpretation, seeing it as simply a "title of honor," and others (especially later in the tradition) favoring a "realistic" interpretation, which affirms true ontological union with God (Russell, 1–2).

4. Aidan Nichols, after an exhaustive study, is able to suggest that Scheeben "is above all a theologian of human deification, a singer of the 'glories of divine grace' . . . ." *Romance and System: The Theological Synthesis of Matthias Joseph Scheeben*, 1st ed. (Augustine Institute, 2010) 287.

energies was a "veritable heresy."[5] Although Palamas had been largely overlooked in recent centuries,[6] a generation of young Orthodox theologians swiftly rose to defend their beleaguered saint, and in the process found a theological method that helped differentiate the Eastern approach. Generally speaking, the basic question that caused the debate between Palamas and Barlaam the Calabrian in the fourteenth century was whether the monks of Mount Athos were, in contemplative prayer, able to "obtain a vision of the Divine Light,"[7] and through this vision, enjoy union with God, transfiguration and deification of mind and body.[8] This question expanded into a wider dispute over whether or in what sense "participation in the divine nature" was possible.

A. N. Williams helpfully points out that any Christian model of deification must negotiate two poles: acknowledgement of an "unbreachable divide" between the transcendent Creator and creation, and the affirmation that human beings, by grace, really do enjoy participation in and union with the triune God.[9] As the great defender of deification, Palamas affirms that in prayer the Hesychasts experience genuine deifying communion with God's uncreated light, and that this is no threat to God's absolute transcendence. For Palamas, the essence-energies distinction is the traditional[10] means by which both poles can be preserved, which is to say, it is the necessary theological context for any doctrine of deification.[11]

---

5. Jeffrey D. Finch, "Neo-Palamism, Divinizing Grace, and the Breach Between East and West," in *Partakers of the Divine Nature: The History and Development of Deification in the Christian Traditions*, ed. M. J. Christensen and J. A. Wittung (Fairleigh Dickinson University Press, 2007) 233. Cf. A. N. Williams, *The Ground of Union: Deification in Aquinas and Palamas* (Oxford University Press, 1999) 13-14.

6. Jeffrey D. Finch, "Neo-Palamism," 233.

7. John Meyendorff, "Doctrine of Grace in St. Gregory Palamas," *St. Vladimir's Seminary Quarterly* 2 (1954) 20.

8. See the introduction by John Meyendorff in Gregory Palamas, *The Triads: The Classics of Western Spirituality*, ed. John Meyendorff (New York: Paulist, 1983) 6.

9. Williams, *The Ground of Union*, 28.

10. Discussion of divine essence and energies is not original to Palamas; he recovers and "radicalizes" the terms from the Cappadocians and Maximus the Confessor. See Thomas Anastos, "Gregory Palamas' Radicalization of the Essence, Energies, and Hypostasis Model of God," *The Greek Theological Review* 38, no. 1-4 (1993) 335-49. See also Alexis Torrance, "Precedents for Palamas' Essence-Energies Theology in the Cappadocian Fathers," *Vigiliae Christianae* 63 (2009) 47-70.

11. John Meyendorff says it succinctly: the distinction "is nothing but a way of saying that the transcendent God remains transcendent, as He also communicates Himself to humanity." *The Triads: The Classics of Western Spirituality*, 20.

In Vladimir Lossky's encapsulation, "This distinction is that between the essence of God, or His nature, properly so-called, which is inaccessible, unknowable and incommunicable; and the energies of divine operations, forces proper to and inseparable from God's essence, in which He goes forth from Himself, manifests, communicates, and gives Himself."[12] It is important to underline the fact that God's essence, in this tradition, is entirely unknown and unparticipable for philosophical and theological reasons.[13] Creatures are united only to the divine *energeiai*, God's operations, or *logoi*. Orthodox theologians in the Palamite tradition are eager to emphasize that the energies are inseparable but really distinct from the essence. They are *not* created, but uncreated realities of the one eternal God. The divine energies illustrate the dynamism of God; according to Orthodox theologian Christos Yannaras, natures are known only through their ecstatic communication, or in other words, "the possibility for nature 'to stand outside of itself,' to become accessible and communicable not as an idea, but as personal uniqueness and dissimilarity."[14] The uncreated energies are a *"mode of being of nature,"*[15] but they are not the divine nature *simpliciter*, since the divine essence is transcendent to the greatest possible

---

12. Vladimir Lossky, *The Mystical Theology of the Eastern Church* (St Vladimir's Seminary Press, 1976) 70.

13. To understand the debate, therefore, it is necessary to understand the philosophical presuppositions about the meaning of "participation." For Palamas, participation necessarily introduces division into that which is participated; Paul Marshall elaborates: "Palamas . . . sometimes seems to think of particulars as participating in their own essence: 'an essence (οὐσία) has as many hypostases as it has participants.' He is therefore naturally reluctant to suppose that created persons can participate in the divine essence, since this would give them the same ontological status as the persons of the Trinity." Bruce Marshall, "Action and Person: Do Palamas and Aquinas Agree About the Spirit?," *St. Vladimir's Theological Quarterly* 39 (1995) 392–93. See also Reinhard Flogaus, "Palamas and Barlaam Revisted: A Reassessment of East and West in the Hesychast Controversy of 14th Century Byzantium," *St. Vladimir's Theological Quarterly* 42 (1998) 15; Rowan Williams, "The Philosophical Structures of Palamism," *Eastern Churches Review* 9 (1977) 29. Reflecting on the model of participation assumed by modern neo-Palamites, Jeffrey Finch says, "But the primary élan behind the neo-Palamite insistence upon a real distinction within God, as indicated earlier, is their common understanding of participation, one that is reductively entitative, having no analogical or causal dimension, thus requiring that an aspect or dimension of the divine nature be protected from involvement with creation in order to protect God's transcendence" ("Neo-Palamism," 239).

14. Christos Yannaras, "The Distinction Between Essence and Energies and Its Importance for Theology," *St. Vladimir's Theological Quarterly* 19 (1975) 235.

15. Ibid., 236.

degree and is not itself communicated.[16] Therefore, names such as grace, deity, love, holiness, and light denote energies of God, God's uncreated activity, which can be truly and fully united to us without endangering God's transcendence. For Thomas Anastos, "Uncreated divine grace is the supernatural 'addition' which enables created beings to transcend their normal capabilities. Grace makes the nous divine, 'uncreating' it so that raised to the proper ontological level it is able to receive divine things."[17]

As suggested by the two poles mentioned above, the basic difficulty of deification has always been whether it is possible for a created being to be ontologically united to God without also being subsumed (pantheistically) into God, and without creating division in God's essence (polytheistically). With the essence/energies distinction, many Orthodox believe that they have a workable answer specific to their own tradition.[18] Insofar as Western theology has been committed to the idea of divine simplicity,[19] which is interpreted to mean that God *is* God's essence and that "whatever is not essence does not belong to God,"[20] neo-Palamite theologians have launched a polemic against Western theology. Yannaras goes so far as to say that, "The problem of the distinction between essence and energies determined definitely and finally the differentiation of the Latin West from the Orthodox East."[21] The orthodoxy of the East is seen in the fact that, unlike the West, Greek theologians are able to embrace and defend

---

16. Thomas Anastos explains how the word 'superessence' was coined to emphasize this point: "The substitution of superessence for essence linguistically dramatized the inaccessibility of God which remains beyond the state of deification. 'Superessence' for Palamas denoted the absolutely transcendent, inaccessible, incommunicable, and imparticipable aspect of God which defines the divine being as what it is" ("Gregory Palamas' Radicalization of the Essence, Energies, and Hypostasis Model of God," 347).

17. Ibid., 338.

18. Insofar as Eastern Orthodoxy is a living theological communion, it is no surprise that there is animated disagreement at many levels, including whether the neo-Palamite approach is *the* Orthodox solution, whether it is an accurate interpretation of patristic precedent, whether it is philosophically tenable, etc. For an overview of the discussion, see Williams, *Ground of Union*, 138–40.

19. Palamite theologians do not deny divine simplicity, though their interpretation is distinct; see Lossky, *The Mystical Theology of the Eastern Church*, 76–79. Orthodox theologian David Bentley Hart is critical of neo-Palamite attenuation of divine simplicity; "The Hidden and the Manifest: Metaphysics After Nicaea," in *Orthodox Readings of Augustine*, ed. George E. Demacopoulos and Aristotle Papanikolaou (St. Vladimir's Seminary Press, 2008) 214 n. 40.

20. Yannaras, "Distinction Between Essence and Energies and Its Importance for Theology," 242.

21. Ibid.

the patristic doctrine of deification in all of its mystical realism. Most offensive to neo-Palamite ears is the idea of "created grace." Commenting on Western theology, Yannaras says, "in the final analysis, the *theosis* of man, his participation in the divine life, is impossible, since even grace, the 'sanctifier' of the saints . . . is created, even though 'supernatural,' as western theologians have rather arbitrarily defined it since the ninth century." From the "Latin perspective," the state of grace can only represent "an objective change of the human intention," and not the participation of our very being in the divine nature.[22] Lossky expands on the same point when he says that, because the West puts emphasis on the "one essence," it must rely on created intermediaries between God and human beings: "Eastern tradition knows no such supernatural order between God and the created world . . . . For eastern tradition the created supernatural has no existence."[23]

The basic claim, then, is that because Western theologians do not recognize a real distinction between the divine essence and energies, therefore "limiting" God to divine essence, two inadequate options remain: either our union with God is an absorption into the divine essence—and therefore human nature is lost—or we are related to God only by other created forms ("created grace"), and thus lack true union with the divine nature. God remains at an infinite distance, and the great hope of patristic soteriology is unrealized. The classic and contemporary question for Scheeben, then, is this. Is he able to affirm deification without (so to speak) losing the human being in God, and without violating the integrity and transcendence of the uncreated and eternal Trinity? Has the West been able to embrace the scriptural affirmation that Christians "partake of the divine nature" (2 Peter 1:4) without relying on a "real distinction" in God?

A FIRST ATTEMPT: NATURE AND GRACE

When painting a picture of Catholic theology at the beginning of the nineteenth century, historians very often use a palette of gloomy colors. For example, Cyril Vollert says that "Catholic theology had reached its nadir," and with similarly dark hues, Nichols describes how Catholic theologians at this time were haunted by Enlightenment critiques of revelation, and struggled to defend theology in the courts of rationalism. Just as problematically, this sometimes led to a counter-reaction in the direction of

22. Ibid., 242–43.
23. Lossky, *Mystical Theology of the Eastern Church*, 88.

fideism.[24] As Catholic thought bounced tumultuously between extremes, a new generation of theologians realized the need for change.

Matthias Scheeben was born just outside of Bonn, Germany, on March 1, 1835. At the age of seventeen he was sent to the Gregorian University in Rome where he studied under such notable scholars as Passaglia, Schrader, and Cercià, but most influentially in these early years, Joseph Kleutgen and Johann Baptist Franzelin. One reason Kleutgen was significant for Scheeben was that he "brought to the German theological consciousness the old Scholastic doctrine regarding the essence and worth of the supernatural."[25] As for Franzelin, he was known for his careful study of Latin and Greek church fathers, whom he brought into conversation with Thomas Aquinas, an approach that he would pass on to young Matthias.[26] Every work on Scheeben emphasizes his deep love for, and profound study of, the fathers, especially the Greek fathers. Given this fact, even if it is possible to say that Scheeben develops a doctrine of deification that is uniquely Latin insofar as it draws on scholastic terminology and insights, his theology is also heavily indebted to the great saints of the East. Vollert says that by reading the fathers, Scheeben discovered his theological vocation: "to make the drab naturalistic world glow again in the light and beauty of grace, to bring back to the consciousness of men the glorious destiny of our conformation to God."[27]

Ordained a priest in 1858, appointed professor of dogmatics in Cologne in 1860, the twenty-six-year-old Scheeben submitted for publication his first full manuscript in 1861, simply entitled *Nature and Grace*. This book is a recovery of the supernatural in a world that could not fathom its existence—or at least, its relevance—and at the same time it is a celebration of the natural in all of its possibility and limitation. The goal, then, was to understand "the difference, opposition, and union of these two orders" (xviii). In the early chapters of the book, Scheeben works to meticulously define and distinguish nature from grace and "supernature," but in the

---

24. Nichols, *Romance and System*, 1–5.

25. Malachi Donnelly, "The Indwelling of the Holy Spirit According to M. J. Scheeben," *Theological Studies* 7 (1946) 247.

26. Cyril Vollert, "Matthias Joseph Scheeben and the Revival of Theology," *Theological Studies* 6 (1945) 460.

27. Ibid., 461. Or, in Scheeben's own words, from the first paragraph of the preface, "My cherished aim is to bring out the supernatural character of the Christian economy of salvation in its full sublimity, beauty, and riches. The main task of our time, it seems to me, consists in propounding and emphasizing the supernatural quality of Christianity." *Nature and Grace* (St. Louis: Herder, 1954) xvii. Parenthetical citations in this section will refer to this text.

last chapter his writing turns rhapsodic as he describes the "marriage" of nature and grace.

In tracing the development of Scheeben's thoughts on deification, we will find two opposing tendencies in *Nature and Grace*. First, there is a resolute desire fully to affirm and defend the soteriological hope of human participation in the divine nature. At the same time, second, one finds in *Nature and Grace* a commitment to assumptions and norms in scholastic dogmatics that impede progress in the direction of the first tendency. We will look, therefore, first at Scheeben's positive affirmation of deification, starting with the intense imagery in the final chapter on the nuptial union between God and humanity, and then turn to those aspects of Scheeben's thought that seem to substantiate neo-Palamite critiques.[28]

Scheeben begins his fifteenth chapter, entitled "The Mystery of the Union in the Christian Economy," with a consideration of three different understandings of nature and freedom that have been presented in the Christian tradition; essentially, three possible anthropologies. First, if nature is broadly defined as the human person's "being and condition such as he has of himself" (306), it is possible to push this to the extreme. As creatures called into existence *ex nihilo*, what do human beings have independent of God? We truly have, and are, "nothing." The only "possessions" that the human being can claim as his own are those aspects of his life that are ordered toward his primordial nothingness; he can claim only "his potentiality, his indetermination to good, and his possibility of falling into evil" (ibid.). Remembering that sin itself is privation, an orientation toward nothing, from this extreme perspective a person could say that by "nature" all she or he has is sin. Therefore, one might identify oneself as only "something imperfect, indeterminate, mean, chaotic" (308). From this angle, nature is the polar opposite of grace, the opposite of the divine life, and must finally be contradicted by grace.

Second, however, when considering nature and freedom from the perspective of the divine caller, from the fact that we have received these gifts from God, a very different picture emerges. Scheeben says "we can also formally regard nature together with its freedom as a definite power

28. This paper supports Balthasar's general assessment of Scheeben: that, given Scheeben's need to correct the inclination of his contemporaries to collapse nature into grace or vice-versa, a large part of Scheeben's early work is given to meticulously distinguishing nature and grace (in fact, Scheeben may overreact in this direction). As Balthasar says, however, the "initial clarity of his conceptual distinctions" prepares the way for a description of the "very profound interpenetration of both realms," *The Glory of the Lord: Seeing the Form* (Continuum, 1982) 109. In the last chapter of *Nature and Grace*, careful attention to this "profound interpenetration" is already evident.

communicated to us by God, and then it is the foundation of all good." It is therefore assumed that our nature is "what it ought to be, to have, and to be capable of in accordance with the will and institution of the Creator" (313). Here, nature and freedom are so exalted that there is an *identity* with grace (316), a perfect correspondence, such that *union* (which by definition implies difference) is equally impossible. Neither model can conceive of the relationship between nature and grace as a marriage, either because grace must absolutely oppose nature, or because the two terms are virtually redundant.

Scheeben has sketched two possibilities: grace as extrinsic, wholly incongruous with nature, and grace as intrinsic, fully identical with nature. But there is a third option in which "natural freedom, in contradistinction to grace, emerges as something independent and good, as a genuine factor alongside grace" (320). Unsurprisingly, Scheeben identifies this as the authentic position of both the Greek Fathers and Augustine. This "middle position" takes into account the theological claim that human beings are from "nothing," and that we retain "a certain powerlessness and indetermination toward the good," but also that this "nothing" has been called to free communion with the triune God, and therefore God has honored us with "a certain power and determination to good" (320). Human nature is lovingly empowered for union with God, and it "advances toward grace with ardent yearning" (321). The erotic element in the relationship between nature and grace is therefore central for Scheeben. True union between nature and grace is conceivable only for this third anthropology.

What does it mean to say that nature "advances toward grace"? Scheeben clearly affirms that God alone has the initiative in approaching human beings, but he also says that the "first capacity for the spiritual life or for union with God ... is already found in man's nature" (322). In other words, God has made human beings capable of receiving grace, it is not repugnant to us, and in fact the divine life fulfills our deepest, even if unknown, longings. While it is possible to speak of a "void" in human beings, finite creatures are helpless to fill the void on their own precisely because it is a longing for another. Nature, given its relation of total dependence vis-à-vis God, cannot force or manipulate God into offering his love; love can only be given freely. But when the light of grace shines on the creature, it "awakens in nature a perception of its inherent lowliness, indigence, and barrenness, and thus incites it to seek help, support, and happiness from grace" (324). Therefore, nature is capable of an awareness of a need which can only be satisfied by grace:

> All the wants of nature are fully met through grace; and to that extent nature has a natural desire for union with grace. But this desire merely makes nature capable of receiving grace; that it may lead nature to grace, it must . . . be enkindled by the first rays of grace itself. If nature is the receptive subject and grace is the celestial dew fructifying nature, and if both strive for union with each other, the real union must actually take place as soon as nature humbly and obediently accepts the invitation issued by grace and throws itself into the arms of grace. (325)

Nature truly has wants and desires apart from grace—even though Scheeben has a doctrine of "pure nature,"[29] it cannot be, in the final analysis, a purely self-satisfied nature. Nature is made for union with God, and feels its "limitations and imperfections" (334), even if it cannot naturally know the supernatural end for which it longs. At the same time, God also "strives" for union with us, a striving most dramatically seen in the incarnation of the Son. Scheeben's theology represents nothing like the "static categories of 'nature' and 'grace'" which John Meyendorff identifies as the Western approach.[30] Both nature and grace are alive with a dynamic, though asymmetrical, desire for communion.

God has invited human beings into relationship; Scheeben draws attention to the word "invited." He says, "The union is not merely natural, like the union of body and soul; it is a true marriage, and consequentially must be free on the side of grace as well as of nature" (325). Nature is not forced, but—notice the seeds of a theological aesthetics—drawn "by a supernatural attraction" (326). At this point, Scheeben's remarkable theological vision comes into focus:

> Thus this wonderful union of the divine nature with human nature in the communication of grace or supernature is brought about by God's merciful, infinite love. It is a chaste marriage. For grace, on its side, unites with nature and fructifies it without violating it; nature, as an image of God, is the undefiled, receptive soil to which grace brings the dew of heavenly energy down from heaven to revive and fructify it, and sheds on it heavenly

---

29. See, for example, the fifth chapter—"Spiritual Nature of Man"—where Scheeben strongly defends the idea that created nature has a proportionate natural perfection.

30. After congratulating Eastern theology for refusing to regard the human being as a "static, 'closed,' autonomous entity," Meyendorff claims that "The dynamism of Byzantine anthropology can easily be contrasted with the static categories of 'nature' and 'grace' which dominated the thought of post-Augustinian Western Christianity . . . " *Byzantine Theology: Historical Trends and Doctrinal Themes* (Fordham University Press, 1979) 2.

light to adorn and warm it . . . Conversely, nature does not defile grace.³¹

Given the fact that *Nature and Grace* culminates in this fervent and lyrical depiction of the fruitful union of human nature and divine grace, ichnographically embodied in the chaste marriage of the Holy Spirit and the Virgin Mary, it would seem that Scheeben's theology could readily embrace and develop the patristic doctrine of deification. Earlier parts of the book both confirm, and complicate, this conclusion. The conclusion is confirmed insofar as Scheeben explicitly wants to embrace the doctrine. This is seen again and again as he refers to deification (113, 135, 178), cites the biblical passages most often identified with deification—1 Peter 1:4, we are made "partakers of the divine nature" (103, 106) and Psalm 81 (82):6, "You are gods all of you the sons of the Most High" (135, 173)—and quotes the most famous patristic articulations of the doctrine—"God became man that man might become God" (103, 124) and "we become by grace what the only-begotten Son of God is by nature" (114). There can be no doubt, based on all of these references and allusions, that Scheeben wants to recover and highlight this sometimes neglected doctrine.

However, as mentioned earlier, Scheeben's status as a Catholic theologian of deification becomes complicated when one looks carefully at just what type of union between divinity and humanity he is able to affirm in this early book. There are multiple ways of considering the nature of the sanctified woman or man's union with God in this text, but perhaps the most direct approach is to look at Scheeben's critical assessment of Denis Petau S.J. (also known as Petavius). Over one-hundred years before Scheeben's work, Petavius controversially argued in his *Theologica Dogmata* of 1644 that just as the hypostatic union is proper specifically to the second person of the Trinity, the divine and sanctifying indwelling in human beings is proper to the Holy Spirit. Petau added that there was a *substantial* union between the graced human being and the Holy Spirit.³²

31. Ibid., 327. It is no surprise that Scheeben seamlessly transitions from this discussion of the marriage of nature and grace to the spiritual marriage of the Holy Spirit and the Virgin Mary; in fact, if one were to re-read this passage, but replace the names "Mary" for nature and "Holy Spirit" for grace, she would have a very nice outline of Scheeben's Mariology. All Christians are called to model Mary in their chastity, in their desire for marriage with the Holy Spirit, and in bearing Jesus Christ in the wombs of their souls. As Scheeben says, "Through grace the Son of God is to be born again in human nature, not in physical unity of person, but in a moral, personal union, by a real image of His divine light and a real sharing of His divine light. The hypostatic union is the ideal, as well as the principle and end, of the union by grace" (328).

32. Donnelly, "Indwelling of the Holy Spirit According to M. J. Scheeben," 245–46.

This theory was not well received by scholastic theologians; due in large part to Thomas Aquinas's famous correction of Peter Lombard's view of charity as the Holy Spirit dwelling in the mind,[33] coupled with the Catholic reaction against the Reformation doctrine of imputed righteousness,[34] Catholic theologians had found it necessary to emphasize the fact that grace truly has a created effect. It does not simply work within us without us, but transforms and elevates created nature. Therefore, Petavius's proposal produced anxiety, and anyone working in soteriology, or especially pneumatology, would be expected to address it. Scheeben joins the chorus in denouncing the Jesuit's teaching. Scheeben cannot deny that aspects of the biblical and patristic witness appear to suggest "that the Holy Spirit is in a certain sense the formal cause of our new spirituality, the soul of our spiritual life, and . . . that He Himself, as distinct from His created goods and the other two divine persons, is given to us" (197). Since this is basically Petau's claim, Scheeben's admission of apparent traditional support is significant. But after a more careful consideration of some of the specific passages from the fathers that Petavius uses, Scheeben offers the following assessment:

> Thus the Holy Spirit is, so to speak, the soul of supernatural life, for He communicates His own life to the creature; He not only *brings supernatural life into existence* as its primary efficient cause, but preserves it and gives it the power of movement by a continuing activity and care. This is the only sense in which we can speak of the Holy Spirit as the formal cause of our higher spatiality and of our supernatural, spiritual life. Consequently *there is no real, substantial union of our nature with His*; we can think of Him as formal cause only to the extent that a formal cause, as in other cases, effects, sustains, and arouses the subject's life. And this comes back more or less to what we said before,[35] that the Holy Spirit is *the external formal cause* of our higher spirituality, the *exemplar* communicating itself by its own power. (202, emphasis added)

See also Del Colle, *Christ and the Spirit*, 87, note 31. Del Colle's book explains in detail the development in Western pneumatology from Scheeben through the twentieth century.

33. Thomas Aquinas, *Summa Theologica* II–II, Q. 23, Art. 2.

34. Nichols, *Romance and System*, 90.

35. The earlier passage reads, "Hence we can call [the Holy Spirit] formal cause, not in the sense of an inhering, formed, and intrinsic form, but in the sense of exemplary and extrinsic form, *virtually containing the form* inhering in the thing" (198, emphasis added).

A Man of the Church

It is important that Scheeben speaks of the Spirit bringing supernatural life *into existence*: insofar as he is referring to something created, it must not be divine in the full sense. God's relation to us is though a created, external ideal; the notion of "real, substantial union" is excluded.

With this in mind, Scheeben's meaning in other areas comes into focus. As mentioned, one of the key terms in the book is "supernature"; while he recognizes that the word is not especially traditional (xxi), he also believes that it helpfully draws attention to the distinction between grace and nature. As the word is used in this text, supernature in human beings is created, and must be distinguished from the infinitely fuller "supernature" of God (31). In his desire to avoid pantheism and Petavian speculations, Scheeben stresses that "supernature is not . . . a new substance in the natural order; and it is certainly not the divine substance uniting itself substantially with nature" (34). Neither human essence, nor its corresponding nature, is substantially changed by grace; at no point do we become something other than human. Following Thomas, Scheeben says that grace—or, in his own terms, supernature—is an "accidental form and nature" (107) that adheres to our created essence, elevating and transfiguring it. Because it is not a substantial form, Scheeben must admit that "the soul does not become divine, that is, a divine substance, but becomes godlike in its condition" (154). Another way of speaking of this same phenomenon, also traditionally Thomistic, is to say that God gives us a "second nature," understood as a *habitus* in human nature.

One should not underestimate the degree to which Scheeben is trying to emphasize that God truly gives us a godlike nature that brings us into a most intimate relation with him. Through this "second nature," we are able to receive perfections, such as immortality and charity, which are exclusive to God. He repeatedly says that this is not a mere rationalistic redirection of intentions, but our nature is elevated to new and previously unimagined life. In the context of nineteenth-century naturalism, the following statement would undoubtedly have turned heads: "[T]he entire being of the soul is altered in its deepest recesses and in all its ramifications to the very last, not by annihilation but by exaltation and transfiguration . . . because it has been granted a participation in the essence of Him to whom the higher nature properly belongs" (30). This is truly a powerful theological vision, but it also remains true that Scheeben cannot, in this earliest work, find a way to affirm formal union between God and human beings. His concern to protect the integrity of human nature is well taken, and entirely in keeping with the tradition. But, as any neo-Palamite theologian would immediately notice, Scheeben must place a created "something," which he calls supernature, between us and God. In his study of created and uncreated grace in Scheeben, Fraigneau-Julien is correct when he says, "In *Nature and Grace*, [Scheeben] insists less on union with the divine persons than on the reality and the properties of created grace. His goal, in effect, consists in conducting a scientific analysis on created grace, a supernatural ontology, based on the data of scripture and tradition."[36] Uncreated grace is largely missing in the theoretical portions of this book, even though the final chapter, with which we started, points toward deeper mysteries. Already in the "Epilogue" to *Nature and Grace*, Scheeben is looking forward to a more complete treatment: "A fuller, more adequate, systematic application of the doctrine about the supernatural character of the Christian economy of salvation will have to await a later work . . . ." (340).

A SECOND ATTEMPT: THE MYSTERIES OF CHRISTIANITY

As mentioned above, Kleutgen likely played a role in bringing the scholastic category of the supernatural to Scheeben's attention. It was also Kleutgen who wrote Scheeben "an encouraging letter" after the publication of *Nature and Grace*, urging him to reassess his views on the inhabitation of the Holy Spirit.[37] Scheeben not only reconsidered, he radically changed his opinion, a transition that has already begun in an intermediate work, *The Glories of Divine Grace*, and which comes to maturation in *The Mysteries of Christianity*. This change also clears the way for a more profound consideration of the doctrine of deification.

To attempt to describe the doctrine of deification in *The Mysteries of Christianity* is a special challenge. While his first book focuses more narrowly on the mystery of grace, *Mysteries* is an entirely different kind of project with an immense scope. Vollert explains that the book "penetrates into the interrelations, the laws, the organism, and the consequences of the great mysteries of Christianity . . . . To do justice to the work, the reader must master it as a whole rather than trace out and follow Scheeben's

---

36. Bernard Fraigneau-Julien, "Grâce Créée Et Grâce Incréée Dans La Théologie De Scheeben," *Nouvelle Reveu Theologique* 77 (1955) 347.

37. Cf. Donnelly, "The Indwelling of the Holy Spirit According to M. J. Scheeben," 247.

personal theories in disputed questions."[38] In this text, the doctrine of deification is discussed nowhere and everywhere. Nowhere, because Scheeben never stops to deal with it in isolation. Everywhere, because in almost every section[39]—page after page, context after context—he returns to deification. This paper can only focus on the portion of the text which deals specifically with the indwelling of the Holy Spirit.

By the time he sits down to write *The Mysteries of Christianity*, Scheeben has almost completely overturned his earlier judgment on the indwelling of the Holy Spirit. In the *Mysteries*, Scheeben says that the individual divine persons "as distinct from one another and especially so far as one proceeds from another, can give themselves to us for our possession and enjoyment."[40] He further explains that precisely because of the unique eternal relations that characterize each of the divine persons, each divine person "possesses the divine nature in a special way" (166), and therefore it follows that each person can relate to creation in a distinct fashion. This theory is confirmed at least in the case of the Son, who possesses created nature in a personal way through his incarnation; Scheeben now asks, "[W]hy should not the Holy Spirit be able to take possession of a created being in a way proper to His own person, by means of a less perfect and purely moral possession?"[41] Scheeben is no longer able to deny the possibility on theological grounds, and closely related to this, he implies that his continued study of the fathers, and he makes special reference to the Greek fathers, has persuaded him that they did in fact teach the unique indwelling of the Spirit.[42]

---

38. Vollert, "Matthias Joseph Scheeben and the Revival of Theology," 462. Vollert is correct, and therefore the following discussion will not be entirely "just," since it must isolate a single thread.

39. Explicit references to deification are found in the sections on the Trinity, Adam's original justice, the incarnation, the Eucharist, justification, and the beatific vision.

40. Matthias Scheeben, *The Mysteries of Christianity* (St. Louis: Herder, 1946) 160. Parenthetical citations in this section will refer to this text.

41. Ibid., 166. The words "and purely moral" may be deceptive, seeming to diminish the substantiality of the union he is here defending. For helpful clarification on what "moral" means in this context, see Donnelly, "The Indwelling of the Holy Spirit According to M. J. Scheeben," 273. In this context, "moral" underlines the fact that it is "a real union between two complete, independent Persons, fully constituted in their own right."

42. Cf. 165–66, 167, 211. He thus overturns his earlier claim that Petavius was misreading the fathers on this point.

Although Scheeben's new teaching was foreshadowed in *Glories of Divine Grace*,[43] here we get a more theologically precise account of the indwelling. Quite significantly, he says that "the Holy Spirit comes to our soul and becomes present in it formally in His own person" (160), and then adds, "Thus the Holy Spirit in Himself, and not merely in His gifts, although supposing and including them—for he can be united with us and we can possess and enjoy Him only through them—is in fullest truth an uncreated and hypostatic gift" (162). There are at least three striking claims in these passages. The first claim is that the Holy Spirit is "formally" present to the soul; this represents a withdrawal of his assertion that the Spirit is not properly a formal cause, but at best an external formal exemplar. The old view is contradicted explicitly: "the Holy Spirit is in a most exalted and marvelous manner not only the efficient and exemplary cause, but in a certain sense also the formal cause of our supernatural sanctity, of our dignity as sons of God, and of our union with the divine persons" (167). This is "in a certain sense" because it is also true that sanctity truly inheres *in us*.

Which leads smoothly into consideration of the second striking claim: that the indwelling Spirit and his gifts are inseparably related. It is now obvious that Scheeben has come to see that the infused gifts which truly transform created being, and which can rightly be called "created grace," are inseparable from the (uncreated) Holy Spirit himself who substantially dwells in and is united to the deified creature. The familiar analogy[44] is that of a ring and wax: as the ring presses into the wax, the wax is transformed by the union. As the Spirit is "pressed" into interior union with human nature, human nature is simultaneously, more and more, transfigured according to the divine image. The two aspects of the single event are mutually necessary. The fact that the human person is genuinely transformed such that she can say that holiness is a property of her graced nature in no way diminishes her actual union with and participation in the Spirit. The uncreated Spirit makes the created effect possible.

Third, there is the phrase "uncreated and hypostatic gift." The first element, "uncreated gift," is a radiant mystery. From the beginning, and especially in the context of the trinitarian debates, Christian theologians have insisted that there is an abysmal ontological gulf separating created from uncreated nature; and Scheeben as much as anyone has drawn attention to

---

43. Matthias Scheeben, *The Glories of Divine Grace: A Fervent Exhortation to All to Preserve and to Grow in Sanctifying Grace* (TAN, 2000) 73–74.

44. Which Scheeben himself uses in *The Glories of Divine Grace*, 72.

the fact that created nature is from nothing, always teetering on the brink. And yet, we are created *spirit*, in God's image and likeness, and thus made for an unimagined union with the eternal. Scheeben affirms that uncreated Spirit makes himself a gift for us, and more remarkable still, makes us capable of receiving the gift without annihilation. Scheeben further says that this is a "hypostatic gift," suggesting again that this gift is proper to the Spirit. It is fitting that the Spirit, as the love uniting the Father and the Son, should be sent to be united with us so as to draw us up into the same trinitarian union. Of course, Scheeben highlights the fact that the Father and the Son are not left on the sidelines: "[the Spirit] must be able to dwell in us as in His own temple, that belongs to Him in a special manner, although, because of the oneness of the divine substance and because of His personal relation to the other persons, He cannot take possession of this temple without them . . . for the other persons give themselves to us in Him" (166).[45]

Even though the word deification is not used in this section of the book, it is clearly on Scheeben's mind, as when he says that "[w]e are made partakers of the divine nature by the mission and the communication of the Holy Spirit" (179). The cherished analogy of marriage is also prominent: "The real indwelling of the Spirit of the bridegroom in His bride is to the spiritual marriage of the Son of God with the soul what corporal union is in corporal marriage, a union to which bride and bridegroom aspire in their reciprocal love" (171). When we expand our scope, direct references to deification proliferate.[46] As Vollert has said, the texts in this book are all interrelated, and Scheeben's bold teaching on the indwelling of the Holy Spirit, specifically identified as *Spiritus Christi* (385), is organically linked

---

45. By linking the hypostatic indwelling of the Holy Spirit to the corresponding indwelling of the whole Trinity, Fraigneau-Julien (echoing Eröss) says that Scheeben broke out of a false dichotomy which had existed in the preceding debate. It had been said that one must either choose the *exclusive* indwelling of the Spirit (which was, apparently, Petavius's view), or settle for an indwelling by appropriation only. Scheeben's solution rejects the dichotomy, suggesting that a true hypostatic and proper indwelling of the Spirit need not and cannot exclude the Father and the Son; Fraigneau-Julien, "Grâce Créée Et Grâce Incréée," 355; cf. Donnelly, "Indwelling of the Holy Spirit According to M. J. Scheeben," 260.

46. For example, Scheeben says, "if the Son of God becomes man, He does so only for the purpose of deifying man" (378), or when he explains our motivation for partaking of the Eucharist, saying, "We must be overwhelmed with the fullness of the Godhead; we must be deified" (487), or finally when he says that both in earthly sanctification through grace and in the heavenly beatific vision, "this transfiguration is a deification of man by his participation in the nature of the Godhead" (654).

to every other teaching on human sanctification and glorification, and especially those passages which teach deification.

CONCLUSION: A WESTERN, NUPTIAL MODEL OF DEIFICATION

Scheeben had just turned thirty when *The Mysteries of Christianity* was published; he would live twenty-three more years, during which time he wrote his master work, the monumental (and, unfortunately, unfinished) *Handbuch der katholischen Dogmatik*. A comprehensive study of Scheeben's doctrine of deification will require careful review of this book.[47] Nevertheless, even in his early work, one finds the raw materials of a theologically satisfying approach to deification informed by Western insights. *Nature and Grace* was ultimately a detailed analysis of the integrity of human nature and its relation to created grace. The trajectory of this work is clearly in the direction of an approach to deification that emphasizes the (*eros*-driven) union-in-difference between the triune God and humanity. The problem is, because Scheeben denies the proper indwelling of the Holy Spirit, or any divine formal causality, the bold theological proposals of his last chapter strain the more traditional scholastic categories of the earlier sections.

By the time of the *Mysteries of Christianity*, however, a major change occurs: Scheeben has overturned his earlier rejection of Petavius's pneumatology. By affirming the substantial indwelling of the Holy Spirit,[48] Scheeben opens the doors for a much fuller, pneumatologically focused account of "uncreated grace." Based on mounting patristic evidence, Scheeben reconsidered contemporary theological conventions, and he is therefore able to break through the occasional (but not universal!) tendency in Latin theology to keep God distant from creatures, a distance created when only

---

47. The *Handbuch* is still untranslated in English. The abridged version that does exist (*A Manual of Catholic Theology: Based on Scheeben's "Dogmatik"* [Kegan Paul, Trench, Trübner, 1906]) is widely considered inadequate, sometimes tempering or obscuring Scheeben's bold theological reasoning. Nevertheless, Nichols' new book on Scheeben is an outstanding overview that focuses especially on the *Handbuch*. The way Scheeben ultimately weaves the two major themes discussed in this paper (created grace and the indwelling of the Holy Spirit) in his most mature work is beautifully described; Nichols, *Romance and System*, 78–94.

48. As when he straightforwardly says, "Undoubtedly this presence of the Holy Spirit is real and substantial, for by grace we are really in Him, just as He is really united to us by a real bond" (*Mysteries*, 165).

divine efficient causality through created grace is acknowledged, or when the Holy Spirit is seen as merely an external exemplar. Scheeben's doctrine on the indwelling of the Holy Spirit tends toward reestablishing the priority of the uncreated Gift in Catholic soteriology. Still, Scheeben does not propose that the Spirit indwells the Christian without transforming and elevating her created nature. Therefore, because Scheeben's perspective of the indwelling has changed, his valuable analysis of "created grace" in the first book needs to be revisited so that the scholastic categories can more effectively contribute to this Petavian/patristic development. This final, integrating step is taken in the *Handbuch*.

Like Scheeben, Gregory Palamas also follows patristic precedent and emphasizes participation specifically in the Holy Spirit, but it is a participation tinted by his theory of a real distinction between the divine essence and energies: "the Spirit is imparticipable in his essence, while in his deifying energy, which is called 'divinity,' 'thearchy,' and 'theosis,' he is participable by the worthy."[49] For the Eastern tradition emerging from Palamas, recognizing the indwelling of the Holy Spirit does not resolve the problem: the essence/energies distinction remains necessary to protect divine transcendence while simultaneously making it possible for the creature to partake in divinity.

Again, models of Christian deification must navigate two "poles": the "unbreachable divide" between Creator and creature and substantial, participatory union[50] between the triune God and human beings. Two elements of an alternative Western approach to the paradox of deification have been developed in Scheeben's work. First, far from impeding the doctrine of deification by propounding static and lifeless categories, Scheeben's teaching on nature and grace is helpful. For Scheeben, "nature" is neither grace, nor indifferent to grace. Using the analogy of marriage, he says that nature erotically strives toward grace, while he also insists that nature is unable to know the one for whom it was made, or take even a single step toward grace, apart from divine self-revelation and help. Scheeben's approach to nature highlights the genuine freedom of the created spirit

49. Quoted by Russell, "Theosis and Gregory Palamas," 370.

50. It should be noted that ambiguity over the philosophical category of "participation" hovers in the background of this debate. The Palamite tradition assumes that the participant necessarily creates division in the participated, and therefore the essence must be protected from participation (see note 13, above). The work of Erich Przywara, a few decades after Scheeben's death, helps to clarify how the divine Being is related to created beings in a non-competitive way, such that the absolute transcendence of divine Οὐσία is in no way threatened by creaturely participation. Przywara's insights contribute greatly to a comprehensive Western approach to deification.

which is inflamed and empowered by the grace of the Holy Spirit. The articulation of a clear distinction between nature and grace helps convey the drama at the heart of Christian revelation. It also helps to underscore the profound ontological difference ("unbreachable divide") between God and creatures, while at the same time highlighting the fact that created spiritual nature is a difference made for union. This shows that, at the level of created nature, there is neither antinomy between God and humanity, nor identity, but the promise and fervent hope of chaste marital union.

Second, for Scholastic theology, Scheeben's work is a turning point toward a renewed awareness of the centrality of uncreated grace. Orthodox theologians are correct that created grace alone is insufficient. A key premise in the patristic trinitarian debates was the conviction that true deification cannot be communicated by creatures; we are deified through communion with divine persons. By affirming the indwelling of the Holy Spirit, Scheeben prioritizes uncreated grace as a formal cause of our deification. Of course, precisely because of the "ever greater" difference between divine Being and created beings, the Holy Spirit does not "dwell" in us like one Russian doll in another. The Spirit does not need to carve out space for himself, as if human nature and divine nature are in competition. In Scheeben's theology, the Spirit can be wholly present in his divinity without destroying or pantheistically absorbing our nature precisely because of the radical ontological dissimilarity. The Thomistic idea, using Aristotelian terms, of the Spirit being substantially present as an accidental yet transfiguring form in created nature is one helpful proposal that Scheeben will use to communicate the real difference and real unity between uncreated and created spirit. These distinctions in Scheeben, between nature and grace, and between created and uncreated grace, seem helpful in protecting divine transcendence while affirming real deifying presence, without reliance on a theologically and philosophically problematic "real distinction" between God's essence and energies.

Deification is not just a "Greek doctrine." It is a Christian mystery that has been beautifully preserved in the East—something Scheeben acknowledges with gratitude —but which has also been developed in a unique and indispensable way with the help of the treasures of the Latin tradition. Hopefully this development can promote further ecumenical dialogue and mutual learning between East and West as the Church learns to breathe, more and more, with two lungs. To that end, Catholics interested in Western models of soteriology must return to the sources: they must retrieve the work of Matthias Joseph Scheeben.

14

Spirit-Christology and the Shape of the Theological Enterprise

ANDREW GROSSO

INTRODUCTION

ONE OF THE PROBLEMS that has emerged from recent studies in Spirit-christology concerns the nature and shape of the theological enterprise as a whole. Questions about the correspondence between christology and pneumatology have evoked additional issues regarding the relationship between these areas of study and other major loci of theological inquiry (e.g., soteriology, trinitarian theology, ecclesiology, etc.).[1] This questioning would seem to confirm Joseph Farrell's critique of Alan Richardson's assessment of the *filioque* controversy: the question of the relationship between Christ and the Spirit involves far more than "verbal trifles" that have no bearing on any "vital theological issue[s]."[2]

This brief study attempts to address the potential ramifications of this ongoing recovery of pneumatology upon the theological enterprise at large. More specifically, I intend to outline a programmatic approach

---

1. For a summary of various "critical dogmatic issues for Spirit-christology," see Ralph Del Colle, *Christ and the Spirit: Spirit-Christology in Trinitarian Perspective* (New York, NY: Oxford University Press, 1994) 26–29.

2. See Joseph P. Farrell, "A Theological Introduction to the Mystagogy of Saint Photios," in Photios, *The Mystagogy of the Holy Spirit*, trans. Joseph P. Farrell (Brookline, MA: Holy Cross Orthodox Press, 1987) 17.

to dogmatic or systematic inquiry that takes seriously the ramifications of Spirit-christology for all areas of theological reflection; this includes, not incidentally, accommodating the pervasive complementarity that emerges between the major themes and concepts of systematic analysis. I will show that, far from having no bearing on any "vital theological issues," the relationship between christology and pneumatology bears on *every* vital theological issue.

The first part of the essay reviews a recent effort to summarize contemporary studies in Spirit-christology. The focus then shifts to a more narrow consideration of the event(s) at the heart of both christological and pneumatological reflection, namely, the four-fold exaltation of Jesus. Analysis of the exaltation then leads to exploration of general questions regarding the nature and purpose of the theological enterprise before zeroing in on questions that pertain to the structure of systematic or dogmatic theology in particular. This essay thus attempts to set the stage for more focused and thorough study and reflection.

2. CONTEMPORARY SPIRIT-CHRISTOLOGY: AN AGENDA

In his book *The Anointed Son*, Myk Habets explores a number of recent efforts aimed at clarifying the place and role of pneumatology in theological studies. His chief purpose is to provide a "comprehensive map" for those interested in navigating "through the many competing proposals for a Third Article theology."[3] Thus, Habets provides an agenda for contemporary studies in Spirit-christology.

Not surprisingly, Habets finds that many of the apparently insoluble tensions in late modern theology arise from a concomitant neglect of pneumatology. Incessant debates about the relative merits of "functional christology" as opposed to "ontological christology," the extent to which one should emphasize the "person" of Christ or the "work" of Christ," or whether one should adopt an anabatic as opposed to a katabatic approach to such questions (i.e., theology "from below" as opposed to "from above") all reveal that theologians have backed themselves into some very unfortunate corners.[4] Rather than force a choice among what he sees as a series of false dichotomies, Habets seeks to demonstrate how attention to the

---

3. Myk Habets, *The Anointed Son: a Trinitarian Spirit Christology* (Eugene, OR: Pickwick, 2010) 7.

4. See ibid., 10–52.

doctrine of the Spirit not only invites a reconsideration of incarnational theology, but also provides a more expansive and integrative perspective on the theological enterprise as a whole.

As one might expect, Habets devotes considerable time and effort to identifying the events and trends in the Western theological tradition that led to the accession of Logos-christology over Spirit-christology.[5] However, despite the fact that Habets believes the Western theological tradition has been impoverished because of its neglect of Spirit-christology, he responds to the question of whether to abandon the legacy of Chalcedon with "a resounding '*no*', and for various reasons."[6] He hopes thereby to avoid some of the problems he finds in the work of those who have self-consciously adopted a "post-trinitarian" perspective (e.g., Roger Haight, Piet Schoonenberg, Geoffrey Lampe, et al).[7]

Taking his cues chiefly from the biblical witness but also from the theological tradition, Habets outlines an approach to incarnational theology that is equally responsive to pneumatology and christology and thus more faithful to both the scriptures and the dogmatic deposit.[8] More specifically, Habets finds that any viable contemporary Spirit-christology will accommodate a number of distinct but interdependent themes. First, there must be consideration of both the "economic" and "immanent" configurations of the doctrine of the trinity. Second, the redemptive economy should be understood in terms consistent with the life of the three divine persons. Third, ontological or metaphysical accounts of the divine life cannot be collapsed into strictly phenomenological or functional accounts of divine presence and activity, even though the latter provide the starting point for all consideration of the former. Finally, the relations between the divine persons must originate in a single, unified, and eternal action that upholds the *monarchia* of the first person while also maintaining the perichoretic relations of all three persons.[9] To these we should also add that any viable contemporary Spirit-christology will be mindful of both the essential correspondence and the necessary distinction between God's creative, redemptive, and consummative activities (each of which, we can expect, will manifest a trinitarian pattern).

---

5. See ibid., 53–80.
6. See ibid., 81–88 (emphasis in the original).
7. See ibid., 193–99.
8. See ibid., 89–187.
9. See ibid., 220–27.

In short, Habets demonstrates that attentiveness to the presence and activity of the Spirit yields a heightened appreciation for the connections between different areas of theological inquiry. Spirit-christology, in other words, may have more to do with recovering an appreciation for the the "scope," the "unity," and the "coherence" of the theological enterprise than it does with understanding one or two specific themes or topics.[10] In some ways, Habets thus points in a direction comparable to the one indicated by Stratford Caldecott in his call for a "renewal of Christian cosmology."[11] As does Habets (albeit in a slightly different way), Caldecott proposes that the "unity-in-distinction" signified by trinitarian theology "is the basis for an analogy that runs right through creation as a kind of watermark," an analogy that thus fosters awareness of both the essential correspondence as well as the necessary distinction between God's creative, redemptive, and consummative activity.[12] The remainder of the current study is devoted to outlining one approach to recovering the perspective both Habets and Caldecott commend.

THE EXALTATION OF JESUS

One of the more significant and potentially fruitful moves Habets makes in *Anointed Son* is to highlight the importance of various "disclosure episodes in the life of Christ" that he suggests are germane for understanding the presence and activity of the Spirit.[13] Specifically, Habets accentuates the following: (1) the conception and birth of Jesus; (2) the baptism and temptation of Jesus; (3) the messianic vocation of Jesus; (4) the crucifixion and death of Jesus; (5) the resurrection of Jesus; and (6) the "two-stage exaltation" of Jesus (i.e., ascension and Pentecost).[14]

Habets is clearly on to something here, and his exposition of each of these "episodes" reinforces that a close reading of the life of Christ should yield both christological and pneumatological insights (and, not incidentally, trinitarian as well). However, it also seems that his first cast may be a bit too wide: rather than try to account for the whole of the life and ministry of Jesus at once, it may be more effective (and true to the data) to begin

---

10. See ibid., 228.

11. Stratford Caldecott, "A Science of the Real: the Renewal of Christian Cosmology," in *Communio* 25 (1998) 462–79.

12. Caldecott, "Science of the Real," 477.

13. Habets, *Anointed Son*, 118.

14. See Habets, *Anointed Son*, 122–86.

with a somewhat attenuated organizing image. To that end, the current study proposes that (1) the most significant single "disclosure episode" in the life and ministry of Jesus is his "exaltation" and (2) this exaltation has four "stages" (i.e., cross, resurrection, ascension, and the gifting of the Spirit), rather than just two.[15]

The rationale for this proposal is two-fold. First, these four episodes are mutually constitutive in ways that other episodes from the life of Jesus are not. While it is of course true that a fulsome account of both Christ and the Spirit require attending to the full breadth of the biblical witness, it is also accurate to say that no four events in the life of Jesus are as inextricably bound up with one another as are these four. Reflection upon the meaning of the cross presumes not only the resurrection, but also the inspiring work of the Spirit, which itself in turn presumes the ascension. Similarly, the meaning of the resurrection depends directly on the cross and anticipates both the ascension and the gifting of the Spirit even as it assumes their actuality (i.e., the inspiring work of the Spirit is just as much a necessary condition for explicating the meaning of the resurrection as it is of the cross). Finally, the meaning of both the ascension and the gifting of the Spirit are as dependent upon one another as they are upon the meaning of the death and resurrection of Jesus. In short, the four-fold exaltation of Jesus signifies what we might call (to borrow from Michael Polanyi) a "polycentric Gestalt," that is, a meaningful whole that evinces multiple complementary dimensions or modes.[16]

The second reason for highlighting this particular account of the exaltation of Jesus has less to do with the interdependence of each of these four episodes on one another and more to do with the influence of the exaltation as a whole (i.e., as a single, unified "polycentric Gestalt") upon the life and witness of the church. Martin Kähler's well-known account of the canonical gospels as "passion narratives with extended introductions" can perhaps be seen not only as a way of making sense of the shape of

---

15. Perhaps it is more accurate to say that the exaltation evinces two two-stage episodes rather than four distinct episodes. Habets, following Moltmann, suggests as much when he notes that (1) the cross and resurrection should be seen as part of a single event and (2) the ascension and gifting of the Spirit should likewise be seen as a single event with two stages; see Habets, *Anointed Son*, 160–86.

16. For Polanyi's account of "polycentric problems," see Michael Polanyi, *The Logic of Liberty: Reflections and Rejoinders* (Chicago: University of Chicago Press, 1951) 171–81. For his account of the role of *Gestalten* in all knowing, see idem, *Personal Knowledge: Towards a Post-Critical Philosophy*, rev. ed. (Chicago: University of Chicago, 1962 [1958]), 57–58, 340–43; idem, *The Tacit Dimension* (Chicago: University of Chicago, 1966) 6–8.

the biblical witness, but also as a hypothesis that affords a unified perspective on the development of the kerygmatic, liturgical, canonical, and theological traditions.[17] In other words, it is fair to say that the whole of the Christian experience involves nothing other than the expatiation of the meaning of the exaltation of Jesus.[18]

Not immediately evident, though, is the bearing of this four-fold event not only on christology but on pneumatology: is the exaltation of Jesus equally an "exaltation of the Spirit," as it were? Answering this question requires attending to the relationship between Jesus and the Spirit in each of the four dimensions of episodes of the exaltation; this will lead not only to a heightened appreciation of the complementarity of christology and pneumatology, but to a better sense of the perspective the exaltation affords on the theological enterprise at large.

That the cross has an obvious and significant bearing on whatever might be said about Jesus seems self-evident; perhaps less clear is how best to understand the Spirit's participation in this event. The biblical narrative(s), however, seem to suggest that the cross is for both Son and Spirit an occasion of submission. Jesus surrenders himself in complete hope and trust to the one he called his Father; his surrender is not passive resignation but an active commitment, a striving after and achievement of a form of unqualified obedience (Phil 2.5–8; Heb 2.10–18).[19] Likewise, the Spirit submits to being completely governed by the faithful acquiescence of Jesus; the presence that inspired and directed the life and ministry of

---

17. According to Kähler, the testimony of the early church is grounded in "the cross and resurrection of Jesus as interpreted in the light of Pentecost. Every testimony to Jesus that we possess has been written and preserved from the perspective of the apostles' encounter with him as the risen Lord," from Carl E. Braaten, "Revelation, History, and Faith in Martin Kähler," in Martin Kähler, *The So-Called Historical Jesus and the Historic Biblical Christ*, ed. and trans. Carl E. Braaten (Philadelphia: Fortress, 1964 [1896]) 24. Cf. Ralph Del Colle's analysis of the work of James D. G. Dunn, in Del Colle, *Christ and the Spirit*, 141–47.

18. It is indeed not too much to suggest that the overall shape of the New Testament canon bears witness to this process of expatiation, i.e., to suggest that the canon itself is organized around a gradual unfolding and elaboration of the exaltation of Jesus, from the earlier and more concise accounts in the Pauline epistles (e.g., 1 Tim 3.16; Phil 2.5–11; Eph 1.3–10, 17–23) to the more developed proclamation of the early church (e.g., Acts 2.14–36) to the even more fulsome accounts provided by the canonical gospels. Cf. Pheme Perkins, *Resurrection: New Testament Witness and Contemporary Reflection* (Garden City, NY: Doubleday, 1984) 331–420.

19. Thomas Torrance affirms the simultaneously passive and active dimensions of the work of Christ, and refers to them as "passive action" and "active passion." See Thomas F. Torrance, *Incarnation: the Person and Work of Christ*, ed. Robert T. Walker (Downer's Grove, IL: IVP, 2008) 80–81; cf. 114–29.

Jesus is now poured out to the uttermost, not in an act of obvious power or glory but rather in abject humility and brokenness (Lk 22.46). Both the incarnate Word and the incarnating Spirit thus experience a *kenosis* of their being, and in so doing experience a *kenosis* of their relationship with one another (as well as their relationship with the one from whom they were both sent).[20] The cross thus signifies the complete identification of Jesus and the Spirit with the brokenness of the human experience; as such, it is an act marked chiefly by mortification.[21] Paradoxically, however, it is in and through this act of complete dispossession that the wisdom, the righteousness, the glory, and the power of God is manifest (1 Cor 1.17–2.5); the cross, in other words, can rightly be considered an act of exaltation.

The resurrection can likewise be considered an act of exaltation, but it is characterized more so by vindication.[22] Jesus is raised in and through the power of the Spirit, once again an act that reveals concomitant passivity and active striving. As at the conception of Jesus (Lk 1.34–35), the Spirit once more brings forth new life; however, the resulting life not only *bears* the Spirit (as at the conception) but has the capacity to *give* the Spirit (Jn 3.34, 7.39). The resurrection thus marks a further stage in the fulfillment of the ministry of Jesus, and the *munus triplex* of his identity and his mission as prophet, priest, and king is clarified and authenticated. The resurrection of Jesus is likewise a vindication of the Spirit, for it ratifies the faithful presence and the power of the Spirit as the source and ground of his ministry (Lk 4.14–21) as well as the horizon wherein his new life and ongoing ministry is situated (Rom 8.1–17).

The ascension signifies a further stage in the exaltation, one marked chiefly by glorification.[23] The transfiguration achieved in the resurrection is in the ascension intensified even further, and portends a new and more

---

20. Cf. Habets, *Anointed Son*, 165.

21. The mortification of Jesus and the Spirit could be further elaborated by exploring the meaning of Holy Saturday and its relationship to the cross (and, indeed, the whole of the exaltation). See, e.g., Edward T. Oakes, "The Internal Logic of Holy Saturday in the Theology of Hans Urs von Balthasar," in *International Journal of Systematic Theology* 9 (2007) 184–99; Alan E. Lewis, *Between Cross and Resurrection: a Theology of Holy Saturday* (Grand Rapids: Eerdmans, 2001).

22. Cf. Habets, *Anointed Son*, 170. See also N. T. Wright, *The Resurrection of the Son of God*, Christian Origins and the Question of God 3 (Minneapolis: Fortress, 2003) esp. 719–36. For background on the theme of vindication and other aspects of the meaning of resurrection in first-century Judaism, see Perkins, *Resurrection*, esp. 39–47.

23. Cf. Gerrit Scott Dawson, *Jesus Ascended: the Meaning of Christ's Continuing Incarnation* (Phillipsburg, NJ: P. & R., 2004) 53–72.

intimate relationship between God and the world: the human experience is now drawn into the experience of the divine life itself (Col 3.1–4). Here again, Jesus is both passive as well as active: he actively bears his own transfigured humanity to the presence of God, a process carried out in and through the Spirit according to the will of the Father. The ascension thus signifies the completion of one stage in the ministry of Jesus (Eph 1.20–23; Heb 1.3–4) and the beginning of another (Heb 9.11–15).[24] This glorification of Jesus is also a glorification of the Spirit, for the ascension testifies to the fact that the power that raised Jesus from the dead is one that is greater than every other power, earthly or otherwise (Eph 1.20–21). Like Jesus, the Spirit is also both passive and active in the ascension, being the one in whom Jesus "takes captive" the whole of the created order and draws it along with himself into the divine life (Eph 1.9–10, 4.7–10) while also being the one in whom he is reunited with the Father.

There is symmetry in the exaltation: just as the cross appears at first blush to be an event having to do primarily with Jesus—but involving just as much the Spirit—so does Pentecost appear at first blush to have to do primarily with the Spirit—but also has to do with Jesus. The coming of the Spirit is indeed an exaltation of the presence and power of the Spirit (Acts 2.14–21), but as such should be understood in terms of the presence and the power of Jesus (John 14.15–21, 15.26, 16.12–15). Through the gifting of the Spirit, the glorification of Jesus signified by the ascension (i.e., his exercise of divine sovereignty) is manifest in the world in concrete terms (Eph 4.1–32). Having rent the veil separating the world from God (Heb 10.19–22), the risen and ascended Christ now pours out the abundance of the divine life in all its eschatological and proleptic fullness.[25] Here again is something like the paradox manifest in the cross: the exaltation of Jesus in the gifting of the Spirit enables humanity to apprehend (and even to share in) the mortification of Jesus (and thus the Spirit) on behalf of the world (2 Cor 4.7–5.10; Col 1.21–29). The distinct character of the gifting of the Spirit can thus be considered one of sanctification (Rom 6.1–23, 8.3–11).

It should by now seem proper to suggest that any account of the exaltation of Jesus requires not only consideration of the complementary

---

24. Cf. Dawson, *Jesus Ascended*, 117–41.

25. Cf. "The trajectory of christological identity, ontologically instantiated as Person[,] moves from the increasingly concrete crucible of history to the eschatologically universal presencing in his glorified humanity. The Spirit, on the other hand, proceeds in the inverse, from the universal public outpouring to the transformation of the particular and the concrete," in Ralph Del Colle, "The Holy Spirit: Presence, Power, and Person," in *Theological Studies* 62 (2001) 333.

activity of Christ and the Spirit, but necessarily includes consideration of the role of the Father as well. The abnegation of Jesus and the Spirit in the cross in part signifies a comparable abnegation on the part of the Father, who does not undergo the suffering of the cross but who does experience the risk of losing his identity as the Father of the Son (Matt 27.45-46; Mark 15.33-34).[26] The resurrection of Jesus likewise testifies to the activity of the Father as the one who raises up Jesus in the power of the Spirit (Rom 8.11; Gal 1.1; Col 2.12), and it is the faithfulness of the Father that is vindicated in the resurrection as much as is anything else.[27] The ascension, as we have seen, involves not only a restoration of the relationship between the Father and the Son but also a transformation of that relationship as the Son returns bearing his own transfigured humanity; the Father becomes, as it were, the Father of the whole world (Gal 3.23 — 4.7). The gifting of the Spirit is almost more a work of the Father than it is of the Son, inasmuch as it testifies to the Father's determination to pour out the gift of the divine life in and to the world (John 3.16-17). In short, what all this suggests is that Spirit-christology may be only a signpost on the way to what needs to be a fully trinitarian theology.

The above accounts do not begin to do justice to the meaning of each of the "disclosure episodes" of the exaltation, let alone their relationship to one another. What should, however, be evident even from this perfunctory examination is that each episode can be seen to bear in different ways on christology, pneumatology, and their relationship to one another (and to trinitarian theology). Perhaps the most succinct way of describing the meaning of the exaltation is to say that it involves something of an inversion (as was noted in my examination of the resurrection): Jesus goes from being the one anointed *by* the Spirit to being the one who anoints *with* the Spirit, a change that is itself part of his vocation and ministry (cf. Mark 1.7-8; John 1.29-34). The Spirit likewise undergoes a transformation: the "spirit of the Lord," the one in whom the life and ministry of Jesus is actualized (cf. Luke 4.16-19), becomes the "spirit of Christ," the one in whom the transfigured life of the exalted Jesus is made available to the world (John 20.22-23; 2 Cor 3.17-18).[28]

---

26. Cf. Habets, *Anointed Son*, 167-68.

27. Cf. "The Father raises Jesus by his own free and sovereign action, which is to bestow his Spirit upon the slain Jesus," in Bruce D. Marshall, *Trinity and Truth* (Cambridge, UK: Cambridge University Press, 2000) 246.

28. Cf. Habets, *Anointed Son*, 162, 173-74, 180.

THE EXALTATION AND THE THEOLOGICAL ENTERPRISE

What wider consequences follow from this approach to the exaltation of Jesus? How does this reading of the cross, the resurrection, the ascension, and the gifting of the Spirit influence the theological enterprise (and, indeed, the whole of the Christian experience)? Answering these questions involves unpacking the six objectives identified above (i.e., the five recommended by Habets and the additional one having to do with the correspondence between God's creative, redemptive, and consummative activity).[29]

The parameters of the current study will, obviously, not allow for a thorough exploration of any of these objectives. The goal herein is much more modest, and intends nothing more than a preliminary examination of the extent to which Spirit-christology, understood in terms consistent with the above account of the exaltation of Jesus, affords a particular perspective on the correspondence of these objectives to one another. In other words, the task at this point is to consider how the insights of the previous section bear on the scope, unity, and coherence of the theological enterprise at large.[30]

In his exposition of the theology of the incarnation, Thomas Torrance provides an insight that helps facilitate this task. In particular, Torrance asserts that the practice of any "science" arises out of efforts "to know something strictly *in accordance with its own nature and activity*."[31] What this means for any understanding of the incarnation, Torrance suggests, is that it must account for a two-fold mystery, i.e., the mystery of the incarnation itself (how it is that God has become human) alongside the equally mysterious means whereby God enables us to recognize the reality and truth of the incarnation.[32]

What this means is that apprehending and understanding the correspondence of christology and pneumatology depends on participation in the redemptive work of God in Christ and the Spirit (1 Cor 2.6–16). In

29. See above, § 2, 4.
30. Cf. Habets, *Anointed Son*, 228.
31. Torrance, *Incarnation*, 4 (emphasis in the original).
32. See Torrance, *Incarnation*, 2–5. Note that Torrance understands "mystery" (*mystērion*) in a technical, distinctly theological manner, one having to do chiefly with God's self-disclosure in and to the world and the purpose (*prothesis*) it signifies, namely, communion (*koinōnia*) between God and the world; see Torrance, *Incarnation*, 164–174. Cf. Eph 1.3–12, esp. vv. 9–10; Col 1.26–27, 2.2–3.

other words, the *ordo cognoscendi* signified by the theological enterprise is itself grounded in the more fundamental *ordo salutis* that constitutes the Christian life.[33] Both of these in turn depend on the even more fundamental *ordo essendi* of the redemptive economy (i.e., the trinitarian life of God as manifest in the created order), which in turn signifies the *ordo essendi* of the divine life in and of itself (i.e., the trinitarian life of God considered in abstraction from God's relationship with the created order).[34] The question of the relationship between these three "orders" is itself a kind of adumbrated account of the parameters of the theological enterprise.

This image can be further sharpened by borrowing from Michael Polanyi insights pertaining to the emergence and development of formal intellective traditions. Polanyi suggests that there are four different types of articulation, each of which signifies a coterminous mode of apprehension or understanding. The most primitive involves the more or less unreflective, strictly instrumental means whereby living things seek to exercise their faculties in the satisfaction of drives and appetites (physical and otherwise). Attempts to organize experience by adopting more precise and symbolic patterns of signification facilitate the emergence of "descriptive" forms of apprehension. The further elaboration of concepts and language alongside the application of the modes of apprehension and understanding that arise from this effort results in greater distance from concrete experience even as it facilitates the emergence of "exact" forms of analysis and reasoning. Finally, "increasing formalization and symbolic manipulation" involves the abandonment of concrete experience entirely and the emergence of purely "deductive" forms of apprehension and reasoning.[35]

Putting Polanyi's account of articulation alongside Torrance's account of the correspondence between the *ordo salutis*, the *ordo cognoscendi*, and the *ordo essendi* of the incarnation thus provides a strategy for sorting out and pursuing the distinct demands of each the six objectives mentioned earlier. In short, what this means is that the development and elaboration of theological forms of awareness and articulation depends on

33. Torrance does not employ the term "*ordo salutis*" in quite the same way it's used here, but his thinking is consistent with the point being made; see Torrance, *Incarnation*, 37, 81–82, 105–14.

34. Cf. Torrance, *Incarnation*, 94, 174–80; Del Colle, *Christ and the Spirit*, 152–57; idem, "Reflections on the *Filioque*," 212–14.

35. See Polanyi, *Personal Knowledge*, 82–87. For further analysis of the correspondence between the thought of Michael Polanyi and the theological enterprise, see Andrew T. Grosso, *Personal Being: Polanyi, Ontology, and Christian Theology*, American University Series VII: Theology and Religion 258 (New York, NY: Peter Lang, 2007) 97–125.

the transfiguration of the mind, a process that itself is part and parcel of the oblation of one's life to God as a "living sacrifice" (Rom 12.1–2). Further, the essential correspondence and the necessary distinction between experience, knowledge, and being both provides for the opportunity to say something meaningful about reality despite the inevitable contingence and limitations of human experience. Perhaps most importantly, it is the prevenient work of God that is seen here as having absolute priority, that is, the creative and redemptive taxonomies of the divine life given to us in Christ and the Spirit.[36]

DOGMATICS IN OUTLINE

What remains, then, is to put this strategy to work in an attempt to demonstrate how the general principles described in the previous section can help organize the various topics and themes one encounters in the study of Christian dogmatics.[37] The limitations of the current study prevent anything more than a quick sketch of how the practice of systematic theology might appear in the light of the insights afforded by the above efforts.[38]

Both the earlier review of the exaltation of Jesus as well as the insights gleaned from Torrance and Polanyi suggest a need to take seriously the importance of *metanoia* as an essential starting point for all theological reflection and inquiry. The exaltation provides an image of the "object" of theological inquiry, namely, the living Christ present in and to the world in the Holy Spirit. Understanding this reality "in accordance with its own nature and activity" (as Torrance puts it) requires nothing less than apprehension of the new creation manifest and signified thereby, for it is the rationality of this order that governs the rationality of theological inquiry.[39] In other words, participation in the *ordo salutis* of God's work in Christ and the Spirit is the point of entry into the *ordo cognoscendi* of

---

36. Cf. Torrance, *Incarnation*, 27–29.

37. Of course, this approach to theological studies will have ramifications not only for the study of systematics but for other theological disciplines as well (e.g., biblical theology, historical theology, theological ethics, etc.), to say nothing of the relationship of these disciplines to one another. The purview of the current study does not extend to such considerations.

38. Cf. Habets, *Anointed Son*, 228–80.

39. Cf. Simon Chan, *Spiritual Theology: a Systematic Study of the Christian Life* (Downer's Grove, IL: InterVarsity, 1998) 15–39. Cf. also Mark McIntosh, *Divine Teaching: an Introduction to Christian Theology* (Malden, MA: Oxford University Press, 2008) 3–15.

theological reflection, both of which are grounded in the *ordo essendi* of the new life of the risen Christ.[40]

The centrality of the exaltation is helpful precisely for sorting out the considerable range of questions and problems that emerge at this point: it is the image of the crucified, risen, and ascended Word present in the Spirit that should govern any consideration of salvation, of God, of human identity and experience, and of the world.[41] In other words, christology and pneumatology together very quickly evoke the need for reflection on soteriology, trinitarian theology, theological anthropology, and theological cosmology.

Here Michael Polanyi is again helpful: his account of the "tacit triad" is a useful way of thinking about the unity-in-distinction of the study of christology, pneumatology, and trinitarian theology. All knowing, Polanyi suggests, involves the coordination of three things: the knower, the known, and the means whereby the former apprehends the latter. Both that which is known and the means whereby it is known are present to the knower; the former, however, is present explicitly (as a "distal" object), but the latter is present only implicitly or tacitly (as a "proximate" object).[42] The relationship between that which is explicitly present and that which is tacitly present can at any time be reversed, but doing so involves transforming what had been an object of knowledge into the means of apprehending some other object(s).[43]

This account of the experience of knowing can serve as a model for understanding the correlation between Christ, of the Spirit, and of the life of the triune God: pneumatology is the means whereby we apprehend the person and work of Christ, and christology is the means whereby we apprehend the person and work of the Spirit. Both Christ and the Spirit refer in different ways to the Father, and thus provide complementary perspectives on the triune life of God.[44] Shifting from one perspective to

40. Cf. McIntosh, *Divine Teaching*, 57–65.

41. Cf. "We recognize the ultimate epistemic right which belongs to Jesus Christ by organizing our total system of belief around the narratives which identify him, crucified and risen. If we ascribe this epistemic significance to Jesus, we shall be unwilling to hold true any belief which we recognize to be inconsistent with these narratives, and, conversely, unwilling to regard these narratives as false for the sake of holding true any other belief, should that belief conflict with them," in Marshall, *Trinity and Truth*, 180.

42. See Polanyi, *Tacit Dimension*, 10–12, 95–96.

43. See ibid., 3–25.

44. Cf. "The Son is related to the Holy Spirit not only in the divine economy but also in the eternal life of God, not by way of hypostatic origination but by inner-trinitarian

another fosters a deeper awareness of all three; the trick is not to allow one's thinking to become so conditioned by one perspective that the others are neglected.

This same complementarity manifests itself in the relationship between (on the one hand) any understanding of God and (on the other) the nature and scope of God's redemptive work: soteriology, in other words, will be immediately informed by trinitarian theology (and vice versa).[45] The above analysis of the exaltation (and in particular of the cross) demonstrated that the exaltation can be read as the revelation of the wisdom, holiness, glory, and power of God.[46] Taken together, these descriptors provide a holistic and integrative way of explicating God's redemptive presence and activity in Christ and the Spirit. Negatively speaking, the exaltation also provides us with an account of the conditions that require God's redemptive work in the first place; soteriology, in other words, is the point of entry to hamartology.

Another essential insight that follows from the exaltation has to do with what might be called its "hypostatic" and "ecstatic" dimensions. On the one hand, the exaltation evinces an image of the presence and activity of God that tracks more in the direction of individuation and incarnation. On the other hand, the exaltation also manifests an image of the presence and activity of God that tracks more in the direction of relation and incorporation. Both dimensions or forms of "in-humanation" are equally christological and equally pneumatological; to say otherwise would be to do an injustice to the integrity of God's self-revelation in Christ and the Spirit.[47] Thus, both theological anthropology and ecclesiology emerge at this point as distinct but related fields of inquiry. Between them, these fields provide the foundation for an account of contingent personal existence that avoids the twin dangers of solipsism and collectivism.[48] Like-

---

manifestation," in Del Colle, "Reflections on the *Filioque*," 206. Cf. also "By stressing that the Holy Spirit is mutually conferred by the Father and Son upon each other as mediated in the divine economy, one is advancing a framework in which the outward procession of the Spirit . . . is contextualized via the inward movement of the Spirit that returns Jesus' love to the Father and, through that same love, that of the church and all creation," in ibid., 212.

45. This is, of course, another way of describing the interdependence of the *ordo salutis*, the *ordo cognoscendi*, and the *ordo essendi*.

46. See above, § 3, p. 8.

47. See Del Colle, "Holy Spirit," 334–38.

48. Cf. Philip Rolnick, *Person, Grace, and God* (Grand Rapids: Eerdmans, 2007) 208–56. See also John D. Zizioulas, *Being as Communion: Studies in Personhood and the Church*, Contemporary Greek Theologians 4 (Crestwood, NY: St. Vladimir's

wise, both fields are amenable to exposition in terms of the multimodal soteriology mentioned above: the pursuit and exercise of divine wisdom, holiness, glory, and power should be evident within both the hypostatic and ecstatic dimensions of the human experience.[49]

Torrance provides yet another insight that helps establish the connection between the exaltation, the doctrine of salvation, and the doctrine of creation. The incarnation, says Torrance, "creates for itself out of our world" its own history by becoming the interpretive key to God's relationship with humanity.[50] The world, in other words, is not a "given" onto which is projected an account of the presence and activity of God. Rather, the notion of the world as creation is a ramification of the redemptive work of God manifest in the exaltation.[51] It seems the apprehension of the world as cosmos (i.e., as evincing an order that is equally rational, moral, and beautiful) depends (both ontologically and epistemologically) on the prior apprehension of the meaning of the wisdom, holiness, and glory of God given to the world in Christ and the Spirit.[52] The fact that it is human beings that are uniquely gifted with the task of bringing this contingent order to light and embellishing it in a manner responsive to God's Word and Spirit refers back both to theological anthropology and to incarnational theology (i.e., to the vocation of Christ).[53]

On a distinct but related note, it comes as no surprise that each of the various dimensions of the theological enterprise thus far identified (incarnation, trinity, soteriology, theological anthropology and ecclesiology, creation) each manifest in different ways and to varying degrees

---

Seminary, 1997 [1985]) 49–65. It should be noted, though, that what is *not* intended here is a correlation between, on the one hand, the distinction-in-unity of what we are referring to as hypostatic and ecstatic existence and, on the other, Zizioulas's account of "biological" and "ecclesial" life. The two forms of life Zizioulas identifies are to some degree inimical to one another, but the two forms or modes of life identified here as "hypostatic" and "ecstatic" are complementary and mutually constitutive.

49. Cf. Del Colle, "Holy Spirit," 330–32.

50. Torrance, *Incarnation*, 38.

51. Cf. Michael Welker, *Creation and Reality*, trans. John F. Hoffmeyer (Minneapolis: Fortress, 1999) 21–28.

52. Cf. Del Colle, "Holy Spirit," 324–29.

53. Cf. Philip Rolnick's observation that the self-conscious participation of human beings in the natural order "is a particularly lovely gift of the creation that is susceptible to the mixed phenomena of givenness and construction, for it allows a threefold integrity: the integrity of the world that communicates its act of being in sundry but dependably law-like ways; the relative integrity of persons who can progressively understand this world; and the interactions of persons and world that becomes the intervening phenomenon of culture," in Rolnick, *Person, Grace, and God*, 136.

an eschatological character. The manifestation of Word and Spirit in the world is itself an eschatological event (indeed, *the* paradigmatic eschatological event), so it is entirely natural that each and every dimension of the theological enterprise grounded in and ordered by the rationality of the exaltation should likewise exhibit an eschatological tenor. As Torrance puts it, "when salvation is lodged fully in Christ then he in his own person fills the whole vista of faith, while the reality of his presence through the Spirit means the reality of the presence of the kingdom here and now."[54] Far from being a mere denouement (as is the case when it is conceived chiefly in terms of the "four last things"), eschatology is here seen to be one of the principal ways that the complementarity of Word and Spirit can be recognized in each and every dimension of the theological enterprise.

In some ways, this leads back to the beginning: if all theology is to some degree eschatological and if eschatology includes (without being exhausted by) apprehension of the presence and activity of God's Word and Spirit here and now, then the question of *metanoia* is one again imperative. Thus, theology can never be about the elaboration of a closed intellectual system, but is chiefly about participation in the redemptive economy of God. The place where theological reflection is most fully manifest, in other words, is in the mutuality of members of the body of Christ, wherein the gifts of those called to this vocation can both be supported by the (sacramental) life of the community and can offer the fruits of their labor in support of the mission and ministries of the people of God. The consummation of theology, in short, is the *leitourgia* of the church on behalf of the world.[55]

CONCLUSION

All of the insights outlined herein require further exposition and clarification; this study takes only a first step on what is a much longer journey. It seems, though, that there are nonetheless three provisional (and closely related) conclusions that emerge even at this stage. First, the ongoing recovery of pneumatology and its application to all areas of theological inquiry offers a profound resource for rethinking the correspondence

---

54. Torrance, *Incarnation*, 299.

55. Cf. "the Christian experience of God is pneumatically mediated as the transformative event/process of sanctification and mission. Being 'set apart' (holiness) and 'being sent' (mission) constitutes the shape of Christian life as life in the Spirit which the human self and the community with power," in Del Colle, "Holy Spirit," 324. Cf. also Chan, *Spiritual Theology*, 102–22.

between the "*being*-of-God-in-his-acts" and the "*acts*-of-God-in-his-being."⁵⁶ Spirit-christology, in other words, is a starting point for a fully trinitarian account of God, the world, and all human experience. Second, Spirit-christology provides a way of pursuing the theological task that accounts for and accommodates (indeed, requires) the pervasive complementarity evident between particular areas of theological reflection. The ubiquitous mutuality of the various dimensions of the *ordo cognoscendi*—to say nothing of the correlation between the *ordo cognoscendi*, the *ordo salutis*, and the *ordo essendi*—is less a problem to be solved and more an opportunity to be embraced. Third, the rehabilitation of systematic theology by way of Spirit-christology cannot afford to neglect the ecclesial context wherein the "renewing of the mind" (Rom 12.2) is made possible. What Spirit-christology ultimately yields is an understanding of the theological enterprise that is ultimately oriented towards participation in and proclamation of the redemptive work of God in Christ and the Spirit on behalf of the world.

---

56. Torrance, *Incarnation*, 85 (emphasis in the original).

IV

Theological Dimensions
of Biblical Interpretation

15

The Facecloth of John 20:7

DAVID COFFEY

IN CONTRAST TO THE Synoptic accounts, in the Johannine account of the visit to the tomb of Jesus (John 20:1–10), a disciple—namely, the one identified as the disciple "whom Jesus loved"—comes to resurrection faith without the mediation of an angelic announcement. Yet it was not the mere emptiness of the tomb that induced his faith. And so we ask: what *did* lead the Beloved Disciple to faith?

In the following pericope (John 20:11–18), we see Mary Magdalene coming to faith through an appearance of the risen Lord. But she had already looked into the tomb and seen two angels, not seen by the disciples in the preceding pericope, "sitting" where the body of Jesus had been, "one at the head and one at the feet." Probably, the empty space between the angels is to be understood as corresponding to the mercy seat of Exodus 25:22, the place where God spoke to Moses, "between the two cherubim," a place, therefore, of divine revelation (cf. Exod 25:17–22, Lev 16:2, Num 7:89). The sitting posture of the angels indicates that in its definitive emptiness this space is a silent revelation of the resurrection, for the body is absent and the fact that the angels are in repose shows that they are not expecting its return. The two pericopes have an interesting point in common: in each, what was seen in the tomb could and should of itself have led to faith, as with the Beloved Disciple, but in fact it did not, with Peter in the first instance, or with Mary in the second.

It seems that despite the differences between the raising of Lazarus and the resurrection of Jesus, the Lazarus story (John 11:1–44) acts in some measure as a control on the tomb story of John 20:1–10. Lazarus, we are told, "had his hands and feet bound with bandages and his face wrapped around with a cloth (*soudarion*)" (11:44). The same word, *soudarion*, is used for the facecloth of Jesus in John 20:7. The linen cloths, therefore, of 20:7 (and 19:40) were presumably bandages for Jesus' hands and feet. Jacques Winandy says they were for his "wrists and ankles, to facilitate transport and to give the corpse a dignified attitude on the surface where it was laid out."[1] With Brendan Byrne I am not convinced by Sandra Schneiders's interpretation of the *soudarion* as a "veil."[2] This interpretation is based on the contention that in the Aramaic Targums the Hebrew word for "veil" in Exodus 34:33–35, a passage concerned with the veil that covered the face of Moses, appears to be translated by *soudarion*. The connection with the Targums is too tenuous, and Schneiders's use of the Exodus passage to refer prophetically to the ascent of Jesus (as distinct from his resurrection) as suggested by Moses' "ascent" to the Lord settles on ascension rather than resurrection as the theological key to our pericope. Bauer says a soudarion is a facecloth for wiping perspiration, corresponding somewhat to our handkerchief.[3] In fact it was larger than this, more the size of a towel. According to Winandy,[4] it was tied under the chin. This makes sense of the word "around" in John 11:44, quoted above, and better sense of the phrase "on his head" in John 20:7.

There is now general agreement that the facecloth is the clue to the Beloved Disciple's coming to faith. The argument proceeds as follows. From outside the tomb no inference could be drawn, as all that could be seen was a disordered bundle of cloths "lying there." But from inside, the Beloved Disciple perceived from the facecloth an order that moved him to infer, in faith, what Peter had failed to infer, namely, that Jesus had been raised. This order was evident in two facts: 1) the facecloth was separate from the other cloths, and 2) it was rolled up, whereas they were in a jumble. This perception enabled the Beloved Disciple to infer, with his superior spiritual insight, exactly what had happened. Where in the

---

1. Jacques Winandy, "Les vestiges laissés dans le tombeau et la foi du disciple (Jn 20,1–9)," *La nouvelle revue théologique* 110 (1988) 216–17.

2. See Sandra Schneiders, "The Face Veil: A Johannine Sign (John 20:1–10)," *Biblical Theology Bulletin* 13, no. 3 (August 1983) 94–97; Brendan Byrne, "The Faith of the Beloved Disciple and the Community in John 20," *Journal for the Study of the New Testament* 7, no. 23 (1985) 83–97.

3. *A Greek-English Lexicon of the New Testament and Other Early Christian Literature*, (1957), s.v. soudavrion.

4. Winandy, "Les vestiges," 218n19.

case of others it was an appearance of the Lord or an angelic announcement concerning the reason for the emptiness of the tomb that led them to faith, in his case it was the perceived separateness and foldedness of Jesus' facecloth.

But why should these features of the facecloth have had this effect? Byrne's answer is that the fact that it was folded supports the inference that Jesus had actively accomplished his own resurrection. But there is no kind of necessity linking this fact with this interpretation. It is at odds with the situation of Lazarus, who had to be unbound by others (cf. John 11:44). Further, it makes no appeal to the separation of the facecloth from the other cloths. It also fails to take account of the nature and purpose (described above) of the *soudarion* as a facecloth. Above all, it fails to appeal to a passage of scripture, which the text itself suggests is the key to the interpretation of the pericope as a whole. In this connection several commentators appeal to Psalm 16:10, but the problem with that is that it involves no reference, direct or indirect, to a *soudarion*.

In this regard we now need to attend to John 20:9, which uses a certain Greek word, *oudepō*, which I shall translate slightly differently from most of the standard versions. For example, the RSV has, "for as yet they did not know the scripture, that he must rise from the dead." Here *oudepō* is translated "not as yet." But in John 19:41—"Now in the place where he was crucified there was a garden, and in the garden a new tomb where no one had ever been laid"—the same word, *oudepō*, is translated "not ever," or "never," that is, *until then*. No body had ever been laid there, but now one would be. The above translations are unimpeachable, but what I am drawing attention to is that they differ according to context. I am suggesting that in the last text *oudepō* would be best translated as "not until then," and I am further suggesting that on a parallel argument this is the most appropriate translation for John 20:9 as well. I note that the NEB and the REB both have this for 20:9 ("until then they had not understood"), but not for 19:41. Further, I would make two more changes to the RSV translation. First, I would say "text of scripture" rather than simply "scripture," because the word is in the singular. A particular text is what the singular form of the word refers to in all 11 occurrences in this gospel, as distinct from its single occurrence in the plural. And secondly, I would drop the comma after "scripture." The verse would then read, "for until then they did not know the text of scripture that he must rise from the dead."

Two further comments are in order. First, the "for" is highly significant. It relates the transition from the absence to the presence of faith in the Beloved Disciple to his insight into a previously not fully understood text of scripture, a text, moreover, in some way involving a facecloth. This text was destined to acquire for them (the Beloved Disciple and Peter, the "they" of verse 9) the status of a prophecy of Christ's resurrection. Not known as such to them before, thanks to the Beloved Disciple it would be so known from now on. And secondly, while Peter was unquestionably the appointed leader of the disciples, the evangelist was firmly convinced that the Beloved Disciple, the revered founder of the Johannine community, was the more perfect model of discipleship, endowed with superior spiritual insight. Significantly, this gospel does not record a special resurrection appearance to Peter, as does Luke's (cf. Lk 24:34), with which it otherwise shares some remarkable common features.

I am suggesting that John 20:9 invites us to search the scriptures for the text that moved the Beloved Disciple to interpret the folded facecloth in the sense of Jesus' resurrection. I would like to suggest that this text was Isaiah 25:7–9. It occurs in what is called the Isaiahan "apocalypse," and, as is commonly recognized, resurrection is an apocalyptic theme. Not that Isaiah 25:7–9 can be interpreted straightforwardly as prophesying resurrection. Hans Wildberger says in his commentary, "This text is not speaking directly about resurrection but says, rather, that there are no longer any limits to how far Yahweh wishes to go in bringing restoration."[5] But this is enough for our purpose.[6] If this text truly lies behind John 20:7, it locates in Jesus' death and resurrection the fulfillment of the Samaritan confession of him as "the Savior of the world" (John 4:42).

Isaiah 25:7–9 runs as follows in the NRSV:

> (7) And he will destroy on this mountain the shroud that is cast over all peoples, the sheet that is spread over all nations; (8) he will swallow up death forever. Then the Lord God will wipe away the tears from all faces, and the disgrace of his people he will take away from all the earth, for the Lord has spoken. (9) It will be said on that day, Lo, this is our God; we have waited for him, so that he might save us. This is the Lord for whom we have waited; let us be glad and rejoice in his salvation.

Against Byrne, I am suggesting that it is *God* who brings Jesus to life, an act symbolized in *his* "unbinding" of him (cf. John 11:44). In any

---

5. Hans Wildberger, *Isaiah* 13–27, trans. Thomas H. Trapp, Continental Commentaries (Minneapolis: Fortress, 1997) 533.

6. This text had special significance for Ralph: he chose it to be the OT passage read at his funeral Mass. (See the Epilogue of this collection.)

case in this context Jesus did not unbind himself, as his hands were not free: he did not miraculously pass through the bonds, just as he did not miraculously pass through through the mouth of the tomb, as "the stone had been taken away" (John 20:1). The use of the passive voice here early in the pericope is a first hint of something confirmed later, namely, that God had been active at the tomb. This inference is supported by a second use of the passive, in regard to the facecloth, namely, that it was "rolled up." This text stands with some others in John that emphasize the corporeality of Jesus' resurrection consonantly with his well-recognized anti-docetic doctrine of the "flesh" of Jesus. The facecloth's separateness and foldedness were particularly significant and suggestive of the Isaiahan text, because they would indicate to a spiritually aware person that God had used the facecloth for its primary purpose, which is to say that with it he had wiped the face of Jesus, who had worn a crown of thorns (cf. John 19:2) and suffered a violent death. The Isaiahan text here presents God's eschatological act as the destruction of death and as salvation, and therefore, in harmony with this part of Isaiah and in virtue of a prophetic interpretation by one with spiritual insight, as the resurrection of Jesus. Of course, in itself it would refer to a general resurrection rather than to that of a particular person, but the New Testament is at pains to present the resurrection of Jesus as the guarantee and indeed inauguration of a "general" resurrection (even if only of the just). For the New Testament it is an important Old Testament text, being quoted explicitly twice in the Book of Revelation (7:17 and 21:4).

I have argued in this account against an active role for Jesus in his resurrection, even though such a role would seem to be supported by John 20:9. However, the expression that Jesus "rose" from the dead is not incompatible with a passive raising, of which this gospel speaks in regard to Jesus in other places, for example, 2:22 and 21:14. It seems likely that while elsewhere the gospel presents the later theology of an active rising, for example, in 10:18, in this story associated with the tomb, which preserves also several other early motifs, it respects the older theology that Jesus was raised by God.

Surely Sandra Schneiders was correct in proposing the kind of argument she did for the interpretation of John 20:3–9. It called for the identification of a particular Old Testament text that would be the key to the meaning of the pericope as a whole. For this she chose Exodus 34:33–35. But surely Brendan Byrne too was correct in criticizing her choice. And so I have proposed as the key a different text, namely, Isaiah 25:7–9, which I claim has clear advantages over Schneiders's choice. But this is not to say that I am necessarily right. Somewhere in the Old Testament, unsuspected by readers generally, there may lie yet another text, which someone, some day, will identify as the right one to the satisfaction of all.

16

The Book of Job and God's Existence

MATTHEW LEVERING

THE BOOK OF JOB, says Stephen Mitchell, "is the great poem of moral outrage. It gives voice to every accusation against God, and its blasphemy is cathartic. How liberating it feels *not* to be a good, patient little God-fearer, scuffling from one's hole in the wall to squeak out a dutiful hymn of praise."[1] Mitchell argues that the power of Job's outrage comes from the fact that he believes in and loves God and therefore anticipates that justice exists, even though he cannot find it. Although the answer that Job receives from God at the end of the book might seem unsatisfying, Mitchell urges us to press further. He notes that ultimately Job's quandary involves not "a question that is addressed, but a person. Our whole being has to be answered."[2] For Mitchell the key is that Job must accept the radical limits of human understanding and let go of all ideas about God. The divine Voice that Job hears causes him to enter "a world of primal energy, independent of human beings," so that Job is placed "among the most elemental realities, at the center of which there is an indestructible power, and indestructible joy."[3] What the Voice reveals is

---

1. Stephen Mitchell, "Introduction" to his translation of *The Book of Job*, 2nd ed. (New York: HarperCollins, 1992) vii–xxxii, at xvii. I also began a previous article on the Book of Job by describing Mitchell's position, although without comprehending all its elements: see my "Aquinas on the Book of Job: Providence and Presumption," in *The Providence of God: Deus Habet Consilium*, ed. Francesca Aran Murphy and Philip G. Ziegler (London: T. & T. Clark, 2009) 7–33.

2. Mitchell, "Introduction," xix.

3. Ibid., xx.

the world's pulsing life-energy and power, beyond good and evil. Our individual lives are caught up within this pulsing power, and nothing is truly good or evil—but we can find peace by awakening to the pulsing life-energy. We can then surrender our personal will, our ego, and no longer be upset by either life or death, because we have made contact with the impersonal, awe-inspiring, creative, and destructive energy of being that pulsates beneath sensible appearances.[4]

Mitchell's perspective is, in my view, a particularly striking reading of the Book of Job and of the mystery of life; his is a nature mysticism that worships the bloody and lustful play of being. By contrast, David Burrell and Gustavo Gutiérrez find God's response to be significant because Job dares to talk to God rather than merely about God. It is not so much what God speaks but that he speaks. Indebted to the medieval Jewish commentator Saadiah, Burrell recognizes that "both performatively and thematically, God's act of responding to Job mirrors the Creator's utterly spontaneous 'speaking' the universe 'in the beginning.'"[5] For his part, Gutiérrez holds that the two speeches of God in chapters 38–41 have distinct themes reflective of God's creative providence: "the first emphasizes the *plan* of God, which enfolds and gives meaning to God's creative work; the second emphasizes God's *just government* of the world."[6]

In what follows, I am particularly interested in the question of how Job knows God. We will see that Job, Eliphaz, and Elihu describe powerful signs of God's existence and providential presence. Yet their arguments fail to lead them to a God whom Job can trust. Job urgently seeks further signs of God. In the end God gives him such a sign, even while affirming the value of the earlier arguments for God's existence and presence. I dedicate this essay to Ralph Del Colle, who sought and found signs of God in the world.

---

4. For a similar view of the meaning of life, see Michael Fishbane, *Sacred Attunement: A Jewish Theology* (Chicago: University of Chicago Press, 2008). See also Friedrich Nietzsche, *Thus Spoke Zarathustra*, trans. R. J. Hollingdale (London: Penguin, 1969).

5. David B. Burrell, CSC, *Deconstructing Theodicy: Why Job Has Nothing to Say to the Puzzle of Suffering* (Grand Rapids: Brazos, 2008) 124. See also Robert Eisen, *The Book of Job in Medieval Jewish Philosophy* (Oxford: Oxford University Press, 2004); J. Gerald Janzen, *Job* (Atlanta: John Knox, 1985).

6. Gustavo Gutiérrez, *On Job: God-Talk and the Suffering of the Innocent*, trans. Matthew J. O'Connell (Maryknoll, NY: Orbis, 1987) 69; cf. 54, 84, 87. Carol Newsom has noted that although there are ancient near-Eastern parallels to Job's complaints to God, "there is no literary precedent for a pair of speeches that set over against one another the voice of a sufferer and the response of his God." See her, *The Book of Job: A Contest of Moral Imaginations* (Oxford: Oxford University Press, 2003) 238.

I. KNOWING GOD IN THE BOOK OF JOB

The Book of Job begins with Job knowing God through moral behavior and cultic ritual. God, however, permits Job to suffer the loss of all his children and property and to be afflicted with sores all over his body. In this situation, Job's wife is no longer able to know God as good, and she urges Job to curse God. Job's initial response, however, is to insist that the God he knows is worthy of praise: "Naked I came from my mother's womb, and naked shall I return; the Lord gave, and the Lord has taken away; blessed be the name of the Lord" (Job 1:21). But Job's response does not end there. He does not curse God, but he does challenge God for allowing him to live and to endure such things. Life is God's gift, but Job curses the day that he received that gift, and he asks why God allows him to live like this. God's gift of life sustains Job in misery, and this seems to Job more like a trap than a gift. Of Job's three friends, Eliphaz the Temanite is the first to rebuke him. Eliphaz simply urges that Job must be guilty of something. In Eliphaz's view, God would never permit those who love him to suffer in this way, unless they sinned against God. Furthermore, even to dare to presume that one is not to blame for one's own sufferings is a sin against God.

Eliphaz then offers a basic statement of God's existence and providence. God "does great things and unsearchable, marvelous things without number: he gives rain upon the earth and sends waters upon the fields; he sets on high those who are lowly, and those who mourn are lifted to safety. He frustrates the devices of the crafty, so that their hands achieve no success" (Job 5:9–12). Rain does not simply come upon the earth at its own volition; rather, there must be a providential Cause of all things who sends rain and who sends all the other necessary things for the sustaining of life. That providential Cause is just, and he will ensure that the gifts that he sends are in proportion to human deeds.

Job responds by again asking what sort of gifts this God provides. The issue is how God could permit his creature to undergo such extraordinary misery. Why won't God simply take away from Job the "gift" of life, which has now been exposed as a curse rather than a gift? Life is profoundly hard and short, even if it is God's gift: "My days are swifter than a weaver's shuttle, and come to their end without hope" (Job 7:7). Job wants to be done with a life like this; he wants to return such a dreadful gift. Even if Job has in fact sinned—which he denies—why does God sustain him in life just to torment him? As Job asks God, "If I sin, what do I do to thee, thou watcher of men? Why hast thou made me thy mark? Why have I become

A Man of the Church

a burden to thee? Why dost thou not pardon my transgression and take away my iniquity?" (Job 7:20–21). Job begs that God either heal him from sin (if there has been any), or take away the supposed gift of life.

The next friend to rebuke Job is Bildad the Shuhite. Bildad asserts that the testimony of the past teaches that the only way to succeed in life is to trust in God. If Job is blameless and trusts in God, God will amply reward him soon. Job responds with an affirmation of God's existence and power: "He [God] is wise in heart, and mighty in strength—who has hardened himself against him, and succeeded?—he who removes mountains, and they know it not, when he overturns them in his anger; who shakes the earth out of its place, and its pillars tremble; who commands the sun, and it does not rise; who seals up the stars; who alone stretched out the heavens, and trampled the waves of the sea" (Job 9:4–8). Obviously God is great. The heavens did not stretch themselves out, the ocean did not make itself, and the movements of the dry land cannot account for how they come to be. God can overturn even the natural order, furthermore, through miraculous acts. It is clear that this world cannot explain its own existence. A simple glance at the movements of the stars, sun, earth, and sea should suffice to tell us that God, who is invisible and all-powerful, "does great things beyond understanding, and marvelous things without number" (Job 9:10).

But this affirmation does not solve Job's problem, because it may be that this God is brutal. Whether Job is guilty or innocent does not really matter, because Job is nothing before the all-powerful God. The giver of life has Job in his clutches. Job admits that nothing can oppose God. Even though he thinks himself blameless, he recognizes that the all-powerful God could "prove me perverse" (Job 9:20). God is an unstoppable, unimpeachable force, and rather than listening to Job or helping Job, God has trapped Job in the utmost misery. The all-powerful God does not really care when humans suffer, as they do in natural disasters, for example. The all-powerful God lets the wicked rule the earth. Even the most holy person will be plunged "into a pit," a naked corpse (Job 9:31). The all-powerful God has willed it so. Why did God bother to make Job, if "the land of gloom and chaos" (Job 10:22) is to be Job's end?

Now the third friend, Zophar the Naamathite, rebukes Job. Zophar accuses Job of babbling about things that far exceed his grasp, and that instead should be left to the all-knowing God. If only Job would concentrate on repentance and holiness, God would reward him anew. Job replies that he used to repeat this same nostrum himself, in the days before he was brought low. Again, Job observes that he knows that God is the sovereign, wise, all-powerful Creator of all things. He knows that God governs human history. But he wants God to meet him face-to-face and let him know why these calamities have happened to him. Even if the reason is sin, Job wants God to relent rather than to punish so severely; after all, humans live such a short time. Job wishes that God would yearn for Job the way that Job yearns for God. Why does God give humans so little time before sending them into oblivion?

Eliphaz answers Job by arguing that Job simply lacks wisdom. God will console those who repent and love him, and God will punish the wicked. Job once more cries out that God has abandoned him. Bildad assure Job that the wicked do not flourish. Job responds that God has treated him as an enemy. Zophar reiterates that the wicked thrive only for a moment before they are cut down. Job argues that the wicked thrive and enjoy a prosperous old age; there is no rhyme or reason with respect to who thrives on earth and who lives miserably and dies alone. Eliphaz accuses Job of various sins, and also accuses Job of imagining that his wicked deeds are hidden from God. He urges Job to repent and pray to God, so as to be rewarded. Job, in reply, imagines himself speaking with God as with a kindly and understanding judge rather than a tyrant; but then Job recalls that God's purpose is unchangeable and that God is terrifyingly great, and he gives way again to fear as he recalls that God allows the wicked to rule the earth. Bildad repeats that God is pure and humans are impure, but Job scornfully replies that the all-powerful God does not need to be defended in such clichéd ways.

This leads Job into a second statement of God's existence and power: "Sheol is naked before God, and Abaddon has no covering. He stretches out the north over the void, and hangs the earth upon nothing. He binds up the waters in his thick clouds, and the cloud is not rent under them. . . . Lo, these are but the outskirts of his ways; and how small a whisper do we hear of him!" (Job 26:6–8,14). God is the one who sustains all things in being, who frames the cosmos—and such work is as nothing for God. Job then proceeds to offer his own affirmation that the wicked gain no lasting good, and he underscores that God alone has wisdom, because God alone made all things. Human wisdom can only be fear of God and an upright life. However, Job still yearns for the days gone by, when he was beloved by God, blessed with children and wealth, and honored by his neighbors, who came to him for help. Now his neighbors scorn him, and God has abandoned him to affliction and death, despite his upright life. He concludes by testifying once again to his uprightness.

A new critic arrives at this point, Elihu the Buzite. Angered by Job's self-justification, Elihu explains to Job that sometimes God chastens us in order to prevent us from falling into pride or into evil deeds. Even when a person is near death, that person may repent and pray to God once more, so as again to be blessed by God. God allows a person to draw near the pit, but God also redeems the repentant person. Elihu accuses Job of thinking that no reward is to be had from loving God, whereas in fact God always rewards and punishes people in accord with justice. It is absurd for a mere human to challenge God's justice. If anyone is afflicted, he or she must repent and praise God's works. God has charge over the whole world, sustains all things in being, and sees everything. As Elihu states, "Behold, God is great, and we know him not; the number of his years is unsearchable. For he draws up the drops of water, he distils his mist in rain, which the skies pours down, and drop upon man abundantly....God thunders wondrously with his voice; he does great things which we cannot understand" (Job 36:26-28, 37:5). Elihu's concluding exhortation to Job consists in urging Job to fear God because God is the one who sustains the cosmos: "Hear this, O Job; stop and consider the wondrous works of God. Do you know how God lays his command upon them, and causes the lightning of his cloud to shine? Do you know the balancings of the clouds, the wondrous works of him who is perfect in knowledge....Can you, like him, spread out the skies, hard as a molten mirror?" (Job 37:14-16,18).

Thus far the affirmation of God's existence and power by appeal to God's framing of the cosmos, which could not frame itself, has appeared four times in the Book of Job (or five, depending on whether one considers Elihu to present it twice). Eliphaz uses it against Job (Job 5), and Elihu uses it against Job (Job 34 and especially 36–37). Job himself uses it twice on his own behalf (Job 9 and 26), but both times he makes clear that it does not solve his predicament; he still does not understand why God's gift of life has been so profoundly undermined by God. In chapter 38 of the Book of Job, we find this "proof" used once again, and this time it extends over four whole chapters and the speaker is God himself.

After challenging Job to answer, God begins at the beginning: "Where were you when I laid the foundation of the earth? Tell me, if you have understanding. Who determined its measurements—surely you know! Or who stretched the line upon it? On what were its bases sunk, or who laid its cornerstone, when the morning stars sang together, and all the sons of God shouted for joy?" (Job 38:4–7). Recall that Job himself had earlier argued that one cannot contend with God, not least because God "alone stretched out the heavens" (Job 9:8) and because God "stretches out the north over the void, and hangs the earth upon nothing" (Job 26:7). Elihu, too, had urged Job to "stop and consider the wondrous works of God" (Job 37:14)—and of course Job had done so. Nonetheless, God presses this line of argument. God describes his power over the sea, over the cycle of day and night, and over the "gates of death" (Job 38:17). God describes his knowledge of the natures and propagation of animals. God has given them life, power, free range, and courage, but he has not given them wisdom; it is by his wisdom that they do what they do.

Depicting Job as a "faultfinder" (Job 40:2), God again challenges him to answer. Job does not dare, but instead professes his own lowliness. God then once more contrasts himself and Job. He tells Job that when Job can abase the proud, as God can, then and only then will God "acknowledge to you that your own right hand can give you victory" (Job 40:14). Job himself, of course, has already proclaimed God's unfathomable power in response to Bildad, and Job has already concluded that "these are but the outskirts of his ways; and how small a whisper do we hear of him! But the thunder of his power who can understand?" (Job 26:14). God describes the power that he has given to "Behemoth," the hippopotamus, and to "Leviathan," the whale. Even the power of these creatures, let alone the glorious power of God, should put to shame the pride that Job has in his own strength.

Job, however, already knew all this and has already confessed it all. It adds little to the affirmations of God's existence and providential power that we have already seen in the Book of Job. The structure of these affirmations or "proofs" is the same each time, although the content varies somewhat: God has given being, power, and structure to the heavens and the earth, to the cycle of day and night, to the weather (especially rain), and to animals. These creatures have a power and order that they could not have given to themselves: all things reflect a source of power and an intelligent orderer. But we recall that all this did not previously impress Job. He was willing to grant the proof insofar as it goes, but he still feared that he had been created by a brutal, tyrant God. He could not understand why God's gift of life involves such misery. Having encountered the depths of human suffering, he judged that the gift of life is a bad gift. As Job earlier said to God, "Thy hands fashioned and made me; and now thou dost turn about and destroy me. . . . Are not the days of my life few? Let me alone, that I may find a little comfort before I go whence I shall not return, to the land of gloom and deep darkness, the land of gloom and chaos, where light is as darkness" (Job 10:8, 20–22). Even granted the "proof" of God's existence and power, Job wanted to return the supposed gift of life; he had discovered that it was no gift, because even righteous humans suffer so profoundly.

Now, however, Job has the opposite reaction: when God speaks the words of the "proof"—words that mattered little when Job himself said them—Job affirms God's words and repents. Job first says what we would expect: "I know that you can do all things, and that no purpose of yours can be thwarted" (Job 42:1–2). From Job's earlier words, we already knew that he thought this. He previously admitted, "With God are wisdom and might: he has counsel and understanding. If he tears down, none can rebuild; if he shuts a man in, none can open" (Job 12:13–14). He previously stated that God "is unchangeable and who can turn him? What he desires, that he does. For he will complete what he appoints for me" (Job 23:13–14). There was no discernible impact on Job when Elihu rebuked him along these same lines: "God is greater than man" (Job 33:12).

Job's next words to God, therefore, should be quite unexpected. He recants his previous statements: "Therefore I have uttered what I did not understand, things too wonderful for me, which I did not know" (Job 42:3). What has brought about this change of perspective? Why does Job now think that he has been speaking of "things too wonderful" for him? He always knew, after all, that God was utterly beyond him. It seems that something new has come, but as we have seen it is not the content of God's words that is new. Job himself, much earlier, had already expressed the basic content of God's words. The new thing comes, clearly, in the encounter with God, and Job says as much: "I had heard of thee by the hearing of the ear, but now my eye sees thee; therefore I despise myself, and repent in dust and ashes" (Job 42:5–6). It is the encounter with God that changes Job's perspective. The proofs, which both he and his friends knew, had no impact on him because he did not trust God to care for him in the face of death and dissolution. When God spoke to him, he knew that God cared, even though God said nothing new.

This should help us to reflect upon the strengths and limitations of "proofs" of God's existence and presence. On the one hand, if the "proofs" had no value, God would not repeat them. There is wisdom in God's reminder to Job that created things cannot account for their existence, but instead receive being from God. The existence and order of the universe are miracles that no empirically based explanation can unravel. God's words remind us that we do not understand how this vast profusion of ordered finite things came to be: "Where were you when I laid the foundation of the earth?" (Job 38:4). God's words recall us to the joy and wonder of being. This is the attitude attributed to the first creatures, when God recalls how "the morning stars sang together, and all the sons of God shouted for joy" (Job 38:7). Likewise, the strength of brute animals and their natural patterns of being what they are should call to mind not only the One who gives them such exultant and powerful natures, but also the mystery of our being able to know them. We are physically weak compared to many of these animals, but like God we can know them. We have something of the perfection of rationality, but we hardly know as God knows. This too gives us a basis for lifting up our minds to God.

These "proofs," then, have value. When God employs them, he reminds Job that God is. He uses created signs to instruct Job about the divine power and presence. If these are the strengths of the "proofs," what are the limitations? Job does not know that God has a real plan for Job, other than to create him and then destroy him. When we love someone, we wish to commune with them forever; we do not wish their annihilation. Job feels himself sliding into death and non-existence. He has loved God, and if God loves Job, how could God allow Job to be in this situation? After speaking of the apparent finality of death, Job begs God: "Oh that you would hide me in Sheol, that you would conceal me until your wrath be past, that you would appoint me a set time, and remember me! If a man die, shall he live again? All the days of my service I would wait, till my release should come. You would call, and I would answer you; you would long for the work of your hands" (Job 14:13–15). Job wants to be remembered by God, rather than annihilated. It is one thing to say, as Job does, that "the Lord gave, and the Lord has taken away; blessed be the name of the Lord" (Job 1:21). But if God's name is truly blessed, if God truly cares for the rational creature that God has made, then God would not obliterate Job. It seems to Job, however, that this is precisely what God has in mind: "Thy hands fashioned and made me; and now thou dost turn about and destroy me" (Job 10:8).

In short, the "proofs" are not much good, if God is brutal and uncaring in his obliteration of humans. Who cares if God exists, if God is not loving and if God gives us only a short taste of the richness of life and of relationship with him, to be followed by everlasting "gloom and deep darkness" (Job 10:21)? Who would want even to be born, if it is simply to hope for a short time and then be utterly obliterated? This is Job's position.

After Job has heard and seen God and has repented "in dust and ashes," God commends the words that Job had spoken to his friends. This might seem strange since God himself has just finished rebuking Job. But we read that "the Lord said to Eliphaz the Temanite: 'My wrath is kindled against you and against your two friends; for you have not spoken of me what is right, as my servant Job has'" (Job 42:7). How is it that Job has spoken of God "what is right"? Job has called upon God with deepest yearning, that God might "remember me" and that God would "long for the work of thy hands." In so doing, Job has spoken truly about God, for God in fact remembers and longs for us. Moreover this God, who does indeed remember and long for us, is none other than the all-powerful One who "laid the foundation of the earth" (Job 38:4). The "proofs" that God uses instruct us that the One who loves us exists and is not another mere creature. Rather, God can do all things and his purposes cannot be thwarted (Job 42:2). God will not be thwarted in caring for his people. Job learns this decisively when he personally encounters God in the midst of his suffering.

II. CONCLUSION

The mysteries of Jesus Christ's life also are signs of God's love, from the Incarnation, to Christ's miracles, to Christ's Passion and Resurrection. In all of these ways, God confirms his extraordinary love and care for us. This does not dispense us, however, from also knowing God through the signs that he has given us in the creation. As we find in the Book of Job, we continue to need to reflect on the existence and order of finite things, so as to raise our minds to the transcendence and glory of the Creator who gives us the gift of life and the gift of salvation. We find ourselves, in other words, always in the position of Job, learning about God through both God's Word and God's signs in the created world. And with Job, we discover that at the very same time that we can truly say that we know God, we also find ourselves admitting that "I have uttered what I did not understand, things too wonderful for me, which I did not know" (Job 42:3).

17

Reformation Controversy and Biblical Interpretation

R. R. RENO

IN AN EDITION OF the New Testament that Luther oversaw, he provides an account of his reading of the New Testament as a whole. There is, says Luther, a canon within the canon, a center that "shows" Christ and his saving truth, and Luther names John's Gospel and first letter, the letters of Paul to the Romans, Galatians, and Ephesians, as well as Peter's first letter as the central texts. The Epistle of James is not part of that center. The letter is on the periphery, for, as Luther says, "it has nothing of the nature of the Gospel about it."[1] It is, as he put it, an *epistola straminea*, a strawy letter.

As you and I look back on Luther's judgment, we can see that the Reformation doctrine of justification by faith guides his assessment of James. Indeed, most Reformation and post-Reformation interpretations of James are highly charged with the doctrinal controversy surrounding the doctrine of justification. This raises a suspicion in most modern readers: is doctrine over-determining interpretation? Don't we want scripture to speak for itself, as it were, rather than being stage-managed to fit into a preconceived dogmatic scheme?

And yet, is our usual way of thinking accurate? Can the diverse witness of scripture "speak for itself"? Does doctrine flatten out scripture, making it serve only as a source of proof texts for dogmas? As I hope to

---

1. LW 35:362.

show in a short survey of Reformation era readings of James, the influence of doctrine heightens rather than diminishes interpretive attention to the context and nuance of scripture. The Reformation debate about justification put pressure on interpreters. They needed to dig deeply and develop subtle exegetical strategies in order to sustain their doctrinal convictions. The result was exegetical innovation—in some cases anticipating the critical insights of modern historical exegesis.

We can see this animating role more clearly if we recognize that in classical, pre-modern exegesis doctrine is neither the premise in exegetical arguments, nor is it a conclusion to be drawn. Instead, doctrine orders the priorities of a reader's relationship to scripture, forcing the reader to find a way to think through the details of scripture so as to sustain these priorities. This is the essential challenge of any overall interpretation of scripture. The Bible has something to say in and through the many things it says. There is a grammar, as it were, that governs its sentences. Working out this grammar sentence-by-sentence requires immense intellectual creativity, which is why, contrary to modern presumptions, doctrine vivifies rather than dulls our reading of scripture.

Let us begin with the way in which Luther analyses James. The problem is patent. James tells us that Abraham is justified by his works, but in Romans, Paul says the opposite. James describes the law as an agent of liberty, while Paul describes the law as sin, slavery, and death. In short, James is not only peripheral; the letter would seem antithetical to the core New Testament texts that Luther reads as teaching justification by faith alone. Its sentences violate the rules of doctrinal grammar. The place of James in the canon prevents Luther from simply editing out this troublesome text. Nonetheless, he is eager to block any backsliding into works-righteousness. To do so, Luther must analyze the odd sentences of James so that it accords with the grammar he takes to be normative for the New Testament.

Luther's argument moves on two tracks. First, he questions the apostolic status of James. He observes that the epistle does not read as a tightly organized document. Rather, it appears to be a loosely organized collection of traditional apostolic sayings that were preserved by a post-apostolic writer. Second, Luther suggests that *Sitz im Leben* for James is a post-Pauline context in which antinomian readings of the doctrine of justification by faith had gained credence. Against this misreading of Paul, the author of James is offering an unfortunately hyperbolic and one-sided corrective. In this double argument, we see a striking anticipation of modern approaches to the New Testament. Luther dates the text, and he establishes the context for its composition. The result is a confirmation of his doctrinal analysis. James is a late epistle that should be read as a response to certain concerns that emerge from the earlier and more decisive writings of Paul.

I do not want to query Luther's nascent historical-critical assumptions or analysis. I simply wish to point out that his mind was stimulated to think through the question of canonical development and context *because of* the pressure created by doctrine. The lens of doctrine would seem to sharpen his historical vision. As Reformation polemics placed soteriological questions in the foreground of exegesis, it became crucially important to account for relevant but anomalous scriptural data. In Luther's case, basic forms of historical-critical analysis emerge as strategies for maintaining the *sola fide* doctrine over and against the apparent works-righteousness of James.

Martin Chemnitz, a second-generation Lutheran, gives further and more detailed evidence that a concern about historical development has doctrinal motivation. In his great work of dogmatics, *Loci Theologici*, Chemnitz prefaces his discussion of the doctrine of justification with an extended reflection on the history of salvation. As befits a man whose life was defined by the increasingly intractable conflict between Protestants and Roman Catholics over a proper definition of salvation, Chemnitz saw the history of humanity, from Adam and Eve to his own time, as characterized by dissension over the doctrine of justification. Thus, Abel anticipated the Reformation view that his sins were lifted from his shoulders by faith in the promise, while Cain foreshadowed the Catholic view "that he could by his own sacrifices and other works remove and take away his sin. . . ."[2]

Chemnitz traces this history through the Old Testament, and he uses the same pattern of dissension to explain the structure of the New Testament, including the emphasis on works that we find in James. According to Chemnitz, the coming of Christ clarifies that justification comes through faith alone and not the works of the law. At this point, the devil must change strategies. Unable to defeat faith by proclaiming works, writes Chemnitz, "the devil foisted Epicurean philosophy [this is Chemnitz's way of describing antinomian rejection of moral constraints] upon the church."[3] This new strategy explains the emphasis upon works in James. "From this," writes Chemnitz, "we find a difference in the writing of

---

2. *Loci Theologici*, Vol. II, trans. J. A. O. Preus (St. Louis: Concordia, 1989) 463.
3. Ibid., 466.

the apostles, so that the earlier epistles are contending against the spirit of belief in the righteousness of the Law, while the later ones are promoting the fruits of repentance and refuting Epicurean notions regarding licentious living."[4] Chemnitz, not surprisingly, follows Luther. James must not be read as defining the nature of salvation, which revolves around Paul's account of the proper ordering of Law and Gospel. Instead, the letter should be read as a corrective response to antinomian misreadings of Paul.

My purpose is not to criticize or to defend Chemnitz's theologically motivated historiography. One rarely reads a contemporary writer discussing the historical development of the New Testament canon in terms of demonic plots, though feminist historiography has a certain formal similarity. Rather, my point is that Chemnitz is concerned to preserve Protestant priorities in his reading of scripture. This forces him to develop a historical thesis, one that describes the authorship of the texts of the New Testament in light of varying communal contexts, allowing us to see how James functions as a subordinate text in the larger canon. Paul is addressing the central soteriological question of how we are saved, while James is guarding against Epicurean or antinomian distortions that corrupt Pauline teaching. Here we can see that establishing the historical priority of Paul and the *Sitz im Leben* for James allows for a doctrinally unified reading of the New Testament as a whole, in this case one that fits with the Protestant view of justification by faith alone.

Not all Reformation interpreters used history as a tool for relaxing the contrast between Paul and James. In his exegesis of James, Calvin adopts a scholastic device in order to read James in a fashion consistent with a reading of Paul as proclaiming justification by faith alone. Calvin's analysis turns on a distinction between two different senses of "faith." On the one hand, faith can mean what Calvin describes as "a bare and frigid knowledge of God."[5] On the other hand, a theologically robust sense of "faith" entails knowledge that involves full participation in Christ. For Calvin, the author of James was faced with adversaries who claim that a mere intellectual knowledge of Christ is sufficient, and to combat them he adopted the rhetorical trope of concession. "Okay"—if I might paraphrase Calvin's analysis—"you say you have faith, but were it true faith, it would manifest the Spirit of Christ." With this gloss, Calvin is able to preserve the plain sense of James in concert with a Reformation interpretation of

---

4. Ibid.

5. *Commentaries on the Catholic Epistles*, trans. John Owen (Grand Rapids: Eerdmans, 1959) 310.

Paul. When James says that Abraham is justified by his works, he is not contradicting Paul. He cannot, since each is using the word differently. Paul teaches the basic truth that by faith we are justified, "but James has quite another thing in view, to show that he who professes that he has faith, must prove the reality of his faith by his works."[6]

One can read Calvin's analysis of James and wonder on just what grounds he might object to Trent and its teaching on justification, for it would seem reasonable to read Trent as joining Calvin by insisting upon the point that he who professes faith must prove its reality in works.[7] However, this is not a paper in ecumenical theology. Instead, I want to focus on the way in which Calvin's doctrinal commitments force him to apply himself to the meaning of the word "faith." He draws attention to the distinction between "bare and frigid" knowledge and a knowing that is participatory and animated. This distinction achieves the same end as Luther and Chemnitz's historical schemes: one can read James literally without colliding with Paul. Furthermore, in achieving this end, Calvin has injected (or more accurately, re-injected, for the distinction is by no means unique to Calvin) semantic texture into his reading of scripture, just as Luther and Chemnitz enrich and fill in a historical narrative that provides a context for the New Testament. In each case, a commitment to Reformation doctrine brings the conflict between James and Paul into sharp relief, and the minds of the interpreters are exercised. Exegesis must become active and creative in order to arrive at a satisfactory, non-contradictory reading.

The Catholic tradition follows the same pattern. Session VI of the Council of Trent treats the doctrine of justification. The canonical relationship between James and Paul is as important to the Catholic as the Protestant position, but at Trent it is inverted. Reading the session in its entirety, one cannot escape the impression that James serves as the governing center of Tridentine New Testament interpretation, with Paul offering important addenda and supplementation.

---

6. Ibid., 314.

7. Compare Calvin's summation of his argument concerning the crucial verses in James 2 with Trent, Session VI, chapter 7. First Calvin: "In this sense we fully allow that a man is justified by works, as when anyone says that a man is enriched by the purchase of a large and valuable estate, because his riches, before hid, shut up in a chest, were thus made known" (315). Then Trent: "Though no one can be just unless the merits of our lord Jesus Christ are communicated to him; nevertheless, in the justification of a sinner this in fact takes place when, by the merit of the same most holy passion, the love of God is poured out by the agency of the Holy Spirit in the hearts of those who are being justified, and abides in them."

A Man of the Church

We see this inversion of Reformation readings in the way Trent deploys quotes from Paul. For example, in the crucial chapter 7 of Session VI, the Fathers at Trent define justification as participation in Christ, a point in line with Calvin's own definition of the true faith that justifies. Such participation is made possible by the infusion of the virtues of faith, hope, and love into the believer. "Hence," Trent concludes in the idiom of James, "it is very truly said that faith without works is dead and barren." Immediately, Paul is brought into the text as a supporting voice: "in Christ Jesus neither circumcision is of any avail nor uncircumcision, but faith working through love [Gal 5:6]." This use of Paul is characteristic of Trent. In numerous instances, the same pattern follows. The independent clause is a paraphrase of James, and the dependent clause comes from Paul. Here is a typical example: "It is the just who should feel themselves bound to walk in the path of justice all the more because, now that they *are set free from sin and are become slaves of God* [Rom 6:22], and are living *sober and upright lives* [Titus 2:12], they can make progress through Jesus Christ, through whom they had access to that state of grace [cf. Rom 5:2]."[8] Elsewhere, Trent exploits passages in which Paul emphasizes growth in faith (e.g., 1 Cor 9:24ff.), divine judgment according to our deeds (e.g., Rom. 2:6), as well as many passages in which Paul condemns immoral acts and exhorts his reader to seek perfection.

While Trent reads Paul as subordinate to James, the Council does not offer an exegetical explanation; it simply pursues a strategy of quotation. For a Catholic account of the essential harmony between James and Paul, I turn to R. P. Cornelius à Lapide, an influential Flemish Jesuit who wrote commentaries on nearly all the books of the Bible in the decades following the Council of Trent.

Lapide's solution to the apparent conflict between James and Paul is to draw attention to the historical context for Paul's many teachings against works. The context is consistently one of circumcision and other aspects of Jewish ceremonial law. By Lapide's reading, "Although the Jews perceived that they were justified by circumcision and the ceremonies prescribed by the Mosaic law, Paul rejects this, and teaches that all these things are insufficient and useless for justification and salvation without the faith and grace of Christ."[9] Here, we find an interesting inversion of the Protestant position represented by Luther, Chemnitz, and Calvin. They read James as addressing a limited problem—a subplot of the devil,

---

8. Session VI, chapter 11.
9. *Commentaria in Scripturam Sacram, Tomus Vigesimus* (Paris, 1861) 133.

to recall Chemnitz—while Paul teaches basic truths about salvation. In contrast, Lapide treats Paul's discussion of works as a limited address to Judaizing Christians in the first century, while James articulates timeless truths about the new law of Christ, which is integral to the Gospel.

It is fascinating that, while Lapide's reading of Paul is motivated by the doctrinal assumptions of Trent and not historical-critical methods, he ends up with results that largely correspond to the scholarly consensus about Paul that has emerged since Krister Stendhal's groundbreaking dissent from the standard Protestant readings. However, it is more important to see that the priorities of doctrine structure commentary; he is not proving doctrine with his exegesis. Moreover, the lens of Tridentine doctrine magnifies and makes visible something rendered nearly invisible by the development of Christian thought in the West: the fact that Paul's account of salvation entails a theology of ritual and law.[10] This insight flows from the pressures created by the conflict between the priorities of Trent and the ways in which Paul lends himself to Protestant readings. Lapide must treat Paul's sentences as troublesome and irregular, and the upshot is a multi-layered, intensive analysis designed to bring them into conformity with the Tridentine rules of grammar.

The sample is very small. Nonetheless, it casts some light on the general relationship between doctrine and scripture in pre-modern exegesis. Readers did not prove their doctrinal assumptions by quoting specific texts that affirm their doctrinal presuppositions. When it comes to the doctrine of justification, that can't be done with a canon that includes both James and Paul. Instead, the commentators offer close analysis in which they show how both Paul and James can be accounted for within the grammatical rules of their doctrines. To do so, they saturate their readings with historical observations, scholastic distinctions, and scriptural context in order to bring us to see how their doctrinally ordered interpretations are apt. To a large degree this saturation is Christian theology, or more precisely, Christian theology is the manifold of intellectual practices that provides historical judgments, conceptual distinctions, and textual nuance that the exegetes deploy in order to sustain their doctrinally governed readings. Without doctrinal priorities, exegesis becomes one-dimensional and flat, all too often falling into set patterns of merely academic routine. This is one reason why older historical-critical interpreters are interesting—even

---

10. Not surprisingly, Lapide makes extensive use of Hebrews in order to harmonize Paul with James.

as they pledged themselves to *Wissenschaft*, they were still animated by doctrinal loyalties—while contemporary academic criticism seems less vigorous and creative. The exceptions are feminist and other ideologically driven interpreters. Their secular doctrines also motivate the development of various techniques for making scripture sing a single tune.

Secular, orthodox, or heterodox, doctrine is the lens through which we organize the scriptures, the world, and concepts so that we can defend, coordinate, and sustain any number of specific exegetical conclusions ordered toward a single vision of what the Bible says. The same holds for the commentators whom I have surveyed. Their doctrinal commitments organize the history of the canon, the concept of faith, and the subject matter of various scriptural passages so that they can prove that Paul and James do not contradict each other. In so doing, they are not proving or concluding with doctrine. To evoke St. Augustine's famous distinction between *uti* and *frui*, they are *using* their doctrinal commitments to achieve focus, to establish the key questions to ask the text, and to order their priorities as readers.[11]

Thus, the crucial question to ask about doctrine is not whether it is "in" the text or can be deduced from the scriptures. Rather, we should judge doctrine according to its "usefulness." Just how we discern and judge this usefulness must be the subject of another, and no doubt longer, essay.

---

11. See *De doctrina Christiana*, Book I. For an example of St. Augustine's own exegetical use of doctrine, see his brief digression into a verse of the Song of Songs, Book II, chapter 6.

18

Baptism, Unity, and Crucifying the Flesh[1]

RODRIGO J. MORALES

I WILL NEVER FORGET the first time I met Ralph Del Colle. Several years ago, when I was on Marquette's campus interviewing for my current position, I was scheduled to meet him in the early afternoon. When he arrived a few minutes late for the interview, he apologized, explaining that he had spent a little too much time in prayer after the noon Mass. Toward the end of our conversation, during which he asked (among other things) about the relationship of my scholarship to the life of the Church, he assured me of his prayers as I continued the process of interviewing for jobs and discerning where I should begin my professional career. These references to prayer came with no hint of embarrassment or affectation. They reflect Ralph's character as a man of integrity, someone who refuses to capitulate to the modern tendency toward compartmentalization and instead lives a unified life of intellectual and spiritual rigor. His prayer life is no doubt one of the many factors that have given his work such richness and depth. In gratitude for his collegiality, for his friendship, for his dedication to the Church, and for his prayers, and with the assurance of my own for him, I offer this brief piece to honor his life and work.

---

1. The research for this essay was made possible by a fellowship from the Alexander von Humboldt Foundation. An earlier version of the essay was presented at the "Galatians and Christian Theology" conference in Saint Andrews on July 11, 2012. I am grateful to the participants at the conference for their feedback.

A Man of the Church

CO-CRUCIFIXION THROUGH BAPTISM?

"I have been crucified with Christ; I myself no longer live, but Christ lives in me" (Gal 2:19b–20a).[2] This statement, one of the most striking in Paul's letters, has long been the subject of debate. Among the many issues it raises is the connection between crucifixion with Christ and baptism. Some have read Paul's startling expression in light of the similar language in Romans 6 ("Our old human being has been crucified [with Christ]") and concluded that Gal 2:19–20 refers to baptism.[3] Others deny a baptismal interpretation, arguing that the connection between co-crucifixion and baptism is a later development in Paul's thought.[4] In this essay, I will argue that Galatians 2:19–20 does in fact allude to baptism, as does the

---

2. Unless otherwise noted, the translations in this essay are my own.

3. Hans Dieter Betz writes, "Most interpreters. . . interpret Romans 6 into Gal 2:19–20." *Galatians: A Commentary on Paul's Letter to the Churches in Galatia*, Hermeneia (Philadelphia: Fortress, 1979) 123. Among the commentators advocating a baptismal interpretation, see Marie-Joseph Lagrange, *Saint Paul: Épître aux Galates*, Études bibliques (Paris: Librairie Lecoffre, J. Gabalda, 1918) 51; Heinrich Schlier, *Der Brief an die Galater*, 4th ed. of the rev. version, Kritisch-exegetischer Kommentar über das Neue Testament 7 (Göttingen: Vandenhoeck & Ruprecht, 1965) 99–100; Franz Mussner, *Der Galaterbrief: Auslegung*, 5th ed., Herders theologischer Kommentar zum Neuen Testament 9 (Freiburg im Breisgau: Herder, 1988) 180–81; Ragnar Bring, *Commentary on Galatians*, trans. Eric Wahlstrom (Philadelphia: Muhlenberg, 1961) 99–100; Thomas Söding, "Kreuzestheologie und Rechtfertigungslehre: Zur Verbindung von Christologie und Soteriologie im Ersten Korintherbrief und im Galaterbrief," in *Das Wort vom Kreuz: Studien zur paulinischen Theologie*, Wissenschaftliche Untersuchungen zum Neuen Testament 93 (Tübingen: J. C. B. Mohr, 1997) 153–82, at 170; cf. recently Wilfried Eckey, *Der Galaterbrief: Ein Kommentar*, Neukirchener Theologie (Neukirchen-Vluyn: Neukirchener, 2010) 147. See also Rudolf Schnackenburg, *Das Heilsgeschehen bei der Taufe nach dem Apostel Paulus: Eine Studie zur paulinischen Theologie* (Munich: K. Zink, 1950) 57–61. Schnackenburg interprets the verses as a baptismal reference based on the aorist verb ἀπέθανον, but reads the verb συνεσταύρωμαι on three levels: Christ's death on the cross, the Christian's death in baptism, and the continuing state of being crucified with Christ (cf. 2:19b, 6:14).

4. Betz, *Galatians*, 123; James D. G. Dunn, *A Commentary on the Epistle to the Galatians*, Black's New Testament Commentaries (London: Adam and Charles Black, 1993) 144n1; Udo Borse, *Der Brief an die Galater*, Regensburger Neues Testament (Regensburg: F. Pustet, 1984) 117; Joachim Rohde, *Der Brief des Paulus an die Galater*, rev. ed., Theologischer Handkommentar zum Neuen Testament 9 (Berlin: Evangelische Verlagsanstalt, 1989) 116n80. Richard N. Longenecker does not address the question in *Galatians*, World Bible Commentary 41 (Nashville: Thomas Nelson, 1990) 92. See F. F. Bruce, *The Epistle of Paul to the Galatians: A Commentary on the Greek Text*, The New International Greek Testament Commentary (Exeter: Pater Noster, 1982) 144. Bruce tentatively connects the saying with baptism, but is quick to suggest that for Paul the experience of co-crucifixion occurred on the road to Damascus rather than in baptism.

reference to crucifying the flesh in Galatians 5:24. For Paul baptism is the means by which one dies to self and puts to death the passions of the flesh.

Showing that the crucifixion language in these verses alludes to baptism is not an end in itself. Rather, I will argue that by its nature as a crucifixion of the self and of the flesh, baptism is ordered to unity, not only in that the rite is open to all (Gal 3:27–28), but also in that, by crucifying the flesh through baptism, the baptized are empowered to overcome the passions and desires of the flesh (Gal 5:24) manifested especially—though not exclusively—in the strife that seemed to be plaguing the Galatian churches (cf. Gal 5:19–21). This reading presents a challenge to the contemporary Church, which is characterized by discord every bit as much as Paul's first-century Galatian communities.

CRUCIFIED WITH CHRIST

The baptismal interpretation of Galatians 2:19–20, based primarily on the language shared with Romans 6, goes at least as far back as John Chrysostom.[5] In typical patristic fashion, Chrysostom interprets these verses in light of other Pauline texts. Thus, the death to which Paul refers is the mortification of the flesh, that is, putting to death the vices (citing Col 3:5: "Put to death your earthly members, which are sexual immorality, impurity, adultery"), and this death initially takes place in baptism (citing Rom 6:6: "'Our old human being was crucified [sic—ἐσταυρώθη],' which took place in the bath").[6] Modern scholars have noted other similarities between Galatians 2 and Romans 6. In addition to the specific terminology of "co-crucifixion" (συσταυρόω), Paul speaks in both passages of dying *to* something: in Galatians, it is his own death to the law (2:19a), in Romans, the death of all Christians to sin (6:2; cf. 6:10). This death results in a life with Christ (Gal 2:20: ζῇ δὲ ἐν ἐμοὶ Χριστός; Rom 6:8: συζήσομεν αὐτῷ), which he characterizes in both texts as a life for God (Gal 2:19: ἵνα θεῷ ζήσω; Rom 6:10–11: λογίζεσθε ἑαυτοὺς ζῶντας τῷ θεῷ).[7]

---

5. John Chrysostom, *Homilies on Galatians* 2 (PG 61, 645) "For in saying, 'I have been crucified with Christ,' he alludes to baptism, and in saying 'I no longer live,' [he alludes to] our conduct after these things, the conduct through which our bodily members are put to death."

6. Ibid. (PG 61, 645–46). Many modern scholars follow Chrysostom in interpreting Gal 2:19–20 in light of Rom 6, but few compare the former text with Colossians.

7. Christian Strecker, *Die liminale Theologie des Paulus: Zugänge zur paulinischen Theologie aus kulturanthropologischer Perspektive*, Forschungen zur Religion und Literatur des Alten und Neuen Testaments 185 (Göttingen: Vandenhoeck & Ruprecht,

In addition to these parallels, the connection between co-crucifixion and justification supports a baptismal interpretation of the texts, particularly when compared with other baptismal references in the Pauline corpus. Galatians 2:19-20 appears in a section of the letter that most scholars, following Hans Dieter Betz, consider its *propositio* (Gal 2:15-21).[8] Although the details of this text are notoriously difficult, the most basic point Paul wants to make is straightforward: human beings are justified by faith rather than by works of the Law.[9] This much is clear from Galatians 2:16. The verses that follow take a number of twists and turns, the details of which do not ultimately affect the present argument. The salient point is that Galatians 2:19-20 serves as part of Paul's explication of justification. This can be seen both in the conjunctions that join verses 17, 18, and 19 and in the thematic connection between verses 19-20 and verse 21 (that is, the question of the Law and of Christ's crucifixion).[10] For Paul, justification is brought about through the death of Christ, more specifically through co-crucifixion with Christ. Some might take this interpretation as an argument against a baptismal reading of the verses: for Paul justification comes through faith, not through baptism. Such a reading, however, fails to account for Paul's appeals to baptism both in Galatians and in the broader Pauline corpus.[11]

We can begin with Galatians. Justification remains a central topic of chapter 3.[12] Paul continues the contrast between faith and works of the Law, once again in the context of a reference to Christ's crucifixion (Gal

---

1999) 254; cf. earlier Udo Schnelle, *Gerechtigkeit und Christusgegenwart: Vorpaulinische und paulinische Tauftheologie*, Göttinger theologische Arbeiten 24 (Göttingen: Vandenhoeck & Ruprecht, 1983) 55-56.

8. Betz, *Galatians*, 113-14.

9. I have deliberately avoided the question of whether to interpret the phrase πίστις Χριστοῦ as "faith in Christ" or "the faith(fulness) of Christ." The question, though an interesting one, does not materially affect the present argument, and as many on both sides of the debate have admitted, the theological differences resulting from the two interpretations are ultimately negligible.

10. On the coherence of Gal 2:15-21, see Scott Shauf, "Galatians 2.20 in Context," *New Testament Studies* 52 (2006) 86-101; cf. Michael J. Gorman, *Inhabiting the Cruciform God: Kenosis, Justification, and Theosis in Paul's Narrative Soteriology* (Grand Rapids: Eerdmans, 2009) 64-67.

11. Cf. Udo Schnelle, "Transformation und Partizipation als Grundgedanken paulinischer Theologie," *New Testament Studies* 47 (2001) 58-75, at 66, 72.

12. See Shauf, "Galatians 2.20 in Context," 95-97. Hans Halter writes, "Kp. 3 ist eine Erhärtung der fundamentalen These von 2,16 und eine Vertiefung und Entfaltung von 2,15-21 überhaupt." *Taufe und Ethos: Paulinische Kriterien für das Proprium christlicher Moral*, Freiburger theologische Studien 106 (Basel: Herder, 1977) 108.

3:1–5), and then appeals to the example of Abraham to support his understanding of justification by faith (Gal 3:6–9). He points to the curse of the Law to reinforce his argument that righteousness does not come from the Law but rather by faith (3:10–14). Similarly, he notes that it is because of the Law's failure to give life that righteousness cannot come from the Law (3:21).[13] He then argues that the Law's role as a pedagogue was meant in some way to lead to justification by faith (Gal 3:24). The argument of chapter 3 climaxes with an appeal to the Galatians' baptism. Though he speaks initially of the Galatians being "sons of God through faith," Paul grounds this sonship in the rite of baptism: "For as many of you as were baptized into Christ have been clothed with Christ" (Gal 3:27). It is through baptism that the Galatians now belong to Christ and therefore are Abraham's seed (Gal 3:29), that is, those who are justified (cf. Gal 3:6–9).[14]

This connection between baptism and justification is not unique to Galatians. Romans 6 also associates justification with baptism.[15] In verse 6 Paul writes of the crucifixion of "our old human being" with Christ, which he explains in the following verse using the language of justification: "For the one who died has been justified (δεδικαίωται) from sin" (Rom 6:7).[16] Though some scholars take this verse as a Jewish maxim about death putting an end to the power of sin, such a reading is difficult to square with Paul's thought more broadly.[17] In light of the context it is much more

13. Note the contrast with the life Paul has been given through his co-crucifixion with Christ in 2:19–20.

14. Cf. Halter, *Taufe und Ethos*, 103–04. For a similar exposition of Galatians 3, see Gerd Häfner, "Taufe und Einheit: Paulinische Tauftheologie in Gal 3,26–29," in Jacques Schlosser, ed., *Paul et l'unité des chrétiens*, Colloquium oecumenicum Paulinum 19 (Louvain: Peeters, 2010) 105–39, at 115–18.

15. It should also be noted that Rom 6 is closely related to Rom 5, which also discusses justification; see 5:1, 5:9, 5:16–19, 5:21.

16. The verb δεδικαίωται is probably better rendered in this context "liberated" or "freed," but it belongs to the word group traditionally translated with the language of "justification" and "righteousness," and in the context of the letter should most likely be connected with Paul's earlier discussions of this theme. For a brief discussion of the translation issues, see Michael Wolter, *Paulus: Ein Grundriss seiner Theologie*, Neukirchener Theologie (Neukirchen-Vluyn: Neukirchener, 2011) 142.

17. In favor of reading the verse as a Jewish maxim, see, among others, Douglas J. Moo, *The Epistle to the Romans*, The New International Commentary on the New Testament (Grand Rapids: Eerdmans, 1996) 376–77; Arland J. Hultgren, *Paul's Letter to the Romans: A Commentary* (Grand Rapids: Eerdmans, 2011) 249–50; Eduard Lohse, *Der Brief an die Römer*, Kritisch-exegetischer Kommentar über das Neue Testament 4 (Göttingen: Vandenhoeck & Ruprecht, 2003) 192. For criticisms of this interpretation, see Conleth Kearns, "The Interpretation of Romans 6,7," *Studiorum paulinorum congressus internationalis catholicus 1961: Simul secundus congressus internationalis*

likely that this death imagery relates to baptism. Earlier Paul describes baptism as a baptism "into Christ's death" and as a being "co-buried" with Christ (Rom 6:3-4). Moreover, the consistency of the aorist verbs in the passage (v. 3: ἐβαπτίσθημεν; v. 4: συνετάφημεν; v. 6: συνεσταυρώθη; v. 8: ἀπεθάνομεν) suggests that they all point to the same event, namely baptism.[18] Thus, in Romans 6 we see a close connection between baptism, co-crucifixion, and justification.

The evidence of 1 Corinthians suggests that this association of justification with baptism was not a later development in Paul's thought. First Corinthians 6 contains one of the few instances of "justification" language in the Pauline corpus outside Galatians and Romans. In a transitional paragraph between his rebuke of the Corinthians over their lawsuits and his criticism of their frequenting prostitutes, Paul reminds them, "But you were washed, but you were sanctified, but you were made righteous (ἐδικαιώθητε) in the name of the Lord Jesus Christ and in the Spirit of our God" (1 Cor 6:11b). Many scholars take the language of being "washed" as a reference to baptism, both because other New Testament texts describe baptism in terms of washing and because the occurrence together of the phrases "the name of the Lord Jesus Christ" and "the Spirit of our God" indicates a baptismal context.[19] If the text is a baptismal reference, then we see two texts in the Pauline corpus, Romans 6 and 1 Corinthians 6, that associate justification with baptism. In light of the similarities with Romans 6 already noted, a baptismal reading of Galatians 2:19-20 is at the very least plausible. The probability that these verses allude to baptism increases when we consider their relation to Galatians 3:26-29, as well as Galatians 5:24.

---

catholicus de re biblica, Analecta Biblica 17-18 (Rome: Pontifical Biblical Institute, 1961) 1:301-307; Robin Scroggs, "Romans vi. 7: ὁ γὰρ ἀποθάνων δεδικαίωται ἀπὸ τῆς ἁμαρτίας," *New Testament Studies* 10 (1963-64) 104-8, at 105.

18. Strecker, *Die liminale Theologie*, 253; cf. Schnelle, "Transformation und Partizipation," 65.

19. On the connection between baptism and washing, see especially Acts 22:16; Eph 5:26; Ti 3:5. In support of a baptismal reading of 1 Cor 6:11, see Lars Hartman, *"Auf den Namen des Herrn Jesus": Die Taufe in den neutestamentlichen Schriften*, Stuttgarter Bibelstudien 148 (Stuttgart: Katholisches Bibelwerk, 1992) 64-66; Schnelle, *Gerechtigkeit und Christusgegenwart*, 179n61; Jacob Kremer, *Der Erste Brief an die Korinther*, Regensburger Neues Testament (Regensburg: Friedrich Pustet, 1997) 117; G. R. Beasley-Murray, *Baptism in the New Testament* (Grand Rapids: Eerdmans, 1962) 163; C. K. Barrett, *A Commentary on the First Epistle to the Corinthians*, Black's New Testament Commentaries (London: A. & C. Black, 1968) 141.

CLOTHED WITH CHRIST

Although he denies a baptismal interpretation of the imagery of being co-crucified with Christ, Betz suggests that Galatians 2:19–20 is most naturally compared with Galatians 3:26–28, and there are good reasons for connecting the passages.[20] Both texts refer to divine sonship: Christ's in 2:20, that of the baptized in 3:26. Moreover, the notion of being crucified with Christ fits with the participatory nature of the sonship Paul describes in 3:26: "*In Christ Jesus* you are all sons of God through faith."[21] And if the language of co-crucifixion in Galatians 2:19–20 is a baptismal allusion as I have argued, then the explicit reference to baptism in Galatians 3:27 would evoke the notion of being crucified with Christ. Such a connection is strengthened if one considers Paul's portrayal of Christ in Galatians and the nature of being "clothed with Christ" in light of this portrayal.[22]

Among the images Paul uses to describe Christ in the letter, the phrase "Son of God" plays an important role, appearing at significant points (Gal 1:16, 2:20, 4:4–6; Christ's sonship is also implicit in the references to "God the Father" in 1:1–4). Given the prominence of this image, it is significant that Paul associates the sonship of believers with baptism. As already noted, it is in the context of the baptismal reference that Paul first reminds the Galatians of their new status as "sons of God." The conjunction γάρ in 3:27 suggests that baptism is the event in which the Galatians have acquired this new status of being "in Christ" and the sonship that this status entails.[23] One might paraphrase verses 26–27 thus: "For through faith you

---

20. Betz, *Galatians*, 122–23. One wonders why he suggests this connection, since he proceeds to warn against interpreting Gal 2:19–20 in light of Rom 6:1–10. For a similar connection, see Beasley-Murray, *Baptism in the New Testament*, 147–48; Jung Hoon Kim, *The Significance of Clothing Imagery in the Pauline Corpus*, Journal for the Study of the New Testament, Supplement Series 268 (London: T. & T. Clark, 2004) 116–17.

21. Though this translation rearranges the Greek word order, it reflects the sense of the verse better than translations that suggest that the phrase "in Christ Jesus" modifies the word "faith."

22. Kim (*Significance of Clothing Imagery*, 122) asks a similar question: "If so, who is 'Christ' with whom the baptized has been clothed; in other words, with whom he has been united?" He fails to consider the centrality of the cross in Paul's portrayal of Christ, however. He focuses instead on the negations of Gal 3:28, 5:6, and 6:15, and he favors a dubious interpretation in terms of Adam Christology.

23. Schlier (*Galaterbrief*, 172–73) suggests that v. 27 grounds only the phrase ἐν Χριστῷ Ἰησοῦ. ; cf. Ernest De Witt Burton, *A Critical and Exegetical Commentary on the Epistle to the Galatians*, The International Critical Commentary 35 (Edinburgh: T. & T. Clark, 1921) 204.

are all sons of God in Christ Jesus, because in your baptism you have been clothed with Christ." This clothing imagery is crucial to understanding the role of baptism in the letter and must be interpreted both in the immediate context of verses 26-29 and in light of the letter as a whole.

In the immediate context, the imagery of being clothed with Christ functions to underscore the unity of the baptized, as the following verse clearly demonstrates: "There is neither Jew nor Greek, there is neither slave nor free, there is no male and female; for you are all one in Christ Jesus" (Gal 3:28). It is hardly surprising that Paul should link baptism with the unity of the baptized. The motif is common in the Pauline tradition, as one can see in 1 Corinthians 12:13, Colossians 3:11, and Ephesians 4:4-6. What distinguishes Galatians from 1 Corinthians and Ephesians is the explanation of how this unity is brought about.[24] In baptism the differences of ethnicity, social status, and gender that alienate people from one another are relativized through the new condition of being clothed with Christ.

But can we say more precisely how Paul understands this language of being "clothed with Christ"? The key to answering this question, I suggest, is the fundamentally cross-centered portrayal of Christ throughout Galatians. It is striking how little Paul makes of Christ's resurrection in the letter, at least explicitly. Apart from the early reference to God as "the one who raised [Christ] from the dead" (Gal 1:1b), the picture of Christ in Galatians focuses squarely on the cross.[25] In the letter opening, Paul refers to Christ as the one "who gave himself for our sins" (Gal 1:4a). His rebuke of Peter, climaxing in Galatians 2:19-21, refers to Paul's own co-crucifixion with Christ, describes Christ once more as "the one who handed himself over for me," and notes, "if righteousness comes through the Law, then Christ died gratuitously."[26] Reminding the Galatians of the terms in which he preached the gospel to them, he notes that he graphically presented Christ crucified before their eyes (Gal 3:1). His discussion of the curse of the Law focuses on the crucifixion (Gal 3:13-14). Those who are pressuring the Galatians to have themselves circumcised, Paul asserts, do so only to avoid persecution for the sake of the cross (Gal 6:12). Moreover,

---

24. Colossians seems to have a similar idea, as the reference to "Greek and Jew," etc. follows a reference to "putting on the new human being" (Col 3:10).

25. The reference to Christ "living in me" in Gal 2:20 also implies the resurrection. Nevertheless, the point remains that throughout the letter Paul describes Christ *primarily* with reference to his self-giving on the cross.

26. I have borrowed the translation "gratuitously" for the Greek δωρεάν from Richard Hays.

belonging to Christ involves crucifying the flesh (Gal 5:24) and being crucified to the world (Gal 6:14).

The point cannot be stressed enough: the Christ of Galatians is the one who gave himself on the cross for our sins. Given the centrality of the cross in the letter, one could naturally conclude that being "co-crucified with Christ" and being "clothed with Christ" are two complementary ways of describing the same event (though this event has implications for how the baptized are to conduct their day-to-day lives, as Galatians 5 makes clear).[27] It is with the *crucified* Christ that the Galatians have been clothed in baptism, and in this way they have become sons of God in Christ Jesus.

The nature of divine sonship in Galatians further supports this reading of the clothing imagery. For Paul Christ's sonship is closely bound up with his self-offering. Twice in the letter he describes Christ as "the one who gave himself for me" in contexts referring to his sonship (see 1:4, 2:20b; cf. 4:4–6, esp. compared with 3:13–14). Thus, it would seem to follow that becoming sons of God by putting on Christ through baptism involves a co-crucifixion with Christ (cf. Rom 6:6) that is to be worked out in a life patterned on Christ's own suffering (cf. Rom 8:17; note that being a child and a co-heir entails sharing in Christ's suffering).

In Galatians 3:29 Paul notes two further effects of being clothed with Christ in baptism. First, as a result of their baptism the Galatians now belong to Christ and so are counted as Abraham's seed (Gal 3:29a). Second, and related to their new status as Abraham's seed, the baptized are now also heirs according to the promise (3:29b). These themes of belonging to Christ and inheritance, as well as the importance of unity among the baptized, reappear with different emphases in Galatians 5.

CRUCIFYING THE FLESH

In 5:24 Paul reminds the Galatians, "Those who belong to Christ (Jesus) [οἱ δὲ τοῦ Χριστοῦ (Ἰησοῦ)] have crucified the flesh with its passions and

---

27. Cf. Beasley-Murray, *Baptism in the New Testament*, 147–48; Bring, *Galatians*, 180–81; Schlier, *Galaterbrief*, 173. Kim (*The Significance of Clothing Imagery*, 117) writes, "When thus the believer's death-and-life relationship with Christ is considered as the centrepiece of the metaphor 'baptism into Christ' (Gal. 3.27a) the expression 'putting on Christ' (Gal. 3.27b) can also be interpreted in the same vein, that is, the putting on of Christ connotes the entering into a death-and-life relationship with Christ." Similarly, Bruce (*Galatians*, 186) suggests, "To 'put on Christ' is for Paul another way of expressing incorporation into him," though he is hesitant to identify co-crucifixion with baptism.

A Man of the Church

desires." This verse shares, albeit with different nuances, the imagery of crucifixion with the reference to being "crucified with Christ" in Galatians 2:19. Unsurprisingly, then, many who already read Galatians 2:19 in terms of baptism offer a similar assessment of Galatians 5:24.[28] In addition to this similarity with 2:19, the notion of crucifying the flesh in Galatians 5:24 bears a resemblance to Romans 6:6, where Paul recalls that in baptism "our old human being was crucified [with Christ] in order that the body of sin might be destroyed." Destroying the "body of sin" and "crucifying the flesh," while not identical in wording, seem to point to the same reality.[29] And yet, as Betz (among others) is quick to point out, Romans 6 was written after Galatians, and we should exercise caution when interpreting the earlier text in light of the later one.[30] Is there evidence within Galatians itself that supports a baptismal reading of this crucifixion language in 5:24?

Even those who deny a baptismal interpretation of Galatians 5:24 recognize shared imagery between this verse and Galatians 3:29.[31] In 5:24 Paul refers to "those who belong to Christ (Jesus) [οἱ δὲ τοῦ Χριστοῦ (Ἰησοῦ)]," essentially the same phrase he uses to describe the Galatians in the baptismal context of Galatians 3:26-29 ("If you belong to Christ [εἰ δὲ ὑμεῖς Χριστοῦ], then you are Abraham's seed").[32] In and of itself such a connection is hardly remarkable, but there are other features in the context of Galatians 5:24 that also point to a baptismal reading of the verse.

In addition to the notion of belonging to Christ, Galatians 5 uses the imagery of inheritance, an image that also appears in Galatians 3:26-29, which notes, "If you belong to Christ, you are Abraham's seed, heirs [κληρονόμοι] according to the promise." Shortly before the reference to crucifying the flesh in chapter 5, Paul warns the Galatians, "Regarding these things [i.e., the works of the flesh listed in 5:19-21a] I warn you, just as I already warned you, that those who do such things will not inherit

---

28. See Rohde, *An die Galater*, 251-52; Mussner, *Galaterbrief*, 390n104; Schnackenburg, *Heilsgeschehen*, 61. Surprisingly, Dunn (*Galatians*, 315) supports a baptismal interpretation of this verse, though not of 2:19-20. Borse (*Galaterbrief*, 206) allows for a loose connection to baptism. Betz (*Galatians*, 289n172) characterizes a baptismal reading as "artificial."

29. So Schlier, *Galaterbrief*, 263.

30. Betz, *Galatians*, 123.

31. Longenecker, *Galatians*, 264; cf. Betz, *Galatians*, 289; Hans Halter, *Taufe und Ethos*, 131; Schlier, *Galaterbrief*, 175, 263.

32. It is worth noting that 1 Corinthians 1 also seems to connect baptism with the notion of "belonging to" someone; see 1 Cor 1:12-13.

[κληρονομήσουσιν] the kingdom of God" (Gal 5:21b).³³ The parallels between these two passages are not perfect. As some have noted, the nature of the inheritance does not seem to be the same in both cases.³⁴ Nevertheless, the combination of inheritance, belonging to Christ, and crucifying the flesh is suggestive. Moreover, the distinctive features of the inheritance language in Galatians 5 further support a baptismal reading of Galatians 5:24.

Scholars have noted three elements of Galatians 5:21b ("those who do such things will not inherit the kingdom of God") that distinguish the verse vis-à-vis the rest of Galatians.³⁵ First, the phrase "kingdom of God," though common in early Christianity, appears somewhat infrequently in Paul's letters.³⁶ Second, the participial phrase οἱ πράσσοντες is unusual in Galatians, where Paul typically uses ποιέω when referring to "doing." Third, as already noted, the use of the inheritance imagery differs from the other uses in the letter. Earlier in the letter Paul connects inheritance to Abraham and the promise God made to him (cf. Gal 3:18, 3:29; 4:1, 4:7, 4:30), but in Galatians 5:21b the inheritance is the "kingdom of God," a phrase with no obvious connection to Abraham.

In view of these anomalies, as well as Paul's statement that he "already warned [the Galatians]," Richard Longenecker suggests that these verses draw on the pre-baptismal catechetical instruction Paul addressed to the Galatians.³⁷ Analogous material can be found later in the *Didache*,³⁸ and we find hints of such instruction elsewhere in Paul's letters. We find in 1 Corinthians 6 a similar conjunction of a vice list and a warning about inheriting the kingdom of God. At the beginning of verse 9 he reminds the Corinthians, "Don't you know that the unrighteous will not inherit the kingdom of God?"³⁹ He follows this reminder with a vice list describ-

---

33. Dunn (*Galatians*, 307) notes connections with Gal 3:18 and 4:6–7, but not 3:29.

34. Cf. Longenecker, *Galatians*, 258: "The use of the verb κληρονομέω ('inherit') here does not match the other instances of the term in Galatians (cf. 3:18, 29; 4:1, 7, 30)."

35. See, e.g., Longenecker, *Galatians*, 258.

36. Rom 14:17; 1 Cor 4:20, 6:9–10, 15:50; cf. 1 Cor 15:24; 1 Thess 2:12.

37. Longenecker, *Galatians*, 258; cf. Betz, *Galatians*, 281: "In addition, v 21 bc shows that the original *Sitz im Leben* of the whole passage was primitive Christian catechetical instruction, most likely in connection with baptism." Considering his interpretation of the verse, one wonders why Betz finds a baptismal reading of 5:24 "artificial" (see n28 above).

38. Longenecker, *Galatians*, 258.

39. Though the point is disputed, the phrase "don't you know" (οὐκ οἴδατε) may function in a way analogous to Paul's note in Galatians that he "already warned [them]"

ing the "unrighteous" and warning once again that such people "will not inherit the kingdom of God" (1 Cor 6:10b). Following this warning Paul reminds them, "And such were some of you; but you were washed; but you were sanctified; but you were made righteous in the name of the Lord Jesus Christ and in the Spirit of our God" (1 Cor 6:11). Again, though some dispute the point, the washing imagery most likely refers to baptism. Moreover, later in the chapter Paul bases his exhortation on the indwelling of the Spirit (1 Cor 6:19-20). Thus, we see a close connection between inheritance of the kingdom, rejecting vices, baptism, and the indwelling of the Spirit.

In Galatians 5 we see a similar constellation of ideas. Paul warns the Galatians against the "works of the flesh" (Gal 5:19-21a) because those who do such things "will not inherit the kingdom of God" (5:21b). Instead, the Galatians are to bear "the fruit of the Spirit" (5:22-23; cf. Rom 6:22-23) and to order their lives by the Spirit (5:25).[40] If the vice list is a reminder of the Galatians' prebaptismal instruction, then the language of "crucifying the flesh," like the language of "washing" in 1 Corinthians 6:11, makes sense as an allusion to baptism, particularly given the other connections we have seen between Galatians 5:19-25 and 3:26-29. Paul's reference to crucifying the flesh seems to point to a decisive event, and moreover to one the Galatians would quickly recognize. Given the connection between baptism and crucifixion elsewhere in Paul's letters (cf. 1 Cor 1:13; Rom 6:3-11), the most obvious candidate for such an event is baptism.[41] Indeed, if Galatians 5:19-21 does reflect pre-baptismal catechetical instruction, then Paul has already prepared the Galatians to hear an allusion to their baptism and its significance.

If the baptismal interpretation of Galatians 5:24 I have offered is correct, then the nature of the works of the flesh sheds further light on the significance of baptism and on why Paul alludes to the rite at this point. The list in 5:19-21 seems tailored specifically to address the problems facing the Galatians.[42] As others have noted, a high proportion of the works of the flesh relate to disunity ("hostilities, strife, jealousy, wrath, selfishness,

---

(Gal 5:21b) i.e., by recalling earlier instruction. Cf. Rom 6:3, where the phrase appears in the context of a baptismal reference.

40. It may also be worth noting the similarity between Paul's designation of the Galatians as "those who belong to Christ" in 5:24 and his reminder to the Corinthians that they were "bought with a price" (1 Cor 6:20a).

41. Even Dunn (*Galatians*, 315), who tends to resist seeing baptismal references in Paul unless they are explicit, suggests a possible reference to baptism in Gal 5:24.

42. So Bruce, *Galatians*, 250.

dissensions, factions, envy"). Moreover, Paul warns against backbiting in verse 15 ("But if you bite and devour one another, take heed lest you be consumed by one another") and envy in verse 26 ("Let us not became vain, provoking one another and envying one another").[43] These attitudes and actions are highlighted among the "works of the flesh" that exclude one from inheriting the kingdom of God (5:19-21). It is precisely these works (among others) that the Galatians "crucified" through their baptism (5:24). A reminder of baptism in the context of a warning against strife makes sense because, as Paul makes clear at the end of Galatians 3 and, indeed, in most of his references to the rite, baptism is ordered to unity among the baptized.

By reading Galatians 5:24 as a baptismal reference and in light of the emphasis on divisive works of the flesh, we see that this baptism is so ordered in at least two senses. First, as Galatians 3:26-29 shows, baptism fosters unity insofar as it is open to all regardless of ethnicity, social status, and gender. Second, Paul's description of baptism as a crucifixion of the flesh shows that the rite is ordered toward unity among the baptized also in the sense that it empowers them to live together by the Spirit in a manner incompatible with boasting and jealousy (Gal 5:26). This unity is a crucial effect of baptism, for, as Paul warns the Galatians, those who live in jealousy, strife, and the rest will not inherit the kingdom of God (5:19-21). A righteous life manifested through unity with the baptized in the present leads ultimately to inheriting the kingdom of God. All of this is rooted in the union with Christ that baptismal co-crucifixion with him initiates (Gal 2:19-20, 3:26-29).

CRUCIFYING THE FLESH THROUGH BAPTISM FOR THE SAKE OF UNITY

The reading I have offered has significant implications for understanding Pauline theology. If my interpretation of these verses is correct, then we see an inextricable connection between various aspects of Paul's thought. The natures of Christ's sonship, of baptism, and of the Church are intimately intertwined. It is by being clothed with Christ in baptism that the baptized become sons of God in Christ. Living out this sonship through suffering and self-giving (cf. Gal 1:4, 2:20; Rom 8:17) confirms this status

---

43. John M. G. Barclay, *Obeying the Truth: Paul's Ethics in Galatians*, Studies of the New Testament and Its World (Edinburgh: T. & T. Clark, 1988) 152-53; cf. Bruce, *Galatians*, 250.

and points ultimately to participation in the kingdom of God (Gal 5:21). This self-giving can be embodied only in relation to others, and so the way the Church lives out the unity that baptism brings about is as important as the availability of baptism to all regardless of ethnicity, social status, or gender.

We live in a time when the Church is plagued by strife and division that makes the situation in Galatia seem tame. Paul's call to unity through co-crucifixion in baptism should confront us in all its stark severity: those who sow division will not inherit the kingdom of God! Though a reminder of the cruciform nature of baptism may not instantly solve all our problems, it would at least refocus our vision and could, by the grace of God, help us cultivate the fruit of the Spirit our fractured Church and world so desperately need. Few people have worked and prayed as tirelessly for the unity of Christians as Ralph Del Colle. May we never tire of working to make his hope and the vision of the apostle a reality.

V

Ecumenical Dimensions of Christian Theology

19

Mary and Inculturation[1]

PETER J. CASARELLA

RALPH DEL COLLE WAS an extraordinary ecumenical theologian (and an extraordinarily ecumenical theologian). He examined the convergences and divergences between Roman Catholicism and Spirit traditions in mainline Protestantism, in Evangelical Christianity, and in Pentecostalism. He forged new paths of understanding ("pathos v. aesthetics" or "charismatic v. sacramental") that beckon both sides to contemplate the possibility of growth towards a differentiated consensus.[2] His genius lay, I think, in the facility with which he could explain centuries of scholastic debate (on nature and grace, for example) with refreshing simplicity and ardor.[3] His uncommon erudition was worn lightly. His faith in the Spirit's efficacy in moving us towards the unity to which we are called by the Lord spoke volumes in its forthrightness. For example, he called upon his

---

1. An early version of this paper was presented during the Roman Catholic-Baptist World Alliance Conversations that took place between 2005–2010, but neither that presentation nor this text should be taken as a draft of the Catholic position in the document that ensued.

2. On "pathos v. aesthetic," see his "Aesthetics and Pathos in the Vision of God: A Catholic-Pentecostal Encounter," *Pneuma: The Journal of the Society for Pentecostal Studies* Vol. 26 (2004) 99–117. On "charismatic v. sacramental," see his essay: "Pentecostal/Catholic Dialogue: Theological Suggestions for Consideration," *Pneuma: The Journal of the Society for Pentecostal Studies*, Volume 25 (2003) 93–96.

3. Ralph Del Colle, "Nature and Grace: Why this Catholic Delineation of the 'Supernatural' is Important for Pentecostals," *Journal of Pentecostal Theology* 18 (2009) 111–22.

fellow Catholics to witness in a distinctively ecclesial manner that brings others through sacraments of initiation to faith in Jesus Christ. "How can bishops, priests, deacons, religious, spiritual directors, and others who exercise ministry," asks Del Colle, "promote the formation of evangelistic apostolates for the future?" [4] His answer: "It all comes down to whether one can share the Gospel of Jesus Christ to one another out of the divine love that mission embodies."[5] Here we see his bold, Ignatian sense of purpose.

Del Colle's work on Mary fits a similarly ecumenical pattern, albeit one more irenic in its Benedictine style of obedience to following the Lord. His essay from 2007 entitled "Mary, the Unwelcome (?) Guest in Catholic/Pentecostal Dialogue" is a sharply cut and finely polished gem.[6] It will suffice to glance at just a few facets. Examining Biblical evidence, *Lumen Gentium*, and the ecumenical practice of the Dombes Group in France, Del Colle posited four intersections between Catholics and Pentecostals: 1) the outpouring of the Spirit upon the disciples gathered in prayer with Mary on the day of the Pentecost, 2) Mary as a singular human instance of how the grace of Christ flows through the charisms of the Holy Spirit in a wholly efficacious manner, 3) the recognition of the Spirit's anointing in fraternal/sororal communion and with that the priority of the Marian over the Petrine dimension of the Church, and 4) praise for God's glory and for the shining examples of God's grace through the communion of the Holy Spirit, both now and in the Parousia. Del Colle challenges Pentecostals to acknowledge the Spirit in the liturgical prayers of Catholics, and he challenges Catholics to see a form of ecclesial communion in Pentecostal/charismatic assembly. Del Colle's robustly ecumenical theology of the Spirit enables him to articulate an integral Mariology: she is neither just a "type" of the whole Church ("ecclesiotypic orientation") nor just an individual example of faith in Christ ("christotypical") who stands apart from the Church. Mary's criterion of belonging is neither adherence to an abstract theorem nor a privately experienced sense of belonging to Christ. *Abiding within the ecclesial communion* and *the concrete praxis of Christian faith* go together in the life of discipleship that Mary teaches us. Catholics see Mary as a watermark of the Church's being (to borrow a phrase from

---

4. Ralph Del Colle, *Talking with Evangelicals: A Guide for Catholics* (Mahwah, NJ: Paulist, 2012) 80–81.

5. Ibid., 81.

6. Ralph Del Colle, "Mary, the Unwelcome (?) Guest in Catholic/Pentecostal Dialogue," *Pneuma: Journal of the Society for Pentecostal Studies* 29 (2007) 214–25.

Hans Urs von Balthasar) only because she can thus point out for each of us individually the path to follow Christ:

> The outpouring of the Holy Spirit is an event among persons of whom Mary can serve as an icon. She witnesses to the fruitfulness of the Spirit's work.[7]

Mary's witness of faith bears fruit within the life of the Spirit. This message presents challenges for both Catholics with a strong Marian piety and those raised in the Spirit traditions. In the rest of this essay, I will follow this extraordinary ecumenical example in addressing another pressing issue regarding Mary's witness.

I. THE ECUMENICAL CHALLENGE OF AN INCULTURATED MARY

When Mary appears to believers and this appearance receives the recognition of the Church, she communicates the message of the Gospel in the language and culture of the believers. Mary of the New Testament is thus translated into a local idiom. This process of translation has taken place and continues to take place across the globe.[8] Pope John Paul II, for example, reflected on the universality of Marian sites like that of Guadalupe, Lourdes, Fatima, and Jasna Góra. He discovered in these encounters a new approach to theological anthropology. The same pontiff who regularly exhorted millions of Catholics to join him in such pilgrimages re-defines the globalized faith in Christ inspired by Mary as "the interior space" re-opened within humanity that the eternal Father can fill with every spiritual blessing.[9] In other words, the measure of success of Marian devotion lies not in her frequent flyer miles. It lies rather in Mary's capacity within the divine plan of salvation to witness to a faith in Christ that opens up to a "new and eternal Covenant."[10] Mary's interior space is the unfathomably wide but largely hidden space of humanity's capacity to say "Yes" to God.[11]

---

7. Ibid., 217. Mary and the saints thus transform elements of temporal existence into manifestations of eschatological and eternal realities according to Ralph Del Colle, "Trinity and Temporality: The Relationship between Time and the Divine Being," *The Spirit & Church* 4 (2002) 36–37.

8. Cf. Lamin Sanneh, *Whose Religion is Christianity? The Gospel beyond the West* (Grand Rapids: Eerdmans, 2003).

9. Pope John Paul II, *Redemptoris Mater*, #3.

10. Ibid.

11. Closely tied to this is the notion introduced by Pope John Paul II at the homily

A Man of the Church

This astute insight into the Christian universality of the Marian fiat has positive repercussions for ecumenical dialogue.

When Mary appears in a distinct culture, this appearance testifies to the seed of the Gospel that faithful witnesses have planted in that culture. The inculturated Mary thus belongs to the harvest that can arise from placing the seed of the Gospel in new soil.[12] Her presence in the language and tongue of a distinct culture is supremely fitting given that her own identity in Scripture is inextricably bound up with her being the spiritual embodiment of the daughter Zion. Just as Mary's witness to Christ becomes more and not less enhanced through her self-presentation as the daughter Zion, so too is her self-presentation as—for example, Our Lady of Guadalupe or Our Lady of Czestochowa—an enhancement rather than a diminishment of her role and self-description as a witness to Christ. The relationship between the Daughter Zion and the Marian apparitions of later centuries is meant only to offer an analogy about the process of inculturation. The image of Mary in the New Testament is already an inculturated presentation of what came before. To acknowledge that a stream of interpretation precedes Mary's unique role in the history of salvation centered on her Son is not to slight the singularity of the Marian fiat. Mary belongs to the Old Testament history of interpretation of the Daughter Zion even as she points to the beginning of an insuperably new era of history. Since Mary of the New Testament is the one who appears in the Marian apparitions of the later centuries, here the relationship is exactly the opposite. Apparitions belong to a stream of interpretation that begins with the Mary of the New Testament, but they represent no decisive break with the Biblical history.

The remainder of this chapter will investigate the theological foundations of the Catholic teaching regarding Mary and inculturation. It consists of three parts. The first part treats the question of the relationship between faith and culture in Catholicism and examines some aspects of this teaching as it pertains to Mary. The second part provides a brief overview of the treatment of popular piety in recent Roman Catholic teaching as it pertains to Mary. In this context, I will examine the distinction in current Roman Catholic thinking between the unique devotion to the Blessed

---

for the announcement of *Redemptoris Mater* that Mary is "the memory of the Church." For further elaboration, see Hans Urs von Balthasar, *Mary for Today* (San Francisco: Ignatius, 1987) 35–45.

12. On the imaging of inculturation as a harvest, see Ferdinand Nwaigbo, *Mary-Mother of the African Church: A Theological Inculturation of Mariology* (Berlin: Peter Lang, 2001) 172–73.

Virgin Mary and the adoration that is reserved for Jesus Christ. The third part advances the argument regarding the necessity and limits of an inculturated Mary by focusing on three particular cases in Latin America.

Recent Catholic thinking about inculturation is well summarized by Pope John Paul II in his post-Synodal Apostolic Exhortation, *Ecclesia in Oceania*.[13]

> The process of inculturation is the gradual way in which the Gospel is incarnated in the various cultures. On the one hand, certain cultural values must be transformed and purified, if they are to find a place in a genuinely Christian culture. On the other hand, in various cultures Christian values readily take root. Inculturation is born out of respect for both the Gospel and the culture in which it is proclaimed and welcomed.... The Synod Fathers saw further inculturation of the Christian faith as the way leading to the fullness of ecclesial *communio*. Authentic inculturation of the Christian faith is grounded in the mystery of the Incarnation. "God loved the world so much that he gave his only Son" (John 3:16); in a particular time and place, the Son of God took flesh and was "born of a woman" (Gal 4:4). To prepare for this momentous event, God chose a people with a distinctive culture, and he guided its history on the path towards the Incarnation.[14]

The Pope ties inculturation closely to the taking on flesh of the Word of God and likewise to the reality of a full ecclesial communion.[15] As the Gospel takes root in a culture, its enfleshment is directly rather than inversely related to the permeation of all aspects of that culture by the Word of God. The Pope underscores that inculturation cannot be limited to a single plane of cultural life. The question of how the Gospel can be presented to indigenous peoples accordingly must be broached with the greatest of tact and intelligence. In the words of Paul VI from a 1969 symposium of African bishops: "It will require an incubation of the Christian 'mystery' *in the genius of your people* in order that its native voice, more clearly and frankly, may then be raised harmoniously in the chorus of other voices

---

13. See also, for example, *Ecclesia in Africa*, #55–71.

14. *Ecclesia in Oceania*, Post-Synodal Apostolic Exhortation of Nov. 22, 2001, #16. See also #6 on the work of Blessed Mary MacKillop among the Aboriginal peoples in Australia. Cf. *Redemptoris Missio*, #52–54 and *Catechism of the Catholic Church*, #854.

15. Cf. Francis E. George, OMI, *Inculturation and Ecclesial Communion. Culture and Church in the Teaching of Pope John Paul II* (Rome: Urbaniana, 1990).

in the universal Church."¹⁶ John Paul II applies this same teaching to the devotion to Mary in the Southwest Pacific. Mary in Oceania, he says, has been a helper in the Church's efforts to preach and teach the Gospel.[17] Titles that have a special significance in the local setting like "Our Lady of Peace" or "Help of Christians" are a function of this evangelizing role. Mary has no entitlement or throne apart from that of service to the person of the incarnate Word of God. To say this is not meant as a dethronement of Mary but rather as a specification of her proper place in the plan of salvation.[18]

II. FAITH, CULTURE, AND REVELATION

The mandate to transform the culture into a culture capable of bearing the fruit of the gospel lies at the heart of the Gospel itself. St. Paul's sermon on the unknown God at the Areopagus (Acts 17:22–31) is a prime example of inculturation because here Paul takes a philosophical teaching of Aratus of Soli and examines it in the light of the revelation of Jesus Christ. Paul engages the culture of the Areopagus. By the same token, he is able to show that knowing the idiom and mode of thinking of the pagan culture serves more than just a strategic end. In spite of the singularity of her witness, the Mother of the Lord for Catholics is still not presented in the New Testament as a bare soul who stands as an individual before God.[19] Catholicism does not place the materiality of culture on a higher plane

---

16. Address to those participating in the Symposium of African Bishops at Kampala, July 31, 1969, 2: AAS 61 (1969) 577, as cited in *Redemptoris Mater*, #54. Italics added.

17. *Ecclesia in Oceania*, Post-Synodal Apostolic Exhortation of Nov. 22, 2001, #53.

18. *Lumen Gentium* #59 still refers to the Mary assumed into heaven as *universorum regina a Domino exaltata*. On this see Pope John Paul II, *Redemptoris Mater*, #41, who links her queenship directly to discipleship. On the connection between the necessity of inculturation and the mystery of salvation, see Vatican II, *Ad Gentes Divinitus*, #10.

19. For certain Lutherans, for example, a focus on Mary's gender, her motherhood, her cultural and therefore religious identity—all of the characteristics tied to her own flesh—are of no real theological value. See, in this regard, the honest and adroit reflections of the Lutheran systematician Lois Malcolm: "What Mary Has to Say about God's Bare Goodness," in *Blessed One: Protestant Perspectives on Mary*, ed. Beverly Roberts Gaventa and Cynthia L. Rigby (Louisville: Westminster John Knox, 2002) 139–141. For a non-polemical Catholic appraisal of the insights of the Protestant Reformation of Marian dogma, one can consult George Tavard, *The Thousand Faces of Mary* (Collegeville, MN: Liturgical, 1996) 103–67.

than spirituality but sees the possibility of having the Gospel bear fruit in the culture through the lens of Mary's total self-giving in body and soul.

One good way to appreciate the Marian witness of faith as an evangelization of culture is through the image of the Daughter Zion. What is indeed significant about this designation of Mary of the New Testament is that the Scriptural motif highlights the "physical substratum" of a spiritual solidarity.[20] If it is the case that the narrative in Luke 1:28–33 has as its model Zephaniah 3:14–17, then some theological conclusions could be justified about Mary as the Daughter Zion.[21] The first and most important one is that Mary accepts the word of the angel and is called to rejoice in that message. Her receptivity is paradoxically the free response of a reflective individual that simultaneously embodies the corporate person of Israel. In the words delivered as a pastoral address in 1975 by then theologian Joseph Ratzinger: "She is in person the true Zion, toward whom hopes have yearned throughout all the devastations of history."[22] Whatever holiness lies in Israel has thus reached its fulfillment in the free and wholly personal response of the Mother of God.

Mary's Jewishness lies at the border between the Old and New Covenant. What, if anything, carries forward from that Jewishness when she assents to the message of the angel? In the words of theologian Ratzinger:

> She is entirely a Jewess, a child of Israel, of the Old Covenant, and as such a child of the full covenant, entirely a Christian: Mother of the Word. She is the New Covenant in the Old Covenant; she is the New Covenant *as* the Old Covenant, *as* Israel: thus no one can comprehend her mission or her person if the unity of the Old and New Testaments collapses. Because she is entirely *Entsprechung* [response, correspondence], she cannot be understood where grace seems to be opposition and response, where the real response of the creature appears to be a denial of grace; for a word that never arrived, a grace that remained solely at God's disposal without becoming a response to him, would be no grace at all, but just a futile game.[23]

---

20. The term "physical substratum" is drawn from the work of Hans Urs von Balthasar and is here used as cited by Malcolm.

21. I have not provided here the textual evidence for this parallel. It can be found in Joseph Ratzinger, *Daughter Zion: Meditations on the Church's Marian Belief* (San Francisco: Ignatius, 1983) 38–47 (who relies upon Heinz Schürmann and René Laurentin). See also Emery de Gaál, *The Theology of Pope Benedict XVI* (New York: Palgrave MacMillan, 2010) 293–94.

22. *Daughter Zion*, 43. See also Pope John Paul II, *Redemptoris Mater*, #3.

23. *Daughter Zion*, 65 (translation altered).

The theological importance of her Jewishness—and even of her whole embodiment—lies in the character of the response. It is not just that Mary perfects the example of a human response to God. She *is* the creature who has become the response.[24] Her word (*Wort*) *is* response (*Antwort*). She gives us the most cogent example of why pure obedience to God is never an abrogation of human freedom.

Mary's embodiment of Jewish faithfulness is presented to view even as she makes possible a new order of history. This pivotal role that she plays in the unfolding of salvation history signifies that the question of inculturation and the attitude of Christian receptivity embodied in the faithfulness of Mary to God cannot be separated. Mary embodies a particular culture, but the witness of faith that she symbolizes is much more than a cultural relic.[25] Nothing is dated in her witness. In accepting the task of being the Mother of the Lord, she completes the task of Israel to witness to the coming of a future Messiah. She responds by making a commitment of body *and* soul. She witnesses as a *Realsymbol*, according to von Balthasar.[26] By disincarnating Mary's witness, these connections are easily lost, and the task of evangelization can be reduced to winning atomized, disembodied souls for a disincarnate Christ. Ferdinand Nwaigbo writes that inculturation is a new mission of the Church for evangelization. Evangelization involves incarnating the Word of God in distinct cultures so that each distinct complete reception of the faith becomes "the Centrum from where Universal Church shares and partakes the *koinonia* with all the particular Churches, through a particular culture."[27]

III. CATHOLIC PRINCIPLES REGARDING THE MARIAN WITNESS IN POPULAR PIETY

Among the most dramatic gesture of the fathers of the Second Vatican Council with respect to ecumenism was the inclusion of the treatise on the Blessed Virgin Mary within the treatise on the Church.[28] But the explicit

---

24. Ibid.

25. Cf. *Redemptoris Missio*, #42–43: "The First Form of Evangelization is Witness."

26. Hans Urs von Balthasar, *Theo-Drama. Theological Dramatic Theory*, vol. 3: *Dramatis personae; Persons in Christ* (San Francisco: Ignatius, 1992) 333. Quoting St. Ambrose, Balthasar says that she realizes in bodily terms what the Church realizes spiritually.

27. *Mary—Mother of the Church of Africa*, 169.

28. Cf. George Weigel, "Reviewing Vatican II: An Interview with George Lindbeck," *First Things* 48 (December 1994) 44–50.

statement in *Lumen Gentium* on the uniqueness of Christ as mediator is equally straightforward:

> There is but one Mediator as we know from the words of the apostle, "for there is one God and one mediator of God and men, the man Christ Jesus, who gave himself as a redemption for all" (1 Tm 2:5–6). The maternal duty of Mary toward men in no wise obscures or diminishes this unique mediation of Christ, but rather shows His power. For all the salvific influence of the Blessed Virgin on men originates, not from some inner necessity, but from the divine pleasure. It flows forth from the superabundance of the merits of Christ, rests on His mediation, depends entirely on it and draws all its power from it. In no way does it impede, but rather does it foster the immediate union of the faithful with Christ.[29]

On the basis of such conciliar emphasis on the uniqueness of Christ's role as mediator, Pope John Paul II made the proposal in *Redemptoris Mater* (March 25, 1987) that the ecumenical "pilgrimage of faith" could be strengthened through a mutual study of the Mystery of the Incarnation and the mystery of the divine Motherhood.[30] The Pope is unswerving in asserting the subordination of Mary to Jesus in the priority of mediatorship, but he still insists upon the role of Mary as a "type" or figure of the Church.[31] By this he affirms the teaching developed by St. Ambrose and, as noted above, supported in *Lumen Gentium*.[32] She exists as an ecclesial watermark to teach discipleship. This feature of Mary means that her role in signifying the Church as a sacrament of salvation is more than that of a moral exemplar but still essentially different from and subordinate to that of the Incarnate Word. Mary's words and actions speak to the greatness of the Lord, but the language she utters is wholly that of God's love for humanity. The designation of Mary as a figure of the whole Church is sometimes linked to her symbolic status as Mother of the Church even though this latter term is not meant to signify that spiritual motherhood is anything less than a task for the whole Church.[33]

---

29. *Lumen Gentium*, #60. See also *Dei Verbum*, #2.
30. *Redemptoris Mater*, #30.
31. Ibid., #42.
32. *Lumen Gentium*, #63, citing St. Ambrose *Expos. Lc.* II, 7: PL 15, 1555.
33. On these points, see Hans Urs von Balthasar, *Theo-Drama* vol. 3 (San Francisco: Ignatius, 1992) 300–305.

A Man of the Church

Principles are needed to highlight the witness character of Marian devotions and safeguard the priority of Christ's mediatorship. In recent Roman Catholic scholarship much attention has been paid to the impulse of a theology from below that is inscribed into divergent forms of popular piety.[34] The magisterium neither condones nor condemns popular Marian devotions by virtue of their popularity. Instead the bishops of the Second Vatican Council in the Constitution on the Sacred Liturgy went to the heart of the matter by subordinating the legitimate veneration (*doulia*) of the Virgin to the adoration (*latria*) of God in the liturgical celebration. The promotion of devotions, including to the Blessed Virgin Mary, are supposed to accord with the rhythms and final goal of the sacred liturgy, which is the pilgrimage of the people of God to God.

> Popular devotions of the Christian people are to be highly commended, provided they accord with the laws and norms of the Church, above all when they are ordered by the Apostolic See. . . . But these devotions should be so drawn up that they harmonize with the liturgical seasons, accord with the sacred liturgy, are in some fashion derived from it, and lead the people to it, since, in fact, the liturgy by its very nature far surpasses any of them.[35]

This key passage also reiterates a central theme of the Council, namely, that the liturgy is the source and summit of the Christian life. At the same time, it recognizes that the people of God can and should practice "popular devotions" in such a way as to uphold the priority of the liturgy.

The *Directory on Popular Piety and the Liturgy: Principles and Guidelines* from 2001 offers additional guidance in interpreting the teaching of the Council. The Directory is unequivocal on the need to maintain a proper balance between liturgy and popular piety:

> Thus, it is important that the question of the relationship between popular piety and the Liturgy not be posed in terms of contradiction, equality or, indeed, of substitution. A realization of the primordial importance of the Liturgy, and the quest for its most authentic expressions, should never lead to neglect of the reality of popular piety, or to a lack of appreciation for it, nor

---

34. See, for example, Peter Phan, ed., *Directory on Popular Piety and the Liturgy: Principles and Guidelines; A Commentary* (Collegeville, MN: Liturgical, 2005), as well as the relevant essays in Peter Casarella and Raúl Gómez, eds., *Cuerpo de Cristo: The Hispanic Presence in the U.S. Catholic Church* (New York: Crossroad, 1998).

35. *Sacrosanctum concilium* Constitution on the Sacred Liturgy (Dec. 4, 1963) #13.

any position that would regard it as superfluous to the Church's worship or even injurious to it.[36]

The *Directory* offers guidelines for pastoral agents to make judgments regarding whether popular devotions are in actual concord with "the primordial importance of the liturgy."[37] More importantly, the *Directory* includes statements that could help to lift the veil of suspicion that obscured the evangelizing potential of popular devotions: "For its part, popular piety, because of its symbolic and expressive qualities, can often provide the Liturgy with important insights for inculturation and stimulate an effective dynamic creativity."[38]

The *Directory* also recognizes other authoritative sources for guidance on the matter that emanated from the Apostolic See and regional episcopal conferences.[39] In this regard, it is extremely important to recall the historic meeting in Puebla in 1979 of the Latin American bishops with Pope John Paul II. In this document, the bishops treat the relationship between *religiosidad popular* (popular Catholicism, popular piety) and evangelization in terms of their ability to complement one another. They specifically cite the need to recognize the pastoral task of "promoting the cross-fertilization (*mutua fecundación*) between liturgy and popular in order to be able to channel with lucidity and prudence the deep desire for prayer and charismatic vitality that today is being experienced in our countries."[40] The Latin American bishops meeting at Puebla in 1979 no doubt faced a strong resistance to the depreciation of popular piety and were also looking for instruments to carry forward the Gospel's message concerning an integral theology of liberation, a debate that would come to the fore in the next seven years with two statements on the theology of liberation from the Congregation for the Doctrine of the Faith. The idea of cross-fertilization was in no way a capitulation to a non-Biblical piety but rather an attempt to confront the problem of inculturating the Gospel from the grassroots, recognizing the strength and evangelical purpose of

---

36. *Directory on Popular Piety and the Liturgy: Principles and Guidelines*, #50.

37. The central concern seems to be the preservation of the centrality of the paschal mystery of our Lord in all pious exercises of faith. This criterion accords rather well with the focus on the crucified embrace of the Lord in Latino/a popular Catholicism. See, for example, Peter Casarella, "The Painted Word," *The Journal of Hispanic/Latino Theology* 6 (November 1998) 18–42.

38. *Directory*, #58, citing the Puebla document discussed below.

39. Ibid., #2.

40. *Third General Conference of CELAM*, Puebla (1979) #465.

popular movements that fervently support pious practices within the context of a liturgical Christian faith.

The veneration of the Virgin retains a certain uniqueness in the cult of the saints in Catholic doctrine and practice. In fact, the *Catechism of the Catholic Church* reiterates the position of the Second Vatican Council that the Virgin Mary merits preeminence in devotion but never adoration.[41] Also affirmed is the conciliar teaching that "this very special devotion . . . differs essentially from the adoration which is given to the Incarnate Word and equally to the Holy Spirit, and greatly fosters this adoration."[42] Beyond Marian prayers, the Church also fosters Marian liturgical feasts with this same end in mind. As Ralph Del Colle has reminded us, her iconic status is and can only be a fruit of grace.

Another recent ecumenical advance appears in the somewhat unlikely venue of a papal letter on the Rosary.[43] Pope John Paul II considered the practice of the Rosary as a means to contemplate Christ through the eyes of Mary. He takes the traditional motif of Mary as a model of contemplative prayer and imbues it with a Christocentric phenomenology that ponders her manifold gazes at the Son of God:

> Thereafter Mary's gaze, ever filled with adoration and wonder, would never leave him. At times it would be *a questioning look*, as in the episode of the finding in the Temple: "Son, why have you treated us so?" (Lk 2:48); it would always be *a penetrating gaze*, one capable of deeply understanding Jesus, even to the point of perceiving his hidden feelings and anticipating his decisions, as at Cana (cf. Jn 2:5). At other times it would be *a look of sorrow*, especially beneath the Cross, where her vision would still be that of a mother giving birth, for Mary not only shared the passion and death of her Son, she also received the new son given to her in the beloved disciple (cf. Jn 19:26–27). On the morning of Easter hers would be *a gaze radiant with the joy of the Resurrection*, and finally, on the day of Pentecost, *a gaze afire with the outpouring of the Spirit* (cf. Acts 1:14).[44]

---

41. *Catechism of the Catholic Church*, #971.

42. Ibid., citing *Lumen Gentium*, #66.

43. Pope John Paul II, Apostolic Letter of October 16, 2002, *Rosarium Virginis Mariae*. I explore some ecumenical dimensions of the letter in my essay "Contemplating Christ through the Eyes of Mary: The Apostolic Letter *Rosarium Virginis Mariae* and the New Mysteries of Light," *Pro Ecclesia* (Spring 2005) 161–73.

44. *Rosarium Virginis Mariae*, #10.

Mary helps the believer to focus his or her whole life on Christ. Through her eyes the believer can pose questions to Christ, can understand him and have empathy with Him, can grieve, can rejoice in Him, and can be overshadowed by the Holy Spirit. The practice of reciting a prayer to God through Mary is thus an *imitatio Christi*.

IV. TWO IMAGES FROM LATIN AMERICA

The Virgin Mary is one of the most common figures depicted in Latino popular religion. The diversity of Latino Marian images is far greater than many realize, but it will suffice here to focus on two: the Mexican-American experience of Our Lady of Guadalupe and the Cuban experience of Our Lady of Charity. Although the devotion to Mary is more significant among Roman Catholics of Hispanic descent than among Protestants, the images have a cultural significance that can transcend these differences.[45] For example, Eldin Villafañe, a leading Latino Pentecostal theologian in the United States, is quite appreciative of the symbolic status, religious significance, and promise for social liberation for all Christians represented by Our Lady of Guadalupe.[46]

Although the devotion to Our Lady of Guadalupe is sometimes perceived as pan-Hispanic, its origins and meaning are "very Mexican."[47] Her liberating function owes much to the appearance to the indigenous Juan Diego, who takes her message with *flor y canto* ("flower and song," an indigenous term that underscores the "truth" of his experience), as a means to convert the reigning bishop to promote a post-colonial Christianity that considered all peoples to be God's people. Mexican American women in particular have found a form of empowerment in the light of her presence.[48] Guadalupe is also known by Mexican Americans as *la Morenita*, the brown skin, brown-faced Virgin with dark hair, an endearing name that also highlights the question of the how colonial Christianity incorporated symbolic aspects of beliefs native to the New World. According to the earliest report of her appearance, i.e., the document written in

45. Nora O. Lozano-Diaz, "Ignored Virgin or Unaware Women A Mexican-American Protestant Reflection on The Virgin of Guadalupe," in *Blessed One*, 85–96.

46. Eldin Villafañe, *El Espiritu Liberador. Hacia una ética social Pentecostal hispanoamericana* (Grand Rapids: Eerdmans, 1996) 52–54.

47. Virgil Elizondo, *Guadalupe: Mother of the New Creation* (Maryknoll, NY: Orbis, 1997), x.

48. Jeannette Rodríguez, *Our Lady of Guadalupe. Faith and Empowerment among Mexican-American Women* (Austin: University of Texas Press, 1994).

the classical Nahuatl tongue of Juan Diego, she appeared in 1531 on the site where there already existed a cult devoted to sun god Tonantzin.[49] She is clothed with a turquoise blue mantle of sun. Much attention is also focused on her eyes, for an image of Juan Diego and the bishop is actually present in her pupils:

> The missioners wanted to destroy the Indians' sacred statues and replace them with Euro-Christian imagery . . . [Guadalupe] is no mere Indian statue nor Christian image, for she has a pleasant voice that speaks the very language of the people. Even more, she has a compassionate face and beautiful eyes in which Juan Diego could see himself reflected in a loving, respected, and accepted way. She speaks their language and looks upon them with love, understanding, and compassion. The beauty and perfection of the eyes continue to fascinate scholars to this day.[50]

The visual encounter with the image is at once liberating, deeply spiritual, and an exchange of genuine love. At the break of dawn on her feast day (Dec. 12), Guadalupan communities throughout the U.S. process her image through the streets and into their parishes.[51] The cultural aesthetic grounded in the Mexican American experience of the image discloses a truth about God's loving relationship to all of humanity.[52]

Our Lady of Charity is the most famous Marian devotion in Cuba and enjoys a devout following among the Cuban Americans living in exile in the United States.[53] During the year 2012 Cubans on the island

---

49. León-Portilla, *Tonantzin Guadalupe* (Mexico City: Fondo de Cultura Económica, 2000). Cf. Jaime Lara, "The Sacramented Sun: Solar Eucharistic Worship in Colonial Latin America," in *Cuerpo de Cristo*, 261–91.

50. Elizondo, *Guadalupe*, 63. Rodriguez, *Guadalupe*, 25–27.

51. Michael E. Engh, S.J., "With her People," *America* Vol. 188, No. 1 (Jan. 6, 2003): 15–16. See also Elaine A. Peña, *Performing Piety. Making Space Sacred with the Virgin of Guadalupe* (Berkeley: University of California Press, 2011).

52. Virgilio Elizondo, "Our Lady of Guadalupe as a Cultural Symbol," in *Beyond Borders: Writings of Virgilio Elizondo and Friends*, ed., Timothy Matovina (Maryknoll, NY: Orbis, 2000) 119–25.

53. For what follows I rely principally upon Alejandro García Rivera, "Wisdom, Beauty, and the Cosmos in Hispanic Spirituality and Theology," in *Cuerpo de Cristo*, 106–33; Miguel H. Díaz, "Dime con quién andas y te dire quién eres: We Walk with Our Lady of Charity," in *From the Heart of Our People: Latino/a Explorations in Catholic Systematic Theology*, ed. Orlando O. Espín and Miguel H. Díaz (Maryknoll, N.Y.: Orbis, 1999) 153–71; and Thomas A. Tweed, "Identity and Authority at a Cuban Shrine in Miami: Santería, Catholicism, and Struggles for Religious Identity," *Journal of Hispanic/Latino Theology* 4 (August 1996) 27–48.

celebrated the four hundredth anniversary of the devotion, and upwards of five million Cubans (of the eleven million on the island) are said to have participated in public processions.[54] According to a common version of the legend, *Nuestra Señora Caridad de Cobre* (as she is known by the Cubans) appeared at sea to three youths: Juan Moreno (African American), Rodrigo de Hoyos, and Juan de Hoyos (two Amerindian brothers). They were in the bay waiting for good weather before embarking on a mission in search of salt. As the waters calmed, they noticed above the foam of the water a wooden *bulto* floating towards them. The image was of a Virgin dressed in white robes holding the child Jesus in her arms. On its base was the following inscription: "I am the Virgin of Charity." The three were amazed that none of her vestments were wet. The image was brought ashore, and numerous miracles became associated with her. The image was processed. It was also said to go out at night and return the next morning with wet clothes. A shrine was established on the top of a copper hill (hence the name *Caridad de Cobre*), which was also the site of a mineshaft into which a local hermit had fallen and was rescued through her aid.

The image and story of Our Lady of Charity bring together many of the points we have been discussing. The narrative relates how salvation is mediated by sacred images. God intervenes through an image and offers hope to those in need in the voice of an image. The floating statue addresses the three sailors with the words: "I am Our Lady of Charity." Even her movements through the Cuban hills and mining community constitute a form of communication. Second, *Caridad de Cobre* signifies a cosmic mediation between the invisible world of divine grace and the visible world of Cuban existence. There are notable cosmic elements in the story: stars, clouds, rain, thunder, lightning, a storm at sea, salt (which was needed to cure meats), and copper. But the story is also about human history—not just the three boys but all the Cubans through the centuries who through her have found solace in the struggles of daily life. The God of Our Lady of Charity displays love and serenity in two ways—in nature and in offering to human beings a tangible hope of liberation from sin and suffering. Third, *Caridad de Cobre* stands by and accompanies her people. In the words of Miguel Díaz, she "walks in solidarity with all marginalized peoples."[55] Her shrine in Miami is not only a tremendous source of national pride, but it is a place where the Cuban community (both Catholics

---

54. There is a whole issue of *Verdad Esperanza* from the Unión Católica de Prensa de Cuba (Año 3, No. 3, 2011) dedicated to this theme.

55. Miguel Díaz, "Dime con quién andas," 161.

and non-Catholics) negotiates its diverse religious identity while living in exile.[56] The Archdiocese of Miami sponsored a pilgrimage of a statue from Cuba through all of its parishes. Thus, the accompaniment of her people that began when she came ashore in 1612 continues today for Cubans in exile and at home.

There is no generic Virgin in the Latino and Latina community. Latinas and Latinos view the world through the eyes of the Virgin who accompanies their community of faith. The complementarity of the two experiences just examined is striking. Each community of faith with its separate Virgin enriches the New Testament picture of Mary, the mother of Jesus, through its inculturation of the Virgin into the life of its community. *La Morenita* (Guadalupe) descends from the heavens and reflects the plight and dignity of the Indian in her very gaze of love. *Caridad de Cobre* (Our Lady of Charity) transforms the shipwreck of exilic existence into a calm vision of beauty and hope. Through both of these images of Latino popular religion, we encounter distinct but compatible visions of God, the cosmos, and of humanity.

These images present a particular challenge to Spanish-speaking Protestants who live in a culture the majority of whose population is Roman Catholic.[57] The situation for Latin American Protestants is different from Latino and Latina Protestants in the United States because of the predominantly Anglo-Protestant milieu of North America, but in both cases there is the often neglected possibility of considering the Marian images as symbols emanating from a cultural Catholicism whose meaning derives from a common Hispanic heritage. The assimilation of some aspect of the cultural symbol by Spanish-speaking Protestants would require a critical examination of attitudes towards Catholicism, towards "the earthly, Latino culture" in general, and towards the presentation of images of women in the Christian community and in the wider society.[58] Here the three revisions introduced by Nora Lozano to what is taken to be the traditional Catholic image of Mary are noteworthy: a holistic sexuality for all women of Mexican descent, a Mary who is active and assertive and capable of making her own choices, and an extension of the model of Mary's active life beyond motherhood to participating in the original group of disciples

---

56. In addition to the article by Thomas Tweed cited above, see his *Our Lady of the Exile* (Oxford: Oxford University Press, 1999).

57. Nora O. Lozano-Diaz, "Ignored Virgin or Unaware Women," 88–90.

58. Ibid., 88.

who started the church.[59] Lozano's challenge to the Catholic understanding of Mary merits serious consideration and could be then compared to the comments made above representing aspects of a Roman Catholic understanding of theological anthropology centered on the person of Mary. If Mary's *fiat* can be understood as "'the interior space' re-opened within humanity that the eternal Father can fill with every spiritual blessing" (as suggested by Pope John Paul II) or as the creaturely response that embodies what it means to be a free answer to unmerited grace (Ratzinger/Pope Benedict XVI), then it would seem that there could be a fruitful dialogue centered on Mary about the nature of the freedom to respond to the divine initiative in the two traditions.

V. CONCLUSION

Latinos and Latinas in the U.S. also maintain a fervent devotion to the cult of saints and have an especially fervent devotion to the Blessed Virgin. But the relationship between the universal call to holiness and the official theology of the saints is also well expressed by a vignette recounted at an academic gathering by the late Cuban bishop from Miami, Monseñor Agustín Román.[60] Román recounts how a young mother and her daughter enter a local church and gaze with admiration at the depictions in stained glass of individual saints. When the girl is later asked by a catechist in the same parish about the identity of the saints, the child blurts out: "The saints, the saints, the saints are the windows of the Church!" After considerable laughter at the child's naiveté, the little girl he offers a startlingly apposite explanation: "The saints are the windows through which the light of Christ enters the Church." The anecdote reveals how the saints—official and unofficial—inform the life of the faithful. To situate the life of holiness equally in the everyday sphere of domesticity and in the public liturgical life of the Church is no diminishment of the role of the parish or liturgy in the Christian life. On the contrary, following the holy women and men of God leads one ineluctably into the sanctuary of the Church for both private and public prayer. We invoke and partake of the communion of saints in the Eucharist because we know they accompany us on the daily journey of faith.

59. Ibid., 90–94.

60. The story is taken from Raúl R. Gómez, SDS, "Veneration of the Saints and Beati," in Peter Phan, *Directory on Popular Piety and the Liturgy: Principles and Guidelines*, 121–22.

A Man of the Church

The universal path to holiness is *un camino* (a path). The Spanish word maintains better than an English translation a direct link to the act of walking (i.e., *caminar* in Spanish).[61] Walking through a city is a very different experience from taking a bus or battling traffic in one's own vehicle. Walking with the Virgin through the streets of a country where Catholicism had recently been banned, as was the case in 2012 in Cuba, is a highly expressive act. When you walk on the street, you are accompanied not only by the Virgin, but whether you like it or not by the poor, the elderly, those hurrying home from a night shift, and many others. In this respect, it is important to recall the lesson from the New Testament regarding the "way" that Christ showed his followers, for the Greek term (*hodos*) used by the writers of the New Testament also conveys the dual sense of a concrete road and a path of learning.[62] We follow and we learn on our pilgrimage to God. Likewise, there is a path to Christ in the Church because Christ offers himself as the path through his relationship with the Father and the Holy Spirit. As Del Colle notes:

> To recognize how Christ's self-giving is always present in the church is not to exchange a personal relationship with him for an external one. Rather the reciprocity between the personal and the communal reveals not only Christ's relationship with us but also his relationality to the Father and the Holy Spirit in the life of the church and the world, without which the fullness of Christ could not be known and communicated.[63]

Holy women and men of God illuminate this path and help us to follow to the Lord.

---

61. The point is basic to the argument of Roberto S. Goizueta's *Caminemos con Jesús; Towards a Hispanic/Latino Theology of Accompaniment* (Maryknoll: Orbis, 1995).

62. Cf. John 14:6; Acts 16:17, 18:25, 18:26.

63. Ralph Del Colle, *Talking with Evangelicals*, 85.

20

Ghosts of Westphalia: Fictions and Ideals of Ecclesial Unity in Enlightenment Germany[1]

ULRICH L. LEHNER

MUCH OF RALPH DEL Colle's work has been devoted to the study of the beliefs and practices that Christian churches share, and it is therefore fitting to reflect on some ecumenical projects of the past and the historical context in which they developed. For the purpose of this paper, the period after the Thirty Years War and the Peace of Westphalia (referred to as Westphalia) is of particular interest because the Holy Roman Empire was a hotbed of ecumenical disputes. I will look first at a few legal instruments of Westphalia for obtaining religious peace and emphasize the fact that this "constitution" of the empire entailed the explicit command for a reunification of the churches. These instruments, such as parity and nonsectarian jurisprudence, prepared the way for an irenic approach to theological differences with an eye toward a reunion of faiths. At the same time, however, they also impeded any potential reunion because of their political consequences. In the eighteenth century, under the influence of the academy movement, the time seemed to have come for a new way of approaching a reunion. While the *Neuwied Academy* conceived such an attempt in a universalist manner that disregarded theological truth claims, the *Fulda Academy* focused on improving mutual theological understanding as the way to overcome differences.

---

1. First presented at the Notre Dame Institute of Advanced Study, Fall 2010.

A Man of the Church

THE GHOSTS OF WESTPHALIA: FICTIONS OF RELIGIOUS UNITY

The Peace of Westphalia of 1648, consisting of the peace treaties of Osnabrück and Munster, not only ended the Thirty Years War but also brought about an armistice between Protestants and Catholics concerning the nature of the true Catholic Church. In order to reinstate order and unity in the realm, the opposing religious parties agreed to regard their confessional differences as unsettled doctrinal conflicts that would no longer fragment the political balance of the empire. What the Empire had achieved in the treaties was therefore not a tri-confessional nation but a legal, constitutional foundation for a reunion of the churches. Any other conclusion would have meant sacrificing the religious truth claim of one of the parties. It was only because the Peace of Westphalia was an instrument for a reunion of the Churches that the severe restrictions on the power of the pope and bishops and the suspension of canon law (e.g., about waging holy war against heretics) were acceptable to Catholic princes.[2] This theological view of the treaty only disappeared in the eighteenth century, when Protestant scholars of jurisprudence began to see the *emergency* laws,[3] which gave Protestant sovereigns rights over the churches, as settled and perpetually established positive law. Catholics, however, continued to interpret the religious peace as an exterior armistice, which only suspended canon law until all Protestants were once more in full communion with the Roman Catholic Church.[4] Only at the end of the eighteenth century did Catholic jurists seem to have given up this notion, especially under the influence of Christian Wolff (1679–1754) and the church reforms of

---

2. Martin Heckel, "Die Wiedervereinigung der Konfessionen als Ziel und Auftrag der Reichsverfassung im Heiligen Römischen Reich Deutscher Nation," in Hans Otte and Richard Schenk, eds., *Die Reunionsgespräche im Niedersachsen des 17. Jahrhunderts: Rojas y Spinola—Molan—Leibniz* (Göttingen: Vandenhoeck & Rupprecht, 1999) 15–38, at 30; Mathias Fritsch, *Religiöse Toleranz im Zeitalter der Aufklärung: Naturrechtliche Begründung—konfessionelle Differenzen* (Hamburg: Meiner, 2004) 5.

3. See the excellent book by Thomas Hahn, *Staat und Kirche im deutschen Naturrecht* (Tübingen: Mohr Siebeck, 2012).

4. Heckel, "Die Wiedervereinigung," 33–34; Fritsch, *Religiöse Toleranz*, 5–6. On the duty of holy war against heretics, see Bernd Mathias Kremer, *Der Westfälische Friede in der Deutung der Aufklärung: Zur Entwicklung des Verfassungsverständnisses im Hl. Röm. Reich Deutscher Nation vom konfessionellen Zeitalter bis ins späte 18. Jahrhundert* (Tübingen: 1989) 40–41; Konrad Repgen, "Der päpstliche Protest gegen den Westfälischen Frieden und die Friedenspolitik Urbans VIII," *Historisches Jahrbuch* 75 (1956): 94–122; Michael F. Feldkamp, "Das Breve 'Zelo domus Dei' vom 26. November 1648—Edition," *Archivum Historiae Pontificiae* 31 (1993): 293–353.

Emperor Joseph II (1780-1790).⁵ The reason for the existence of the state was now seen solely in the welfare of the people without any reference to religion. This new principle also served as legitimization for Catholic princes to absorb more powers over ecclesial property.⁶ The more sovereigns controlled church possessions and policy (*jus circa sacra*), however, the less likely it became that they would reduce such precious influence for the sake of Christian unity. Thus, a crucial part of Westphalia, the demand for a reunion of faiths, had become a fiction nobody paid much attention any more.

Another result of the peace treaties that initially appeared to settle religious dispute was that of religious parity.⁷ The best example for the parity of religious groups was the *Imperial Diet*, the *Reichstag*, where majority votes on religious topics were suspended. Instead, the two confessional bodies of the *Imperial Diet*, Protestants (Lutherans and Calvinists in the *Corpus Evangelicorum*) and Catholics (*Corpus Catholicorum*) were expected to vote on religious issues separately (*itio in partes*) so that one body could not impose their majority vote upon the other.⁸ These bod-

---

5. Kremer, *Der Westfälische Friede*, 29.

6. Fritsch, *Religiöse Toleranz*, 31-53.

7. Kremer, *Der Westfälische Friede*, 119-152; Fritsch, *Religiöse Toleranz*, 7-12; Winfried Schulze, "Pluralisierung als Bedrohung: Toleranz als Lösung," in Heinz Duchhardt, ed., *Der Westfälische Friede. Diplomatie—politische Zäsur—kulturelles Umfeld—Rezeptionsgeschichte* (Munich: Oldenbourg, 1998) 115-140. On parity in the Empire in general, however, with almost no material on the confessional corpora, see Lothar Weber, *Die Parität der Konfessionen in der Reichsverfassung von den Anfängen der Reformation bis zum Untergang des alten Reiches 1806* (Bonn: J. Fuchs, 1961).

8. Kremer, *Der Westfälische Friede*, 177; Fritsch, *Religiöse Toleranz*, 8; Martin Heckel, "Itio in partes: Zur Religionsverfassung des Heiligen Römischen Reiches Deutscher Nation," in idem, *Gesammelte Schriften*, vol. 2 (Tübingen: Mohr Siebeck, 1989) 636-737; idem, "Zu den Anfängen der Religionsfreiheit im konfessionellen Zeitalter," in Mario Ascheri, ed., *Ins Wasser geworfen und Ozeane durchquert: Festschrift für Knut Wolfgang Nörr* (Cologne et al.: Böhlau, 2003) 349-401. On majority decisions of the *Imperial Diet*, see Winfried Schulze, "Majority Decision in the Imperial Diets of the Sixteenth and Seventeenth Centuries," *Journal of Modern History* 58. Supplement (1986): S46-S63. For the development of the *itio in partes*, see Klaus Schlaich, "Maioritas-protestatio-itio in partes-Corpus Evangelicorum: Das Verfahren im Reichstag des Hl. Römischen Reichs Deutscher Nation nach der Reformation," in idem, *Gesammelte Aufsätze: Kirche und Staat von der Reformation bis zum Grundgesetz*, Ius Ecclesiasticum 57 (Tübingen: Mohr Siebeck, 1997) 68-134. Indispensable for the legal background of the two corpora is still Fritz Wolff, *Corpus Evangelicorum und Corpus Catholicorum auf dem Westfälischen Friedenskongress: Die Einfügung der konfessionellen Städteverbindungen in die Reichsverfassung* (Münster: Aschendorff, 1966): While the concepts *Corpus Catholicorum* and *Corpus Evangelicorum* are not entailed in the Peace Treaties of Osnabrück and Münster, they are contained in the

ies, however, were not officially and constitutionally recognized as the corporate voices of Protestantism and Catholicism, but were somewhat semi-official. While centuries later the *itio in partes* has been recognized as a means of keeping religious peace, contemporaries disliked it because it easily became an impediment to the regular activities of the *Imperial Diet* and was therefore only invoked in extreme cases (only ten times between 1672 and 1806).[9]

The Peace of Westphalia also guaranteed for the first time that Reformed Churches would have equal rights in the Empire's ecclesial landscape. Consequently, institutions that were sworn to religious parity had to provide the Reformed Church with an equal number of offices, just like the Lutherans and Catholics. An interesting application of this newly conceived parity was the Imperial Cameral Court (*Reichskammergericht*), the highest court of the Empire (together with the *Imperial Aulic Council* in Vienna), where Reformed judges had sat on the bench since 1654.[10] A simple majority vote of the judges was sufficient to decide a case, and every judge was perfectly free in his decision and at least officially protected from external influences.[11] The statutes of the court also made clear that every judge or court member had to declare his religion unmistakably so that *absolute* parity could be exercised. Thus, the case of a Catholic judge, who was married to a Reformed wife and who raised his daughters in the Reformed Church, looked suspicious as to his Catholicity as late as 1760,

---

relevant protocols. However, judicially the term *Corpus Evangelicorum* was not used until 1691, and *Corpus Catholicorum* not until 1714 (Peter Brachwitz, *Die Autorität des Sichtbaren. Religionsgravamina im Reich des 18. Jahrhunderts* (Berlin and New York: de Gruyter, 2011) 73; Wolff, *Corpus*, 124–128).

9. Härter, "Das Corpus Catholicorum," 76.

10. For the conflicts regarding the appointments to the Imperial Cameral Court, see the detailed description and analysis at Sigrid Jahns, *Das Reichskammergericht und seine Richter: Verfassung und Sozialstruktur eines höchsten Gerichts im Alten Reich* vol. 1 (Cologne at al.: Böhlau, 2011) 168–327. A good survey of the legislative landscape of Germany and especially the importance of the *Imperial Aulic Council* (*Reichshofrat*) is given in Edgar Liebmann, "Reichs- und Territorialgerichtsbarkeit im Spiegel der Forschung," in Anja Amend et al., eds., *Gerichtslandschaft Altes Reich* (Cologne et al.: Böhlau, 2007) 151–172; Volker Press, "Der Reichshofrat im System des frühneuzeitlichen Reiches," in Friedrich Battenberg and Filippo Ranieri, ed., *Geschichte der Zentraljustiz in Mitteleuropa: Festschrift für Bernhard Diestelkamp zum 65. Geburtstag* (Cologne and Vienna: Böhlau, 1994) 349–365.

11. Wolfgang Sellert, "Richterliche Unabhängigkeit am Reichskammergericht und am Reichshofrat," in Okko Behrends, ed., *Gerechtigkeit und Geschichte: Beiträge eines Symposions zum 65. Geburtstag von Malte Dießelhorst* (Göttingen: Wallstein, 1996) 118–132.

especially because a convert would lose his seat on the bench.¹² Despite much research on the *Reichskammergericht*, its religious dimension and its impact on religious history has been utterly neglected; nothing has been written about its role in religious matters in the eighteenth century, although it was arguably the best working tri-confessional institution of the realm and protected most efficiently the religious rights of the Emperor's subjects, while simultaneously keeping the idea of a united realm alive. The statutes of the court, which propagated a "non-sectarian jurisprudence,"¹³ reminded the judges to be tolerant of each other's religious convictions:

> Judges of the [three]. . .religions as well as all persons of the Cameral Court must not despise others for their religion, nor scorn at each other, or give in to ill will, but must be always friendly to each other and of good will, and have to demonstrate in every way that they work peacefully and tranquilly together and will so in the future.¹⁴

Following this rule, the court did not reject religious truth claims, but only suspended its judgment on religious matters and solved cases pragmatically. Mutual disagreement and corruption brought the court to a lame-duck-position in the midst of the eighteenth century. Until its end in 1806, the court never fully recovered, and all plans for a reform were

---

12. Dagmar Feist, "Der Fall von Albini—Rechtsstreitigkeiten um die väterliche Gewalt in konfessionell gemischten Ehen," in Siegrid Westphal, ed., *In eigener Sache: Frauen vor den höchsten Gerichten des Alten Reiches* (Cologne and Weimar: Böhlau, 2005) 245–270. For the *Reichskammergericht* in the eighteenth-century, see Monika Neugebauer-Wölk, "Das Alte Reich und seine Institutionen im Zeichen der Aufklärung: Vergleichende Betrachtungen zum Reichskammergericht und zum Fränkischen Kreistag," *Jahrbuch für fränkische Landesforschung* 58 (1998): 299–326.

13. Benjamin Kaplan, *Divided by Faith, Religious Conflict and the Practice of Toleration in Early Modern Europe* (Cambridge, MA: Belknap, 2007) 232.

14. Johann Wilhelm Ludolff, ed., *Concept der neuen Kayserlichen und Reichs-Cammer-Gerichts-Ordnung* (Wetzlar: 1717): *Cammer-Gerichts-Ordnung of 1613*, title 4, § 4 (http://virr.mpdl.mpg.de/virr/view/escidoc:414781/image/38—retrieved 24 November 2010). This valuable edition of the statutes of the Cameral Court, visitation protocols, commentaries on the statutes etc. contains over 1,300 pages but is inconsistently paginated. For each part the page number begins with 1; therefore I have decided to indicate also the image number of the scan of the digitized online-version to make it easier for the reader to check the apposite page. For the 1654 decree of the Imperial Diet, see Arno Buschmann, ed., *Kaiser und Recht: Verfassungsgeschichte des Heiligen Römischen Reiches Deutscher Nation vom Beginn des 12. Jahrhunderts bis zum Jahre 1806 in Dokumenten*, vol. 2, 2nd ed., (Baden-Baden: Nomos, 1994) 180–273, *Recessus Imperii Novissimus* of 17 May 1654, § 23 at 194.

either blocked or never implemented.[15] The idea, however, that a court of non-sectarian jurisprudence, using law and reason alone, would resolve religious (and political) problems, remained a crucial ideal for the formation of the reunion academies.

A UNION OF ALL RELIGIONS: THE NEUWIED ACADEMY

The *Free Society for the Renewal [Aufnahme] of Religion* was founded in 1754[16] by the Reformed theologian Johann Heinrich Oest (1727–1777) in the Frisian Islands. For Oest, religion had become marginalized in society and divided people into two categories: those who were overzealous in religious matters and those who were disinterested in religion. Both groups were the target of society, since it explicitly desired to overcome fanaticism and indifferentism. In October 1756 the Count of Neuwied-Runkel was introduced to this project and immediately gave it his special protection. He even lifted any restrictions of censorship from the society. Oest was appointed head of the academy and received the title "professor of polemics." From then on, the society was called the *Academy of Neuwied for a Reunion of Faiths and for the Continuous Improvement of Religion* and was the first institutionalized attempt at ecumenism on German soil.[17] On 1 January 1757 the establishment of the academy was publicly announced in a 72-page brochure.[18] The academy's organization echoes the judicial context

---

15. See, for example, Karl Otmar von Aretin, "Reichshofrat und Reichskammergericht in den Reformplänen Kaiser Josephs II." in Bernhard Diestelkamp and Ingrid Scheurmann, eds., *Friedenssicherung und Rechtsgewährung: Sechs Beiträge zur Geschichte des Reichskammergerichts und der obersten Gerichtsbarkeit im alten Europa* (Bonn and Wetzlar: Arbeitskreise selbständige Kulturinstitute, 1997) 51–81. For an English description of the German judical system, see Joachim Whaley, *Germany and the Holy Roman Empire*, vol. 2 (Oxford: Oxford University Press, 2012).

16. *Schriften der Ostfriesischen freyen Gesellschaft zur Aufnahme der Religion* (n.p.: 1756). The only surviving copy is in the ducal archive in Neuwied. This archive also holds a number of archival files about the Neuwied Academy. The files are not accessible. See Johann Mathias Schroeckh, *Unpartheyische Kirchen-Historie: Alten und Neuen Testaments . . . Vierter Theil, in welchem die Geschichte vom Jahr nach Christi Geburt 1751 bis 1760 enthalten sind* (Jena, Hartung 1766) 698.

17. One of the few, accessible archival documents about the academy (especially about the quarrels in 1757) can be found in the *Haus-, Hof-, und Staatsarchiv Vienna*: Kleinere Reichsstände 537-1-1, including a membership diploma.

18. *Nachricht, Einrichtung, Rechte und Gesetze der Hoch-Gräflich Neuwiedischen Akademie zur Vereinigung des Glaubens und weiterer Aufnahme der Religion* (Neuwied, 1757). Also published in *Acta historico-ecclesiastica* 120 (1758) 582–621, on

of Westphalia, namely a sense for parity, neutrality, and high regard for nonsectarian, mere "reasonable" judgment. Because of its name, one can also detect a strong influence of the European academy movement, which aimed at organizing scholarship and free discussion in academic societies.

The aim of the academy was to bring "enlightened" minds together in order to extract the truths from all "religions" and confute doubts about God's existence and revelation. This society was headed by a clerk (*Greffier*), who was supposed to collect the theological opinions from other members. These statements were then to be read by all society members in private. No meetings were ever to occur, nor any discussions. Surprisingly, the *Neuwied Academy* did not discriminate in its membership policy on the basis of gender, religion, or nationality. Also, the number of members was not limited. One could become a scholarly member, and only as such was one expected to participate in the theological discussion, if one had written a "good essay about one or more and especially disputed" theological propositions.[19]

The introduction to the statutes of the academy called religion the "Inbegriff," the core of the most important truths of humanity, which the society was founded to re-discover by resolving the differences between all (!) religions. The underlying belief was that the conflicting truth claims of religions demonstrate that God and his revelation must have been misunderstood by some or even all religions. In order to bring about one faith for all people and in order to silence agnostic as well as atheist doubt, one had to confute the wrong concepts and uncover the real truth about the divine. A necessary presupposition for this, however, was that members could speak their mind; therefore, freedom from censorship was considered essential.[20] Although the statutes speak frequently of differences between Christian theological systems, mostly they use "religions" and mention at times Judaism, Islam, and even Paganism, therefore one can understand why most contemporaries read this document as a manifesto of syncretism, as did most contemporaries.

The *Neuwied Academy* renounced the conversational methods of earlier reunion attempts and understood itself as a community of unprejudiced academics. Unlike earlier reunion attempts that often ended in the heat of oral discussions, exclusively written communication was used in order to avoid ambiguity and emotional distress. This was supposed to

---

which I rely here.

19. *Nachricht*, 612.
20. *Nachricht*, 585–586.

be a more serious, undisturbed and intelligible way of communicating.[21] The statutes read: "We write and read. . . . The community among us consists not in congregations or talks, but in written communication. . .of our thoughts."[22] Such written communication was not entirely new since other major literary or academic societies had begun using it a few decades earlier. However, to make it part of an ecumenical or universalist strategy was a major innovation.[23]

To ensure that the members would speak their minds, all members had to be kept unaware of the identities of the others, except for the main clerk and the secretary. Each person was asked to submit statements, which were then condensed and edited without indicating the identity of the author.[24] This policy also ensured that the discussion was about arguments and that the arguments were taken seriously regardless of the reputation of the authors.[25]

Already by July 1757, a number of critics attacked the academy because they believed it was a successor to the *Neuwied Ducats Society*, a lottery ponzi scheme.[26] The Giessen professor and Lutheran pastor Johann Hermann Brenner (1699–1782) thought a reunion of all faiths and common worship were impossible. The new academy did not convey the necessary message of Christian irenicism but rather of religious pluralism because it also sought to bring non-Christian religions into dialogue with

---

21. For the advantages of written "conversations," see, for example, the reflections of Dirk Baecker, "Hilfe ich bin ein Text!" in Klaus Kreimeier and Georg Stanitzek, eds., *Paratexte in Literatur, Film, Fernsehen* (Berlin: Oldenbourg, 2004) 43–52, at 45; on academic communication in early modernity, see Martin Gierl, "Res publica litteraria—Kommunikation, Institution, Information, Organisation und Takt," in Klaus-Dieter Herbst and Stefan Kratochwil, eds., *Kommunikation in der frühen Neuzeit* (Frankfurt: Peter Lang, 2009) 241–252; idem, "Kompilation und die Produktion von Wissen im 18. Jahrhundert," in Helmut Zedelmaier and Martin Mulsow, eds., *Die Praktiken der Gelehrsamkeit in der frühen Neuzeit* (Tübingen: Niemeyer, 2001) 63–94. For an excellent overview of the Christian reunion attempts in the form of personal dialogues, see Otto Scheib, *Die innerchristlichen Religionsgespräche im Abendland*, 3 vols. (Wiesbaden: Harrassowitz, 2010).

22. *Nachricht*, 588.

23. Cf. Rudolf Vierhaus, "Die Organisation wissenschaftlicher Arbeit: Gelehrte Sozietäten und Akademien im 18. Jahrhundert," in Jürgen Kocka, ed., *Die Königlich Preussische Akademie der Wissenschaften zu Berlin im Kaiserreich* (Berlin: Akademieverlag, 1999) 3–22.

24. *Nachricht*, 589.

25. *Nachricht*, 612.

26. Arwid Liersch, *Dukaten-Sozietät und Glaubens-Akademie: Zwei Wiedische Gesellschaften des 18. Jahrhunderts* (Neuwied, 1904) 47–48.

the churches.²⁷ Some German sovereigns also protested against the academy because they feared that by circumventing censorship, the academy could publish polemics against basic Christian convictions or against the established parity of confessions in the realm. Especially troublesome was the fact that the academy could consider one or perhaps all of the three officially acknowledged denominations as inferior and attempt to reform them without ecclesiastical or imperial mandate. Moreover, a successful reunion of the Christian denominations would have ended the sovereigns' say over church affairs. Theologically educated sovereigns feared that the Neuwied project could lead to a fourth religion in the realm, one of syncretism or indifferentism. In light of this, it became necessary for the count of Neuwied to respond to these charges. He claimed that such dangers did not exist and were based on a misinterpretation of the statutes of the academy. He also revoked the freedom from censorship the academy had enjoyed and ordered that the academy proceedings be regarded as a scholarly journal that was bound by Imperial censorship law.²⁸ Since the academy never attracted a sufficient number of members, and also because famous German theologians like Johann David Michaelis (1717–1791) protested against it, it soon fell into financial trouble.²⁹ In order to prevent a pending lawsuit of the Protestant count of Hessen-Darmstadt, as well as the Catholic Electors of Cologne and the Palatinate, the count of Neuwied withdrew his protection of the academy and dissolved it in August 1758. Thus, the threat and insult to the established churches was eliminated.³⁰

27. Johann Hermann Brenner, *Prüfung der neuen Aufrichtung einer Hochgräflich-Neuwiedischen freyen Akademie zur Vereinigung des Glaubens und Aufnahme der Religion* (Giessen: 1758), idem, *Zeugnis über die Neuwiedische Anstalten* (1758). On Brenner see *Das neue gelehrte Europa* 17 (Wolfenbüttel, 1762) 941–953.

28. Liersch, *Dukaten-Sozietät*, 55.

29. Michaelis rejected the Neuwied Academy also because he considered its democratic way of resolving theological issues, namely by majority vote, as inadequate. See Johann David Michaelis, "Briefe von der Schwierigkeit der Religions-Vereinigung, an Herrn Pastor Aurand, Secretaire der Neuwidischen (sic!) Unions-Academie," in idem, *Syntagma commentationum* vol. 1 (Göttingen, 1759) 121–70. Johann Michael von Loen (1694–1776), Goethe's uncle, and Johann Daniel van Hoven (1705–1793) were ardent supporters of the Neuwied project (see Joris van Eijnatten, *Liberty and Concord in the United Provinces: Religious Toleration and the Public in the Eighteenth-Century Netherlands* (Leiden and Boston: Brill, 2003) 135–36). For Loen, see his *Des Herrn von Loen kurzer Entwurf der allgemeinen Religion, zur Beförderung des Glaubens der Christenheit: Nebst einer näheren Erklärung an die Gesellschaft der Wissenschaften zu Göttingen von J. D. von Hoven* (Lingen: 1754).

30. The dissolution decree mentions explicitly the threat of the academy to the established churches, at Liersch, *Dukaten-Sozietät*, 58: "... dennoch zum Theil einiger

A Man of the Church

MUTUAL THEOLOGICAL UNDERSTANDING: THE RE-UNION ACADEMY OF FULDA

This reunion project began at a time when the Protestant willingness to actively tolerate Catholics had begun to decrease and slowly gave way to a vibrant anti-Catholicism that lasted well into the twentieth century.[31] Nevertheless, the intellectual climate was still friendly enough to motivate the Protestant Erfurt scholar Jakob Heinrich Gerstenberg (1712–1776) to publish his thoughts about a possible reunion with the Catholic Church in 1773.[32] Surprisingly, he had been intrigued by Johann Friedrich Bahrdt's (1713–1775) universalism insofar as it attempted to come to a purely rational Christian theology, which all denominations could share.[33] Such an attempt was in Gerstenberg's eyes necessary in order to protect Christianity against the forces of atheism and deism. Among his personal friends and supporters was the Catholic sovereign of Erfurt, the future archbishop of Mainz and then vice-regent of Erfurt, Carl Theodor von Dalberg (1744–1817). Dalberg was also devoted to the unity of Christianity and publicly declared in his *Reflections on the Universe* (1778), very much to the dismay of his Jewish correspondent Moses Mendelssohn (1729–1786), who believed that "religious pluralism, not uniformity was the design of Providence,"[34] that all societies, including religions, aim at unity in God.[35]

Orten als anstössig und wohl gar denen im Reich gebilligten Kirchen und Religionen zuwider angesehen werden will."

31. Olaf Blaschke, "Das 19. Jahrhundert: Ein zweites konfessionelles Zeitalter?" *Geschichte und Gesellschaft* 26 (2000) 38–75. Manuel Borutta has argued that Protestant Enlighteners viewed the Catholic South of Germany very much like the Orient—a region that had to be cultivated, and speaks therefore of a Protestant "Orientalism" as basis for the renewed anti-Catholicism (Manuel Borutta, *Antikatholizismus: Deutschland und Italien im Zeitalter der europäischen Kulturkämpfe* (Göttingen: Vandenhoeck & Ruprecht, 2010)).

32. See Christoph Spehr, *Aufklärung und Ökumene: Reunionsversuche zwischen Katholiken und Protestanten im deutschsprachigen Raum des späteren 18. Jahrhunderts* (Tübingen: Mohr Siebeck, 2005) 85–107.

33. Spehr, *Aufklärung und Ökumene*, 105–6. See Carl Friedrich Bahrdt, *Neueste Offenbarungen Gottes*, 4 vols. (Riga, 1773–1774). One of Bahrdt's conversation partners was the Catholic convert and former Lutheran pastor Johann Justus Herwig (1742–1801).

34. Alexander Altmann, *Die trostvolle Aufklärung: Studien zur Metaphysik und politischen Theorie Moses Mendelssohns* (Stuttgart-Bad Cannstatt: Frommann-Holzboog, 1982) 225; Karl Theodor von Dalberg, *Betrachtungen über das Universum* 3rd ed. (Mannheim: 1787).

35. Dalberg, *Betrachtungen*, 6, 100, 105. ibid., 136: "Gesetz des Universums. Einheit ist vollkommen in Gott. Die Schöpfung strebt sich der Einheit zu nähern. Religion

This unity, he perceived, was best embodied in the Catholic Church and therefore he expressed his hope that "the time will come when the light of religion will be preached to all humans of the earth without exception.... Be it that the desire of good hearts be fulfilled! May the different Christian religious parties (*Religionspartheyen*) return to the motherly lap of the Church!"[36] Two years later he composed a *Plan for a Reunification of Religions* which he sent to his friend Johann Gottfried Herder (1744-1803), the text of which is unfortunately lost.[37] Also, other Catholics like the Franciscan Jacob Berthold (1738-1817) in Bamberg argued that mutual denominational tolerance was insufficient but that a real reunion of the churches was desirable.[38] However, only the plan of the Benedictine Beda Mayr (1742-1794), who proposed in 1777/78 an academy for the reunification of the churches, caused a stir among his peers because he suggested a restriction of ecclesiastical infallibility.[39] In contradistinction to Mayr, five Benedictines of Fulda under the leadership of the Reformed theologian Johann Rudolph Piderit (1720-1791) began to work on a reunification academy the same year, which deserves more serious attention.[40] It was inspired by the works of Gerstenberg and Dalberg.

The project leaders among the Benedictines were Peter Böhm (1747-1822) and Karl von Piesport (1716-1800).[41] Piderit, however, seems to have been the main author of the statutes of the *Reunion Academy* and its theological plans. The main idea of this group was similar to that of Neuwied: An academic society for the purpose of a reunification of the three main churches should be founded. Just as at the Imperial Cameral Court, one aimed at strict parity. Besides Piesport (Böhm was an extraordinary member), other members included the Lutheran theologians Wilhelm Franz Walch (1726-1784) and Christian Wilhelm Schneider (1734-1797), while the Reformed were represented by Heinrich Otto Duysing (1719-1781)

---

ist Weg zu dieser Annäherung. Also Einheit ist Urquelle, Zweck und Grundgesetz des Universums."

36. Dalberg, *Betrachtungen*, 134.

37. Konrad Maria Färber, *Kaiser und Erzkanzler: Carl von Dalberg und Napoleon am Ende des Alten Reiches* (Regensburg: Mittelbayerische Verlagsgesellschaft, 1988) 24.

38. Jakob Berthold, *Cogitationes pacis et unionis inter religiones christianas* (Würzburg, 1778).

39. See Ulrich L. Lehner, ed., *Beda Mayr—Vertheidigung der katholischen Religion* (Boston and Leiden: Brill, 2009).

40. Jahns, *Das Reichskammergericht und seine Richter*, vol. 1, 297-342.

41. Spehr, *Aufklärung*, 153-61.

and Piderit and Petrus Abresch (1735-1812).[42] Members were sought out through private letters and conversations. From the Catholic side one could find the support of Johann Gertz (1744-1824), one of the first exegetes who tried to implement historical criticism, but most Catholics were hesitant since the recent censoring and punishment of modernizing theologians deterred them. The statutes of the new society were finished by April 1779. Also, Johannes Schmitt, a dogmatic theologian from Mainz, of whom nothing else is known, was asked to join, since he had greatly sympathized with the plan. Even the Mainz Archbishop Friedrich von Erthal (1718-1802) seemed to sympathize with the newly created society or at least paid careful attention to the plan when he received Schmitt and Böhm in private audience in 1780. Erthal even ordered Schmitt to inform the Elector of the Palatinate, Karl Theodor (1742-1799), of the society. The Elector's advisor, however, prelate Johann Kasimir Häffelin (1737-1827), vehemently rejected it and finally motivated Schmitt also to withdraw his support. Häffelin, a seasoned diplomat, could not imagine that the project of a few theologians could really bring about change, let alone theo-political alterations. Other enlightened theologians also declined membership, mostly because they feared wasting time if the discussions were not supported by any ecclesial authorities.[43] Other concerned Catholic theologians complained to the papal nuncio about the new academy and feared that the project gave up essentials of Catholic teaching. Nuncio Giuseppe Garampi (1725-1792) wondered what common basis the three denominations could have in case of a reunion, "a Catholic, a heretical one or newly invented devilish invention."[44] He went so far as to protest at the Imperial Chancery in Vienna in 1780 against the Fulda plan. The chancery, however, decided to request reports about the activities of Böhm and Piderit but not to intervene, not even when Garampi warned about potential "seditious" consequences of a reunion of the churches. The nuncio's fear was increased by the sympathy important Catholic church leaders, especially the Archbishop-Electors of Trier and Mainz but also the Prince Abbot of St. Blasien, showed towards the reunion plan. The Curia

42. Ibid., 162-63.

43. Ibid., 184-95. On Häffelin see Rudolf Fendler, *Johann Kasimir von Häffelin, 1737-1827; Historiker, Kirchenpolitiker, Diplomat,* Quellen und Abhandlungen zur mittelrheinischen Kirchengeschichte 35 (Mainz: Gesellschaft für Mittelrheinische Kirchengeschichte, 1980).

44. Spehr, *Aufklärung,* 167. On Garampi see Dries Vanysacker, *Cardinal Giuseppe Garampi, 1725-1792: An Enlightened Ultramontane* (Bruxelles: Institut historique belge de Rome, 1995).

now acted promptly. On 10 June 1780 Pope Pius VI issued a secret brief that admonished the monks to abstain from their plans since all previous ecumenical dialogues had been unsuccessful. Moreover, the pope warned about the danger of receiving theological knowledge from Protestant theologians. It could destroy the faith of the Benedictine monks, he feared. Finally, the pontiff insisted that the Benedictines had no proper authority for their ecumenical endeavor. The Bishop of Fulda, simultaneously Abbot of Fulda, was ordered to stop the project immediately. Heinrich VIII of Bibra (1759–1788) was a man of the Enlightenment, but he obeyed. Nevertheless, he did not punish his Cathedral Chapter, consisting only of Benedictine monks, which outright rejected the papal decree and wanted to go ahead with the academy plan. He was pleased with so much self-confidence and allowed the monks to appeal directly to Rome. The pope, of course, never responded to the appeal, which only confirmed Böhm's conviction that the brief had been written *not* by the Bishop of Rome but by the "archenemy" of Christianity.[45]

The last resort of the academy to gain support was to do so by publishing its plan. Piderit as a Reformed Christian was not bound by any papal proscription and went ahead with this plan. The publication in 1781 really stirred up broad interest.[46] Most readers, however, associated the new academy with the universalist project of Neuwied or the rationalism of Bahrdt.[47] Piderit responded that everybody who actually read the plan of the new academy would see that they were not at all interested in "uniting all religions by suppressing the name of Jesus."[48] Instead, the academy aimed at a reunion without giving up the essentials of Christianity and

45. Spehr, *Aufklärung*, 178. On Bibra see Michael Müller, *Fürstbischof Heinrich von Bibra und die katholische Aufklärung im Hochstift Fulda (1759–88): Wandel und Kontinuität des kirchlichen Lebens* (Fulda: Parzeller, 2005).

46. Johann Piderit, *Entwurf zum Versuche einer zwischen den streitigen Theilen im Römischen Reiche vorzunehmenden Religions-Vereinigung* (Frankfurt and Leipzig: Bayrhoffer, 1781). The plan (*Entwurf*) was published initially without an introduction so that a few months after the original publication, a new edition was printed with a 141-page-long introduction by Piderit. Idem, *Einleitung und Entwurf zum Versuche einer zwischen den streitigen Theilen im Römischen Reiche vorzunehmenden Religions-Vereinigung von verschiedenen Katholischen und Evangelischen Personen, welche sich zu dieser Absicht in eine Gesellschaft verabredet haben* (Frankfurt and Leipzig: Bayrhoffer, 1781).

47. See, for example, Johann Jakob Moser, *Unterthänigstes Gutachten wegen der jezigen Religions-Bewegungen, besonders in der Evangelischen Kirche wie auch über das Kayserliche Commissionsdecret in der Bahrtschen Sache* (n.p.: 1780) 4–5; on the constitutional aspect, ibid., 32–42.

48. Piderit, "Einleitung," in idem, *Einleitung und Entwurf*, 9.

A Man of the Church

explicitly despised indifferentism. The mutual dialogues of the academy were not intended to dilute differences but to educate the members. A tolerance that would sacrifice truth claims, a wrong-headed indifferentism, was not the aim of the academy members, Piderit insisted.[49] Mutual education about the varying theological traditions would bring about a new, nobler tolerance and finally harmony among faiths:

> Tolerance. . .[combined] with education [*Belehrung*]. . .is elevated to a noble level. . . . Tolerance leaves a human person . . . in uncertainty. . . . Education has the intention to eradicate gradually all prejudices and maxims that hold the heart . . . captive. If this is achieved, one has harmonious opinions [*einerlei Gesinnungen*].[50]

The plan of Piderit and the Benedictines made clear that the members understood the society as a loose congregation of private persons and the academy's work as private business until a plan was worked out that deserved to be shared with the public.[51] The plan invokes already on its first page the Peace of Westphalia, which itself had prescribed a reunion of the Christian faiths. All discussions among members were considered private and no suggestion was supposed to cause any church any disadvantages or advantages until a final decision was reached. The members would discuss whatever was best for a universal church and conducive for a restoration of universal peace between the confessions. If such proceedings were published, they would not be intended to bind any party to them or to force anybody to accept them. Instead, the theologians understood themselves as a think tank for peaceful, interdenominational theology which declared explicitly its trust in divine providence and its conviction of human frailty.[52]

Only persons who could subscribe to the high ideals of mutual theological education and tolerance and to the uncertainty of the outcome of the project (for example, that one tradition could be utterly wrong) could become members. Every member had to be willing to eradicate error and prejudice, and converse according to "the law of love . . . and let go of any personal displeasure and to embrace . . . ways of peace."[53] This brotherly love should become the key to solving confessional disputes, because it

---

49. Ibid., 141.
50. Ibid., 36–37.
51. Ibid., 4.
52. Ibid., prologue and § 1, 1–6.
53. Ibid., § 3, 9.

demonstrated a deeper commitment, namely that of one's heart to the cause. This did not mean an indifferent embrace of diversity: "Error will remain error and will have to be called as such: a member will always to free... what is perceived as error an error... but without slander."[54] Unlike Neuwied, the Piderit-Fulda Project did not seek to establish a universalist religion and did not threaten the interior or exterior constitution of any church.[55] Whatever was passed by the society members in majority vote could never be binding law or oblige any church unless it was officially accepted and implemented by the relevant church authority.[56] It is also remarkable that the members of the society regarded their business as so important that they wanted to disconnect their work from their academic personas so that the "business," working in mutual tolerance and education for a reunion of faiths, would continue until its completion.[57]

Like the Imperial Cameral Court, the society would consist of twelve ordinary members. The ratio of these members according to their confessions, however, was different from the court as six were supposed to be Catholic and six Protestant. Nevertheless, the idea of an *itio in partes* of two separate bodies is explicitly invoked when it is stated that doctrinal differences among Protestants should be handled solely among them. A reunion should only come about as the result of a search for truth.[58] Therefore the members should regard themselves as "servants" in the vineyard of God and should be ready to suffer for the cause.[59] Although it was left up to the confessional groups how they wanted to name and appoint members, the statutes demonstrate great sensitivity when they state that before a member was appointed the other members were to be informed so it would be clear if anybody had something against this person. Only

---

54. Ibid., § 4, 11.

55. Ibid., § 6, 14: "Nach allem diesem, was bisher angeführet worden, verstehet es sich von selbsten, dass diese vorläufige brüderliche Vereinigung, in der inneren und äusseren Verfassung einer jeden Kirche, keine weitere Aenderung oder Irrung mache."

56. Ibid., § 6, 14: "Alles dasjenige, was in dieser Vereinigungs-Gesellschaft genehmiget, und mit der wahren christlichen Religion genehmiget, und mit der wahren christlichen Religion übereinstimmend, oder der gesammten Christlichen Kirche, nützlich und nothwendig erkannt wird, kann niemalen reichsgesetzmässig, niemalen ganzen Gemeinden und Kirchen verbindlich werden, als bis solches unter dem Ansehen derjenigen, welche hierin etwas vestzustellen [sic], und zu verordnen das Recht haben, auf eine sich rechtfertigen lassende Weise, für ganze Kirchen und Gemeinden ist eingeführet worden."

57. Ibid., § 8, 17.

58. Ibid., § 10, 23.

59. Ibid., § 10, 24.

if nobody objected could the appointment be made. Another paragraph speaks explicitly of the "good friendly harmony" (*gutes, freundliches Einverständnis*)[60] between the members, which sounds very much like the constitutional principle of an *amicabilis compositio* (friendly compromise) of the Imperial Diet or the statutes of the Cameral Court about friendly interaction. Every new member had to sign an oath in which he professed to accept the suggestions of the academy and to be a "loving co-worker of the savior."[61] Once all slots of the society were filled, the oldest two members, a Protestant and a Catholic, would preside as presidents of the academy for one year. On the Protestant side a member of the other confession could be appointed co-president, especially if important discussions pertained to the theological heritage of this group; for example, if a Lutheran were president, a Reformed could be co-president and full president the following year, and so on. Since the presidents would not meet in person, the statutes prescribed one real presider among the presidents, an office that was to alternate between Catholics and Protestants.[62]

Most important, however, was that every member worked "in true fear of God, through prayer, holy obedience and sacrifice of one's heart to the faithful guidance of our Savior and the Spirit he has given us, so that everything a member does can be regarded a real fruit of the spirit of Christ."[63] While unanimity was required for the ultimate solution of doctrinal issues, for other questions, for example, themes to work on, a simple majority of vote was considered sufficient. This majority was not just the majority of simple votes. Majority meant for the society the amount of votes which showed most consensus even if, taken together, the actual number of votes was smaller. It was measured according to the *grade* of consensus; only common votes [*vereinigte Stimmen*] counted! "According to this principle four Catholics and four Protestants who vote for one solution count more than six Protestants and two Catholics, or six Catholics and two Protestants."[64] The doctrinal question that should be investigated was then handed over to a Catholic and a Protestant so that they could write up how this issue was treated in their respective theological traditions. Their statements had to be checked by their churches and

60. Ibid., § 13, 33.
61. Ibid., § 12, 31.
62. Ibid., § 15, 34–52.
63. Ibid., § 18, 62.
64. Ibid., § 19, 73. Spehr's description that a "majority vote" decided the themes of the discussion is insufficient, see Spehr, *Aufklärung und Ökumene*, 223.

authorized. It was crucial that such a statement be based only on approved theological sources an definitive theological judgments, and not on theological school opinions. Two other appointed members of the society then read these documents to find where they agreed and disagreed. The result was shared with the other members, and if nobody objected the "real business" began.[65] Since the differences between the confessions were now clearly stated, the statements could now go to the respective denominational camps for discussion as to how to the doctrinal difference could be resolved. When the issue at question did not pertain to the basic beliefs of either confession, then the camps could reach a compromise [*Vergleich*] and would attempt to enlighten each other in friendship and love over time, but were not to waste time in heated discussions or let a minor issue, even if it was considered an error, impede a reunion.[66] It were, however, also possible that one side considered an issue as minor while the other considered it as shaking the foundations of their church.[67]

As we saw above, the idea to use the power of corporate reason, an academy, for resolving theological differences was not new. However, Böhm and Piderit had learned from the temptation of indifferentism that brought the academy of Neuwied down, as well as from the failures of the constitutional institutions to suspend judgment on theological truth and instead resolve problems pragmatically. Like the judges of the Imperial Cameral Court, the theologians of the academy had to agree on a common constitution. While for the judges it was predominantly the Peace of Westphalia, for the academy members it was the Bible in its Hebrew and Greek original, but as a concession to Catholics the Vulgate was also accepted. Piderit and Böhm thought that such a biblical approach would

---

65. Ibid., § 22, 84–87.

66. Ibid., § 23, 92: "Wenn demnach der streitige Punkt so beschaffen ist, dass derselbe den Grund des Glaubens, wie er von den andern geleget ist, nicht zerüttet, vielmehr solchen wie er liegt unverändert liegen lässt, nur aber nicht nach aller Vollkommenheit darauf bauet, so ist zwar der [!] Gegentheil nicht schuldig, den Irrthum, aus allzugrosser, und in der That tadelhafter Gefälligkeit, Wahrheit zu nennen, und solchem als richtig nachzugeben: Gleichwohl kann doch dieser Irrthum, nach Beschaffenheit der Umstände, und wenn sonst nichts om Wege steheet, kein Hindernis machen, mit dem Gegentheile einen Vergleich zu errichten, und den Irrthum, auf seinen Einsichten und seinem Gewissen, bis dereinst etwa erfolgenden besseren Aufklärung, zumal, wenn man die ausdrückliche Absicht hat, für solche Aufklärung noch ferner zu sorgen, und sich dazu wechselweis die Hand zu bieten, ungerügt stehen zu lassen: und vergeblich, wenigstens unschicklich würde es seyn, durch itzt unzeitiges Disputiren, das ohnehin nach getroffenem Vergleiche, freundschaftlicher und mit mehr kaltem Blute, geschehen kann, die Vereinigung aufzuhalten."

67. Ibid., § 23, 94–98; § 25, 100–101.

eliminate excessive doctrinal differences, "false mysticism, enthusiasm and fanaticism."[68] Like the judges, the theologians were supposed to be free in their judgment and should come from different German states so that no sovereign could overly influence or pressure the outcome of the discussions. Like the Neuwied Academy, the members of the Fulda Academy rejected personal meetings and preferred written correspondence.[69] Likewise, each theological tradition had to express its teachings in a creedal statement, which was supposed to be forwarded to the other members as a foundation for the dialogues. From such documents the theological differences could be derived, themes identified and difficulties resolved. Only the Catholic members sent their creedal statement, namely the *Professio Tridentina* (1565), in 1782. The monks, however, never received an answer or a similar document from their Protestant peers. It was this lack of cooperation and not papal interference that ultimately killed the project in 1783.

CONCLUSION

The Neuwied and Fulda projects testify to the fact that there were two fundamentally different ways of ecumenical dialogue in eighteenth-century Germany. While Neuwied aimed at a universalist union by means of a smallest common denominator, the Fulda project saw mutual understanding of creedal traditions as the key to theological harmony. By shedding light on such ecumenical projects of the past, I do not propose that contemporary ecumenical theologians can learn from the past how to shape the theological future but rather that historical theology improves our sensitivity to the fact that we are standing in a cloud of witnesses whose successes and failures we should remember in order to sharpen our self-reflection. When I encountered the statutes of the Fulda Academy for the first time and read about its desire to have true servants of Christ as

---

68. Spehr, *Aufklärung*, 226; cf. 230. However, if the Vulgate deviated from the original, the Protestants were allowed to use the original text for a rebuttal. Other sources besides scripture were not to be used or only to a minimum. In view of understanding a biblical passage, explanations of the Fathers were admissible and even regarded as "witnesses of truth."

69. The Göttingen scholar Christoph Meiners (1747–1810), who was not involved in any ecumenical enterprises, regarded academic "Geselligkeit" and oral conversation as superior to written correspondence. See Marian Füssel, "Akademische Aufklärung: Die Universitäten im Spannungsfeld von funktionaler Differenzierung, Ökonomie und Habitus," *Geschichte und Gesellschaft: Sonderheft* 23 (2010) 47–73, at 69.

its members, who are also willing to suffer for the truth, the first person that I could associate with such a model theologian was Ralph Del Colle. His search for truth, his love of Christ, and his willingness to suffer the consequences of his belief in humility and joy have made him a theologian I daily look up to for inspiration.

21

"An Irony of Enthusiasm": The Reversal of Luther's Epithet in the Enlightenment

For Ralph Del Colle

PAUL R. HINLICKY

RALPH AND I MET when he came to Union Theological Seminary in New York for his M.Div. degree while I was a doctoral student there. We discovered that we had parallel concerns. He had left the Catholic faith of his youth wondering where the Spirit went, whom he had discovered in the Pentecostal movement. I had similarly wondered how the Spirit disappeared in Lutheranism, though I could not square this experience of Spiritless Lutheranism with the texts of Luther that I was studying. Since then Ralph found his way back to Catholicism and has had a fruitful theological career insisting with St. Thomas Aquinas that—lest we confuse God and His work—our profession of 'one holy Church' is "directed to the Holy Ghost, Who sanctifies the Church; so that the sense is: 'I believe in the Holy Ghost sanctifying the Church.'"[1] Ralph has worked, accordingly, to see that "ecclesial life rests on an integrated Christological and pneumatological foundation"[2] that is faithful to the Church of Rome's best insights and thus ecumenically open.

---

1. Ralph Del Colle, "The Church," in *The Oxford Handbook to Systematic Theology* (Oxford: Oxford University Press, 2009) 251, citing from "ST 2a2ae. I, 9 ad 5 in Aquinas, 1948."

2. Ibid.

In an incisive contribution to the *Cambridge Companion to Christian Doctrine* on "The Triune God," Ralph argued that the decisive question touching upon both the contemporary renewal of Trinitarian theology and the ecumenical rapprochement of the divided Church turns on the reintegration of the Spirit: the "nature of the communication is so intrinsic to the divine life that the understanding of God can no longer be rendered as simple, absolute, undifferentiated monotheism."[3] That is to say that the divine self-giving in the economy of the Incarnate Word's cross and resurrection refers essentially to "the self-communication of divine life that is at the heart of Christian faith known and received in the Spirit."[4] This argument deepens and extends the "truism" that "trinitarian theology stands or falls on the basis of whether or not it maintains a vibrant pneumatology."[5] The integration of divine self-giving Christology with divine self-communicating pneumatology not only keeps the faithful church open in the Spirit; it also keeps trinitarian theology grounded in the Biblical narrative of the economy of God.

Here the immanent trinity is and remains an *induction*, so to speak, to which faith comes and there *remains*. "[T]he trinitarian naming of God points to the Christian understanding that the event of Jesus Christ and the sending of the Spirit reveal the loving mystery of the saving God whose transcendence in the mystery is the basis for its communication and invitation to the creature."[6] But If the immanent Trinity ceases logically to exist as this induction of faith, i.e., as the explication of the implied belief that the revealed Trinity is antecedently capable, competent and willing to keep the commitments made in Christ by the Spirit; and if, instead, the immanent Trinity becomes a revealed truth taken on mere authority more and more detached from its soteriological basis and existential function; then the notion of an immanent trinity invites speculation about the conditions of transcendence as such that must apply. The ironic result, however, is that such transcendental speculation (in the traditions of both Thomas and Palamas) have ended in a self-defeating apophaticism, i.e., in

---

3. Ralph Del Colle, "The Triune God," Chapter Seven in *The Cambridge Companion to Christian Doctrine* ed. C. E. Gunton (Cambridge: Cambridge University Press, 1997) 121.

4. Ibid., 121–22.

5. Ibid., 130. "The recognition of the divine persons in their proper relations to the world is essential if trinitarian theology is to be prevented from losing its grounding in the salvific activity of God" Ibid.,131.

6. Ibid.

the "conundrum" that in the final analysis "the redeemed human creature does not actually know or participate in the actual being of God."[7]

That penetrating analysis brings us to a present impasse: "Either the Christian knowledge of God identifies the very being of God in the revelation of the divine persons and in this manner preserves the transcendence of God, or trinitarian language amounts to a triadic representation of God in history according to the receptive capacity of the human subject and nothing more. In ultimate terms this latter position eventually yields to apophatic agnosticism concerning the being of God."[8] This latter implication—and implied criticism—reflects my own view and I would like in what follows to tell a little tale about the disappearance of the kataphatic Spirit in Lutheranism and the devolution from there to apophatic agnosticism under the purified modern transcendentalism stemming above all from Immanuel Kant. In conclusion I will pick up Ralph's hint that the genuine transcendence of the Triune God is to be found and preserved in, and not in spite of or beyond, the revelation of the divine persons.

LUTHER'S VERBUM EXTERNUM

During 1516 Martin Luther was deeply engaged in the writings of the medieval mystic, Johannes Tauler (1300–1361).[9] Here he found a "critical alternative to the image of man in scholastic theology ... insight into man's own inability and thus his humble dependence on God."[10] During his time at Wittenberg, Thomas Müntzer (1489–1525), of later notoriety for agitating the Peasants' Revolt, absorbed Luther's edition of (what was presumed to be Tauler's) *Theologia deutsch*. On Luther's recommendation, Müntzer became the preacher in Zwickau in 1520; there he met the layman, Nicolas Storch, who "possessed a remarkable knowledge of the Bible" but "emphasized special immediate revelations and illuminations." This claim to immediacy fascinated Müntzer, along with Storch's rejection of "special orders of ministers" and his initiation of "conventicles" to inspire true reformation. Untrained in theology, but believing "that he possessed the Spirit, Storch now developed a strong sense of mission and felt himself called to be a reformer of the church. One consequence

---

7. Ibid., 133.
8. Ibid., 136.
9. Martin Brecht, *Martin Luther: Shaping and Defining the Reformation, 1521–1532*, trans. J. L. Schaaf (Minneapolis: Fortress, 1990) 137–39.
10. Ibid., 142.

in his circle was the rejection of infant baptism."[11] After the radicalized Müntzer's departure from Zwickau, and while Luther was in hiding following the Diet of Worms, prophets from Zwickau under the leadership of Storch appeared in Wittenberg. From the distance of the Wartburg Castle, Luther urged his colleagues "to test the spirits"; but yet another coworker, Andreas Karlstadt (Luther's fellow professor at Wittenberg and partner at the Leipzig debate against Johannes Eck), was captivated by the new prophesy. With two colleagues now lost, Luther wrote the 1525 polemical treatise, *Against the Heavenly Prophets*. He linked Karlstadt's abandonment of his calling to theological scholarship to Storch's spell of prophetic immediacy, as if he could now "learn something better and more unusual than God teaches in the Bible,"[12] also then without the hard work of scholarly theology. Martin Brecht observes: "Thus, for the first time, one of the difficult problems of the Reformation period was raised. The Bible and the office of preaching also were no longer regarded as means of obtaining the transcendent Spirit."[13]

Luther went on in the tract to articulate a doctrine of the *mediation* of divine revelation, the *Verbum externum*. It is not simply a matter of the Bible's formal authority over against private interpretation or of learned hermeneutics over against reader-response speculation, though Luther makes such arguments. More profoundly, for Luther, the Word from God that matters tells a narrative and hence constitutes a unique and recognizable event; it comes as news from outside the self and as such meets and transforms the existing self, as it was figured, in giving *new birth*. The word that does this is not any word, not even any word in the Bible, but "the pure gospel, the noble and precious treasure of our salvation. This gift evokes faith and a good conscience in the inner man." Since the gospel's news of Christ's coming in mercy to befriend sinners is not innate, "outwardly [God] deals with us through the oral word of the gospel and the material signs" of Baptism and Supper. "Inwardly he deals with us through the Holy Spirit, faith, and other gifts . . . The inward experience follows and is effected by the outward . . . Observe carefully . . . this order, for everything depends on it."[14] In Luther's integration, then, the Spirit works *per Verbum*, by the Incarnate Word, thus as a *Verbum externum*, to give new

---

11. Ibid., 36.

12. *Luther's Works: The American Edition* 58 vols. (Philadelphia: Fortress, 1955–2011; hereafter LW followed by volume and page number) LW 40:111.

13. Brecht, *Shaping*, 36.

14. Ibid., 146.

birth. The sequence is essential; it reflects the narrative structure of this new birth by which it is identified, recognized, and distinguished from imposters. If we "tear down the bridge, the path, the way, the ladder, and all the means by which the Spirit might come," we end up teaching "not how the Spirit comes to you but how you come to the Spirit." Or, what is the same, we give heed to some other spirit than the Spirit of Jesus and His Father. That precisely is what Luther tagged as "enthusiasm," as if one had "devoured the Spirit," as he wrote sarcastically thinking of the figure of the dove from Jesus' baptism, "feathers and all."[15] Luther transposed the term into German as *Schwärmerei*. It denoted the same "self-delusion, a mistaken conviction that one had become a receptacle of a divine possession" as "enthusiasm." But in German *Schwärmerei* connoted "contagion and mass frenzy," like "bees swarming around a hive," by which Luther could stigmatize his spiritualizing opponents, "the mobs that followed self-appointed field preachers or rampaged through churches, smashing the statues . . ."[16] Enthusiasm/ *Schwärmerei* would be for Luther the wrong kind of integration of the Spirit—to the antecedent self, rather than with the Incarnate Word—so that together Word and Spirit transform the antecedent self and thus form believers into the Body of Christ and Temple of the Holy Spirit.

Luther holds tightly together justifying faith or regeneration and the particular news of Christ's coming for those lost to God. He can hold them together because the Spirit who led Jesus in filial obedience and raised Him from the dead is recognizably the same Spirit who raises those dead to God to new life by faith in His crucified and risen Son. In the ensuing centuries, however, Luther's economically sequenced and theologically integrated unity of Word and Spirit was sundered in his would-be followers. Rival anthropocentric theologies "of the heart" and "of the head"[17] eclipsed Luther's Trinitarianism[18] with different claims to "enlightenment." The metaphor of "enlightenment," to be sure, has a long history going back at least to Plato (*Republic* VI:508–11, VII:514–17). This makes claims for "the" Enlightenment specious historically, as post-modern

---

15. LW 40:83.

16. Anthony J. La Vopa, "The Philosopher and the *Schwärmer*: On the Career of a German Epithet from Luther to Kant," *Huntington Library Quarterly* 60 (1997) 88.

17. See forthcoming, Paul R. Hinlicky, "The Use of Luther's Thought in Pietism and the Enlightenment," in *The Oxford Handbook to Martin Luther* ed. R. Kolb et al. (Oxford: Oxford University Press, 2013).

18. Wilhelm Mauer, *Historical Commentary on the Augsburg Confession*, trans. H. George Anderson (Philadelphia: Fortress, 1986) 239–70.

thought increasingly realizes. In the tradition of Augustinian theology to which Luther belongs, *illuminatio* is the aforementioned work of the Holy Spirit, who bathes the transfigured Jesus in divine light, so that faith is born by this revealing-and-seeing-and-hearing of the Father's Son, Jesus who descends the mount to give His life for the many. Christine Helmer's pioneering analysis of Luther's Trinitarianism[19] shows Luther at work with this Augustinian *illuminatio,* the Spirit's attestation of the Word Incarnate at the Father's command, *Hunc audite,* bearing witness to those united with Jesus by faith that they too are children of God by the pouring of divine love into their hearts (Rom 5:5, the bishop of Hippo's favorite Bible verse). Such "enlightenment" is at once intellectual and affective[20]—very much in contrast to "the" Enlightenment.

IRONIES OF ENTHUSIASM

Luther's epithet, enthusiasm, consequently suffered a strange reversal in the course of the Enlightenment. What happened historically is this: the Cartesian-Kantian ambition of clearly separating sensible and supersensible realms[21] predominantly worked to consign Luther with the Pietists to the reactionary private realm of emotion with its false, fervid imaginations—the unfounded source of all error. Alongside of this, however, there was another possibility of a more positive, if somewhat muted relation to Luther's legacy. The reformer's critique of enthusiasm could be utilized, though no longer in service to the *Verbum externum.* In Kant's words from the Orientation essay: "Thus if it is disputed that reason deserves the right to speak first in matters concerning supersensible objects such as the existence of God and the future world, then a wide gate is opened to all enthusiasm, superstition and even atheism."[22] Indeed, as this categorical

19. Christine Helmer, *The Trinity and Martin Luther: A Study on the Relationship between Genre, Language and the Trinity in Luther's Works 1523–1546* (Mainz: Philipp von Zabern, 1999) 230–70.

20. Paul R. Hinlicky, "Luther's Anti-Docetism in the Disputatio de divinitate et humanitate Christi (1540)" in *Creator est creatura: Luthers Christologie als Lehre von der Idiomenkommunikation* ed. O. Bayer & Benjamin Gleede (Berlin & NY: Walter De Gruyter, 2007) 139–85.

21. Immanuel Kant, "The Inaugural Dissertation: 'Genuine Metaphysics without Any Admixture of the Sensible," in Manfred Kuehn, *Kant: A Biography* (Cambridge: Cambridge University Press, 2001) 188–93.

22. Immanuel Kant, "What Does It Mean to Orient Oneself in Thinking?" in *Religion and Rational Theology,* trans. Allen W. Wood & George Di Giovanni (Cambridge: Cambridge University Press, 2001) 15.

claim indicates, the irony of Luther in the Enlightenment is that Luther's epithet, enthusiasm, was appropriated by the Tribunal of Reason to rule out of bounds Luther's own theology of the Spirit at work through the external Word.[23] Thus rationalism could claim to have "fulfilled" or "completed" Luther's reformation, more consistently than Luther, albeit against his Christian intentions.

A kind of lazy Kantianism, however, befogs much modern theological scholarship which consciously or not follows Ritschl[24] under the assumption that Luther's reasons for rejecting metaphysical speculation are the same as the great *Aufklärer*.[25] This Kantianism blocks perception of the great irony involved in the fate of enthusiasm. Among philosophers, however, any lineage running unproblematically from Luther to Kant is far more suspect, especially with regard to the utility of Luther's *Verbum externum* for secular reform and ethical activism.[26] In response to this modern suspicion, not only of Luther's supposed rejection of "good works," but especially of "reason, the devil's greatest whore" several essential studies have appeared that patiently explain how for Luther human reason is the divinely appointed lord of the earth, as per Genesis 1:26-28, which paradoxically falls when it tries to rise to the heavens (*sicut deus eritis!*), as per Genesis 3:4-6.[27] Truly good works are those of the former human vocation at home on the earth; "good works," falsely so-called, are the religious bribes and human sacrifices made in the latter quest for self-transcendence. Important recent studies have further probed Luther's enduring debt to advancements in logic produced by the medieval *moderni* in which he was schooled[28] and Luther's complicated relation to

---

23. See Immanuel Kant, *The Conflict of the Faculties* 7.63 in *Religion and Rational Theology,* 283 and the discussion in Paul R. Hinlicky, *Paths Not Taken: Theology from Luther through Leibniz* (Grand Rapids: Eerdmans, 2009) 44-57.

24. Risto Saarinen, *Gottes Wirken auf Uns: Die transzendentale Deutung des Gegenwart-Christi-Motivs in der Lutherforschung* (Stuttgart: Franz Steiner Wiesbaden, 1989).

25. *Paths Not Taken,* 17-24.

26. Lewis White Beck, *Early German Philosophy: Kant and His Predecessors* (Bristol, England: Thoemmes, 1996) 99.

27. B. A. Gerrish, "The Reformation and the Rise of Modern Science," Chapter Ten in *The Reformation Heritage* (Chicago: University of Chicago Press, 1982) 163-78; *Grace and Reason: A Study in the Theology of Luther* (Oxford: At the Clarendon Press, 1962). See also the recent *The Devil's Whore: Reason and Philosophy in the Lutheran Tradition* ed. Jennifer Hockenberry Dragseth (Minneapolis: Fortress, 2011).

28. Graham White, *Luther as Nominalist: A Study of the Logical Methods used in Martin Luther's Disputations in the Light of their Medieval Background,* Schriften der

Aristotle.[29] These are important works of clarification, though they hardly allow Luther's seminal critique of epistemology and revision of metaphysics to surface and sound on their own terms.[30]

One searches for the rare reference to Luther, or detailed knowledge of his theology, among the leading lights of European enlightenment. A certain cliché emerged, which Ernst Cassirer reproduced in the following generalization: "For Luther, as also for Calvin, dogma becomes the real support and core of theology. The break with humanism had thus become inevitable. It is consummated in Luther's work *On the Enslaved Will* with unstinting clarity . . . The hope of a universal religion, as it had been entertained by Cusa and expressed in his work *On the Peace of Faith* had perished; peace of faith had been supplanted by the most implacable spirit of religious controversy."[31] Broadly speaking, what is at issue for the thinkers of European enlightenment are the "humanist" possibilities of the autonomy of reason and the self-determination of the will, which are presupposed in any re-founding of human society on a universal and secularist basis. Connected with this political motive is the repudiation of the Augustinian notion of corporate sin in Adam in favor of a view focused exclusively on individual acts of transgressions, the visible "crimes" which transgress civil order.[32] What is subversive of a new secular order as such is any assertion of an alternative sovereignty, especially one mystified as a putative theonomy. All such claims can now be squelched with the epithet, enthusiasm.

Spinoza acutely identified this threat under the term, "religious authority": "everyone knows how much importance the people attach to the right and authority over religion, and how they all revered every single word of him who possesses that authority, so that one might even go so far

---

Luther-Agricola-Gesellschaft 30 (Helsinki: Luther-Agricola Society 1994).

29. Theodor Dieter, *Der junge Luther und Aristoteles: Eine historisch-systematische Undersuchung zum Verhältnis von Theologie und Philosophie* (Berlin & NY: Walter de Gruyter, 2001).

30. Martin Heidegger saw that in the young Luther's commentary on Romans 8 but immediately utilized the insight for his own, non-theological purpose. See Benjamin D. Crowe, *Heidegger's Religious Origins: Destruction and Authenticity* (Bloomington and Indianapolis: Indiana University Press, 2006) 44–66. See forthcoming Brent Adkins and Paul R. Hinlicky, *Immanence and Imminence: Rethinking Philosophy and Theology with Deleuze* (Continuum, 2013).

31. Ernst Cassirer, *The Philosophy of the Enlightenment* trans. F.C.A. Koelln and J. P. Pettegrove (Princeton, NJ: Princeton University Press, 1979) 140.

32. Ibid., 141, 160. Cassirer rightly connects these repudiations with the emergence of legal positivism, 239.

as to say that he to whom this authority belongs has the most effective control over minds."³³ Contrasting the (supposed) agreement of Moses with natural law and reason, Spinoza not inaccurately reviews "the origins of the Christian religion . . . " to expose its enthusiasm. "It was not kings who were the teachers of the Christian religion, but men of private station who, despite the will of those who held the sovereignty and were their rulers, were long accustomed to address private religious assemblies, to institute and perform sacred rites, to make all arrangements and decisions on their own responsibility without any regard to the state."³⁴ This enthusiastic assertion of an alternative sovereignty, in Spinoza's reading of Christian history, culminated in the massive enthusiasm of the Pope of Rome, who "began gradually to establish his ascendancy over all the kings until he actually attained the pinnacle of dominion." All the efforts of "monarchs by fire and sword" to liberate themselves from the bewitchment, however, failed. In the one allusion Spinoza permits himself to make to Luther and his followers, he points out that it was fellow "churchmen [who] succeeded in doing by pen alone," i.e., by a new assertion of religious authority through the Word, what the secular sovereigns could not accomplish. The moral of the story which Spinoza draws is that Luther's reformation "in itself provides a clear indication of the strength and power of religious authority, and gives further warning of the necessity of the sovereign to keep it in his own hands."³⁵ In drawing this remarkable conclusion, Spinoza was following Hobbes.

Luther does not appear by name in Hobbes's *Leviathan*, but the specter of the Reformer's assertion of "religious authority"—as in *De servo arbitrio*: "Take away assertions and you take away Christianity!"—is everywhere being exorcized, although Hobbes's Protestant biblicism can disguise that. As A. P. Martinich puts it: "Hobbes's fideism is part of a respectable aspect of Reformation Protestantism . . . [b]ut he did not mean by this what Luther did. 'By the captivity of our Understanding [to faith] is not meant a Submission of the Intellectual faculty to the Opinion of any other man, but of the Will to Obedience where Obedience is due.' [Hobbes] favored dictated doctrine."³⁶ In a penetrating study, political philosopher Joshua Mitchell overturns the customary views (themselves

---

33. Baruch Spinoza, *Theological-Political Treatise* trans. S. Shirley (Indianapolis, IN: Hackett, 1998) 225.

34. Ibid., 227.

35. Ibid., 226.

36. A. P. Martinich, *Hobbes: A Biography* (Cambridge: Cambridge University Press, 1999) 107.

inspired by Hobbes and Spinoza) of the relation of Luther's theology to the origins of secularism by showing 1) how early modern discourse was inextricably entangled in Christian theological categories, and 2) how the theological understandings of the relation of Moses and Christ, who each "impersonate" one of two kinds of "righteousness," bore far-ranging implications for the emerging understandings of liberty.[37]

Luther, in Mitchell's account, opens up "the potential for disruptions of political order which emanate from [his understanding of] Christian righteousness" since "the powers of this world" can have "no power over Christians . . . " (cf. Luther's hymn text: "Take they goods, fame, fortune, child or spouse, they yet have nothing gained . . . "). What rescues Luther from a utopian antinomianism, however, is his "dialectical view" that the "law must be fulfilled," that "Christians must pass through the old law to supersede it."[38] Christ surpasses Moses by beating Moses at his own game, so to say, over-fulfilling the law by love for those it condemns in order to inaugurate a new regime of grace beyond the domain of works. This dialectical relation to political sovereignty, which claims to be the holy guardian of divine law, is disruptive, effectively so just because it is not willing to be marginalized into a realm of interiority within the closed system of secularism. Rather it comes to assert another sovereignty in public, alongside political sovereignty, albeit a paradoxical "power in powerlessness." For Hobbes by contrast "Luther's claim that Christ supersedes the truth of the Old Testament" (in the dialectical way just described) "had to be countered if there was to be civil peace at all." Hence, just like Spinoza, "Hobbes finds in Moses the foundations of unified sovereignty: political and religious."[39] The Hobbes of the second half of *Leviathan*, in turn, just like the Spinoza of the *Theological-Political Treatise*, "is not a theologian rather than a philosopher. He is both—and must be to unify sovereignty."[40]

In a further study, Mitchell argued that Locke's seminal plea for toleration is a conceptual cognate of Luther's dialectical relationship between Moses and Christ: Moses,' i.e. the state's claim is limited to the visible realm of works; conscience, belonging to Christ, is beyond its jurisdiction

---

37. "Luther and Hobbes on the Question: Who Was Moses, Who Was Christ?" *The Journal of Politics* 53 (1991) 676–700; here 682.

38. Ibid., 686.

39. Ibid., 687.

40. Ibid., 698. Similarly, Mitchell's own paradigm-altering analysis does "not substitute a Christian view for an enlightenment view, but rather substitute[s] one Christian view for another['s]" since "Christian speculations on the meaning of (biblical history) are essential to early liberal thought" (ibid.).

A Man of the Church

and competence. Indeed, in the event of conflict, conscience can "appeal to heaven." There is a right to dissent, even revolution.[41] If Locke unconsciously followed Luther's lead in his political and moral philosophy in order to oppose Hobbesian absolutism, however, it is a somewhat different story in regard to the muted Christology (which Leibniz came to regard as Socinian) resulting from Locke's foundationalist epistemology: "What God has revealed, is certainly true; no doubt can be made of it. This is the proper object of *faith*: but whether it be a divine revelation, or no, reason must judge: which can never permit the mind to reject a greater evidence to embrace what is less evident, nor allow it to entertain probability in opposition to knowledge and certainty."[42] As an example of Reason's custodianship over theology, Locke mentioned in passing: "we can never assent to a proposition that affirms the same body to be in two distant places at once, however it should pretend to the authority of a divine *revelation*." To do so would "be to subvert the principles, and foundations of all knowledge, evidence and assent whatsoever."[43] The allusion here is not only to Thomist transubstantiation but also to Luther's Christology, which provided the theological basis for his assertion of "religious authority" in his controversial teaching of the ubiquity of Christ's glorified body.[44]

Locke's remark elicited an extended, learned rebuke in Leibniz's *New Essays*.[45] Leibniz affirmed Locke's embrace of rationality, but precisely for the sake of faith, as this Lutheran philosopher understands faith, *not* then as a blind or arbitrary leap: "Faith is a firm assent, and assent, regulated as it should be, can only be given upon good reasons. Thus he who believes without any reason for believing may be in love with his fancies, but it is not true that he seeks the truth, nor that he renders lawful obedience to this divine Master . . . unless to believe signifies to recite or repeat or to let pass without troubling themselves, as many people do . . . I commend you strongly, sir, when you wish faith to be grounded in reason: without this why should we prefer the Bible to the Koran or to the ancient books of the Brahmins?"[46] Rejecting theories of double truth, Leibniz denied that

---

41. Joshua Mitchell, "John Locke and the Theological Foundation of Liberal Toleration: A Christian Dialectic of History," *The Review of Politics* 52 (1990) 64–83.

42. John Locke, *An Essay Concerning Human Understanding*, Abridged (Indianapolis: Hackett, 1996) 328.

43. Ibid., 326.

44. LW 37:62–65.

45. Gottfried Wilhelm Leibnitz, *New Essays concerning Human Understanding* trans. Alfred Gideon Langley (LaSalle, IL: Open Court, 1949) 610–11.

46. Ibid., 580.

any truths, even of revelation, are ultimately beyond reason or without reason, since the God of revelation is and must be conceived of as the *ratio ultima* of His creation. "St Paul speaks more justly when he says that the wisdom of God is foolishness with men; because men judge of things only according to their experience, which is extremely limited, and everything not agreeing therewith appears to them an absurdity. But this judgment is very rash, for there is indeed an infinite number of natural things which would pass with us as absurd, if they were told us, as the ice which was said to cover our rivers appeared to the king of Siam. But the order of nature itself, not being of any metaphysical necessity, is grounded only in the good pleasure of God, so that he may deviate therefrom by the superior reasons of grace, although he must proceed therein only upon good proofs which can come only from the testimony of God himself, to which we must defer absolutely when it is duly verified."[47] Does this latter affirmation of the "superior reasons of grace" make the rationalist philosopher Leibniz an inconsistent "enthusiast?"

Leibniz's epistemic theory, as is evident, is not foundationalist but perspectivalist. It is not that human knowledge can be founded by a penetrating act of insight into what an apparent object is in and for itself, as Locke seems to think. Nor is perception reality, for the perception of any creature is but a glimpse of the whole, hence misleading and indeed morally culpable pride when its little vision claims comprehension. Only God has a whole and intuitive knowledge of creatures, and God has this knowledge by virtue of His own free act of good pleasure, according to His own wisdom. Just this is what faith believes, when it believes in *God's* revelation and *understands* what it believes. What faith believes –against appearances, against the evidence of its own fragmentary perception, against the wisdom derived solely yet proudly out of its own partial perspective—are those meaningful signs "duly verified" of the "superior reasons of grace." This sign is the appearance in the world of Jesus Christ. As Leibniz put it early on in the programmatic *Discourse on Metaphysics*, this "Jesus Christ has revealed to men the mystery and admirable laws of the Kingdom of heaven and the Greatness of the supreme happiness that God prepares for those who love Him,"[48] echoing the Pauline theodicy of faith in Romans 8.

Leibniz's perspectivalism has at least one of its sources in Luther's theodicy at the conclusion of *De servo abitrio* in the teaching on the three

---

47. Ibid., 582.

48. G. W. Leibniz, *Discourse on Metaphysics and Other Essays* trans. D. Garber and R. Ariew (Indianapolis, IN: Hackett, 1991) 40.

lights of nature, grace and glory, which Leibniz expressly appropriated in his own *Theodicy*.[49] The three lights[50] reflect Luther's breakthrough in disentangling the cosmic Pauline-apocalyptic dualism of the Spirit and the flesh from the Platonic-Gnostic anthropological dualisms pitting mind against matter. But the Pauline dualism is not just lying there in the nature of things to be discovered. It must come on the scene. It must break through to appear. It must be revealed, as when One incognito enters a strong's man's house to bind him and plunder his goods (Mark 3: 27). As tamed as Luther's volatile apocalyptic theologizing becomes in Leibniz's hands, it is still recognizably Luther's assertion of "religious authority" by the sign of offense, the appearance of Jesus Christ in the world. Not only is such Christological affirmation exceedingly rare among the champions of European enlightenment, it is not accidentally related to Leibniz's "moderate" (in his language, i.e., ecumenically oriented, Calixtian) Lutheranism. Leibniz, indeed, is the only major figure of "the" Enlightenment who knows Luther theologically and engages profoundly with his vexing, but also most insightful treatise on the collective bondage of human choice to Adam's rebellion. But Pietists accused Leibniz of crypto-Spinozism; Rationalists complained of him, as they had of Luther, as of one still entangled in the Christian, even worse, Catholic superstition. His was a path not taken.

CONCLUSION

The great tragedy of Western Christianity was the non-reception by Leo X of Luther's theology of the Spirit working through the Word for the reform of the church, as irenically expressed in the 1530 Augsburg Confession.[51] I regard this as a tragedy, though Luther regarded it as a sin, the very sin of "enthusiasm." As he fatefully wrote in the polemical 1537 *Smalcald Articles*, "The papacy is also purely religious raving in that the pope boasts that 'all laws are in the shrine of his heart' and that what he decides and commands in his churches is supposed to be Spirit and law –even when it

---

49. Gottfried W. Leibniz, *Theodicy: Essays on the Goodness of God, the Freedom of Man and the Origin of Evil* trans. E. M. Huggard (Chicago and La Salle, IL: Open Court, 1998) 99–101.

50. Thomas Reinhuber, *Kämpfender Glaube: Studien zu Luthers Bekenntnis am Ende von* De servo arbitrio (Berlin & NY: Walter de Gruyter, 2000).

51. Hinlicky, *Luther and the Beloved Community: A Path for Christian Theology after Christendom*, with a Foreword by Mickey L. Mattox (Grand Rapids: Eerdmans, 2010) 258–300.

is above or contrary to Scriptures or the spoken Word."⁵² Today, neither a Catholic theologian like Ralph Del Colle nor a Lutheran theologian such as myself would concur in these fateful mutual condemnations. We both see in the recovering doctrine of the Trinity the right kind of integration of Word and Spirit that establishes koinonia even against our divided church and thus veritably impels us into new relationships and new explorations, owning the divisions between us as mutual problems. Yet as Ralph showed, "communion ecclesiology can be as diverse as the theological trajectories that inform it."⁵³ That important insight leaves us with much work to do in tracing forgotten trajectories at work in the very categories we so unconsciously employ. I hope to have contributed to that work in this study by inducing Lutheran theologians to look self-critically at the fate of their dearest convictions in the course of "the" Enlightenment, a fate which aligned them in the eyes of the Tribunal of Reason together with the scorned enthusiasts and even the popes. But a more edifying note may be sounded too: recovering the mutual and essential referencing of the Word and Spirit by firmly grounding Trinitarian theological discourse in the Biblical economy of God cannot but draw us all together.⁵⁴ It remains true: as the Spirit draws us to Christ, so we are drawn together to the glory of the Father and for the good of the suffering creation. For this insight, the church on the way to the unity the Lord wills is thankful for the theological ministry of Ralph Del Colle.

---

52. *The Book of Concord*, ed. Robert Kolb & Timothy J. Wengert (Minneapolis: Fortress, 2000) 322.

53. Del Colle, *The Church*, 264.

54. Such has been my own endeavor in Paul R. Hinlicky, *Divine Complexity: The Rise of Creedal Christianity* (Minneapolis: Fortress, 2010).

22

Reading Kant Ecumenically: Prolegomena to an Anthropology of Hope in the Aftermath of Modernity

PHILIP J. ROSSI, S.J.

I. SITUATING KANT

WHERE TO LOCATE KANT and his work on the theological "map" of modernity is a matter of long-standing contention among his readers and interpreters. While there has been a tradition of speaking of Kant as "the philosopher of Protestantism"[1] that goes back to the end of the 19th century, Kant's work has also been appropriated—not without controversy—in service of so-called "transcendental Thomism," which constituted one important stream of the neo-Thomism that set the prevailing style for Catholic philosophy and theology for at least a century. Throughout the same period, however, Kant was—and continues to be—also the object of fierce polemics, conducted from a variety of Christian theological perspectives that viewed him among the thinkers who planted the most important intellectual roots of the forms of late modern atheism.

I should add a cautionary note here: Christian theologians do not constitute a unique cadre of those who would locate Kant (or Kant's

---

1. E.g., Friedrich Paulsen, *Kant der Philosph des Protestantismus* (Berlin: Reuther & Reichard, 1899); Julius Kaftan, *Kant, der Philosph des Protestantismus* (Berlin: Reuther & Reichard, 1904).

heritage) as a key source for some important philosophical strategies of modern atheism, for the shaping of intellectual cultures of unbelief, or for the rise of a "secularity" that marginalizes or privatizes religious belief. For instance, philosophers, historians, and social scientists (among others) who subscribe to what Charles Taylor calls the "subtraction story" of the rise of modernity, in which scientific knowledge and technological control increasingly displace and replace religious faith and practice, would most likely consider Kant and Kant's heritage to have provided crucial intellectual impetus to such a secularizing trajectory.[2]

More recently, some Kant interpreters in the English-speaking world have endeavored to position Kant as at least a friendly ally to Christian theological perspectives that make robust affirmations of orthodox renderings of Trinitarian and Christological doctrines.[3] In addition, there have been recent efforts, particularly in Germany, to counter the long-standing animus with which Catholic philosophers and theologians had most often treated Kant in the hope of making his work a locus for constructive engagement with important elements of the Catholic intellectual tradition.[4]

These efforts—whether they seek to engage Kant's work as constructive resource for theological inquiry, or they find his work irremediably hostile to the central elements from which theological inquiry originates—must grapple with important historical and interpretive issues posed by his texts, as well as by the trajectories of both his personal and public life.

2. In Taylor's alternate account of secularity, put forth in extensive detail in *A Secular Age* (Cambridge, MA: Harvard Univ. Press, 2007), which is explicitly offered to counter such "subtraction stories," Kant's work and its reception also plays a major role, but that role is not simply a negative one that pushes religion and faith to the sidelines; it also reconfigures in a positive way what is at stake morally and anthropologically when humans take a stance of faith in the face of the transcendent.

3. E.g., Chris L. Firestone and Stephen R. Palmquist, eds., *Kant and the New Philosophy of Religion*, Indiana Series in the Philosophy of Religion (Bloomington: Indiana Univ. Press, 2006); Chris L. Firestone and Nathan Jacobs, *In Defense of Kant's Religion*, Indiana Series in the Philosophy of Religion (Bloomington: Indiana Univ. Press, 2008).

4. E.g., Norbert Fischer, ed., *Kants Metaphysik und Religionsphilosophie*, Kant-Forschungen 15 (Hamburg: Meiner, 2004); Norbert Fischer, ed., *Kant und der Katholizismus: Stationen einer wechselhaften Geschichte*, Forschungen zur europäischen Geistesgeschichte 8 (Freiburg: Herder, 2005); Aloysius Winter, *Der andere Kant: Zur philosophischen Theologie Immanuel Kants*, Europaea memoria: Reihe I, Studien 11 (Hildesheim and New York: Olms, 2000). Other contemporary Catholic constructive engagement with Kant in Germany can be found in the works of Richard Shaeffler and Thomas Pröpper. For a proposal for a Catholic reading of Kant, see Philip J. Rossi, SJ, "Reading Kant from a Catholic Horizon: Ethics and the Anthropology of Grace," *Theological Studies* 71 (2010) 79–100.

Dealing with these trajectories might well be called "the quest for the historical Kant," so it may be useful for me to make it clear at the outset that the kind of "mapping" which I am most interested in examining is not one that tries to discern in detail the "historical Kant's" personal religious commitment with respect to the ecclesial terrain of 18th-century Prussia. The most prudent response to the questions about this dimension of his views on Christian faith, practice, and theology may be to consider him as at least aspiring to exemplify the attitude of what he intriguingly calls, in *Religion within the Bounds of Mere Reason*, a "catholic protestant," that is, a "human being whose frame of mind (though this is not that of their church) is given to self-expansion."[5] He seems to take such a person to exhibit crucial elements of the proper bearing that a critical use of reason would endorse with respect to the concrete forms that Christian belief and practice had so far historically developed. This outlook would most centrally include an acknowledgement that there is a (moral) universality proper to the fundamental religious claim that our reason places upon our finite humanity, but that this universality may not be identified *in toto* with the concrete historical form given to such a claim by the particular "ecclesial" faith to which one may, in fact, adhere.

Though Kant's view here is neither fully articulated, nor unproblematic, it does seem, first, to indicate a principle from which Christian ecumenical conversation—or even an interreligious conversation–might begin and, second, to be congruent in important ways with aspects of the "cosmopolitan perspective" so central to Kant's effort to articulate principles for a harmonious world order of peace among nations. Such congruence between Kant's outlook upon religion and his outlook upon international relations, moreover, should be unsurprising in view of the observation he makes in a footnote added to the second edition of *Religion*, that differences in language and differences in religion constitute the "two mightily effective causes" that stand athwart the efforts that are driven by the practical interest of reason to have us work for the establishment of a harmonious world order.[6]

---

5. *Religion within the Bounds of Mere Reason*, in Immanuel Kant, *Religion and Rational Theology*, trans. and ed. Allen W. Wood and George Di Giovanni, The Cambridge Edition of the Works of Immanuel Kant (Cambridge: Cambridge University Press, 1996) 14; German text: *Kants Gesammelte Schriften*, Bd. 6 *Die Religion innerhalb der Grenzen der blossen Vernunft, Die Metaphysik der Sitten*, Ausgabe der Königlichen Preußichen Akademie der Wissenschaften (Berlin: G. Reimer, 1914) 109.

6. *Religion within the Bounds of Mere Reason*, 153; German text: *Kants Gesammelte Schriften*, 6:123.

The main claim of this present essay, which will be put forth in sections II and III, is that Kant's work can function as a useful resource for articulating a theological anthropology of hope to help address some of the philosophical and theological questions about humanity and its meaning that seem most urgent for a culture in the aftermath of modernity. Before doing that, however, let me indicate why I have chosen not to focus on placing the "historical Kant" in direct conversation with these questions. A key reason for this choice is that Kant's work—and, perhaps even more significantly, the reception of Kant's work—has served to change in a significant way the context in which such questions need to be asked. We—at least those of us whose ambient intellectual culture has been that of late Western modernity—are all "post-Kantians." I use this term in the sense neither that we have simply left Kant behind such that his thought is now only a matter of "mere" historical interest, nor that we have realized that he is a carrier of an infectious conceptual syndrome for which we best seek a cure.[7] I call us "post-Kantians" in the sense that Kant's work has played a role in determining how we may construe the very meaning of what it is to be human in our relation to one another, to the cosmos, and to the transcendent Other that Christian discourse names "God." Kant's work and its reception has been, at least for those who have been carried about on the main intellectual currents of Western modernity, one of the forces that have set the trajectory of that current, even as it encounters the under-currents and counter-currents we have come to call "post-modernity" and, as these mingle, rush through seemingly uncharted rapids of global cultural, intellectual, and social change.

Within such a context, any efforts to find a starting point for ecumenical conversation in a reading of Kant—as a thinker of the past who is worth engaging as we grapple with the insistent theological issues of today and tomorrow—needs to be carried on at multiple levels. The most basic level is constituted by Kant's own complex philosophical discourse. At this level, it is hardly surprising that Kant's interpreters disagree over many matters, including some that are as basic as understanding the aim and the finality of his great project of critique. My dissertation director, Alexander von Schoenborn, first drew my attention to what I have come to call "the many faces of Kant." He knew that one large issue that led me to study philosophy was the seemingly unbridgeable chasm between the regnant Anglo-American "analytic" style of philosophy and the various styles of

---

7. See, for instance, Nicholas Wolterstorff, "Is It Possible and Desirable for Theologians to Recover from Kant?" *Modern Theology* 14 (1998) 1–18.

philosophy that, from the analytic perspective, were often casually lumped together as "continental." In his efforts to persuade me to focus my dissertation on Kant, one reason he offered—and the one I still recall most clearly—was that Kant is the last philosopher of historical importance that everyone, analytic or continental, reads. The inference from this (which he let me draw for myself) was that, if I hoped to help build even a small footbridge across that philosophical chasm, some of the more effective tools and useful materials for doing so might come from Kant. It has since become clear to me that a similar dynamic is also at work in Kant's relation to theology: dealing with Kant, even if only by way of rejection, has been an unavoidable point of reference for most Protestant and Catholic theologies for more than two centuries

In the course of efforts to articulate an understanding of Kant that might have a philosophically or theologically "ecumenical" import, an important lesson I have learned from Kant's own work is that it is crucial to attend to the orientation with which one approaches any conceptual terrain, including Kant's own. Thus, in the case of the writings that explicitly constitute his project of critique, the scope, the trajectory, and the results of that enterprise take on a different configuration when approached from the works that constitute its end point than they do when approached from the works with which it was initiated.[8] Similarly, if we align the central trajectory of his critical project along epistemological coordinates, by seeing that project as providing a mediating track between empiricism and rationalism, our reading of the overall import of the project and of the role played by its various parts will come out differently than if we align—as some recent Kant interpreters have argued that it is appropriate to do—that central trajectory along moral and anthropological coordinates, by conceiving his critical project as a track mediating primarily between skepticism and dogmatism.

At least one crucial textual basis for orienting a reading of Kant's critical enterprise along moral and anthropological coordinates is the well-known passage from the first *Critique* in which he enumerates the three questions that articulate the defining "interests" of reason: "What can I know?" "What should I do?" and "What may I hope?"[9] That text does not directly include the fourth question which Kant, in at least two other texts,

---

8. In fact, I think a particularly useful touchstone for testing one's own point of orientation for reading Kant can be found in the questions "Did Kant *complete* his critical enterprise, and, if so, in which one of his writings did he do so?"

9. *Critique of Pure Reason* A804–5/B 832–33.

put forth as gathering together the other three: "What is humanity?"[10] I believe a strong case can be made—as is done in the work of Susan Neiman—that these passages indicate that what Kant understands as the fundamental dynamic of human reason, namely, a drive to render intelligible, to make sense of, what it is to be human, provides the fundamental thrust and trajectory to his critical project. Of course, simply making a plausible case for a basic anthropological thrust to Kant's critical project is hardly enough to render Kant philosophically, let alone theologically "ecumenical"; Kant's account of what it is to be human is by no means uncontroversial. But the way that Kant's work can be considered "ecumenical" is not that he provides an account of the human on which we can agree with little controversy. It is "ecumenical" in that it provides a focus that all of us can recognize as fundamental and unavoidable, a focus upon which we all need to articulate our understanding if we hope to engage one another in productive conversation about important philosophical and theological differences. Kant's work is "ecumenical" in that it requires us to hold one another's "feet to the (conceptual) fire" with respect to our understanding of the human, with respect to what we take to be the best philosophical and theological account we can give of our humanity, its hopes and its destiny, as we stand in relation to one another, to the world, and to the transcendent divine.

So, if it is correct to take the trajectory of Kant's work to be oriented by human *reason's* effort to render its very humanity intelligible, then the further suggestion I have made, namely, that it provides a locus for *theological* engagement requires both explication and justification. Those familiar with even the smallest part of the long-vexed controversies over faith and reason (or grace and nature or revelation and reason) will realize that the kind of juxtaposition I am proposing walks directly into deeply disputed territory. One may appropriately ask, how can an anthropology such as Kant's, in which all seems to be measured by the capacity of human reason, claim to offer itself as a resource for theology, which has its origin in the initiative of the Other that exceeds reason? This challenge is as old as Tertullian's question, "What does Athens have to do with Jerusalem?"[11] In a range of current theological discussions, we can see this concern, for example, in the work of the proponents of various forms of "post-liberal theology" or "Radical Orthodoxy," or in the dynamics of

---

10. The fourth question is posed in the Lectures on Logic (Jaeske) and in a letter to Carl Friedrich Stäudlin, dated May 4, 1793.

11. *De praescriptione haereticorum*, chapter 7.

controversy among Catholic theologians who would pit von Balthasar against Rahner or *ressourcement* over against *aggiornamento*. There are many dimensions of these controversies, but the one most germane for my purposes concerns the role of the "anthropological" with respect to the "theological": to what extent is it (theologically) proper and legitimate to claim that what we come to understand about our humanity provides us with a place from within which we may encounter and articulate truth about the divine Other, who is (definitively) revealed in Jesus the Christ? As an initial step in approaching this question and in rendering an answer that constructively engages Kant's thought, it may be useful to reconsider the standard epistemic reading of his critical project, in which the "limits of reason" become the wedge for dislodging "faith" and to propose, in its stead, a reading in which recognition of the moral finitude of our human condition in our practical, that is, moral, use of reason provides the place from which we are empowered to act in hope.

II. BEYOND "THE EPISTEMIC KANT"

Once upon a time we thought we knew the story of modern philosophy and how that philosophy played its role in shaping the culture of the West. It all started with Descartes, and it all had to do with epistemology; the key questions were about the possibility, the legitimation, and the scope of human knowledge. It was a story shaped by the interplay between empiricists and rationalists, between whom Kant tried to shape a middle path. But it is also a story which subsequent *philosophical* controversy has not yet brought to conclusion; we have yet to come to a point in the story in which we might be able to say, "They lived happily ever after." Yet there is a certain way in which this story *has* ended, even though no one seems to have told the philosophers. The story has ended through the emergence of a secular, technological culture, which has opted for the empirical, the testable, the marketable, and what works, as the measures of what we know and what is true. In the face of such apparent cultural hegemony, the philosophical telling of the story seems to have been rendered not so much untrue, but irrelevant.

Philosophy itself had a role in making this story irrelevant, but that ironic complicity is not the main point of calling to mind how culture "on the ground" may have rendered moot the long history of philosophical battles over epistemology. Even as academic philosophy (especially in the English speaking world) continued to wrestle with the heritage of

Descartes' rooting of knowing in the indubitable certainty and clarity of what presents itself to reflective consciousness, there were voices within the philosophical world that were offering alternative accounts of the career of modern philosophy (and, implicitly, about the career of modern culture). Some of those voices proposed a return to the skepticism that brought about Descartes' efforts to secure certainty in knowing—and in that they resonate with the voice of David Hume, who is the precursor of a very important form of the postmodern. Others sought to circumvent the impasse by turning attention away from thought and consciousness to language as it is embedded in human activity and practice. Yet many of these voices did not fundamentally challenge the story that "it all began with Descartes." There were exceptions: Nietzsche is surely one of them, to the extent that he took the story to be not about knowledge, but about power. In doing so he provides one of the markers along the way in which an important contemporary interpreter of Kant, Susan Neiman, has recounted the story of modern philosophy and Kant's role in it.[12]

On Neiman's reading, the story of modern philosophy has not primarily been about what can we know and how can we know it; it has been about the problem of evil. It has been about philosophy's efforts to render intelligible the difference between the world as it is, where things go terribly wrong, and the world as it ought to be, where things go as they should. This is the fundamental "fracture" that we encounter in the world, a fracture to which she sees Kant so attentive that she speaks of it as his "metaphysic of permanent rupture."[13] Neiman's rereading of Kant has a variety of sources, for example, her keen awareness of the manner in which philosophy and culture interact. But a particularly important source of her reinterpretation of Kant she shares with a number of other Kant scholars who have also been "rereading Kant" (the subtitle of her first book, *The Unity of Reason*). They are looking at this project from two opposite directions, not just from the perspective of its extensive initial articulation in the 1st Critique (which is the way it is looked at in the standard story), but also from the perspective provided by the 2nd and 3rd Critiques, as well as by many of the writings Kant produced in the 1790s in which he continued to struggle to bring his critical project to its completion. Looking at Kant's critical project from the former perspective makes plausible "the epistemic Kant" of the standard story, a Kant who is primarily interested

12. *The Unity of Reason: Rereading Kant* (Oxford: Oxford University Press, 1994); *Evil in Modern Thought: An Alternative History of Philosophy* (Princeton: Princeton University Press, 2002).

13. *Evil in Modern Thought*, 80.

in dealing with the aftermath of Descartes' rooting of knowledge in self-consciousness. Looking at Kant's project from the latter perspective—one that takes into account writings such as *Religion within the Bounds of Mere Reason*, *Perpetual Peace*, *The Metaphysics of Morals*, and *The Strife of the Faculties*—we see him grappling with an issue in which the epistemic is just a part. This issue concerns the human place in the cosmos; it focuses upon trying to render intelligible our human status as the unique juncture of freedom and nature.

For Kant, moreover, rendering intelligible our human status of being this unique junction of nature and freedom is not merely a matter of theoretical concern; it is a matter of urgent practical interest, for on it he sees hanging the possibilities that human beings have for taking responsibility for participating in the shaping of their own destiny as a species. It should be emphasized, moreover, that Kant does not think that our destiny is totally in our hands. As Neiman strikingly puts it, "[o]f the many distinctions Kant took wisdom and sanity to depend on drawing, none was deeper than the difference between God and the rest of us. Kant reminds us as often as possible of all that God can do and all we cannot. Nobody in the history of philosophy was more aware of the number of ways we can forget it."[14] Kant is neither Nietzschean nor Promethian, but he does affirm that for our destiny to be truly ours *as human* we must have a genuine hand in its making, even if it also depends at least as fundamentally upon the workings of what he variously calls "nature" or "providence."

At the heart of Kant's account, on Neiman's reading of it, is what she calls "dissonance and conflict at the heart of experience"[15] that renders problematic human reason's effort to resolve it. The world "as it is" presents itself to the theoretical use of reason as the "appearance" of a nature that, in its causal dynamism, works at best indifferently to the ends and purposes that the practical use of reason proposes as befitting the dignity of our finite human freedom. Neiman notes, "It would be easy to acknowledge that not controlling the natural world is part of being human, were it not for the fact that *things go wrong*. The thought that the rift between freedom and nature is neither error nor punishment, but the fault line along which the universe is structured can be a source of perfect terror."[16]

So as mightily as Kant labors in the *Critique of the Power of Judgment*, as well as in his occasional essays on history, politics and culture,

---

14. Ibid., 75.
15. Ibid., 80.
16. Ibid., 80–81.

to legitimate the application of categories of purpose to the workings of nature, that legitimation is not put forth as the basis for a claim about how the world "is." Whatever purposes, if any, the world of nature may have "as it is" "in-itself" remain opaque in principle to the theoretical use of finite human reason. Even more important for Kant is the fact that whatever *moral* purposes we may think are necessary for our making sense of the world are not features *of* the world but rather a demand that our reason *brings to* the world. Bringing to the world "as it is" the demand of practical reason to fashion the world "as it ought to be" is central to what Kant affirms as the primacy of the practical use of reason. The exercise of our finite reason brings those purposes to the world not in the mode of theoretical knowledge but in the mode of a practical, enacted hope that, by heeding the dictate of practical reason to do as we ought, we make it possible for the world to have, in a least some small measure, a moral order of which it would otherwise seem devoid.

Kant used a various pairs of coordinate terms to characterize this basic duality of our human experience, the two basic ways in which we engage the world. The distinctions between such paired terms, perhaps most famously and problematically that between "phenomenon" and "noumenon," have vexed generations of sympathetic and hostile commentators alike. It has rarely been the case, however, that the question of radical evil that Kant articulates in *Religion within the Boundaries of Mere Reason* has been pressed into service as a key interpretive guide to the contours of the fissure that he sees running through our human engagement with the world. That discussion of the moral structure of evil seems to offer little promise for interpretive purchase upon distinctions fundamental to the critical project so long as Kant's affirmation of a duality of nature and freedom is understood—as it has often been—as a response to epistemic and metaphysical issues that are taken to stand in isolation from moral and anthropological ones. In consequence, his explicit engagement of the question of human evil in the later phases of the critical enterprise, as well as the maturation of his thought about the "highest good" as the social object of the practical use of reason, has often been considered marginal to the main conceptual and argumentative strands of his monumental endeavor to delimit the scope of human reason's engagement with the cosmos of which it is a part, in which it functions, and beyond which it drives itself to aspire. Similarly, as long as the vantage point from which Kant's writings are read remains epistemic, his various accounts of the "highest good" can also be seen as mere appendages to his efforts to vindicate the theoretical use of reason. Once the focus shifts, however, to the vindication of reason's practical (moral) use, which Kant called, in the Preface to *Critique of Practical Reason*, "the keystone"[17] of the critical enterprise, the role of "the highest good" becomes far more important, inasmuch as it is the object of the practical use of reason, which has primacy both individually and socially.

III. TOWARD AN ANTHROPOLOGICAL GRAMMAR OF GRACE AND HOPE

I hope that the discussion so far has provided some coordinates for understanding the way Kant sees our human condition in terms of a "metaphysic of permanent rupture." Let me now briefly sketch how, in response to these fractured human circumstances, Kant also provides the basis for constructing what may be termed "a grammar of hope" or an "anthropology of hope," in connection with what we are called upon to do with and for each other in the face of a fragmentation that presents itself to us in a variety of modes. This proposal is one that deliberately crosses back and forth between philosophical and theological modes of discourse and in which a key point of juncture is signaled by the space it then provides for using a grammar of "grace."

This proposal focuses on possibilities for engaging what I term Kant's "anthropological grammar of hope" so as to articulate that hope as a discourse of "grace." In particular, I propose that Kant's understanding of hope, which arises from his account of the fragility of our human freedom, offers a basis for an anthropology that renders us receptive to welcoming that which comes in and through the fractured dynamics of our human circumstances as an invitation to encounter the work of "grace."[18] Kant situates our human freedom in the contingency of the cosmos; his account manifests a deep sense that the common fragility of our finite human freedom stands inextricably coordinate to the dignity that we must recognize in one another's humanity in the moral community he terms the "ethical commonwealth." A relationality that is deeply embedded in

---

17. *Practical Philosophy*, trans. and ed. Mary Gregor, The Cambridge Edition of the Works of Immanuel Kant (Cambridge: Cambridge University Press, 1996) 139; German text: *Kants Gesammelte Schriften*, 5:3–4.

18. For a more extensive discussion, see Philip J. Rossi, "Finite Freedom, Fractured and Fragile: Kant's Anthropology as Resource for a Postmodern Theology of Grace," in *Philosophie et théologie: Festschrift Emilio Brito, SJ*, ed. Éric Gaziaux (Leuven: Peeters, 2007) 47–60.

our common human fragility is thus a key element for constructing an anthropology that inscribes human freedom in the embodied conditions of spatio-temporal finitude. Insofar as we each stand alone, our finitude provides thin and tenuous protection to our core dignity of spirit; under these conditions, our human power for bringing about good, rooted in the fragmentary, fragile exercise of a finite practical reason, stands on a slender and precarious footing. Human fragility stands in need of what it cannot provide of itself; yet, if it is to act responsibly, it must move forward in the hope that what is needed to overcome fracture will be offered. In this respect, both "hope" and "grace" may be construed as openness to the empowering presence of otherness.

One of the ways in which Kant suggests such an anticipatory movement in the direction of awaiting grace is, I would argue, is the mutuality and social character of his characterization of autonomy. This, of course, should be surprising—even outrageous—to those schooled in understanding Kantian autonomy as a lonely and noble moral individual heroism. I would argue, however, that a more accurate reading of autonomy in Kant is one in which awareness of the reciprocal connection of freely offered respect within which one stands to all other human agents—in Kant's terms, awareness of one's membership in a "kingdom of ends"—brings with it a deep sense of the fragility of our finite human freedom, a fragility that goes along with the dignity that we accord to one another through our mutual respect. This fragility of human freedom is inscribed in the embodied conditions of our spatio-temporal finitude. Insofar as we each stand alone, our finitude provides thin and tenuous protection to our core dignity of spirit. The human power for bringing about good thoroughly pertains to, and is rooted in, the fragmentary, fragile exercise of a finite practical reason. The ultimate bulwark for our finitude is not so much the solitary resoluteness that Iris Murdoch once so eloquently described in her depiction of Kantian autonomy[19] as it is the mutual recognition and respect we accord each other for the fragile and vulnerable freedom we each embody. Kant's recognition of the inestimable dignity of the power of human freedom to effect good is equally a recognition that such power resides in agents who are themselves profoundly fragile, who exercise that power in a correspondingly fragile way, yet who are capable of empowering each other's freedom in mutual respect for one another's

---

19. "Kant's [autonomous] man had already received a glorious incarnation nearly a century earlier in the work of Milton: His proper name is Lucifer." *The Sovereignty of Good*, Studies in Ethics and the Philosophy of Religion (1970; repr., New York: Schocken, 1971) 80.

fragility. As embodied, moreover, our freedom is rendered fragile not simply by the inconstancy of intention that Kant marks out as the "inversion of our maxims," nor only by the inattention and distraction with which we thoughtlessly descend into evil's banality. Our embodied freedom is also made fragile by a vulnerability of both body and spirit to violence and violation.

The anthropology that I am suggesting can be drawn from Kant's account of finite freedom is thus one in which moral agency is exercised from a locus of human vulnerability and human solidarity that takes full account of the social and relational dynamisms that are central to Kant's understanding of finite human reason.[20] This fact has important anthropological implications. Once we take full account of those social and relational dynamisms, Kantian autonomy can be understood to have its most significant exercise in the context of a clear recognition of the fragility and vulnerability that form the matrix in which human finite reason finds that it must function. The mutual recognition of human vulnerability thus constitutes a central locus for the dynamisms of hope and of grace.

I believe a case can be made that coordinate to this social anthropology of finite reason is a grammar of moral hope that provides the structure for a syntax of moral recognition, a syntax that places constraint upon both explicit and implicit claims of self-preference, which constitutes the core of what Kant means by "radical evil." Such syntax can be found in the "universal law" formulation of the categorical imperative, which places a veto on the self-preferential obduracy of individual moral agents.[21] It is also operative in the discourse of mutual respect appropriate to membership and shared responsibility in what Kant terms "a kingdom of ends." In this context, a syntax of moral recognition functions to clear a social space within which agents address not only questions of individual human interaction but also those dealing with the social governance of human life.[22] On Kant's account, a grammar of hope functions to break the grip of

20. For an extensive discussion, see Philip J. Rossi, SJ, *The Social Authority of Reason: Kant's Critique, Radical Evil, and the Destiny of Humankind*, SUNY Series in Philosophy (Albany: State University of New York Press, 2005).

21. Placing this formulation in the context of the self-preferential obduracy of radical evil suggests that its focus is more on the veto it imposes on self-preference and self-exemption as stratagems that issue from "the dear self" than on a formal claim of "universalizability" that generations of Kant's critics have castigated as a moral version of "one size fits all."

22. John Rawls' device in *A Theory of Justice* of "the original position" in which (ideal) agents deliberate about the terms of their social governance captures an important dimension of the social space that is a function of a syntax of mutual recognition.

self-preferential obduracy with respect both to the moral life of individual agents and to the structure and dynamics by which human agents mutually govern their social, political, and cultural interaction.

As a result, within the larger social framework that human autonomy provides, *the fragility of human freedom stands coordinate to its dignity.* As we each stand alone, our embodied state provides thin and tenuous protection to our core dignity of spirit. As I have mentioned already, the ultimate bulwark of that dignity is the mutual recognition and respect we accord each other for the fragile and vulnerable freedom we each embody. I noted above that Kant's recognition of the inestimable dignity of the power of human freedom to effect good is equally a recognition that such power resides in agents who are themselves profoundly fragile, who exercise that power in a correspondingly fragile way, yet who are capable of empowering each other's freedom in mutual respect for one another's fragility. In Kant's account, moreover, the finitude of the human freedom that is exercised in the community of mutual respect that he calls "the ethical commonwealth" has moral intelligibility in virtue of its standing in relation to a divine transcendence that affirms human moral responsibility in the shaping of history.[23]

In providing the moral space for human finite agency to have a genuinely constitutive role—though not the sole one—in shaping the trajectory and outcome of human destiny, divine transcendence thus opens a locus for the work of grace. In this case, grace functions in the moral space of mutual respect for freedom. A divine respect for human freedom holds humanity morally accountable, and a human respect for divine freedom acknowledges that human finitude cannot comprehend the mode of that divine freedom's enactment, save in terms of its steadfast respect for the exercise of human freedom, a respect to which I think it would be apt to apply Charles Taylor's characterization of a principle at the heart of the transformative activity of God: "God's steadfast resolve not to abandon humanity in its worst distress."[24]

---

23. See Philip J. Rossi, "Faith, Autonomy, and the Limits of Agency in a Secular Age," in *At the Limits of the Secular: Catholic Reflections on Faith and Public Life*, ed. William Barbieri (Grand Rapids: Eerdmans, forthcoming).

24. *A Secular Age*, 654.

Epilogue

The Homily Preached at the Funeral of Ralph Del Colle

JOSEPH G. MUELLER, S.J.

Readings: Isaiah 25:6a, 7–9; Philippians 3:17—4:1; John 12:23-28.[1]

ACCORDING TO TODAY'S PROPHECY from Isaiah, on Mount Zion in Jerusalem, God will destroy death forever and wipe away all tears of sadness. But no surprise if our first reaction to this promise is to ask, "When, Lord, when will you kill death for good?" We see the casket before us draped in white. We recall so vividly the vital man whose absence from us this casket now betokens. Even as numb as we are, we begin to feel the void Ralph's death has opened in our lives. And we know full well that Mount Zion in Jerusalem, placed as it has been at the center of so much violent contention for so long, is not the first place to look these days to see death spinning down the drain. God himself must know that believer and doubter, mourner and refugee—indeed, every human person with so much as a few moments to reflect—cries out, "When will death be taken away? Why not right here, right now!"

Ralph Del Colle knew the pain of this question. An enthusiastic student of military history, Ralph was attracted to conflict. He could smell it and would head straight for it, to say his word as clearly as possible, to engage in the struggle to hear and to respect others, to listen to them and to create a space of expectation that invited their act of friendship to meet his, even and perhaps especially when he knew the disagreement would perdure. Conflict with friends wounded him, perhaps most of all when he thought he had made it worse by excessive forthrightness, by

---

1. These readings were chosen by Ralph for his funeral Mass.

Epilogue

stubbornness, or by failure to place love above his wanting to be right. He knew that disunity kills us, he prayed for his own conversion from this death, and he lived this prayer in his family and professional life, always as a Christian straining to take in God's word as his only staff of life, his heart breaking to share that bread ever more fully, especially with those who had made God's word a means of division among themselves, that is, especially with so many of us.

So when Ralph told me last week the prophecy he wanted for this mass, he knew we would ask, as he so often had asked, "When, Lord, will you take death away?" Today's second reading from Paul's letter to the Philippians answers that question. When Jesus comes back from heaven as the savior at the end of the world, he will change our lowly body to conform it with his glorified body, so that like him we will be deathless, immortal in our bodies and souls. Then the God of all, through Christ, his eternal Son made human and risen from a shameful death, will subject all things to himself. Then death, the deepest insult to the God of life ever devised by his besotted creatures, will be no more. The prophecy of Isaiah will be fulfilled. Our mortality and our struggle against death will slough off of us and rot away. Our fight against the forces of bodily death, our defensive attacks against the forces in our spirit that kill love and hope and comfort—all of this will evaporate like haze beneath the rising sun of divine glory.

I am not the only one who saw this begin to happen in Ralph. As he sat on the porch or lay in bed in his last weeks, where was the worrier temperament that always wondered whether he had done enough to welcome God's grace, to examine his faults and to struggle against them, to work for perfection? Boiled off in the growing heat of an ever-closer encounter with his Lord, the tense straining for holiness gave way to mirth before his weaknesses and those of the people around him. It gave way to uncomplicated and transparent expressions of love. It gave way to acceptance that some of his last hours would not be spent thinking of God or his family because his body wouldn't let him think any more. His failing strength and the late hour even made his obsession to have things just so seem ridiculous to him, even if it didn't entirely leave him. The man who loved the intricacy of accuracy, both in Christian doctrine and in the spiritual life, was now telling us how simple and uncomplicated God was. Ralph and I talked almost every week about theology and spiritual things for over ten years. Over that time, we marked together the grinding progress of his constant effort to reach Christian integrity through a kind of war of attrition. But in the last weeks of his life, Ralph walked out of the dank trenches into the beauty of a calm field where the battle was done. To see him reach so much of what he had strained for took my breath away.

It showed me what happens when a grain of wheat falls to the ground and dies. Ralph fell and died before our eyes, and as he did so we saw a new life dawning across his tired face. As Jesus teaches in today's gospel, the way to resurrection morning at the end of the age is not a pretty stroll. It passes through an hour that made even the eternally begotten Christ blanch and consider a course correction. We saw Ralph face that moment, too. How quickly his dire prognosis had come upon him, he remarked. When he heard how much time he had, he suddenly had too much to do, too little time in which to do it. But in the end, he let that all go, and he relaxed into confident unity with his Lord in prayer: Father, glorify your name. This was his prayer during the last mass and vespers he celebrated with us in the upper room of his house, as he waited for our risen Lord to come. Where you are, Lord Christ, there also let your servant be.

But Ralph's hour is not ours. This casket is his alone, and we remain to gaze at it and at the ground that will cover it. We are still here to remember him, to pray for him and his family, to offer them our renewed friendship. But most especially, we remain to work as Ralph did for so long, to strain forward, to fall back, wondering when we will ever see the progress we so desire, struggling to live on God's clock and calendar, whose numbers are always just out of focus for us. As we work and wait for the Father's day and hour, as we reach for Christ's hand on a tiring road, we can recall one thing. The Holy Spirit raised up a witness among us. The Spirit of God worked powerful things in this imperfect man. Ralph's wisdom was God's. His goodness was Christ's gift. His peace was the fruit of the Spirit. Through Ralph God showed us he can work in us to propel us toward love and peace, no matter how hard that might be for us. To learn this divine lesson, we have to let God teach it to others through us, just as Ralph let God teach it to us through him. God hear Ralph Del Colle's prayers for us, even as we pray for him.

Opera: The Theology and Witness of Ralph Del Colle (1954–2012)

COMPILED BY RICHARD J. BARRY

PROFESSIONAL ECUMENICAL INVOLVEMENT

1998–2007, 2011–2012	Member, International Roman Catholic/Pentecostal Dialogue
2003–2012	Member, U.S. Catholic/Evangelical Dialogue
1996–2012	Member, United Methodist/Roman Catholic Dialogue (Co-chair 2008–2012), Archdiocese of Milwaukee
2003–2010	Member, U.S. Catholic/Reformed Dialogue
2001–2004	Member, International Roman Catholic/Seventh-day Adventist Consultation
1996–2002	Member, Archbishop's Consultation for Theological Issues, Archdiocese of Milwaukee
1998–2001	Member, U.S. Roman Catholic/Reformed-Presbyterian Consultation
2001	Ecumenical Delegate for the Pontifical Council for Promoting Christian Unity and the National Conference of Catholic Bishops (U.S.) to the General Assembly of the Presbyterian Church (USA), Louisville, Kentucky
1999–2000	Consultant, Wisconsin Council of Churches Faith and Order Commission

1998	Member, Roman Catholic Delegation to the 8th General Assembly, World Council of Churches, Harare, Zimbabwe
1995	Member, Steering Committee, Academic Track, North American Congress on the Holy Spirit and World Evangelization, Orlando, Florida

SOCIETY OF PENTECOSTAL STUDIES

Second Vice-President, 2000; First Vice-President, 2001; President, 2002

BIBLIOGRAPHY

Books

Christ and the Spirit: Spirit-Christology in Trinitarian Perspective. New York: Oxford University Press, 1994.
Talking with Evangelicals: A Guide for Catholics. Mahwah, NJ: Paulist, 2012.

Edited Books

Co-editor with David S. Cunningham and Lucas Lamadrid and primary author of the Introduction (xix–xxiv), *Ecumenical Theology in Worship, Doctrine, and Life: Essays Presented to Geoffrey Wainwright on his Sixtieth Birthday.* New York: Oxford University Press, 1999.
Editor and author of the Foreword (iii–vi), *Is the Reformation Over? Catholics and Protestants at the Turn of the Millennia,* The Pere Marquette Lecture in Theology, 2000, by Geoffrey Wainwright. Milwaukee: Marquette University Press, 2000.

Articles

"David Bentley Hart and Pope Benedict: *Atheist Delusions,* the Regensburg Lecture, and Beyond." *Nova et Vetera* 9 (2011) 297–318.
"The Implications of 'Religious Experience' for Catholic-Pentecostal Dialogue: A Catholic Perspective." *Journal of Ecumenical Studies* 45 (2010) 525–42.
"Ecumenical Dialogues: State of the Question." *Liturgical Ministry* 19 (2010) 105–14.
"On Becoming a Christian: Commentary on the Fifth Phase Report of the International Catholic/Pentecostal Dialogue." *One in Christ* 43 (2009) 98–121.
"Nature and Grace: Why this Catholic Delineation of the 'Supernatural' is Important for Pentecostals." *Journal of Pentecostal Theology* 18 (2009) 111–22.
"Whither Pentecostal Theology? Why a Catholic is Interested." *Pneuma: The Journal of the Society for Pentecostal Studies* 31 (2009) 35–46.

"Oneness-Trinitarian Final Report, 2002–2007: A Catholic Response." *Pneuma: The Journal of the Society for Pentecostal Studies* 30 (2008) 255–62.

"Catholic-Methodist-Pentecostal: A Trialogue?" *Ecumenical Trends* 37:8 (2008) 7–9, 15.

"Inspiration and Inerrancy in Scripture." *Chicago Studies* 47 (2008) 25–38.

"Mary, the Unwelcome (?) Guest in Catholic/Pentecostal Dialogue." *Pneuma: The Journal of the Society for Pentecostal Studies* 29 (2007) 214–25.

"Catholic vs. Pentecostal Missiologies: Toward Reconciliation by Catholic Reception of Baptism in the Holy Spirit." *Missiology: An International Review* 35 (2007) 337–45.

"Aesthetics and Pathos in the Vision of God: A Catholic-Pentecostal Encounter." *Pneuma: The Journal of the Society for Pentecostal Studies* 26 (2004) 99–117.

"Christ and the Spirit: Dogma, Discernment, and Dialogical Theology in a Religiously Plural World." Co-authored with Amos Yong, Dale T. Irvin and Frank D. Macchia, *Journal of Pentecostal Theology* 12 (2003) 15–83.

"Pentecostal/Catholic Dialogue: Theological Suggestions for Dialogue." *Pneuma: The Journal of the Society for Pentecostal Studies* 25 (2003) 93–96.

"Trinity and Temporality: The Relationship between Time and the Divine Being." *The Spirit & Church* 4 (2002) 27–37.

"John Wesley's Doctrine of Grace in Light of the Christian Tradition." *International Journal of Systematic Theology* 4 (2002) 172–89.

"Commentary and Reflections on: *Speaking the Truth in Love: Teaching Authority among Catholics and Methodists*: Report of the Joint Commission between the Roman Catholic Church and the World Methodist Council, 1997–2001, Seventh Series." *Information Service-Pontifical Council for Promoting Christian Unity* No. 107 (2001/II–III) 118–26.

"Person and Being in John Zizioulas' Trinitarian Theology: Conversations with Thomas Torrance and Thomas Aquinas." *Scottish Journal of Theology* 54 (2001) 70–86.

"The Holy Spirit: Presence, Power, Person." *Theological Studies* 62 (2001) 322–40.

"Toward the Fullness of Christ: A Catholic Vision of Ecumenism." *International Journal of Systematic Theology* Vol. 3 No. 2 (2001): 201–211.

"The Pursuit of Holiness: A Catholic-Pentecostal Dialogue." *Journal of Ecumenical Studies* 37 (2000) 301–20.

Review Essay, "Communion and the Trinity: The Free Church Ecclesiology of Miroslav Volf—a Catholic Response." *Pneuma: The Journal of the Society for Pentecostal Studies* 22 (2000) 303–27.

"Incarnation and the Holy Spirit." *The Spirit & Church* 2 (2000) 199–229.

"Postmodernism and Pentecostal/Charismatic Experience." *Journal of Pentecostal Theology* 17 (2000) 97–116.

"Fruits of Witness: Reflections on *Evangelism, Proselytism and Common Witness*." *One in Christ* 36 (2000) 354–64.

"*Evangelism, Proselytism and Common Witness*: A Roman Catholic Response." *Ecumenical Trends* 29:10 (2000) 3–7.

"The Holy Spirit and Ecumenism." *Ecumenical Trends* 29:6 (2000) 10–16.

"Schleiermacher and Spirit Christology: Unexplored Horizons of The Christian Faith." *International Journal of Systematic Theology* 1 (1999) 286–307.

"The Content of Our Hope." *The Living Pulpit* 8 (1999) 26–27.

"Theological Dialogue on the 'Full Gospel': Trinitarian Contributions from Pope John Paul II and Thomas A. Smail." *Pneuma: The Journal of the Society for Pentecostal Studies* 20 (1998) 141–60.

Opera: The Theology and Witness of Ralph Del Colle (1954–2012)

"Ecumenism and the Holy Spirit: The Pneumatological Center of Ut Unum Sint." *The Living Light* 34 (1997) 37–47.
"Reflections on the Filioque." *Journal of Ecumenical Studies* 34 (1997) 202–17.
"Oneness and Trinity: A Preliminary Proposal for Dialogue with Oneness Pentecostalism." *Journal of Pentecostal Theology* 10 (1997) 85–110.
"Trinity and Temporality: A Pentecostal/Charismatic Perspective." *Journal of Pentecostal Theology* 8 (1996) 99–113.
"The Two-Handed God: Communion, Community and Contours for Dialogue." in *Religions of the Book, The Annual Publication of the College Theology Society* 38 (1992) 35–48. Edited by Gerard S. Sloyan. Lanham, NY: University Press of America, 1996.
"The Theological Significance of Trinity Sunday." *Chicago Studies* 33 (1994) 165–78.
"Spirit-Christology: Dogmatic Foundations for Pentecostal-Charismatic Spirituality." *Journal of Pentecostal Theology* 3 (1993) 93–114.
"The Experience of the Divine." *Chicago Studies* 31 (1992) 290–300.

Book Chapters

At Press, "An Ontology of the Supernatural: the Contribution of the 'Lyrical Scholasticism' of Matthias Scheeben to Charismatic/Pentecostal Theology with reference to the Latter Rain Movement." In *Renewal History and Theology: Essays in Honor of H. Vinson Synan*, edited by Christopher C. Emerick and David Moore, Cleveland, TN: Center for Pentecostal Theology Press, 2013.
"Miracles in Christianity." In *Cambridge Companion to Miracles*, edited by Graham Twelftree, 235–53. Cambridge: Cambridge University Press, 2011.
"Christian Theology: The Spirit." In *The Blackwell Companion to Paul*, edited by Stephen Westerholm, 561–75. Chichester, West Sussex: Wiley-Blackwell, 2011.
"Neo-Scholasticism." In *The Blackwell Companion to Nineteenth-Century Theology*, edited by David Fergusson, 375–94. Chichester, West Sussex: WileyBlackwell, 2010.
"The Church." In *The Oxford Handbook of Systematic Theology*, edited by John Webster, Kathryn Tanner, and Iain Torrance, 249–66. Oxford: Oxford University Press, 2007.
"Life as a Holy Penitent: The Catholic Call to Conversion." In *Repentance in Christian Theology*, edited by Mark J. Boda and Gordon T. Smith, 231–50. Collegeville, MN: Liturgical, 2006.
"The Outpouring of the Holy Spirit: Implications for the Church and Ecumenism." In *The Holy Spirit, The Church, And Christian Unity*, edited by D. Donnelly, A. Denaux, and J. Fameree, 247–65. Leuven: Leuven University Press, Peeters, 2005.
"Parousia and Christian Hope." In *A Heart for The Future: Writings On The Christian Hope*, edited by Robert Boak Slocum, 48–58. New York: Church Publishing, 2004.
"Spirit Baptism: A Catholic Perspective." In *Perspectives on Spirit Baptism: Five Views*, edited by Chad Owen Brand, 40–44, 101–3, 169–73, 232–35, 241–79. Nashville: Broadman & Holman, 2004.
"The Holy Spirit and Christian Unity: A Case Study from Catholic/Pentecostal Dialogue." In *Kirche in okumenischer Perspektive*, edited by Peter Walter, Klaus Kramer, and George Augustin, 290–305. Freiberg: Herder, 2003.

Opera: The Theology and Witness of Ralph Del Colle (1954-2012)

"A Response to Jürgen Moltmann and David Coffey." In *Advents of the Spirit: An Introduction to the Current Study of Pneumatology*, edited by Bradford E. Hinze and D. Lyle Dabney, 339-46. Milwaukee: Marquette University Press, 2001.

Editorials

Editorial, *International Journal of Systematic Theology*:
  Vol. 14, No. 2 (2012) 128-30.
  Vol. 13, No. 1 (2011) 1-2.
  Vol. 11, No. 1 (2009) 1-2.
  Vol. 9, No. 2 (2007) 131-33.
  Vol. 8, No. 2 (2006) 125-27.
  Vol. 6, No. 4 (2004) 335-36.
  Vol. 5, No. 3 (2003) 259-60.
  Vol. 4, No. 3 (2002) 253-54.
  Vol. 3, No. 3 (2001) 235-36.
  Vol. 2, No. 3 (2000) 245-46.
  Vol. 1, No. 3 (1999) 229-30.

Other Publications

Foreword to *Gifted Response: The Triune God as the Causative Agency of our Responsive Worship*, by Dennis Ngien, ix-xii. Colorado Springs: Paternoster, 2008.
Introduction to "Christ the Savior: Cur Deus Homo? 1:3, 14, 24; 11:7, St. Anselm of Canterbury (CA. 1033-1109)." In *Introduction to Theology*, Second Edition, edited by John D. Laurance, 149-51. Boston: Pearson Custom, 2006.
"Perspective on Pieter Claeissins I *Madonna and Child* (1550)." In *Perspectives on Art at the Haggerty Museum*, by Marquette University Faculty and Staff, 7. Milwaukee: The Haggerty Museum of Art, Marquette University, 2006.
"A Reasonable and Possible Joy." *Traces: Communion and Liberation International Magazine* 6 (2004) 15.
"Toward Human Flourishing." In *A Generative Thought: An Introduction to the Works of Luigi Giussani*, edited by Elisa Buzzi, 128-32. Montreal: McGill-Queen's University Press, 2003.
"John Paul II exemplifies the power of prayer and action." *Milwaukee Journal Sentinel*, Crossroads Section 3J, Sunday, October 12, 2003.
Primary drafter: "Sharing Life Together." In *Interchurch Families: Resources for Ecumenical Hope, Catholic/Reformed Dialogue in the United States*, edited by John C. Bush and Patrick R. Cooney, 1-10. Louisville: Westminster John Knox; Washington, D.C.: United States Conference of Catholic Bishops, 2002.
"Was the Gulf Conflict a 'Just War'? A Theologian Sorts Out the Moral Issues." *Saint Anselm Magazine* 33:2 (1991) 26-31.
"Democratic Socialism and the U.S. Catholic Bishops' Letter on the Economy." *Religious Socialism* 8:4; 9:1 (1984-1985) 1-2, 24.

www.ingramcontent.com/pod-product-compliance
Lightning Source LLC
Chambersburg PA
CBHW061423300426
44114CB00014B/1520